Emerson.

Château-Thierry
Omaha Beach—
Normandy

Quebec
Brookfield Concord
Ticonderoga Bunker Hill
Fairfield
Gettysburg
Bull Run
Harrison's Landing

Utuado—
Porto Rico

M.J. CAPEHART

By Townsend Scudder

Letters of Jane Welsh Carlyle
(*Edited, with Introduction*)

The Lonely Wayfaring Man

Jane Welsh Carlyle

Concord: American Town

Concord: American Town

Concord:
American Town

TOWNSEND SCUDDER

Boston

Little, Brown and Company

1947

COPYRIGHT 1947, BY TOWNSEND SCUDDER

ALL RIGHTS RESERVED, INCLUDING THE RIGHT
TO REPRODUCE THIS BOOK OR PORTIONS
THEREOF IN ANY FORM

FIRST EDITION

Published April 1947

Published simultaneously
in Canada by McClelland and Stewart Limited

PRINTED IN THE UNITED STATES OF AMERICA

*"There is no great and no small
To the Soul that maketh all."*

To the Reader

THIS book grew from my search for a more human approach to America's story than is possible when the nation is dealt with as a whole. Why not choose some noteworthy place and then funnel the course of history through the personalities and actions of each of its generations, sought and found in the records? Such a scheme should prove closer to the reader's own experience — for what is happening comes home to every one of us by means of what he hears and sees and reads and does in the familiar environment of the community to which he belongs.

As a point of focus, I might have used some great city. But the number of persons involved through the centuries would become confusing. For its own interest and because it suited the purpose, I chose active, articulate Concord, a little town both typical and unique. Of course some of Concord's responses are bound to be biased, such as those to the Civil War. But such prejudices and partisanship belong also to the picture. Some national experiences might entirely pass the town by. Yet the documents show that Concord's awareness of what was going on and its participation from the start to the present have left very little untouched. That in itself is an important part of the story of America.

T. S.

Contents

CONTENTS

Concord: American Town

CHAPTER I

This Founding Enterprise

"WE are in the Lord's hands," said Dr. Ripley, raking his hay very fast as he glanced from time to time over his shoulder at the thunder-gust rolling up beyond Sted Buttrick's ridge across the sluggish little river. It was just as though the parson had said to the Lord, "You know me; this field is mine — Dr. Ripley's — Thine own servant!"

And like as not, after copious sweating — for the old man gathered his hay in the same broadcloth and old-fashioned knee breeches that he wore in making his parochial visits — the parson and his helper would drive the load into the barn of the Manse before the first giant drops spattered into the dust of the neighboring cornfield.

When Ralph Waldo Emerson was writing the historical discourse his fellow townsmen had asked him to give at Concord's two hundredth birthday anniversary, he found his thoughts often preoccupied with the significance of people. How recognize simple human faith without knowing Dr. Ripley? The acres Dr. Ripley farmed to supplement his five-hundred-dollar stipend, his neighbors good and bad whose souls he considered his special obligation, the little town, were for Dr. Ripley the United States of America, the world itself, the past, present, and future.

How understand the integrity and strength of man, without living near Squire Hoar, the town's first citizen? Or the dignity and beauty of women but for the Squire's wife, daughter of that Roger Sherman who signed the Declaration of Independence, the Articles of Confederation, the Constitution — the three great charters of the nation? How know selfish rascality without listening to the baser village politicians? Deacon Jarvis could stand for practical wisdom, with Yankee parsimony thrown in; Deacon Hubbard for honesty and thrift. Hugh Quoil, soldier of Wellington, living in a shanty up the railroad cut and drinking himself into every Concord gutter, shows the fate that sometimes overtakes heroes. Fools and clowns and sots make the fringe of everyone's tapestry of life, and give dimensions to the picture. What could we do in Concord — Emerson asked himself — without Bigelow's and Wesson's barrooms and their dependencies? What without such fixtures as Uncle Sol and old Moore who sleeps in Dr. Hurd's barn, and the red poorhouse over the brook? And yet, as Emerson warned his often sardonic British friend, Carlyle, it does insult to human capability to emphasize the negative.

Through the tavern windows, round the stove and cracker barrel at the grocery store, Emerson could watch men talking politics, hear them laugh boisterously or whisper some sly remark to a grinning neighbor. Eagerly, from his door, he watched the boys and girls come from the East Primary schoolhouse directly opposite. They, too, had much to say that he wished to know.

With his bag of lectures, Emerson had traversed the nation — Chicago, Milwaukee, San Francisco, Fond du Lac in Wisconsin. He had visited Malta and Florence and Paris and Rome. In London, as elsewhere, he had conversed with the great. Yet the best society, he insisted, could be found in the little club he belonged to at home. Twenty-five citizens — doctor, lawyer, trader, miller, mechanic — the solidest men, who yielded the solidest of gossip.

In London, in Boston, in New York — those cities of make-believe — one finds great ostentation bolstered up on a myriad of little ones. I think — Emerson liked to say — we get closer to reality in a village. In Concord there is the milk of life; we are not so raving-distracted with wind and dyspepsia. People go a-fishing and know the taste of their meat. They cut their own whiffletree in the wood lot; they know something practically of the sun and the west wind, of the underpinning and the roofing of the house, and the pan and mixture of the soil.

Does not perceiving presuppose a unit of measure? How form one's notion of the world without a yardstick? That ninety feet of barn back of the house will prove very useful; the six-acre lot where we learned our plowing; the mile walk from the river to the First Parish Church. The Amazon becomes the Concord, only larger. Annursnuc Hill and wooded Punkatasset are the Alps and Andes.

Simon Willard, thirty-year-old Kentish soldier, English adventurer, shrewd trader, expert surveyor, a co-founder of the town along with

Puritan minister Peter Bulkeley, surely had known how to pick a site. Seven natural ponds; more than nine miles of beaver-haunted, fish-abounding river, bordered by meadows of lush grass that Willard figured would be excellent for cattle; any number of lesser streams on which to build mills; several small cornfields already under Indian cultivation, and plenty of rich bottom land for clearing, were included in the six-mile tract granted in the wilderness by the Great and General Court, governing body of the Colony of Massachusetts Bay, at its meeting on the twelfth of September, 1635.

Though Willard had come to the New World to further his fortunes, there was also the matter of faith which helped him decide to cast in his lot with such gentlemen of Puritan inclination as Thomas Dudley, Sir Richard Saltonstall, and John Winthrop. However, let the parson take care of the settlers' souls; he would look out for his own and their temporal welfare.

By force of character and ability, during a long and energetic lifetime, Willard was to make himself one of the first great men of Concord and a leading citizen of the Colony. From the town's founding, by annual election, he was named Clerk of the Writs. He was chosen captain of the militia company. He became the town's first deputy to the Colony's General Court, its first Assistant to the Governor, its first judge or magistrate. Before his death, he was to serve as commander in chief of the Colony's forces in the Indian trouble. Yet unlike many Puritan leaders, he was no bigoted despiser of the red men. His fortune in the fur trade grew from his knowledge of how to handle Indians. In recognition of his gifts, he was made commissioner of the Colony's traffic in pelts, with further handsome returns. Because of his skill as woodsman and explorer, Massachusetts sent him inland to establish its northern boundary. His initials are still visible on a boundary rock near Lake Winnepesaukee.

Concord's first minister, Peter Bulkeley, a gentleman and landowner in his native Bedfordshire, England, and a heavy investor in this founding enterprise, was, like Willard, also shrewd, though a godly man. He had taken care to reserve for himself the gristmill rights at what was to become the center of the village. Peter Bulkeley ran his mill by deputy, and could scarcely be blamed for his man William Fuller's occasional rascalities. Though the bargain with the town forbade such practices, William was not above slyly raising the splashboards of the sluice to give him greater head of water — flooding the cellars of near-by houses and causing to overflow the stinking tan pits presently located beside the pond.

Because he would have further dealings with them, and possessed a conscience, Willard had concluded a treaty with the natives. Standing in front of the minister's new-built house near the little mill brook, he handed over to the Indians — their sachem a squaw — one parcel of wampum, several knives and hatchets, some hoes to replace their cultivating sticks and clamshells, some cotton clothes and shirts. These, for the land. Simon Willard raised his arms. He pointed east and west, north and south, to signify possession. There had been special gifts, also, for the treaty makers. To the medicine man — the squaw sachem's husband — a suit of cotton cloth, a high-crowned hat of heavy English felt, shoes, stockings, and a great-coat.

Emerson's Indian-loving friend Thoreau, in his own blunt way, whenever he thought of this ancient bargain, held it sheer robbery.

Round Jethro's Oak, where the treaty was consummated, the town had done most of its growing.

The pioneer settlers got their first glimpse of the location as they goaded their oxen northwestward along the newly broken-out, incredibly rough trail from the coastal settlements — the Bay Road, or Great Road, as it came to be called. By vote of the people, this was to be kept a right of way, four rods wide.

In front lay the little river. To the right, cutting off winds from the north, stretched a long, uneven, sandy ridge with a crook in its elbow, the forearm bent northward. In this ridge, the ten or a dozen families scooped crude dugouts, where they lived through that first hard winter. Simon Willard knew all about wigwam dugouts, copied from Indian storage pits by ingenious white men. Aided by the steepness of the slope, it was not too hard to fashion an eight-foot square, level with the surface on the downhill side, with the bank itself for a wall in back. A frame of boards served as a front wall. Timbers ran from this wall to the rear, as a roof, with bark and dirt on top to keep out most of the rain.

Probably the first real house built was the minister's, or the trader's. Right afterwards would follow the meetinghouse for congregational worship. After the minister's house came other permanent dwellings along the sunny side of the Bay Road beneath the ridge where the dugouts were caving in. Small houses, smaller than most yeomen's cottages in Kent and Suffolk and other British shires, from which their lines were copied, built of boards instead of English brick or stone, the wood soon seasoning to a wasp-nest gray. Sedge from the river meadows, in place of English thatch, for the roofs, though the

General Court, because of the fire hazard, had forbidden its use. With a spirit of independence fostered by the distance from the Bay — for Concord had the peculiarity of being the first inland settlement on the northeastern seaboard — the town paid no more attention to such regulations than it wished to, preferring to be counseled by expediency.

Round every house, the committee made a land allotment — six acres, more or less, in outright ownership. By order of the General Court, all house lots were to be within a half-mile radius of each new town's meetinghouse — to promote Christian fellowship, safety, schools, and other good ends. But in Concord, because of the lay of the land, this rule presented difficulties. So the lot makers let themselves be guided by topography.

In England, they had practised farming in common. What went at home seemed proper here. So those portions of the grant most obviously suited for tillage were presently divided into planting fields. Within them, strips were parceled out. Around the whole, a fence would be built, each holder responsible for a share of its upkeep. For pasturage, some upland meadow was similarly divided, though for the most part settlers planned fattening their cattle in the great meadows by the river.

The husbandmen soon encountered difficulties in these common fields. Much space seemed wasted by rights of way. Every farmer found himself losing time and effort going from his several shares and returning to his home lot. The English system simply was not working. So by complicated swaps and bargains, each man began to exchange his parcels till at last he had most of them together. Often enough the shift from many little lots to a single large one meant building a homestead far beyond the center. For good and sufficient reasons of his own, Simon Willard had put up his house and trading post on the fallow land southwest of Nashawtuc Hill, not far from where the Sudbury River runs into the Assabet to form the Concord, and about a mile, as the crow flies, from the minister's house. To this spot, for the fishing, the local Indians and their tribal relatives had been coming for generations. Willard had obtained from the Governor's Council the only permit in the region for the sale of strong drink, which he used prudently as a further lure. Here he developed his acres and his steadily rising traffic in pelts. The Penacooks, the Nashaway, and the Pawtucket Indians who came down the Merrimack to enter the Concord where that sluggish stream, flowing inland, loses itself in the larger river, found Willard's truck house a full day's journey closer than Boston with its traders. And Simon Willard, to keep his advantage, pushed his trading outposts ever farther inland — to Chelmsford, settled largely by pioneers from Concord, to Groton and Lancaster.

For several years, in all likelihood, the only way to reach his place from the center was by ferry, till South Bridge was built to match North Bridge at the other end of town. Thus further access was had to outlying farms. Like veins in an egg that holds a living embryo, the primitive bridle trails became highways. Peter Bulkeley could more readily reach his ministerial wood lot, west of Nashawtuc, and the nine acres granted him in the black muck lands beyond the bulge in the Sudbury — later called Fairhaven Bay — whence that district came to be known as Nine Acre Corner. Joseph Jenks and his associates who were seeking iron ore in the bogs about half a mile up the Assabet could now get to their mines.

Later settlers, finding much of what they considered the best land gone, clamored for further grants to the town till its bounds nearly doubled the original. Land starvation in the Old World led to land greed in the New — far beyond practical digestion. Land brought to each pioneer a possessive joy denied to all but the rich and the nobility in baronial England. Here each colonist became master of his castle. *This is my land* — he could say — *free of all rents, all feudal fees and fines. Here I can add further acres; clear more tillage. This earth I can leave to my sons.*

As Emerson worked on the anniversary speech, he could visualize Concord's pioneers, with their military captain and their pastor, clearing the land. He had hoped to use Concord's earliest records. The town books, he liked to remark, are the diary of a living municipality. But these, up to 1664, had been mostly lost, burned up when Willard's house caught fire. But Emerson, a direct descendant of Peter Bulkeley, could draw on his ancestor's book, *The Gospel Covenant.*

Bulkeley's friend, Edward Johnson, who started several towns on the Bay and believed he and his colleagues functioned under God's immediate direction, left a description of Concord's settlement which fascinated Emerson. The adventurous old Puritan told how these pioneers had fought their way through unknown woods, through swamps, through thickets, clambering over fallen trees where if they missed their footing they plunged into an uncertain bottom of water below. Wearied with this toil — continues Johnson

— they came at last on a scorching plain, thick with prickly bushes that scratched their legs. If undefended by boots or buskins, their flesh was torn, blood trickling down at every step. Sometimes under the burning sun, sometimes with the driving snow on their backs, they pressed on into the wilderness. . . .

Now Johnson may have been thinking of his own exploring, or Willard's. Certainly the families of Concord's settlers, who suffered hardships enough, met with no such preliminary ordeal.

In ascribing the settlers' determination to piety alone, Johnson certainly weighted his account in favor of morals. There must have been facts about these pioneers which Johnson did not choose to relate and which Emerson, from his limited sources, written mostly by puritanical, churchly men, could hardly be expected to know.

In the surviving records of the first fifty years, Emerson could find names still current in Concord. Buttrick, Hosmer, Wheeler . . . The men who bore them, like other settlers of New England, must have been yeomen, mercers, and shoemakers, smiths and tallow chandlers, linen weavers and glovers, ostlers and soap-boilers, tanners and wheelwrights, with a pepper-and-salting of gentlefolk.

What little these goodmen and villeins knew of the continent to which they were tending had seeped down from their parish vicars and curates in villages and towns where the clergy were turning Puritan. What they learned about this promised land made up in glamour what it lacked in accuracy.

At the time of the great migration to Massachusetts Bay, wars in Europe, with pikemen overrunning Flanders, had ruined trade. Handicraftsmen were becoming paupers. Clothmakers were forced to sell their looms. All towns complained of the burden of their poor. Surely — said the proselyting Puritan clergy — England grows weary of its inhabitants, and a man has less consequence than a horse or sheep. For five years crops had failed. Yeomen farmers were also starving.

Why stay in England, toiling over an acre or two, when a hundred or more for each settler are assured overseas? Even the English freeholder owes work and tenurial duties to the Lord of the Manor. Pity most the poor tenant! If I die in this rotten, aged realm, my widow, if she would keep her cottage, must pay a fat swine to the landlord. If my daughter marries, there's another fine or fee — the Church as well as the liege lord devouring my stock. Bishops and archdeacons, along with magistrates, rule our lives and our deaths at their courts.

Hear ye, hear ye, all who are discontent! Gather your wives and children; take ship for the Land of Canaan.

Unlike most of the settlers, the Reverend Peter Bulkeley — former fellow of St. John's College, Cambridge, University preacher, then rector at Odell in Bedfordshire, where his father had preached before him — had come to New England as an older man, not as an adventurer hoping to better his lot. This gave proof of his willingness to sacrifice comfort and security for his religious convictions. He could have remained quietly in England, for he had influence. The well-known family he sprang from was endowed with wealth and land. The town of Bulkeley, in Cheshire, owed its ancient name to his stock. His first wife was a daughter of manorial nobility. His paternal grandmother was a Grosvenor. The St. Johns were his kinsmen, and he was to dedicate *The Gospel Covenant*, first published book of sermons from New England, to his nephew, Oliver St. John — formerly King Charles's Solicitor General; eventually, chief justice of the common pleas in England.

These great ones, had Peter wished them to, could very likely have saved him from persecution for the radical heretical beliefs he was espousing. He had been suspended from his ministry for failure to attend a visitation of Sir Nathaniel Brent, Vicar General of the Church of England. Behind this refusal lay his unwillingness to wear a surplice when he preached or to hold a crucifix when performing baptisms. Such forms — he insisted — were mere superstition and dissentient to the Word of God.

Nec Tempere Nec Timide ran the motto under his family crest. It was time to obey it. Why live privately in his views when, in New England, he might publicly exercise the talents God had given him?

Only a very few British clergymen thought and felt as did Peter Bulkeley. The great majority, state-supported and secure, were content to stay within the structure of the established Church. The gentry, too, that came to New England for the sake of their beliefs, formed a very small minority of all the immigrants.

With his newly wedded second wife — Grace Chetwood, daughter of Sir Richard, whose family held the manor at Odell — Peter took the road to London. As a nonconformist minister, he would encounter his difficulties. Without a certificate of conformity he would not be allowed to sail. Without an official permit or license, no subsidy man, or high tax payer, such as he, could leave. But at the Ports of Embarkation, officials could be found ready to wink at the law. Four of Peter's sons — Thomas, aged eighteen; John and Joseph, fifteen and eleven; Daniel, the youngest, nine — were listed separately on different days at the shipping office so as not to arouse suspicion. Grace Chetwood Bulkeley was even entered for a different vessel, then switched places, at the final moment, with another woman aboard her husband's ship.

They sailed in May, 1635; midsummer saw them safely in Boston Harbor.

Ten months and three days after receiving the grant that made it a town, Concord formally organized its church. Since each meeting was supposed to have two elders — a teacher and a pastor, though these offices presently were merged — Concord chose Peter Bulkeley and John Jones, the latter having also settled in the town soon after his arrival from England, where, like Bulkeley, he was a silenced minister and a Cambridge man.

The pattern had been set in 1629 at Salem, with the establishment there of the first Congregational church in Massachusetts: a company of persons gathered in holy covenant with one another and the Lord. Thus, the Puritans held, the Apostles had founded their churches of old. Each Massachusetts meeting thenceforth elected its own pastors. There were to be no bishops or priestly hierarchy above them. Each church would practise the privilege of admission and expulsion of members and have power to conduct worship according to the rules set forth in the Holy Scriptures. These rules the elders of the churches — the Council of Ministers — were even then in process of clarifying, and woe betide that group or church that saw another slant to the light! With absolute truth from God, how can there be two allowable interpretations? Mistress Ann Hutchinson, for example, was soon to have her views challenged and be forced from the Colony.

Because Concord, as an inland town, would be hard for visiting elders to come to, the formal gathering of the Church took place at Newtown. Already Peter Bulkeley, having left quarrels behind in England — as he thought — had met with new difficulties. Bulkeley's brand of Puritanism held that man himself had something to do with his soul's saving. A powerful faction in Massachusetts insisted that man's salvation lay entirely in God's election.

Because of his disagreement with this bleak belief, Bulkeley found that some whom he counted his closest friends had passed by him, as if he were a man they did not know, when first he came to Boston. Governor Harry Vane and his adherents had pointedly stayed away as Peter Bulkeley read the covenant drawn up by himself and his people:

We do bind ourselves one with another this day before the Lord, henceforth to walk as becometh the people of God. And more particularly do we covenant before the Lord, that, whereas he hath brought us from under the yoke of men's traditions to the precious liberty of his ordinances, we will stand for the maintenance of this liberty to our utmost endeavor.

Bulkeley's discovery that there could be trouble even in this Land of Canaan must have had its influence. The covenant concluded:

Considering that we are members one of another and have civil respect, we do therefore here solemnly promise before the Lord that we will carefully avoid oppression, griping, and hard dealing, and walk in peace, love, mercy and equity towards each other, doing to others as we would they would do to us.

In the wilderness, Concord's inhabitants were to find they could not, by simple resolution, keep earthly trouble away. The town's second winter proved worse than the first. The summer before, many had gone barefoot. Now some went without shoes even in icy weather. Snow fell early and stayed late, and when grain was planted in the spring, frosts blackened and blasted it. The summers that followed were so wet and cool that English grain rotted in the ground, while even Indian corn refused to ripen.

After girdling and felling great trees, after backbreaking toil with mattock and hoe, what good did the new land bring? At seedtime, pigeons and blackbirds pecked out the grain. Wolves dug up the corn, planted Indian-fashion, to eat the dead fish put as fertilizer into each hill. Unexpectedly the river rose to drown the lowland crops. The meadow grass, so lush to look at, proved too rich for the cattle, causing many to sicken. As for the swine supposedly confined at Hogpen Walk to prevent their rooting the corn, several escaped and the lynxes ate them. Death was filling the little churchyard, with many children's graves among the others.

As if troubles from natural causes were not enough, man-made troubles came, too.

There had been great rejoicing in Puritan New England when news at last traveled over the sea telling of King Charles's downfall.

Oliver Cromwell's Commonwealth would bring regeneration to England. "The glory of the Lord is rising upon thee!" exulted Peter Bulkeley in a sermon of thanksgiving.

But with the Puritan cause triumphing at home, immigration to the New World came almost to a halt, with few ships to carry back colonial produce. This dislocation of New England's economy led to temporary chaos. Without commerce, prosperity faded. Prices of cattle and timber — Concord's chief source of income aside from Willard's monopoly — fell in the coastal towns; those of imported necessities rose to prohibitive heights. Many sellers, few buyers, and a desperate lack of currency.

Each of the Bay towns felt the pinch, but Concord, because of its greater remoteness, had a season of actual panic. Its period of respite from colonial taxes had ended. Raising rates to run its own affairs — building the meetinghouse, paying the ministers, tending to roads and bridges — had been hard enough. The General Court, with Simon Willard and Thomas Flint as members from Concord, came to the rescue by permitting payment in kind. A bushel of Indian corn stood for five shillings. But the town had little grain to spare, so was allowed to settle its debt in cattle — a debt with a penalty on top of it, since Concord, independently minded frontier town, had been fined for illegally permitting nonfreemen to vote for its General Court representatives. Because all take part in the affairs of local government — reasoned the town — why not in those of the Colony?

Under pressure of these difficulties, the town's inhabitants grew increasingly restless. *Not in Concord, but in fertile Connecticut, lies the Land of Canaan. A victory over the fierce Pequot tribe to the south has opened a safe path from the Bay. In the fair fields of Uncaway, twenty-five miles below the port of Quinnipiac, or New Haven, a town is already founded. Kinsmen of families in Concord are settled in Fairfield.*

In 1644, in the summer, when overland travel is best, the Reverend John Jones, with nearly a seventh of Concord's population, headed for Fairfield. Some of the best men were going; some of the closest family ties were being snapped. The Reverend Peter Bulkeley was losing two of his sons — Daniel, seeking property, and Thomas, recently married to Sarah, John Jones's daughter.

This was not to be the last exodus, since New England enterprise was to carry men of Concord stock over all the enormous land. But New England cussedness, persistence, and shrewdness would come repeatedly to the rescue of the town. Now the thrifty bought dirt-cheap the cleared lands of those who were leaving. Having made a beginning here, there were those who refused to abandon what they had built. And the covenant to establish a church they had made together in the sight of the Lord held many to their purpose.

Several estates, like Peter Bulkeley's, heretofore able to carry more than a proportionate share of the burden of settlement and of taxes, had considerably shrunken. Relief was imperative. So the General Court, honoring a plea from the inhabitants, reduced the allotment of the colonial tax, and passed a law sharply restricting further immigration from the inland towns — for Concord had some neighbors now — lest the frontier be weakened and the Bay exposed to the ever-present menace of Indian attack.

The winter following the departure to Fairfield began with an encouraging mildness. Peter Bulkeley's favorite doctrine of God's Covenant with man, which he preached over and over to his little flock, heartened both himself and his fellow settlers. "Look how it would joy a poor man," he told them, "if a rich friend were to say to him, 'Come unto me in all your wants; I will help you.' So should it be with us. Though we are poor in wants, yet we have a rich friend in heaven, the Lord Jesus Christ, and he will open the rich treasure of his goodness to us, if we go unto him."

Peter Bulkeley became a tower of strength not for the town alone, but for the Colony. With Thomas Hooker, of Boston, he served as co-moderator of a great synod of elders from all the Congregational churches to pass upon matters of doctrine. When a committee was named by the General Court to investigate high prices, Bulkeley was a member.

Later he found himself on an even more important commission, charged with assembling and publishing the laws of the Colony so that all men could know them. Each town meeting was to send in its suggestions, from which an abridgment would be made. The elected deputies of the towns had started this movement because they distrusted the smaller body of Governor's Assistants which, with magisterial powers, might impose a too personal rule. To check any such tendency, a code of fundamental law — a Magna Carta for the Colony — was needed. Because the task ran into years of work, Bulkeley, lest his duties to his parish be neglected, felt at length compelled to withdraw. But when the town received this *Body of Liberties* for its comments and corrections, he was there to explain and clarify the document.

Even a flattering offer from Oliver Cromwell to found a Puritan stronghold, with state aid, in Ireland, could not lure Peter away. His name stood at the top of a list of six prominent men of Massachusetts who replied to the proposal. Unless Cromwell could guarantee them a healthful site, permission to elect their own officers of government, liberty to worship according to their personal practice, and the means to establish free schools and a college, they preferred — they said — to remain in New England. These things they enjoyed, or hoped to enjoy, right where they were.

Till the year of his death, Bulkeley, as pastor of his flock, visited even the remotest farms in his parish. His sermons and his presence were mighty factors in keeping culture alive on the tough frontier. He lent his books to such as would borrow them. He championed education.

He could not persuade the town's secular fathers to go as far as he wished in the matter of the children. With so much pioneering to be done, who could spare a lad to go to school? So, instead of choosing a schoolmaster, the selectmen preferred annually to pay the five-pound fine levied by the General Court on any town of fifty or more householders which failed to appoint a teacher of reading and writing, lest, as the edict ran, "learning be buried in the grave of our fathers" — a prophecy eventually all too true in Concord, where earliest settlers, literate men, reared up children unable even to put their names to the deeds of land which were becoming the symbols of life's most immediate interest.

But Peter Bulkeley had little trouble in winning the town's support for newly founded Harvard College. Forty-two of its citizens compacted to give the sum of five pounds annually to the college for seven years. They sent also their ablest sons. John Bulkeley was one of the nine young men who made up Harvard's first class to graduate.

His address almost ready, Emerson, interested in the evolution of government, determined to describe a town meeting resolution of 1654, in which Concord voted to forgive the North Quarter three pounds of its assessment, in consideration of that section's greater expense in building and maintaining bridges. "Fellow citizens," he would say, "this first recorded political act of our fathers, this tax assessed on its inhabitants by a town, is the most important event in their civil history, implying, as it does, the exercise of a sovereign power, and connected with all the immunities and powers of a corporate town."

Where did this political practice come from? In vain look for the inventor. It was a philosophy made by no man. "The germ" — wrote Emerson — "was formed in England. The charter gave to the freemen of the Company of Massachusetts Bay the election of the Governor and Council of Assistants." This charter permitted Governor and Assistants to elect more freemen, all freemen having the right to make the Colony's fundamental laws. When presently the freemen grew so numerous that a meeting of all became unwieldy, the system of electing deputies followed.

The towns had soon learned to exercise a right of expressing opinions on every question before the country. "In a town meeting, the great secret of political science was uncovered, and the problem solved, how to give every individual his fair weight in the government." In consequence of this institution — Emerson was ready to point out — not a schoolhouse, bridge, meetingplace, or milldam could be set up, or pulled down, or altered, or bought, or sold, without the whole population — both rich and poor, just and unjust — having a voice in the matter.

Leafing through two hundred years of town records, Emerson had met with plenty of evidence of fallibility. He would warn his audience against expecting perfection. Indeed, every private grudge, every suggestion of petulance and ignorance, was as likely to come out in them as altruism, duty, and remembrance of the public weal. In the human story, who can expect to find a church of saints, a metropolis of patriots, enacting nothing but wholesome and creditable laws? "If the good counsel prevailed, the sneaking counsel did not fail to be suggested; freedom and virtue, if they triumphed, triumphed in a fair field. And so be it an everlasting testimony for them, and so much ground of assurance of man's capacity for self-government!"

In the settlement of North America, certain early colonies had endured — the pioneers had stuck it out; others had failed. Sir Walter Raleigh, in the sixteenth century, established settlers at Roanoke, Virginia; he sought them again in 1590, and never found them. In 1609, the Spaniards made a town on the Rio del Norte that runs into the Rio Grande and the Gulf of Mexico, and called it Santa Fe. That same decade, Virginia was settled. The year before, far to the North, Frenchmen built a fort on a high rock and named it Quebec. Then came Plymouth, then the Bay Colony, with a solid success. The difficult climate should have ended these New Englanders. But perhaps it strengthened them. Perhaps they could also attribute their survival to the system of government they developed, with the characteristics it in turn gave to the settlers. Moreover — felt Emerson — though pioneers like the Reverend Peter Bulkeley were unprepared for the hardships they encountered, they possessed armed and determined minds; finer equipment, even, than hardihood of body.

What is history? A river sprung from the thoughts and acts of men? Every revolution is first an idea or feeling in one man's mind. When the same thought occurs to another, is it not the key to an era? History must be read actively — not passively — in the people's experience. Does not history walk incarnate in every man? The human spirit goes forth from the beginning to embody in appropriate events each faculty, each idea, each emotion which belongs to it.

> I am the owner of the sphere,
> Of the seven stars and the solar year,
> Of Caesar's hand, and Plato's brain,
> Of Lord Christ's heart, and Shakespeare's strain.

With the town clerk's ledgers, at last intact, for a diary; with the testimony and the power of the people — history hardly needed an intermediary. From the top of the ridge behind the house his grandfather had built, Emerson could see Concord River journeying out of the gray past into the green future. A greater stream, not shut within the banks, flows in its water, through its rocks, in the air — through darkness, through men and women, passion and thought. Emerson heard and saw its eternal passage.

CHAPTER II

The Tawny Vermin

CONCORD first got the news of Indian trouble in late June, 1675. At Swansea, where the neighboring Plymouth Colony touches Narragansett Bay, the Wampanoags, under Philip, had killed half a dozen settlers.

Unlike Massasoit, who had befriended the Pilgrims during the early difficult years of the Plymouth venture, his son Philip, since becoming chief, had shifted bit by bit from passive to active hostility. If any white man could have attended one of Philip's councils, he might have learned the reasons. With increasing restlessness, Philip and other sachems had watched the usurpation of their hunting grounds and seen the flight of game before the settler and his plow. Milldams in many streams were holding back the spring runs relied on for the year's supply of smoked fish. Also, what would become of a sachem's power if more and more Indians submitted to English rule?

Eleven years before John Endicott entered Boston Harbor to start the Bay Colony, the coastal Indians had been nearly exterminated by what literal-minded men called a plague but the Puritans laid to God's providence. Philip's tribe was insignificant now, dwindled to a poor remnant of what it once had been. But the leaders of the Plymouth and the Massachusetts Bay Colonies had long suspected Philip as a plotter against them. This was the time to crush him, they decided, and put an end to the danger. So Massachusetts mustered three companies to join the troops from Plymouth.

New England's settlers — especially those of the Bay Colony — had grown confident and careless as their numbers increased; as more towns — Brookfield, Groton, Lancaster — thrust the frontier further inland. Now that pelts were growing scarcer, how could the Indians bring in enough of them if not allowed guns, powder, and shot? Everyone knew that laws forbidding sale of arms to the natives were no longer effective. If Indians did not get them from Massachusetts traders less scrupulous than Simon Willard, they bought them from the Dutch and French whose settlements flanked New England. It was thriftier to legalize the business and require every English trader to pay a fee to the Colony Treasurer for each gun sold, each pound of powder.

As a measure of precaution, the General Court instructed every town to put up one or more garrison houses where women and children could seek refuge in case of attack. With other things to do, most had been slow to carry out the order. At Concord, however, men from that village and from neighboring Chelmsford, Billerica, Lancaster, and Groton had organized a frontier troop of cavalry to keep an eye on those Indians who persisted in living in the vicinity. Thomas Wheeler — no Indian lover, though Willard's local associate in the fur trade — was chosen captain.

The men raised to capture Philip marched off from Boston in gay spirits. This would be like a Muster-Day parade, only more exciting, with celebrations and plenty of rum when the job was finished. There was no real danger, folks told one another, of a serious war. The victory over the Pequots, back in 1637, had taught the red men a lesson. Soon the time would come when these tawny vermin would be driven wholly from the region to make room for a better race.

Concord and the Bay towns settled back to await the conclusion. It came sooner than expected.

Militiamen and volunteers began to straggle back with an alarming story. Just when the raw and inexperienced troops thought they had the enemy cornered at Pocasset Neck where it juts out into Fall River, Philip and his warriors built rafts, and, at low tide, shortly before daybreak, ferried themselves over the salt channel to the deep woods that led to the Nipmuck country. An attempt to pursue them had been disastrous. Bullets came from nowhere to strike down the bewildered troopers who crowded forward in close formation. The very bushes seemed in league with the Indians. The occasional Wampanoags glimpsed by the soldiers had fastened green boughs to their bodies. They shot their muskets at close range, then faded back into cover while Englishmen died looking for an enemy to fight.

The little conflagration shifted to abundant tinder. Like phan-
toms, Philip and his braves slipped into Massachusetts. The chief
had kinsmen and adherents among the tribes within the Bay Colony
and Connecticut and possessed a persuasive tongue. There was no
telling where the fire might break out. And here were the so-called
"Praying Indians" within the very gates of the English settlements!

Right from the time that the practice began, hard-headed fron-
tiersmen had looked with disfavor at efforts of men like John Eliot,
of Roxbury, to Christianize the Indians and bring them within the
bastion of the white plantations.

Having quickly got the knack of their language, Eliot had preached
to the Indians in their own tongue. He held to the theory that these
red men were the lost tribes of Israel, hence God's strayed children.
At the very start of his missionary labor, he had seen the advantage
of friendship with Simon Willard. Together priest and trader probed
the interior — Willard for his truck in furs; Eliot, like a second John
the Baptist, clad in buckskins, with a leather girdle round his waist,
to carry God's word to the heathen. They had voyaged by canoe
northwestward on the inland waterways as far as the territory of
Passaconaway, sachem of the Penacook tribe, a branch of the
Abenakis of French Catholic Canada. This sachem was a witch doctor as well as a chief, whose people believed he could make water
burn, bring green leaves to a frozen branch in winter, or turn himself into a spirit of fire.

Wherever he could, Eliot tried to convert the leaders, trusting
that the tribesmen would follow. And Passaconaway, with an eye
on the English goods that would come if he traded with Willard,
had proved hospitable and friendly.

Nearer the Bay, the fur factor had been able to help his friend
set up Christian villages, till seven had been established in Massachusetts — with the hesitant blessing of the General Court, which
granted them lands and charters. Closest of these towns to Concord
was Nashoba, six miles to the westward. Tahattawan, its chief, along
with several petty sagamores, including Waban and the squaw
sachem from whom Concord had bought its land, had been persuaded by Simon Willard and Thomas Flint to place themselves
under the Colony's rule in exchange for protection against the Mohawks from the north.

*Would they worship the only true God, who made heaven and
earth?*

Yes. The English, they saw, throve better under this God than they did under theirs.

Would they do no unnecessary work on the Sabbath?

That was easy; they did little on any day, and could readily take their ease on the Sabbath.

Would they give speedy warning of any conspiracy against their white neighbors?

Yes; they would be brothers.

Eliot hoped to teach these converts to cultivate the soil and be industrious. He encouraged them to make brooms, baskets, and eelpots which white settlers would buy. Concord presently got used to Indians with cropped hair — English-fashion — padding across the Milldam. On the Sabbath, a solemn row of them would fill the back bench of the meetinghouse, to hear the words of "the Big Pray," as they called Peter Bulkeley. Some came dressed from head to foot in English clothes. Those who had not assembled a full outfit wore at least a cast-off Monmouth hat or English blanket.

Eliot's Indian towns — with Bulkeley and Willard keeping a paternal eye on Nashoba — seemed in a fair way toward becoming new Jerusalems for the once-lost tribesmen.

But no one with an interest in the matter could fail to notice that white men were growing daily more grasping in their tactics. Willard's associates in the fur trade at Chelmsford — like the pioneers all along the frontier — were petitioning for more and more territory, much of it promised to the Praying Indians by previous grants of the General Court. At last Willard's sense of justice whipped him into making a protest. In a report to the legislature, he drew attention to the way in which the English were taking over the best lands from Eliot's towns.

The report proved unpopular.

And now that Philip was rousing the tribesmen, the original objectors to the practice of placing any confidence in these vermin felt themselves justified — too late to avoid the danger.

After the fiasco at Swansea, and Philip's escape, Concord became very uneasy when its troop of horsemen, under Captain Thomas Wheeler, was ordered to proceed inland thirty miles toward newly settled Brookfield. Notwithstanding the presence of the militia company of foot soldiers, the town felt safer when its mounted scouts also were close at hand. What's more, drafts on Concord's militia had reduced its strength in order to furnish soldiers for Major Simon

Willard's patrols ranging the line of frontier towns that formed a protective semicircle round the Bay.

Captain Edward Hutchinson, a pioneer recently in the Brookfield region, and on good terms, he believed, with the local sachems, had orders to seek a parley there with the Quabaug tribe of the Nipmuck Indians. Brookfield, midway in the wilderness between the Bay towns of the coast and the river settlements of Hartford and Springfield, must be held at all costs, lest inland Connecticut be cut off from Massachusetts. Philip was promising the Indians of the interior that with their aid he would drive the English back across the sea. Hutchinson must dissuade the Quabaugs from joining the conspiracy. Wheeler's cavalry scouts were to serve as the emissary's bodyguard.

On July the twenty-seventh, at ten in the morning, Wheeler with twenty of his troop reported at Boston. Next morning, Wednesday, when the horsemen rode through Cambridge, they had added four members to their company. Three were Praying Indians from Natick — Joseph and Sampson Petuhanit, brothers, and George Memecho, their kinsman. Since early spring, Waban, the Christian sagamore, making good his promise, had been warning the settlers. After the leafing of the trees — he repeated — watch out for trouble. Now that his prophecy had come true, the colonial government, which had paid little heed before, was ready to take Waban seriously. Guides and interpreters would be needed successfully to carry out this mission. The three Christian Indians had been brought along at Hutchinson's insistence, though they drew black looks from inveterate Indian haters among Wheeler's scouts.

Ephraim Curtis was the fourth member. Well known in Concord as owner of a farm just over the bounds in Sudbury, he had become a trader with the Nipmucks and was perhaps the most skillful woodsman and explorer in the Colony. It was he who had brought word of restlessness among the Indians near Brookfield. Returning now with this show of force — small as it was — he hoped to try the power of persuasion on the Quabaugs.

The troopers rode through Concord, over the South Bridge, then past Nine Acre Corner. They walked their horses in single file on the narrow road through the swampy fields toward Sudbury. Here they spent the night, and on Thursday turned westward into the Nipmuck country.

Now on the outermost rim of settlement, they threaded along through lonely forests, with very rarely a tiny village or trading post on the line of march — Marlborough, once Okamakamesit, one of

Eliot's Praying Indian towns till white men claimed the meadows; Quansigamug, where Curtis kept a truck house.

Thursday and Friday they rode through the woods, past Indian villages lately deserted — no sign of life; refuse freshly dumped on the kitchen middens; campfire ashes not yet washed away by the rain.

On Saturday, early in the morning, the spell of the empty country was broken. Ahead, at a widening of the trail, the troopers caught a glimpse of two red men with a horse — obviously a settler's. Wheeler hoped to speak with them, but the pair, abandoning their booty, vanished among the trees.

Curtis advised a halt. The scouts turned left toward Brookfield. Around noon next day, Sunday, they reached the village.

The inhabitants were amazed to see the troop. They had heard nothing of Philip's rising. Trouble with the friendly Quabaugs, they insisted, was most unlikely. Up to a few days ago, members of the tribe had been working for hire in the settlement's cornfields.

That Sunday afternoon, Wheeler delegated Ephraim Curtis, with two Brookfield men and an Indian guide, to go find the local tribesmen. The news which the messengers brought back was scarcely good to sleep on. Yes, they had met the Indians. About one hundred and fifty warriors, as far as Curtis could judge. The young braves of the party had made big talk, and brandished the muskets they were armed with. But the sachems had quieted the bucks. They had promised to meet the English next day for a council.

The meeting place was a field three miles from town; the time was to be eight in the morning.

Soon after sun-up, Wheeler mustered his troop. He also brought along Sergeant Prichard and Corporal Coy, of Brookfield's militia, and John Ayres, selectman, with whom the Quabaug chief, Matamap, had professed close friendship.

Not a sign of an Indian — the council field was empty. Hutchinson, Wheeler, and his men waited, the silence broken only by the neighing of a restless horse, a phoebe's occasional call, and the low voices of the Christian Indians talking in their own language. The sun rose higher. It was well past eight o'clock. Wheeler and Hutchinson, with the support of most of the troopers, and at the earnest entreaty of the Natick Indian scouts, were for going back. But the men from Brookfield ridiculed the notion of a trap. No, the lazy Indians were just waiting at their camp in the swamp. It would be no great job to find them.

Wheeler at last motioned the cavalcade to advance.

For several miles the route lay through an open valley. Then it narrowed — a rocky hill with stunted scrub oak thickets on the right; on the left, the tangled undergrowth of a sizeable swamp. The ridge pressed the trail to the very edge of the sphagnum.

When the hindmost trooper had come about sixty rods past this dark entry, a volley of musket shot raked the strung-out horsemen all along the line on the swamp side. Even had the footing been good, retreat was impossible — the way now blocked by a horde of screeching Indians.

Instinctively every man not badly hit or whose mount had not been shot from under him turned his plunging horse up the slope. Indians lay in ambush there also, but not so many. Captain Wheeler found himself part way up the hillside before his mind started working and he realized some of his men must have dropped in that first blast. He reined his horse back toward the swamp.

Along with shots from the place of original ambush, there was now a cross fire from Indians who had worked their way to higher ground. Wheeler felt the smash of the bullet that shattered his right arm. A moment later, his horse collapsed. Painted warriors rose yelling from the bushes.

At this nick of time, the old captain heard the clatter of a horseman. It was his son William, who had seen his plight from the ridge. Jumping off, he set his badly injured father on the horse, gave the beast a slap to start him up the hill, then, despite a hip wound he had got in the very first volley, began fighting his way back on foot. He would never have made it had not a riderless horse, just then, thrashed up through the thickets. Young Wheeler caught it and got somehow in the saddle — though another bullet had just made his left arm useless. A moment later, father and son were back with what was left of the troopers.

The survivors got over the ridge and into an open valley beyond. The Indians, busy plundering the bodies of the dead, did not press their immediate advantage.

There was no time to bandage the wounded or count the missing. All three Brookfield men, however, had died by that first volley. There was no one left who knew the lay of the land — and the town, with its garrison house, was easily ten miles distant.

Joseph and Sampson, the two Natick Indians — the third had disappeared — now guided the retreat. Knowing that the enemy would be sure to lie in wait on the back track, they circled away from it.

Skillfully they kept the little party in the open fields, the troopers, many on injured horses, riding slowly and painfully at a pace not too jarring for the wounded. After what seemed an eternity, the cluster of Brookfield's houses came in sight.

News of the disaster flashed quickly through the village. By the time the last trooper dragged himself wearily into the blockhouse of John Ayres, whose widow had just learned of his death, most of Brookfield's inhabitants — some fifteen or sixteen families — had taken refuge there.

Selectman Ayres's place, used as an inn by travelers bound for the Connecticut settlements, was stoutly built. Here for a while at least the little garrison might repel attack. Fifty women and children were packed in the building, but Brookfield's losses in the swamp had cut down her fighting men to scarcely a dozen. And with so short a warning, the women had been able to snatch up little food.

Thomas Wheeler was in no shape to direct the defense. With Hutchinson also badly wounded, Wheeler appointed Lieutenant Simon Davis, Willard's nephew from Concord, to take over active command, along with two Chelmsford men — James Richardson and John Fiske.

Monday afternoon was already well along. Any moment the Indians would attack. But for two hours the deserted outskirts of the village remained in silence. Perhaps there was a chance for a messenger to slip through with news of the plight of the town. Wheeler and Hutchinson called on Ephraim Curtis. He would take with him Henry Young of Concord.

In the yellow light just before sunset, the folk in the garrison watched them mount their horses. But they were hardly out of sight before two shots echoed through the quiet. Curtis and Young, their muskets smoking, were back at a gallop. The Indians, they reported, surrounded the town and were already pillaging the outermost homesteads.

Anxiously the people looked toward Sergeant Prichard's. His young son had just gone there to try to fetch more supplies. They saw him run from the doorway, then drop as a thrown tomahawk caught him.

Yelling in triumph, the Indians cut off their victim's head and began kicking it about like a football. Keeping just out of effective range, they brandished their weapons at the garrison. Then they stuck young Prichard's head on a pole and set it up just in front of his house — the dead eyes, in the failing light, briefly visible to the makeshift fort's defenders.

At dusk, the Indians grew bolder. They circled round, yelling like fiends possessed, and firing their muskets. Henry Young, watching from a window for a chance to blaze away, fell with a shot through the shoulder.

With only a small quantity of powder and ball, the defenders limited their fire. The night, with no moon, grew pitch-black. Under cover of darkness, the enemy crept closer. Splinters from the walls, as bullets struck them, fell in showers on the crouching refugees. Two women who were pregnant and near their time, their pains brought on by the terror and excitement, gave birth prematurely.

Near three o'clock, a waning moon rose. By its light the Indians piled hay at a corner of the garrison, then lit it. Simon Davis ordered the defenders to try a burst of musketry. During this diversion, three or four men, running from the door, put out the fire.

The stock of ammunition was much lower; the number of unwounded defenders was narrowing from threescore toward less than two dozen. Wheeler again called on Curtis. But Curtis found the Indians still an impassable ring. Toward morning, he tried again — creeping like a snake from the briefly unbolted oak door.

Later that morning — Tuesday — the Indians renewed their assault. A group of them had taken over the meetinghouse, about two hundred feet away, and were using it as an outpost. Now and again they would burst into a noisy imitation of psalm singing to mock the beleaguered garrison. By way of reply, the defenders poured in a steady fusillade. That evening they had the satisfaction of watching the Indians carry several wounded or dead from the building. But from the greater number of Indians visible, it was plain the attackers had received reinforcement.

The second night was like the first — only worse. The Indians shot flaming arrows at the roof, but the defenders, watching at holes cut for the purpose, put them out before the shingles caught. A fireball fell through one such opening into a mass of flax and tow, but a soldier doused the flames before they could spread. Again the Indians set fire to an outer wall, this time rushing to the door to shoot down any defenders coming out to fight it. But Davis ordered the men to smash a couple of planks for an opening nearer the fire, and avoided the trap.

It was Wednesday morning, the third day of the siege.

In addition to the meetinghouse, the Indians had now taken over the barn of the garrison, close at hand, which they fortified with posts and rails against the settlers' musket balls.

The defenders' plight was shifting from bad to desperate. Because of the Indians' incessant yelling, sleep was impossible. Most of the little remaining stock of ammunition was used up. The supply of water, so vital for fire fighting, was almost gone. Thomas Wilson, volunteering to get some, received a shot through the neck and upper jaw as he reached the courtyard. His screams of agony drew a derisive whoop from the red men.

That day the Indians devoted themselves to a new invention to burn down the blockhouse. For hours the defenders could see them gather pairs of cartwheels from the barns. These they fastened two by two between shafts till they had a narrow, many-wheeled contraption almost twenty-five yards long. At the forepart, in barrels, they put hay, flax, and candlewood. Maneuvering this vehicle from the rear, the attackers counted on being less exposed to the garrison's guns.

By evening they had two of them ready.

Just as they got them lighted and in motion, a sudden thundershower put out the flames. In the shouting and confusion that followed, and the gloom of the storm, the garrison's defenders became suddenly conscious of what seemed like English voices near by.

Straining to hear, Wheeler thought he could distinguish Major Simon Willard's. He ordered the bugler to sound a call. At the first few notes, there was a rush of horsemen outside. It was indeed Willard. He and his troopers gained the courtyard before the attackers realized that reinforcements had slipped through.

The next moment, old comrades had found each other — Hosmers, Healds, Barretts, and other Wheelers from Concord and the vicinity joining the defense by the side of their kinsmen.

The Indians, uncertain as to what was going on, set fire to the barn they had fortified, then burned the meetinghouse. But though this gave them light through which to see, by the number of horses, that a considerable reinforcement had arrived, it deprived them of cover. They retreated to the further shadow and their shooting stopped.

Presently, one by one, the remaining houses of the village burst into flames.

When dawn broke on Thursday morning, not an Indian was to be seen in the blackened ruins of Brookfield.

* * *

While the exhausted garrison rested, Willard's men tended the wounded and set guards. But the next two days remained quiet, and on Saturday afternoon Captain Thomas Lothrop's troops arrived, the first contingent of relief sent from Boston.

Presently all the Middlesex Troop able to travel set out for home. Ample reinforcements were arriving. Captain Richard Beers and his company had already joined with Lothrop's men — troopers from Springfield and Hartford, Connecticut. Swashbuckling Samuel Moseley with sixty dragoons had cantered in. A privateer in the West Indies — some called him plain "pirate" — before Philip's war, Moseley was as independent and unscrupulous an adventurer as his equally tough soldiers could wish for. With Moseley there, and his Indian-killers, there seemed little likelihood of renewed attack.

Hampered by wounds and lack of horses, it took five days for Wheeler and his group to reach Marlborough. There Captain Hutchinson grew worse and died. Wheeler saw him buried, then pushed on for Concord.

Rumors of the Brookfield disaster had prepared Concord for the shattered troop's return. With Philip and his allies anywhere and everywhere, security had vanished. Every remote farm, every settlement, was in peril.

During the succeeding weeks, the news that came to Concord remained of the worst. Captain Beers and his entire company were wiped out at Northfield. A few days later, catastrophe struck near Hadley, where Captain Lothrop and his men were massacred in ambush — English blood crimsoning the near-by brook as seventy in the troop of eighty died. Deerfield and Springfield went up in flames.

In spite of Captain Wheeler's sworn certificate that his Praying Indian guides at Brookfield had been chiefly instrumental in the escape from the swamp and had acted throughout with faithfulness and courage, Concord's inhabitants looked toward the Christian Indian village of Nashoba with increasing fear and hate. Were not all red men the same? Would not these also, like serpents in the grass, twist and kill?

When the Governor and Council, heeding popular clamor, ordered all Praying Indians confined within the limits of their towns, Concord rejoiced. The added provision that any Indian found a mile beyond the center of his village could legally be shot on sight — the white settlers told one another — was a good decree.

Prevented thus from cultivating their cornfields, cut off from their livelihood of trade with the whites, the Christian Indians of Nashoba soon faced starvation. Even under slightly better earlier conditions, their numbers had been shrinking till only fifty-eight were left — mostly squaws and children. On Eliot's appeal, the General Court ordered them moved to Concord where they could be kept under surveillance and given work. Daniel Gookin, Superintendent of the Christian Indians, was appointed with Simon Willard to see to the business.

At Concord, the commissioners could find only one citizen, John Hoar, willing to undertake the responsibility of looking after this remnant. Hoar had the reputation of being a cantankerous man. At William Buss's public house, Concord citizens had heard him speak of Reverend Edward Bulkeley's prayers as so much empty babbling. Those honest enough to contrast the feeble pompous son with the father he had succeeded must have agreed about the second Bulkeley's windy periods. But Hoar had run afoul of the pulpit's uncontradictability, and was made to pay the ten-pound fine. For other hotheaded explosions he had been disbarred from the courts. Perhaps because of his history, perhaps in spite of it, Willard and Gookin decided to accept his offer.

With forty pounds of his own money, Hoar built his charges a stockade and workshops near his house. At risk of his life from hostile Indians, he drove his team to Nashoba to save what he could of his wards' winter supply of corn. He was determined they should neither starve nor lack work. At least they would be better off than the rest of the Praying Indians, who had been herded together on bleak Deer Island, at the mouth of blustery Boston Harbor, with so little grain that they were forced to dig clams to keep alive.

That fall, the military council of the Colony gave up pursuit of marauding Indians by heavily armed troops. Militiamen no longer bragged that one white man could account for ten Indians. Concord and other inland towns were thankful that some of their soldiers were ordered back for home garrison duty. With every able-bodied man under arms, the harvests had suffered.

Meanwhile, the vulnerable inland towns of Massachusetts waited.

On February tenth, before dawn, a hard-riding messenger from the Bay galloped into Concord. Three hundred Indians from the west at Wachusett, he warned, were moving on Lancaster. The news, he said, had been brought at midnight to Daniel Gookin at Cambridge by a Praying Indian, Job Kattenanit, set free from Deer

Island to serve as spy. Arriving exhausted and famished at Gookin's house, this man had traveled eighty miles by snowshoe with the tidings.

Concord had close ties with Lancaster. Lancaster's minister, Joseph Rowlandson, was related to the Hosmers by marriage. The Prescotts and other families had kinsfolk in both towns.

The first relief to arrive, Captain Samuel Wadsworth with forty soldiers, found half the town in flames. Wadsworth's men, barely escaping ambush, defended themselves in Cyprian Stevens's palisaded house — one of several blockhouses in the spread-out village. When eighty horsemen at last got there from Concord, forcing the Indians back into the hills, most of the town was in ruins. Rowlandson's garrison, where nearly forty people were said to have taken refuge, was a burnt-out horror — the bodies of the dead hacked and charred. At first the soldiers feared Lancaster's minister had been killed, till survivors from other garrison houses explained he had left several days before to plead with the Governor for better protection for his town. His wife's body was not among the victims. Evidently she and her three children had been carried off by the marauders. Subtracting the number of dead from the total thought to have been in the blockhouse, Selectman White guessed about twenty-four captives must have been taken.

At Nagog Pond, near the deserted Praying Indian village of Nashoba, Isaac Shepard, with his brother Abraham, was threshing grain in the barn. News of the attack on Lancaster had increased the household's caution. To warn of danger, the men posted their fourteen-year-old sister, Mary, on a boulder part way up the snow-covered hillside behind the house.

But the pounding of the flails drowned the girl's shriek, A moment later, Isaac Shepard sprawled in death near the musket he had not had time to fire; his brother Abraham lay unconscious near him. From the barricaded house, the two men's wives saw Indians make off with the girl.

Abraham Shepard rallied enough to set out through the snow with his dead brother's wife, his own wife, and his wife's small baby, for refuge at Concord.

A week later the Shepard girl rode into the village. She told how the Indians had taken her on a three days' journey inland to Winnisimmet — their camp northwest of ruined Brookfield. Many Indians, she said, were at this place. She thought they had other prisoners with them. There, in the night, she had slipped from her captor's wigwam, untethered a horse, then followed her back track home.

Concord felt in no mood to temporize. The neighborhood was rife with rumors that Praying Indians still at large had taken part in the Lancaster massacre and raid on the Shepard farm. On the Sunday following Mary's return, just as the people were filing into meeting, a troop of horsemen clattered into town. At their head was Captain Samuel Moseley.

Several of the congregation — aware of what was stirring, having indeed started the motion by sending secretly for Moseley — exchanged knowing looks.

The dark-faced captain sat impassive through Edward Bulkeley's prolix sermon. Then he spoke to the people:

Did they not have some heathen in town, committed to one Hoar, who were a trouble and disquiet to them?

Heads nodded assent.

If the citizens wished it, he would take these vermin to Deer Island.

Again heads nodded. Two or three men spoke in favor of the plan, while the rest, by their silence, gave Moseley all the consent he needed.

As the meeting broke up, the captain strode to the workhouse and stockade John Hoar had built south of the millpond. The whole congregation — men, women, and children — determined to miss nothing, streamed behind. At Moseley's peremptory thumping, John Hoar opened the gate.

Where were these Indians? the captain demanded.

For once keeping his temper, Hoar checked them off, one by one, on his list. All, he replied, were accounted for.

"I will leave a corporal and soldiers to secure them," said the captain.

That would hardly be necessary, Hoar pointed out. *He* was their security. They had been committed to his care by order of the Court. Nor — added the lawyer firmly — would he give them up.

For the time being, Moseley was daunted.

Next morning, however, he was back in force, demanding surrender of the Indians.

"Where is your order from the Court?"

Moseley could not produce one — all he had was his commission to fight Indians. Hoar refused to accept this authority.

Checked far beyond the point he usually tolerated, Moseley thrust the custodian aside and ordered a corporal to smash the workhouse door. Though the captain made some pretense at stopping the plunder, the soldiers at once fell to stripping the Indians even of their shoes and shirts. Then all fifty-eight were lined up between two files and led toward Boston. Among them went the wife of Joseph Petuhanit, who by his skillful guiding had saved Captain Wheeler's company after the massacre in the swamp at Brookfield. Joseph himself, despairing of good treatment from the English, had sought refuge with King Philip.

During the rest of February and into March, old Simon Willard divided his time between emergency meetings of the Governor's Council and directing the companies of scouts that patrolled the woods. Yet despite his efforts, many of the inner girdle of towns, by the end of March, had been attacked, with several abandoned. Groton, Willard's present residence, vanished in flames. Luckily the major had moved his family to Charlestown, but his big farmhouse was burned to the ground. "Major Willard and loving Sir," wrote Edward Rawson, Secretary of the General Court, "I am requested by the Governor . . . upon . . . information of the enemy's resolution to destroy or ruin Marlborough, Concord, Sudbury, Watertown, Cambridge, Charlestown, and Boston . . . that you, with your forces thereabout, keep . . . ranging towards Marlborough, and further prevent what mischiefs may be."

Thus far Concord had escaped. But roving bands of Indians, down from their winter quarters in the north and west, were all about. After daybreak on Tuesday, April 18, when the town chanced to be empty of all soldiers save for its own little garrison, the warning came. Five miles up the river, at Sudbury, Indians were attacking.

Not one of its own militia officers was in Concord to command the group of a dozen townsmen that set out to the aid of the neighboring village. But with Josiah Wheeler, a veteran of Willard's relief of Brookfield, and with Daniel Comy, Jim Hosmer, and the rest all experienced militiamen, they started with plenty of confidence on their dangerous venture. Most were family men. Comy was father of six children. At all costs, the Indians must be turned back from Concord. Joe Buttrick, son of an original settler of Concord, had double cause for anxiety — his wife's family lived at Sudbury.

As usual for that season, the river was in flood, the South Bridge almost impassable. Sloshing about the men's knees, the water felt icy.

When they drew near low-lying Sudbury, the musket men were forced to quit the river road, which was inundated, and take to the edge of the flooded meadows.

Ahead, near the west bank — the side they were following — stood the garrison house of Walter Haynes. Across the river, eastward, the men of Concord could see columns of smoke from several burning houses. As they cautiously approached Haynes's place, the swollen waters of the Sudbury on their left, they saw what looked like half a dozen Indians making ready to attack the garrison. Apparently the red men had not seen them. By a quick rush over the wet meadow, they hoped to rout the attackers and gain the shelter of the blockhouse. With a yell to disconcert the Indians, they made a dash for it.

They almost reached safety, their feet heavy with the river mud, when Indians hidden in the brush all along the right flank of the meadow, above and some already behind the men, opened fire. The bullets that missed their mark splashed into the water beyond. Most of Concord's little group fell in the first moment of ambush. Jim Hosmer, seeing every other way of escape cut off, jumped into the river to swim across, only to have a musket ball crash through his head.

More shots — and not a man was left alive.

Not till the following day, Wednesday, did Concord get anything but confused reports. The rest of that Tuesday remained a day of uncertainty and terror. From messengers hurrying to seek reinforcements, the inhabitants heard that over fifteen hundred warriors were attacking the neighboring town. By noon and later, fresh troops were marching through. All afternoon, word that came back was that the fighting continued. Captain Wadsworth's command — first to have come to the rescue of Lancaster — was surrounded, men said, on a hill west of Sudbury.

In the all-night defense of the hilltop, Wadsworth's troop was to lose all its officers and more than half its men.

But by Wednesday morning, the Indians were through.

This unexpected turn had an explanation. Actually, they had attacked in no great numbers. To fool the white men, they had made their squaws carry staves to look like braves armed with muskets. Losses among their warriors, as more and more troopers converged from Marlborough, Watertown, Boston, made flight essential. Furthermore, the natives found themselves matched against Indians fighting in the English ranks. On Gookin's repeated urging, the war

Council had at last enlisted the services of the Praying Indians from Deer Island. A company of them had reached Sudbury in time to help rescue Wadsworth's battered survivors.

Throughout the early summer, though small bands of Indians still shifted between marauding and flight, the conspiracy was drawing ever closer to disintegration. The Indians were out of food and had failed to find enough at Sudbury to supply their needs. During the past autumn and winter, the partners in Philip's loosely-knit league had lost most of their corn through raids by white soldiers. And Willard's scouts had kept them from their annual spring fishing. The back of Philip's hope for victory was almost broken.

Kept guessing by the almost invisible enemy, however, the settlers, lacking a clear picture, had little reason for confidence. They had just suffered a different kind of blow. Toward the end of April, Concord's inhabitants and the rest of the Colony had been shocked by news of Simon Willard's death, at Cambridge, after a brief illness.

Fearing the constant threat along the border, not every man of Concord who wanted to could attend his former townsman's funeral at Charlestown. The six companies which paraded that day in his honor marched directly afterwards to Concord — their rendezvous for patrolling the frontier.

The great news in Concord, near the first of May, was that Mrs. Rowlandson and other Lancaster captives might be ransomed.

They had vanished into the woods without a trace. Though Reverend Joseph Rowlandson's frantic appeals to the Council prompted several raids into the Nipmuck country, the soldiers came back empty-handed. The Council refused to risk any more scouting parties.

But Commissioner Daniel Gookin presently started the minister on another track. If any Praying Indian at Deer Island could be induced to seek out the captors in their winter quarters, negotiations for ransom might be got under way.

Mindful how little they owed the English, the Praying Indians showed scant interest. But at last Tom Doublet, who had been a ward at John Hoar's, consented to try. Near Wachusett Mountain, thirty miles from Concord, he found what he was seeking.

The peril of starvation — for weeks they had lived mostly on ground nuts — had forced the Lancaster raiders to abandon their winter quarters in the hope that something would turn up nearer the coast. Though at first they threatened Tom's life, the prospect of supplies by way of ransom was tempting. Yes, most of the captives, they said, were alive. If the Council would send a representative, the sachems might be willing to make talk.

The one man in the Colony likely to be able to enter the Indian camp and not get killed was John Hoar of Concord. Rowlandson pleaded with him to try it.

With Tom Doublet and Peter Conway, another Christian Indian, John Hoar took the trail for Wachusett. At a large rock in the eastern valley near the foot of the mountain, he met the sagamores.

Why, he asked, did they not stop this war, and promise to fight only in defense?

They so wished it, they answered; they wanted only to be left alone by the white men so they could plant their corn.

By handing over the captives — replied John Hoar — they could put true heart behind their words.

To prove she was alive, the sagamores let him speak to Mrs. Rowlandson. Though gaunt as a skeleton, she had survived the ordeal of almost constant travel as the Indians moved from camp to camp. Her daughter Sarah, hurt during the siege, had died eight days after the fall of the garrison. Though she had been separated from her other children, the Indians insisted both still lived.

To free Mrs. Rowlandson at once, Hoar promised supplies from his own stock in addition to the regular ransom. Quitting the camp before the Indians could change their minds, he got Mrs. Rowlandson safely to Concord.

In the next few weeks, thanks to John Hoar's courage and diplomacy, the other survivors won release.

That summer, the Indian conspiracy reached final collapse. By mid-August, men gathered at Buss's tavern or waiting for their grain to be ground at Bulkeley's mill swapped accounts of how King Philip had met his end.

He had died at his hideout in the swamps of Pocasset near his tribal home on Narragansett Bay.

All through July and after, soldiers with their Indian guides had been tracking down starving, demoralized bands of fugitives. The Indians themselves had become the victims of ambush and massacre, squaws and children — as the seed of the trouble, said the English — dying with the remnants of the warriors or sold into West Indian slavery.

A bullet through his heart, Philip had fallen face downward in the mud. His quartered body was hung on a tree; his head carried in triumph to Plymouth.

This was right — men declared — the heathen dog was justly punished.

With the rest of the Colony, Concord, on Thursday, November ninth, 1676, celebrated Thanksgiving. The Reverend Edward Bulkeley, now a man of sixty-two years, who limped more than ever as he walked, read the proclamation from his pulpit:

God hath been pleased to look with favor on his people, helping them to repel the heathen that had burst like a flood upon so many of our towns. Of the several tribes risen up against us, there now scarce remains a name or family in their former habitations but are either slain, captive, or fled into remote parts of this wilderness. Let us give praise to God for His singular and fatherly mercies.

With the end of the Indian menace, Concord could total up. It had lost one sixth of its men in the fighting. Among others, Captain Wheeler and his son, before the war was out, had died from wounds received at Brookfield.

But there was good mixed with ill. Sturdy citizens and people of ability — the Prescotts from Lancaster, families from Groton and other burnt-out towns — having found refuge in Concord, decided to stay there. The number of these new inhabitants considerably exceeded that of the men the town had lost.

Concord's importance in the interior was now solidly established. As the colony recovered from the fighting and entered what gave promise of becoming an era of prosperity, the town found itself excellently placed to share in the gains. Concord even had a leader to take Simon Willard's place. Men were saying that Squire Peter Bulkeley, Edward's son, had all his grandfather's remarkable energy of mind and practical sense.

CHAPTER III

Old and New Loyalties in Conflict

THE second Peter Bulkeley was a birthright son of Concord, born in his grandfather's manse near the millpond while his father Edward, already twenty-seven years of age, was still hopefully awaiting a call to some newly gathered church in the settlements. A few months after his son's birth, Edward was chosen by the congregation at Marshfield, in the Plymouth Colony, on the low-lying, swampy coast near the boundary brook that marked the Massachusetts border. With his parents and his older sister, Elizabeth, Peter had left Concord for this village of the Pilgrims, in a region where men like Captain Miles Standish, Elder William Brewster, John Alden, and the White family — parents of Peregrine born on the *Mayflower* — had pushed northward along the shore to seek more land for pasturage, founding Duxbury, then, some of them, Marshfield — incorporated as a town in 1642, the year of the parson's arrival.

Though nothing much ever happened in Marshfield, this was a time of restless movement in the world at large. Oliver Cromwell died in 1658 and the great leader's easygoing son left the door ajar for the return of the Stuarts. In the Bay Colony, to which Peter presently returned as a student at Cambridge, the processes of government moved on with the energy and pains typical of growing institutions.

The Bay had become increasingly strong and self-sufficient. It established its own mint and more and more was coming to regard itself as a commonwealth in junior partnership with Britain. Even the Navigation Act (a favorite measure with Cromwell), passed by Parliament in 1651 — forbidding all ships save those that flew the English flag to trade between Europe and the colonies — had not greatly upset the Commonwealth's independence and self-esteem. Massachusetts was on excellent terms with Cromwell. This bill, it knew, was aimed principally at the rascally, grasping Dutch. Besides, Massachusetts merchants were perfectly well aware that they could violate the Act with impunity.

In 1660, the year the monarchy was restored, young Peter, just graduated from Harvard, returned to Concord, where his father now was preacher. Peter felt no inclination toward the ministry. A public career was what he craved. He could launch himself into it from his native town — for a town was the surest springboard into politics. As was fitting, he married a Wheeler — Rebecca — and got lands along with a bride. His marriage was the second in the family, his sister Elizabeth having become the wife of a certain Joseph Emerson who preached in the Congregational church at Mendon.

Old inhabitants, delighted to find in Peter the Second the abilities — though differently applied — of Peter the First, began to speak of him as a suitable man to represent Concord. In his thirty-second year they elected him deputy.

Peter more than satisfied his constituents. Each annual election they returned him to office with an almost unanimous vote. In the crisis of King Philip's War, when the inhabitants of Concord wanted to be sure that the Colony's leaders would be mindful of the town's exposed position, it was comforting to know that their fellow citizen, Peter Bulkeley, had been elected speaker of the lower house in the special session called by Governor Leverett to carry on the battle for survival.

Proud of its native son, Concord named Peter the chairman of its committee of militia — though the claims of the speakership rather diverted his attention from local duties. So did another matter which had been long a cause of trouble, reaching its culmination right on the heels of the Indian war.

Years before the calamity of Philip's attack, the Bay Colony, sure of its power, ignoring the northern boundary marked by Simon Willard, had begun to edge its jurisdiction into territories regarded as their own by the heirs of Sir Ferdinando Gorges, English royal patentee for Maine, and of John Mason, who claimed New Hampshire. These men, supporters of the Stuarts, could not hope for a hearing from Cromwell. But now that a second Charles was on the throne, the heirs were quick with their complaints. It is high time, they argued, that British authority look to this bumptious

Massachusetts Colony that likes to exercise the prerogatives of a sovereign state.

The Charter that his royal father had granted to the Bay — Charles knew — had been stretched to justify the Colony's every action, even such as ran counter to his realm's defense and commerce. There could be no surer rebuke to Massachusetts — some of his counselors were urging — than to revoke the Charter. The King decided to investigate.

England's first delegation charged with bringing home a report had met chiefly with rebuff. A Massachusetts committee consisting of Governor Leverett, Simon Willard, and three others resorted to the simple expedient of delay, declaring the time too short for action on all the proposals of the Royal Commission. So Charles sent over strict-minded, efficient Edward Randolph, a firm believer in centralized government for the realm.

Randolph confirmed British suspicions. The mint, the do-as-we-please attitude, the dominance of the Congregational Church in politics, the arrogant spirit of independence hidden beneath lip-service loyalty to England — all this and more, reported Randolph, characterized the present situation. And year after year the Bay was proving less and less willing to accept the reasonable view that a colony, to England's advantage, should restrict its trade within the realm. "The laws of England," Massachusetts baldly declared, "are bounded within the four seas, and do not reach America." Recent enforcement acts were being openly flouted. The Bay was carrying on an active commerce with Holland, Spain, France, and their possessions — causing loss to England and gain for her rivals.

To explain these matters and answer the Mason and Gorges claims, the King ordered the Bay Colony to send agents to London.

Willard had been among those named to parry the earlier charges. Now another Concord man, up-and-coming Peter Bulkeley, was chosen with William Stoughton to ward off interference from England.

In dealing with British demands that she act like a colony, the self-created "Commonwealth of Massachusetts Bay" had thus far found evasion an effective policy. So she instructed her delegates to declare themselves empowered to deal only with the Mason and Gorges claims. As for any other charges, they must plead lack of authority to act. If privately they could influence the Bay's old friends —

several had survived the Restoration — to work for the preservation of the threatened Charter, this they should do.

"Lord pity them!" exclaimed venerable John Eliot, close friend of Peter's grandfather, when he thought of the treacherous diplomatic ice over which the agents would be skating. But Peter was not dismayed. The appointment flattered his vanity. He could readily afford to leave little Concord for wider service. Eagerly he looked forward to the sight of England. There he would meet his kinsmen, the high-born Grosvenors. He could wait on the family of his cousin, St. John, former chief justice of the common pleas, to whom his grandfather had dedicated *The Gospel Covenant*.

On Wednesday, September 6, 1676, Peter and his fellow agent sailed for London, armed — in lieu of answers — with an offering of New England cranberries for the King.

After protracted hearings, the Gorges and Mason claims were upheld against Massachusetts by the English court. But the agents managed secretly to purchase Maine from the Gorges heirs, nullifying the effect of the judgment.

Having finished one part of the business, the Privy Council went right on with its catechism of the Massachusetts representatives. Under these allegations, which he must strive neither to admit nor to answer, William Stoughton squirmed uncomfortably. But Peter Bulkeley, finding very pleasant the social life of London which his family connections opened to him, treated this inquisition as a minor nuisance and soon acquired a courtier's skill in privy chamber and palace.

Though he missed his family — Rebecca his wife, young Edward, Joseph, and John — Peter did not greatly mind the delay. Little, primitive, forest-girt Concord seemed unreal and very far away, here in this city with its sophisticated court. While waiting, Peter was having his portrait painted by Sir Godfrey Kneller, the fashionable artist. He was enjoying himself attending the King's levee. Very pleasantly he widened the circle of his influential friends — the Earl of Angelsey; Sir Joseph Williamson, Secretary of State; the Right Honorable Henry Coventry.

When finally, after three years, the Massachusetts agents were permitted to sail, Peter quitted London with regret. On a bleak Tuesday in the fourth week of December, 1679, he found himself once more in Boston Harbor.

*   *   *

The agents and their predicament had often been the subject of anxious debate in the General Court and Governor's Council. Nor had their personal affairs been neglected. In his first year away, regardless of the fact that he probably could not soon take his seat, Peter had been voted into the upper house. He had been named captain of Concord's company of militia. To tide her over during Peter's absence, the General Court had advanced Rebecca funds enough to maintain her comfortable style of living.

At Concord, his constituents stared with interest at this man returned like a stranger from England. His embroidered coats with gold buttons, the little rapier he carried, his fringed gloves, looked oddly out of place as he entered his house by the millpond. But the first Peter, men recalled, had enjoyed such luxuries of life as could be brought into the wilderness and had spoken wistfully at times of England. Certainly Squire Bulkeley was become a gentleman of distinction! Even his physical appearance had changed. The vigorous, energetic young man Concord had known was gone. In his stead sat this heavy-lipped, beef-faced, ruddy Englishman, with well-fleshed hands that rested comfortably on his stomach. At Heywood's tavern, where strong waters could be bought, stronger language poured out freely in derisive blasphemy over the foreign feathers of Captain Peter.

When the Middlesex Militia, grown oversize by 1680, was separated into two regiments, Peter, with the title of major, took command of the inland division. Like his grandfather before him, he was presently named to a commission charged with revision of the Commonwealth's laws. In addition to his office as Assistant, he was chosen by the General Court to serve as one of the two Massachusetts Commissioners to the Council of the United Colonies of New England — that loose confederation for mutual advice and aid made up of the Massachusetts, the Plymouth, the Connecticut, and the New Haven Colony which had been a factor for white survival during the Indian trouble. Though he could hardly qualify as "a magistrate unconcerned with the Mason claims" — the way the General Court described him — he sat as a justice on such cases against the Mason heirs as Massachusetts could bring within her jurisdiction.

Meanwhile, England's displeasure had reached a threatening pitch. Edward Randolph, the first royally designated official assigned to New England, had found his efforts to carry on as Collector of Customs blocked at every turn — the sister colonies of the confederation following the lead of the dominant Commonwealth of the Bay. Randolph returned indignantly to England.

The next thing Massachusetts knew, her Charter had been revoked — that precious Charter she had always looked to as the basis of her civic life and independence.

No longer would the voters elect their Governor — a Governor was to be named by royal decree. No longer would the towns choose their representatives — since the General Court was to be dissolved. No longer would the inhabitants share in the choice of the eighteen Assistants — that body also was disbanded.

To Concord, as to the other towns of the Bay, this turn of events came as a sudden shock — for it burst on the citizenry more precipitously than on the forewarned leaders. Always the inhabitants had lived in the belief that Commonwealth and town managed their own affairs. Like the quarterly military trainings, election had become an uproarious holiday. With only town officers to vote for, much of the zest would be gone.

To Peter Bulkeley, the change brought a disconcerting problem. As agent of the Bay he had gone to England resolved to defend the Charter. But his three years' stay in London suggested another attitude. One could see there was a certain justification for the royal point of view. Unable to forget what he had learned, Peter had been troubled by the suspicious glances of some of his associates in the General Court on his return from England. Now, meeting a far more hostile attitude in Concord, Squire Bulkeley, with his ambitious temperament, faced a harder dilemma.

Why bother? With no elections, he did not need his old constituents to further his career. Indeed, the new Royal Governor *pro tem*, Joseph Dudley, had already appointed him to the reorganized Council — though several of Peter's old colleagues refused the honor, Simon Bradstreet and Nathaniel Saltonstall among the number.

When King James named Sir Edmund Andros "Governor and Captain General in Chief of all his Majesty's Territories in New England" (submerging Massachusetts to a common level with the colonies she had thus far lorded it over), Peter Bulkeley was continued on the Council.

Andros had the reputation of being a conscientious servant of the Crown, an ardent supporter of the Stuarts, and a resolute soldier expecting obedience. Peter could not help recalling his earliest encounter with Sir Edmund. It had taken place during King Philip's War, while Andros was Royal Governor of New York. Bulkeley, Massachusetts agent along with William Stoughton, had spurned the offer made by Andros to aid the New England colonies. The delegates had been instructed thus to refuse, lest Massachusetts be thought to owe an obligation to the Crown. As justification of the rebuff, he and Stoughton had charged Andros with secretly arming the Indians against the Bay; a charge which Andros — with justice — had angrily denied. Would Andros hold this episode against him? Peter rather approved of Andros. He liked his aristocratic, hawk-nosed, intelligent face, with its compressed lips and deceptively bland expression. In public hard and arrogant when crossed, Andros, Peter knew, could be charming in his circle of friends, bringing to New England a quality found heretofore only in London.

Evidently Bulkeley's name had come before Andros with high English recommendation. Two years after becoming Governor of an even greater territory lumping together all of New England, New York, and New Jersey, Andros named four men to the bench of the highest court of his dominion. These were Joseph Dudley, Chief Justice, and, as associates, John Palmer of New York, William Stoughton, and Peter Bulkeley of Massachusetts.

Steering his difficult course as royal governor, Andros met with increasingly stormy seas. Yet he would not take in sail or change direction.

More than most observers, Judge Bulkeley, when home in Concord, could gauge the rising winds. From its early isolation, from the hardships it had surmounted, from its fight to win fruitful lands in the wilderness, Concord had learned to cherish a rugged freedom. Men who had been Peter's friends did not hesitate to denounce Edward Randolph, the most hated official in New England and Peter's associate on the Council. Even Peter's name, in the place he had once represented, was sometimes linked with the word "traitor."

With bitter violence, in clandestine meetings, Concord spoke out against the royal regime.

Had not Andros levied money and made laws without the agreement of the people? Better to hand over a shilling in taxes by our own consent in general assembly than to pay a copper penny by force!

With the servile consent of the rump members of his Council (Squire Bulkeley among them), why had Andros passed a decree prohibiting town meetings except for once a year? Was he afraid of the voice of the people?

In Boston, men from Concord had seen the soldiers brought over from England by Andros to enforce his rule — a heretofore undreamed-of show of royal power in Massachusetts.

More serious still, what is this talk that with the Charter has gone all title to the lands we hold? These farms — arable, pasture, wood lot — have been won through the sweat and toil of a first and second generation. They have been consecrated by the blood of men who fell at Sudbury and Brookfield. Is not ours the right to pass them on — as we choose — to a fourth and fifth generation?

Let the timid merchants in Boston pay a quit-rent to confirm their titles, as exacted by the thieving representatives of Andros. No Concord farmer — even if he has the money — will be so cowardly thus to acknowledge a lack of freehold!

These were the more serious charges — but there were others. Since the coming of Andros, prices had soared. Those avaricious horseleeches, his agents, were extorting uncommon fees for common services till even the probate of a will cost as many pounds as it once cost shillings. Had not the councilmen declared in open session that the inhabitants had no right to expect the privileges of Englishmen to follow them towards the ends of the earth? Did Magna Carta not hold good in *New* England?

Might not Andros even send the militia thousands of miles out of the country — as he claimed his right — leaving the homes of Massachusetts undefended?

No danger of their being sent, however, against the popish, intrusive Frenchmen at the north! All men knew where Charls and James had spent the years of their exile. What if Andros should hand over New England to France? Was not his being Governor part of a plot aimed at the extinction of the Protestant religion? Men hinted King James was an implacable Catholic who would not stop till he had delivered England to the Pope. Old Edward Bulkeley, still Concord's minister, had often warned his people of the scarlet whore of Rome — even as his son Peter, the friend of Andros, sat in his father's congregation displaying fine clothes that hinted of Babylon.

*   *   *

Some of these charges against the Governor, Peter realized, had been cooked up by those bitter opponents of Andros, the leaders of the Puritan hierarchy of Massachusetts. But some were based on wrongs actually suffered by his fellow townsmen. All — hearsay, fact, and falsehood — had now grown into the mass grievance of the people.

More and more, Peter found himself torn between an old and new loyalty. He could not quite forget the promise he had given, when he had sailed to England, to defend the liberties of Massachusetts. He had thought himself ready to do so.

But as with all disputes, there were two sides, he knew, to this one. England, fighting for her commercial supremacy, had a case, as well as the colonies. Massachusetts and the rest of New England, his English friends had argued, formed a large and fruitful land. Suppose it should continue to prosper not only in husbandry but in manufacture — making the very things on which England depended for her export trade? Would this not ruin England? If Massachusetts held her government in her own hands, such a threat could not be controlled.

There was even something to be said — Bulkeley acknowledged — for James's policy of a centralized colonial government, provided it could be made effective. Surely men of English blood ought not to object to a closer dependence. As for that suspected Royal Proclamation for Liberty of Conscience — though perhaps not made from the most ingenuous of motives, it did not really interfere with the practice of Congregationalism, though it opened the door to other sects.

Finally, Judge Bulkeley believed, Andros was an honest, upright man. It was unfortunate that the Royal Governor received the blame for the rapacious conduct of some of his underlings, in a government perhaps too large for effective control.

As for the attitude of his own critics, Bulkeley told himself, it was scarcely fair. If the Governor wanted a measure, he declared it passed, regardless of dissent, without bothering to sample the opinion of the Councillors. As a justice, what could Peter do but enforce the law?

A sensitive man, Bulkeley went out less and less in the village. "Honest Major Bulkeley is quite tired out and can hardly be persuaded to come to Boston," Edward Randolph told Peter's associates on the Council, describing him somewhat later as drowned in melancholy.

*   *   *

On Friday, May the twenty-fifth, 1688, in his forty-ninth year, Peter died, ending a career which had begun with such brilliant promise.

The people had grown away from the gentleman who would not represent them. Even Squire Bulkeley's estate had shared in his decline. "Brook Meadow," his farm at Concord, was knocked down to Stephen Hosmer. The ironworks in which Peter held a major share turned out to be worthless. The tract of land he had got, by way of speculation, from the woebegone residue of the Praying Indians of Nashoba never was given a clear title, and his heirs, for five shillings, gladly sold the claim.

The events so largely responsible for Peter Bulkeley's decline soon ran their course. Next year, during the night of April eighteenth and into the morning that followed, Concord was kept awake by a confusion of alarms. Only one thing was certain — before dawn the militia company, under Captain John Heald, were to muster on the green.

As Concord's soldiers gathered in the gray light, they added up what they had heard. The colony was rising against Andros. Now — men said, and spat as they said it — was the time to throw the tyrant out. News had just been brought over the Atlantic that there was glorious revolution in England; that Andros's master, the Catholic James, was being pushed from the throne by William of Orange with the backing of England's protestants.

Barrett . . . Buttrick . . . Davis . . . Hayward . . . Hosmer . . . Minot . . . Prescott . . . Wheeler — through the muster roll. Then the company shouldered their heavy flintlocks. Down the Bay Road they marched, past the willows leafing into green along the millstream.

Rumors of dangers ahead flew from lip to lip. A French fleet of thirty sail, they say, is hovering off the coast, ready to seize Boston when Andros gives the signal. The Mohawks, in league with the French, are about to swoop from the North. Andros has secretly honeycombed Boston with mines so he can blow the town to blazes.

Shortly before noon, when the company ended its fourteen-mile stretch to the water's edge at Charlestown, where militia companies from other towns were also gathering, Boston was seen to stand tranquilly enough across the quarter-mile reach.

New England's counterpart of the glorious revolution was already bloodlessly over. Andros, taken by surprise through the quick action of conspirators — few men had known what was planned, though the people, once the alarm was given, took up arms with surprising unanimity — had prudently given up, impressed by the show of strength of the militia. He and his supporters were prisoners. Old Simon Bradstreet, last governor elected under the Charter, along with other members of the General Court before its dissolution, held control.

As suddenly as the citizen soldiers had taken up arms, they laid them down, once again to become farmers and blacksmiths, millers, wheelwrights, and tanners.

Back in Concord, where town meetings could again be held without molestation, they passed a resolution. Let the old plan of government under the Charter be restored, and the former deputies take their places. Other towns in Massachusetts were passing similar resolves, but Concord's had teeth in it.

If we are not granted this privilege by England — declared the townsmen — let the people of Massachusetts hold a council of war and fight for their rights.

After tempers had cooled, King William, though friendly to the Bay, saw fit to grant a charter keeping the governorship a royal appointment. But he legalized the General Court and restored to it most of its functions. The Court, of course, would levy taxes and disburse the money.

Very quickly Massachusetts found that control of the purse-strings put an effective check on the Royal Governor. With the exit of Andros, the brief day of autocracy had closed.

Concord liked to recall the part it had played in Andros's overthrow and arrest — though Andros, at William's request sent back to England, had won exoneration in a British court. Ebenezer Prout, Clerk of the Town, had served as clerk of the revived Massachusetts house of representatives. It was he who, right after the uprising, had signed the warrant on which Andros had been locked up in the fort that defended Boston Harbor. There Sir Edmund proved a slippery prisoner. Disguised in woman's clothing, he had walked past two of the guards before a third, glancing at the boots he forgot to change, caught him.

Its land secure, its town meetings saved, its size and prosperity increasing, Concord turned once more to its affairs, forgetting Andros and Squire Bulkeley, his supporter.

CHAPTER IV

The Tradition That Won the Land
for the English Race

EVERYBODY knew about Captain Lovewell. He was back in Boston now, according to Thursday's *News Letter*, March 11, 1725, recruiting for a third expedition. Lovewell was the most successful Indian hunter since Captain Moseley's time. From the day that the Abenakis, armed and encouraged by the French, began to pillage and burn the vulnerable settlements of Maine and New Hampshire, claiming they had never sold the land, Lovewell, without loss of a single man, had been leading raids deep into Indian territory. He and his forty scouts had just returned with the scalps of ten Abenaki warriors, each scalp worth one hundred pounds by act of the Massachusetts Assembly.

One thousand pounds for Lovewell and his company! In a single month one could gain more money Indian hunting than during several lifetimes tilling the land. Right now, with spring planting to be done, was an awkward time for leaving. But Lovewell's volunteers from Concord were promising themselves a richer harvest. Nine had signed up, mostly kinsmen: the brothers David and Eleazer Melvin; Jacob and Joseph Farrar, cousins, both experienced scouts, both past thirty with children to support; two Davises; two Whitneys; and Josiah Jones.

Lovewell was assembling his men at Nashua on the Merrimack, gateway to the Indian country which eighty years before, through its beaver trade, had brought wealth to Simon Willard. Many were sib to one another. Lieutenant Josiah Farwell, of Dunstable, was a grandson of Henry Farwell who had pioneered at Concord, while the other lieutenant, Jonathan Robbins, native of Chelmsford, had ties of blood with many in Simon Willard's first town. Seth Wyman and John Harwood, old campaigners with the captain, were Lovewell's ensigns. The only comparative stranger was Jonathan Frye, of the class of '23 at Harvard and preparing to enter the ministry. He was volunteering as chaplain, he affirmed, but the scouts soon found that their headstrong and impetuous young religious counselor's chief concern was plenty of scalp money on which to take to wife a fourteen-year-old girl his purse-proud, well-born family did not approve of.

Forty-seven men in all were under Lovewell's command, with Toby, a Mohawk Indian, for a guide.

This year, spring was late — snow still lingering in the denser woods. Several days of bad weather held up the company. But on Wednesday, April fifteenth, the cold rains stopped. Lovewell headed north along the Merrimack.

Flood water blocked the customary upriver passage by canoe; the three sharp rips just above Nashua were quite impassable. To complicate matters, right at the start the Indian guide fell sick and had to be left behind. There would have been no difficulty following the carries around the rapids, but the Indian trails along the quieter reaches, even if they could be found, would be sure to be overgrown because so seldom used. Much of the way led through tangled thickets, with alder swamps between, and only here and there an open grove of hemlock or pine.

From the day they started, William Cummings, of Dunstable, had been troubled by an old wound. It was much worse now. Lovewell decided to send him back, with a second member of the troop to look after him.

The forty-five that remained struck northward toward Winnepesaukee and the Pigwacket country. Indians were scarce nearer the coast. Grown careless after their sack of Brunswick and other settlements along Merrymeeting Bay, they had let a force of two hundred English surprise their encampment at Norridgewock. Eighty red men had been killed, along with their Jesuit Priest, Sebastien Rale, long suspected as the secret agent of the Papist French in Canada. Since that defeat, the Indians were staying closer to their hideouts among the White Hills of New Hampshire.

With Contoocook, some thirty-five miles beyond Nashua, behind him, Lovewell followed the tactics that had brought success to his earlier expeditions. Two things are all-important in Indian territory — to catch, and not to be caught. The troop traveled slowly, with scouts ahead on the lookout for Indian signs, and a scout to cover the track. Five to fifteen cautious miles made a good day's average, ending early in the afternoon at a strategic camp site. Then the scouts, having bivouacked their packs, would fan out by twos and threes for more methodical hunting — on the lookout for a fresh-used trail, a recent camp, or smoke in a distant valley. With the trees just leafing and last year's ferns flat underfoot where the snow had left them, it was easy for an experienced hunter to comb the woods.

But even the most likely places yielded no Indians — the salmon-trout in the little rivers swam unmolested; the fish camps had not been used. In that whole region, the Indian villages were deserted.

With abundant game, food was no problem for Lovewell. The thing to do was to work further inland towards the stockaded Indian town at Pigwacket.

Early in May, when they reached Great Ossipee Pond, Lovewell called a halt. Here, on the sandy west shore, they would build a stockade to retreat to, in case of emergency. In front, the lake would give protection. To the rear, the thin, scraggly stand of scrub pine that grew on the sandy flat plain westward, where the White Hills hovered like a mirage in the spring mists, would guard against surprise. Benjamin Kidder, of Nutfield, had taken sick. It would be best to keep him here with the company's doctor, William Ayer of Haverhill. Leaving a garrison of eight, including the Whitney boys from Concord, Lovewell, with thirty-four men, headed north again into the interior.

This was a denser, more difficult country through which they were traveling. Hemlocks darkened the woods. The Saco, after its rush through the northern mountains, was caught here in a level basin which changed it from a flashing stream to a black and sluggish river. Like a pinned snake trying to escape, it doubled and twisted in repeated loops. To see any distance ahead in the sphagnum swamps was next to impossible. Full of an uneasy sense of being followed, the scouts kept glancing backward. Every time, far off, a pigeon woodpecker thudded intermittently, they stopped to make sure of the sound. The fort lay some twenty to thirty miles behind them.

On Saturday night, May eighth, the guard woke the camp, positive he had heard Indians. But nothing could be seen in the darkness. The only sounds were those belonging to the woods — the snort of a deer clearing its nostrils better to catch the man scent; the hooting of a great horned owl in the distance.

That Sunday morning, Lovewell kept the men in their camp near the mouth of a little brook which flowed into Saco Pond. The Sabbath was not the day for pious men to go hunting. So Jonathan Frye led prayers as the scouts rested and the pickets, sent out to guard against surprise, watched the distant approaches. The Saco River, three miles east, was an Indian thoroughfare, with a carry to the near-by pond used as a short cut to rejoin the river below one of its most time-consuming bends.

Between nine and ten, the picket from the pond came back. He had spotted a lone Indian, a hunter, on the westerly shore. The Indian had failed to see him.

Lovewell was for lying low. Deliberately to track an Indian on the Sabbath would lead to no good end. But Jonathan Frye, fervent and excited, impatient of delay and disappointed that no scalps had yet been taken, began to argue with the Captain.

Have we not all along prayed God we would meet the enemy? he asked. The enemy now lies in our grasp. Shall we return empty-handed, and be called cowards for our pains?

What harm, when the chaplain himself urged action on the Sabbath? Against his better judgment, Lovewell called for a show of hands. The majority favored attack.

The scouts saw to their guns and knives and shouldered their packs. Cautiously they worked their way parallel to the water till the curve of the shore southward should hide them from the Indian. They came out at an open place by a second brook where there were few trees and very little brush. Near the water's edge were the marks of several canoes — the little ridges of heaped-up sand still moist. Near this clearing, Lovewell ordered his company to hide their blankets and supplies. Watching every step lest a dry twig snap, the scouts headed left, close to the pond.

The sun rose higher, falling on the men's backs. They had come perhaps two miles. A further bulge of land just ahead, with a bay beyond, cut off their view. As the cove opened before them, Ensign Wyman dropped to one knee. Not more than four or five rods off walked the Indian, quite unconscious of his danger. His eyes searched the fresh growth of pickerel weed, out from the shore. In one hand he held two ducks by the feet, in the other, his gun. A second musket was slung at his back.

Wyman let him draw closer, then fired — the men behind him rising from their cover to see the effect. But the slug went wide. Quick as thought, the Indian snapped first one gun, then the other, loaded for duck, at his attackers. A scattered hail of beaver shot cut the bushes and peppered the English. Lovewell, hit in the stomach, doubled over. Samuel Whiting also was wounded.

As the Indian turned to run, Wyman, having reloaded, dropped him in his tracks. Frye ran forward to scalp him.

His scouts gathered around Lovewell. He could walk, he insisted, he was not much hurt — the shot had not gone very deep.

With two men thus unexpectedly wounded, it was best to retrieve the packs and make a bee line for the protection of the stockade at Ossipee. Though Lovewell made no complaint, his face was pale and blood was trickling to his boots. In their haste taking little advantage of cover, the men followed the open shore to the place where they must turn off for their packs near the pine grove. Climbing the waist-high bank, they were within two hundred yards of their blanket rolls when a soldier stopped abruptly.

"An Indian!" he shouted.

Not one Indian. The grove ahead, the sheltering banks of the stream, seemed full of them. From every log and tree trunk they opened fire, while shots and yells from the side and rear warned the English they were nearly surrounded. Lovewell and a third of his company were hit. Each soldier left alive dove for the nearest cover. Benjamin Hassell, closest to the captain, saw him fire his musket, struggle to reload, then collapse and lie still. Dropping his own gun, Hassell made a dash toward the only flank where as yet there were no Indians. That was the last his companions saw of him.

Both lieutenants had been seriously wounded. For a moment it looked as though the company had lost every officer. Then Ensign Wyman's voice steadied the men. While the Indians were reloading, he told them, they must themselves attack, pick up their wounded, then run for the breastwork of the lake shore.

With a yell the English broke forward. The boldness of the onslaught caught the red men by surprise. Several Indians dropped at the volley and the rest fell back. In the confused melee, the circle was broken.

At the pond shore, with their backs protected, the men, under Wyman's skillful direction, took up a defensive position along the bank behind a couple of fallen trees. On the right, the mouth of the brook, on the left, a little rocky point gave shelter at the flanks. A swampy space between them and the pines, providing scanty cover, would help hold back the Indians. Yet Lovewell's men could reckon how desperate were the odds. Eight of their number lay dead at the place of ambush. Of the twenty-five men left, nine were wounded; and Hassell had disappeared.

Fifteen unscathed scouts to keep off a pack of Indians . . .

Wyman would not let their spirits flag. "If your courage don't fail" — he told them — "then the day will be yours." Each man still had thirty rounds of ammunition. With these, they must keep the Indians off till nightfall.

The sun, past its zenith, was slipping westward. Little fountains of water on the lake behind the men jumped into the air whenever an Indian's bullet overshot. But others found their mark. Jonathan Frye, the chaplain, was hit. Then Lieutenant Robbins, already injured, was wounded again, along with another man. Several scouts, hit earlier in the fight, were failing — though most could still keep shooting at the enemy.

At first the Indians, confident the white men could be overwhelmed, came in at close range. But a growing heap of their dead taught them caution. Out of range, they waved ropes at the English as a sign to surrender. But Lovewell's men, afraid they would get no quarter, yelled defiantly back and the Indians went on fighting — howling and yelling like wolves and shaking their scalping knives and hatchets.

On either end of the line the best marksmen in the company — Chamberlain from Groton, Wyman himself, and the Melvins — guarded against flanking. Late in the afternoon the chief himself had tried it, only to be killed by Wyman.

The death of their leader rattled the attackers. By sundown, firing had diminished. Presently it stopped altogether.

In the darkness, the scouts could hear their enemies dragging off the dead.

The exhausted survivors had eaten nothing since morning, their rations having been lost with the packs. During the fighting, they had been able to do little for the injured. Now, while a lookout kept watch, they tended the wounded and brought them water. Jacob Farrar was found dying by the edge of the pond where he had crawled for a drink. Robert Usher of Dunstable was also nearly dead. Lieutenant Robbins, in spite of his wounds, had fought all day. Now he lay on his back, too weak to move.

Had the Indians really given up and gone off with their injured? It made little difference — they would be back with the morning.

The only salvation lay in making for the fort at Ossipee, where help and supplies waited. Of the eleven wounded, not counting the nearly dead Robbins, Farrar, and Usher, all insisted they were strong enough to travel. Lieutenant Farwell had lost much blood since the ambush. Young Frye, the chaplain, was also very weak. Josiah Jones and Eleazer Davis of Concord both were suffering from stomach wounds, and Davis's right thumb had been shot away.

Shortly before twelve, the moon, a wan half-circle, filtered its dim light through the trees. Now was the time to make a try for it.

They said good-by to Robbins. At his bidding, they left two loaded guns. If he lived till morning — he said — he would see if he could knock off a couple of Indians when they came back looking for scalps.

Wyman led his file of nineteen weary, bleeding men along the lake shore and up the bank into the woods. Their ears still ringing from the uproar of fighting, each scout waited for the quiet darkness to be shattered by an Indian screech. But only the labored breathing of the severely wounded as they forced their stiffening bodies into motion broke the silence.

Wyman urged on the file of soldiers for a mile and a half more. Then they rested. When the column again was ready to start, four scouts — Lieutenant Farwell, Chaplain Frye, and Jones and Eleazer Davis from Concord — were too exhausted to get up. The others, they insisted, must go without them. So the line moved off — Wyman promising to send back help from the fort.

Seth Wyman did not dare stop for many rests. Not till dawn did they venture a little sleep.

Ahead lay a sandy tract of scrub with a dense growth of bracken underfoot. Sixteen men, tramping single file through these brittle ferns, would be sure to leave a trail for Indians to follow. Yet to split up the troop seemed as great a danger. Finally three men in one group, two in another, set out for the fort by different routes while the main party of eleven, risking pursuit, stuck together. Hours later, they reached the fort.

It was deserted.

Not till summer was well along did all survivors from Concord return to their town. The Whitneys, back first, told what had happened at the fort. Hassell had burst into the stockade to tell how Lovewell and all his company had been killed. The Indians, he said, were on his track. He had traveled all day and night to bring the warning.

Leaving some food for possible survivors, Sergeant Wood and his men had pulled out for Dunstable.

The Melvins and Joseph Farrar were the next to return. They told how they had been forced to leave Eleazer Davis and Jones, expecting to return with reinforcements from the stockade. After finding the fort deserted, they also had fetched up at Dunstable.

The inhabitants of Concord never expected to see Eleazer Davis and Jones again — yet they did.

The story these two men told was scarcely believable — but there they were to prove it. For several days, with Lieutenant Farwell and Jonathan Frye as the group's third and fourth members, they had waited for rescue from the fort. The water they drank from a near-by brook merely aggravated their abdominal wounds, which filled with maggots and began to stink and fester. In their agony, they sometimes wished the Indians would return and finish them off.

Movement was better than waiting, even if it killed them. So, pausing often to rest, they had struggled toward the fort. Even at the slow pace of the others, Jones had not been able to keep up. Presently the three men realized they could no longer hear him behind them. He must have strayed from their trail.

Three days later, Jonathan Frye could go no further.

For a week or more — never certain of the way — Farwell and Davis dragged themselves painfully toward Lake Ossipee. At last they came to a stream they thought they recognized. Thus far they had found nothing but berries to eat. With a little more strength, they might reach their friends at the fort. Davis told how at that moment he spotted a trout in the water. There it lay, in a pool under an overhanging rock. Fashioning a noose from thongs cut from their moccasins, Davis let it drift with the current. A jerk, and the trout was theirs.

After eating his share, Davis felt better. But Farwell got rapidly worse. Davis waited for the lieutenant to rally. Instead, he was soon too far gone to stand. If help could be brought from the stockade, Farwell might be saved. Davis set out alone.

Like the men before him, he found the place abandoned.

But enough salt pork and flour had been left for him to keep alive. Building up his strength, he tarried several days. By great good fortune, no Indians were following. Farwell, he knew, must be dead. He struck out for the settlements. There he was cared for till well enough to go home.

Even more incredible was Josiah Jones's escape. Almost dead from the putrefaction of his wound — the cranberries with which he was trying to keep himself alive, he said, kept coming out of the opening — his clothes torn nearly from him, and his ribs jutting like a skeleton's, Jones, after thirteen days in the woods, had stumbled into the town of Saco near the river's mouth.

Such was the inside story; but stranger still, perhaps, for those who knew the truth, was what presently happened to the account of Pigwacket.

Parson Thomas Symmes, of Bradford, New Hampshire, close friend of the Fryes and young Jonathan's preceptor, shocked at the idea of hunting blood-money on the Sabbath — especially when the chaplain himself had urged it — set skillfully to work shifting the date to Saturday, the eighth. Seven days after the fight he had preached a memorial sermon. His written account of the disaster, given to Boston's three papers, named Saturday as the day. In a widely distributed pamphlet, he published a further account. He even got an attestation from Seth Wyman and two other survivors — though Wyman's consent to sign hung up Symmes's clever qualification: "We can't each of us, indeed, attest to every particular article and circumstance in it, yet we can aver that the substance of it is true, and are well satisfied in the truth of the whole."

Old Judge Samuel Sewall, inveterate diarist, gave his tacit approval of the change, lest there be further scandal in the colony. In his private notebook he had recorded Sunday, but said no more about it. Colonel Eleazer Tyng, commander in the Dunstable region, had named the Sabbath in his report to his superiors. So the Governor and Lieutenant Governor knew and sanctioned the shift. Soon Saturday was taking the Sabbath's place in public opinion, by the power of the printed word and with the help of a popular ballad composed by Benjamin Franklin, whose nephew, Ben, was also a printer, at work for himself at Philadelphia, in Penn's thriving colony.

For obvious reasons, Symmes had praised Frye's piety and courage. Presently, men were to call a new settlement on the Saco after the chaplain. And Lovewell got his memorial, too, with Saco Pond henceforth known by his name.

But Seth Wyman, whose fortitude and skill had saved the day, won his peculiar reward — in addition to the captain's commission and the presentation sword given him by the Council at Boston. The veterans of the fight never forgot what they learned from Wyman. They passed on their knowledge and fighting skill to their sons. Blood like theirs could never be idle. At Fort William Henry — to the west and Detroit — at the Forks of the Allegheny — with Rogers's Rangers, they or their sons or grandsons kept in the thick of it. The tradition they were building was to help win the land for the English race.

In Concord itself, while that place, along with Cambridge, became a bustling shire town, its inhabitants, already famous for the love they bore their village, nevertheless kept right on showing a restless knack for roving. At home, men might thrive through commerce. As Boston became a city with a highly lucrative oceanwide commerce, many of the goods she sent in trade to the interior passed through Concord along the highroad under the hill. The returning stream brought grain, hay, lumber, cattle — to which Concord added her share. Why not save the farmer farther inland a whole day's journey to the coast? So Concord's shrewd traders saw to it that their shops were well stocked with goods to suit the needs of the frontier that moved ever westward.

But though business prospered at home, men left Concord to settle many a distant place. Through the turbulent years from William's reign through Anne's and those of two of the Georges, Concord also watched her soldiers setting out for the wars. Some went as drafts from the militia; some as volunteers. The fights they fought in (just as Lovewell's fight had been) were parts of greater conflicts that bore strange names — War of the Palatinate; War of the Spanish Succession. Concord's soldiers knew nothing of these names, nor cared a rap for the confused origins of the conflicts. They were simply fighting enemies they hated and feared — the popish French and their Indian allies. They asked few questions as they fought.

Sometimes, to the town's bewilderment, her soldiers were shipped to places seemingly remote from the obvious danger. A grandson of Squire Bulkeley, Captain John Prescott, and eighteen militiamen, in the King's service, went from Concord in 1741 to the West Indies. Only three came back — their comrades having mostly died not from wounds but from fever. Generally, however, the way lay north and westward.

When Concord's veterans returned the town learned to speak

of their exploits in terms of battles won or lost, and, if they were wounded, forgave them their poll tax: William and Thomas Robbins, present when Port Royal, on the Bay of Fundy, surrendered. Captain David Melvin, whose exploits as an Indian fighter were becoming legendary, returning wounded from the assault on Louisburg, in the Gulf of Saint Lawrence — his brother Eleazer among the dozen or more from Concord who helped take the Fort. Concord soldiers in Acadia when England stripped that land of the people who had settled it. On Lake Champlain when the British took from the French the forts at Crown Point and Ticonderoga.

When Captain Thomas Wheeler returned with his men after Quebec had fallen and Wolfe and Montcalm lay dead on the Plains of Abraham above the city — the Englishman in victory, the Frenchman in defeat — he brought home with him pits from the choice plums that Frenchmen grew in Canada. When he planted them in his orchard, they flourished.

This final peace — said gossip on the Milldam — would open to English settlers all the land clear to the Mississippi.

CHAPTER V

Minister Trouble

PARSON WHITING — there could be no doubt about it — was under the influence. To put it bluntly, he was drunk. The words of his sermon came thickly to the ears even of those members of his congregation most well disposed towards him. Nor was this the first offense. The trouble had been steadily increasing since that cheerful fourteenth day of May when charming John Whiting, with the good wishes of the celebrants, had been ordained to usher in a new and friendly era on the scuffed heels of the Reverend Joseph Estabrook's unpopular ministry. And now it was nine years later, 1730, and the parson was drunk.

Ever since Peter Bulkeley's death, Concord had been going through minister trouble. The sole balm she could lay to her hurt was the fact she was not unique — sooner or later almost every town in New England became similarly afflicted. Even the Reverend Peter had known one or two detractors, but the town honored him as a great and good man, and the presumptuous critics had been called to account. With lame Edward, his son, the chief trouble had been feebleness of body. When Edward presently asked for a co-pastor to lighten his burden, the town had acquiesced. Joseph Estabrook, three years out of Harvard College, became Edward's assistant. Having two ministers was of course a drain on the town's resources, but with the Reverend Edward in such poor health, that situation would not last. Besides, the town had got young Estabrook at a bargain.

But with the desperation of feeble men, Edward hung on for twenty-nine years longer. At last, two years before his death, he petitioned the town to retire him on thirty pounds a year.

While Edward Bulkeley lived, few persons had bothered to probe deeply into the religious views of his assistant. On the pittance handed him by the town, the Reverend Joseph Estabrook managed to build a house north of the river, raise his family, and preach sermons the brilliance of which few people were qualified to judge. True, Dr. Philip Reed, a newcomer to Concord, had dared to remark that Edward Bulkeley was unworthy even to carry the books of the assistant preacher, and was fined twenty pounds for his temerity. What Concord first noticed, when Estabrook took charge, was his dissatisfaction with his salary. There had been times, he declared, when even the small amount promised had not been paid. So the selectmen gave out warrants to constables Stow and Dakin summoning all inhabitants to the meetinghouse to treat with Mr. Estabrook concerning his yearly pay.

Seated with his fellow townsmen, Parson Estabrook listened to the first motion: that he be given eighty pounds a year in cash. Cash was something few townsmen saw much of. Thus far, at least in part, they had paid their ministers in goods. The resolution was defeated. Another motion was put forward — to pay thirty pounds in money and the rest in grain, with an extra seven pounds' worth for good measure. Three times, distinctly and slowly, so that every man would understand, the moderator repeated the proposal. It was so voted.

Estabrook, grateful to be placed on a minister's regular salary, thanked the town, declaring himself satisfied with what Concord now promised.

The Reverend Joseph Estabrook had a Delft plate which had come from England. For many years he had cherished it — a dainty thing with beautiful decorations: the cross of the Saviour, the three nails of the crucifixion. To his mind those symbols brought warmth and passion to a faith grown cold. An alms basin, he would put it back to the use for which it was intended.

At meeting, the minister made his prayer and preached his sermon. Then, as the congregation waited in that benignant trance of self-approval which men fall into when they are about to give alms, he handed the plate to the deacons for the collection. A horrid crash fractured the spell. Noticing on the plate the signs of English episcopacy, someone had dashed the basin to the floor. The minister's oldest son, Captain Estabrook, sprang from the family pew to where the dish lay shattered. Tenderly he gathered up the pieces, then stalked from the meeting.

Ever after, there had been warfare in the parish. A few men sided with Estabrook; most said he was rightly served. When the pastor got that portion of his wages which was paid in grain, the ears of maize were lean, the wheat and barley smutted. His petitions to be paid in money were promptly voted down.

After forty years of service, Mr. Estabrook asked for an assistant. But the thrifty villagers knew a trick worth two of that. To escape the usual fine for failure to support the grammar school, it was necessary to hunt up a master. Ready at hand was Samuel Estabrook, the parson's younger son, a student of divinity. For twenty pounds a year the town hired him to keep school — with the proviso that he should help in the pulpit without additional pay.

Five years later, when Samuel left to take over the church at Canterbury, Connecticut, Joseph Estabrook, seventy-five years old and very feeble, again begged help. But the selectmen, attached to their thrifty expedient, refused to be hurried. They would search for another teacher-preacher. While they were hunting for this beast of burden, the Reverend Joseph Estabrook died.

In Boston, the comment was heard that Joseph Estabrook had been too bright a star to be muffled up in the wilderness. Angered perhaps by this remark, Concord refused even to help with the funeral expenses.

The town intended to be very careful in its choice of the next incumbent. Deacon John Heywood and selectmen Benjamin Whittemore and William Wilson were chosen for a committee to invite three leading candidates to deliver two sermons apiece before the people. After the trial period, at town meeting, by a large majority the election fell to Mr. John Whiting.

In the past, through paying the minister partly in goods, there had been much trouble. Henceforth, the town decided, the salary would be in currency — one hundred pounds a year to be raised like other taxes at a rate fixed by the selectmen. Eager to be generous with her new pastor, Concord further voted a liberal fee to encourage his settlement.

Concord felt proud of its new minister and the wisdom shown in choosing him. Though only thirty, he had served as librarian, tutor, then corporation member of his alma mater, Harvard. He had, men said, a tidy fortune of his own. He was known as a good companion and man of spirit. His mother was a Danforth, daughter of the Colony's Deputy Governor. Through his great-grandmother, Sarah Bulkeley St. John, he had the blood of Concord's first minister in his veins. Finally, in his religious views, John Whiting was safely orthodox.

Concord's pride, its new meetinghouse, was finished just in time for the ordination. The town had raised a generous fund for the festivities, but even at that it was not sufficient to pay for all the baked meats, the pies and puddings, the cider, the brandy, the Madeira and Canary wines, the rum, consumed in honor of the occasion. Captain Jonathan Prescott, master of ceremonies, made up the difference — willing to be paid back later, if at all. This ordination had been a splendid thing for business and for the town. As the last inhabitants, with careful tread, wove homeward, everyone agreed it had been a memorable occasion.

For a while, all went smoothly — everything save the minister's fixed salary. But that was not the fault of either the town or Mr. Whiting. Whiting had shown himself a lover of mankind, a man of openhandedness and hospitality. Many of his parishioners had become his closest friends — especially those successful, conservative townsmen who, like their minister, enjoyed convivial life. Not since its first pastor had there been a clergyman in Concord, like John Whiting, whom its inhabitants were glad to honor by appointment to town committees.

But even committees had no power over the currency. Something was very much amiss with the paper money that Massachusetts kept on printing. When it first appeared soon after the turn of the century, merchants in town rejoiced, for easy cash had the look of great prosperity. But as time went on, more and more money bought less and less. Though Mr. Whiting had inherited an estate, he presently complained that he and his family were pinched for means. The inhabitants, recognizing the justice of his requests, did what they could. By contributions, or an increased rate, his pay was kept afloat on the rising flood of paper notes and inflation.

It had been another tide, at last, that threatened to overwhelm him. At the start, there were ways to meet it. The captain and Town Moderator's son, versatile young Timothy Minot, keeper of the grammar school, who could preach as well as teach, was glad to relieve his friend the minister whenever Whiting could not appear. But writing sermons is hard labor, and presently Timothy began to charge the town three pounds each time he filled the pulpit. At its spring meeting, Concord paid the bill. But in voting the minister's salary as usual, the town did so with the emphatic provision that if Mr. Whiting could not handle his own preaching, he must pay the substitute.

An empty pulpit brought the crisis.

To judge its minister, Concord summoned from the neighboring churches a council of the pastor's peers.

Whiting, decreed the council, must consider himself suspended from his pastoral office till ready to make solemn and public promises of repentance and reformation. This he did in full meeting, and the shepherd was taken back into the fold.

Less than a year thereafter, Timothy Minot was again supplying the pulpit.

After a night of cold rain, one October morning, ministers from seven churches met for a second council in the presence of the entire congregation. Though earnestly requested by his church and the visiting clergy to plead his case, John Whiting refused to appear. After public testimony heard and considered, the Reverend John Hancock, of the Lexington church, as moderator, rose to address the assembly:

"We advise and direct the Church of Christ in Concord to remove the Reverend John Whiting from his pastoral office because of lapses of a more aggravated nature, after public promise to reform. . . . We can assure the people that we have come to this decision with distress of mind and grief of heart. Nothing could have constrained us to it but regard for the honor of Christ, the credit of the ministry, and the welfare of the souls of this people, and if our consciences had not been impressed with such awful scriptures as these: 'Do not drink wine, nor strong drink, thou, nor thy sons with thee, when ye go into the Tabernacle of the Congregation, lest ye die.' "

Sorrowfully Concord pondered the advice of the Reverend Council. Meanwhile, a substitute minister must be found.

Daniel Bliss looked like a brilliant, though venturesome choice. True, he was very young — perhaps too young — not yet twenty-five. He was also from that new and upstart college, Yale, down at New Haven, where Jonathan Edwards showered fire and brimstone on the people, roaring that only the few elect would be saved. But Samuel Chandler, Concord's representative at the General Court, and Deacons Joseph Dakin and Samuel Meriam, the committee that examined him, found Bliss an earnest zealot who would never bring on the parish trouble such as Whiting's. He had been one of ten candidates come by invitation to show their wares. After his seventh sermon, the congregation, by a reasonable majority, decided to accept him, the town concurring.

Taking into account the disconcerting antics of paper money, the town voted five hundred pounds as fee for the minister's settlement, with a salary of two hundred and fifty pounds a year. Bliss's reply to this offer was a trifle alarming. If the value of old tenure continued to decline, wrote the minister, he would expect the town to make good the difference. They would also provide his firewood annually, he trusted, according to custom. Considering the extent of the ministerial work, especially in so wide-flung a town, he hoped they would be ready upon special occasions to afford some friendly help in the pulpit. And should his later circumstances require it, the town, he assumed, would stand prepared to make needful additions for his support.

Concord was willing to be generous, but not to be dictated to. A tactful remonstrance brought less painful words from the new incumbent. The minister would leave these matters to the town's generosity.

For the pastor's ordination, Concord — mindful of past difficulties — voted just enough money to provide suitable and decent entertainment. At Holdin's tavern, that evening, the inevitable remark was made about passage from a state of drunkenness to one of bliss. The Reverend John Whiting did not appear throughout the day.

Young Daniel, taking over his new sheepfold, soon discovered that it bore closer resemblance to a lion's den. The children, and some adults of the parish, showed persistent signs of misbehaving. By vote at town meeting, Pastor Daniel Bliss was desired to warn heads of families that they must caution those under their charge. A stranger, and very young, Bliss found it no easy matter to confront grizzled patriarchs on such a mission. But his greatest trial was brought about by the man he had replaced.

Whiting would make no confession of his fault, nor would he attend the church. At last a committee, including such good friends of his as Deacon Miles, were sent to his house to make remonstrance. But Whiting, declaring it was he that was wronged, refused to receive the delegation and asked for a written statement from the church. On the return of the ambassadors, the congregation forthwith put the question to the vote. With a certain satisfaction, Daniel Bliss spread the record on the Parish Book: "That Mr. John Whiting, late pastor of the Church in Concord, being deposed from his pastoral office by the advice of venerable Council, be suspended from communion with us in the ordinance of the Lord's Supper, until such time that the Church shall have further satisfaction from him in order to his making Peace with this Church wherein he hath offended."

That might have ended the business, but it did not. On the succeeding Sabbath, the congregation was electrified to see the old minister, with all his family, cross the threshold of the meetinghouse. Obediently, conforming to ancient usage, the communicants rose as he marched up the aisle. Straight to the bench behind the pulpit he made his way. His family — Mrs. Whiting and her four large children — sidled into the minister's pew. There would be very little room for Phoebe Bliss. Daniel, with his predecessor breathing over his shoulder, struggled to get through the service.

Concord, thinking to compromise, voted a new pew built for the former pastor. Meanwhile, Whiting continued to sit behind the preacher. And in the minister's pew, till the new one was completed, Phoebe Bliss could not without eclipse display, in all due modesty, the pretty clothes she had brought, as a bride, from Connecticut.

Mid-October, in the second year of Daniel's ministry, found Concord — and for that matter the neighboring countryside, all Massachusetts, and all New England — in a state of intense excitement. George Whitefield, the revivalist from England, was cause of the turmoil. He would preach today in Concord.

Since early that crisp morning, people from neighboring villages had been pouring into town. Now, toward noon, several thousand visitors were crowded on the common around the giant oak where Willard had made his treaty with the Indians. Whitefield, just arrived, was resting at Daniel Bliss's house beyond the Milldam. He had already spoken that morning before great crowds in Boston. No church could hold the multitudes which came to hear him. He would speak in Concord at noon in the open air.

Inhabitants of the town who stood nearest the two men, as Daniel and his guest made their way from the preacher's house toward the big tree on the common, were startled by their young minister's face. His usual earnest, eager look bore an expression of intenser zeal, and though he was dwarfed by the portly, white-wigged, cross-eyed man beside him, the drawn, sharp lines of Bliss's mouth, his startling pallor, drew glances away from Whitefield's dominant figure.

A hush fell as Whitefield raised his puffy hands above his shoulders in the attitude of prayer — a gesture he repeated frequently to emphasize his preaching. It was an extraordinary voice that floated out on the still October air — tender, soft, persuasive — a voice with a caressing, naked intimacy. Whitefield spoke in tones seemingly meant only for his nearest neighbor, yet they carried beyond the limits of the crowd, giving all hearers an uneasy sense that the preacher was exhorting each of them personally. He spoke as though he had caught sight of an actual heaven above their heads and could see the marshaled hosts of the Lord. Then, as he described the flames of hell that crackled and snapped like serpents' tongues for the many, his voice gained greater power. Avenging angels and messengers of Grace, he shouted, were hovering over every man and woman in the multitude. Only God's elect, only the chosen, could win to glory.

Somewhere in the crowd a woman shrieked. Whitefield wove the scream into his sermon. Behold, in their midst, the holy spirit working! Through such manifestation lay the way to salvation!

No longer masters of themselves, men and women cried out or fainted dead away. Like an autumn field of wheat rippled by the wind, the crowd swayed to the revivalist's preaching. Turning, at the end, to the young minister beside him, the evangelist, face glowing, pronounced him a child of God. Whitefield had gathered in his harvest.

Many of Concord's graver citizens were offended and shocked by the scene they had just witnessed. From the moment they had laid eyes on that round face and triple chin, they had been suspicious of Whitefield. If they had not actually seen and heard this tumult, they would not have believed such extravagance possible. This singing and shrieking, this clapping of hands, this roaring — what had these things to do with religion? Was it not closer to an affront of the Blessed Spirit and a barefaced flouting of common decency? Here was a drunkenness far worse than that of wine.

Matters were not improved when Whitefield denounced Harvard College as destitute of godliness. The Reverend John Hancock of neighboring Lexington refused to open his pulpit to the evangelist, and in other parts of Massachusetts several members of the clergy who had at first been friendly shifted to open hostility.

But fervent young Daniel Bliss remained loyal to the new light and its most brilliant, dramatic source of inspiration. More and more he preached extemporaneously, with a vehement enthusiasm — eschewing the time-honored practice of following a bundle of manuscript, new or old. No longer was there need for Tithingmen Jonathan Buttrick and Stephen Hosmer to make use of the foxtail at the end of their staffs to tickle into wakefulness a drowsy congregation. Instead, many were buffeted into a state of righteous indignation by what they heard. Was their new preacher becoming a second Whitefield? Why, he was even encouraging laymen to testify and exhort publicly! And by what right did he disturb other churches by wandering from town to town preaching?

What did he mean by declaring from his pulpit that it was as great a sin for a man to gain an estate through honest labor as through dice and cards, if he had not at heart the furtherance of God's glory? Concord's hard-working, more successful inhabitants could not let any such statement pass without rebuttal. And had not pastor Bliss wronged the truth by declaring that only the rare elected can pass the narrow gate?

The critics of the minister included some of the most substantial citizens. The objectors privately laid their complaints before a committee of the neighboring clergy, then asked their own congregation to summon a council. At church meeting, by a single vote, the motion was lost.

Daniel Bliss rose to defend himself. When had he sought to force his beliefs, he demanded, on an unreceptive people? Have not most — at least some of you — joined with me at the communion table many times since you pretended to know this? Where were your bowels of kindness that you should live in the same town and never acquaint me with your fears and apprehensions? Have you not offended God in laying this thing before a number of churches without giving me opportunity to speak with you concerning it?

By their actions — he told his accusers — they had exposed themselves to the heavy abiding wrath of God.

The young minister had rent the veil of the temple. Concord lay split in two. Minots were arrayed against Minots and whole families were divided.

The malcontents, a good third of the congregation, withdrew from the parish and set up preaching of their own. John Whiting, now a soberer, wiser man, became their pastor. Because the town, by a narrow margin, defeated each attempt of the West Church, as it called itself, to gain the use of any public building, the separatists moved over the mill brook to the Black Horse Tavern for meetings, nor could the pointed remarks of ribald critics dent their dignity. They won from the General Court an order relieving them from the financial support of their former church and minister, with the result that Daniel Bliss, as the Colony's paper money continued its misbehavior, found himself badly pinched to provide for his growing family.

At last his own congregation agreed to call a council — nor was it the last one to consider Concord's religious problems. Elders from fourteen churches assembled to reconcile the two factions. They declared Bliss not incorrigible but carried away by an unwholesome fervor. He must temper his statements and publicly retract some of them. This he agreed to do, but members of the Black Horse church, unwilling to risk offenses by the man of zeal, stood pat. Though for many years the peacemakers continued to pour oil, the waters remained troubled.

Not till John Whiting died, thirteen years after Daniel's arrival, did certain members of the second parish seek readmission to the original church. Time had made it hard to tell the black sheep from the white. Two meetings were an expense, and often an inhabitant, through some mistake, found himself called on for a double assessment. At last the Black Horse Tavern resumed its primary function and all but the stubbornest rams returned to the fold.

The shepherd himself had mellowed. In New England, the glare of the new light sank to a milder glow. Even when Whitefield, in 1764, made another visit, no flare-up followed. The hectic days of the revival were over.

On Sunday, March 11, Whitefield was again in Concord. That morning, Daniel Bliss preached; in the afternoon, the famous visitor. "If I had studied my whole life," said Whitefield of his host's discourse, "I could not have produced such a sermon." The people of Concord were inclined to agree. Their minister had given the better discourse.

Concord was proud of its fiery patriarch. She was proud of his family of four strapping boys and three pretty daughters — Phoebe, the oldest daughter, winsome as the friendly little bird that called her name from the woodlands at Walden.

After that famous sermon, the Reverend Daniel Bliss never again spoke from his pulpit. Full of scars, years, and honors, he died later that spring, and Concord paid the expenses of a handsome funeral.

CHAPTER VI

Very Bad Subjects of His Majesty

THE day town meeting heard the letter of acceptance from Daniel Bliss's successor, Concord also had other important business. For one thing, the selectmen wished to know the minds of the people as to what instructions should be given their representative, Charles Prescott, to guide him in the General Court's debate over the Stamp Act just imposed by England's Parliament on all her North American colonies.

Already there had been plenty of trouble about that tax. Every bill of sale, every judgment, every will and testament, must have a stamp on it, paid for in specie. With so little hard money in the town — and in the Colony — this impost would drain away all that was left. With no hard money to buy stamps and also pay the lawyer's fee, a citizen could no longer sue for damages in Squire Minot's court when a neighbor's pig broke through his fences. The inhabitants dearly loved their lawsuits, and would be loth to give them up. The lawyers in Concord were angry, too. They had hoped to see Concord the only shire town in Middlesex, with Court Week four times a year. Now their thriving business threatened to wither at the roots.

As long as Hancocks and other rich merchants of Boston were the only ones getting their purses pinched in a trade war with England, Concord and the back country had refused to become greatly interested. It was fun to laugh at the outraged squawks of the Bay's merchant aristocracy. But now everyone's pocket was being picked — the farmer's, artisan's, lawyer's — along with the merchant's. Everyone in Concord was talking about the riots in Boston — how Deputy Governor Thomas Hutchinson's fine house had been sacked and his papers trampled into the mud. Some men deplored it; many felt it served him right for being England's tool. The conspicuous tree that stands southeast of Boston Common, facing Dorchester Neck across the flats, was blossoming, in this summer and fall of 1765, with peculiar fruit — the effigies of those traitors to the people who had agreed to be England's agents. Let them look to themselves, lest the branches bend with a heavier weight!

At the Boston Court House, Concord's representative met with assemblymen of the other towns to vote that a circular letter be dispatched inviting all the British colonies in North America to send delegates to centrally placed New York for a Stamp Act Congress which should devise united measures to oppose the tax.

The Sons of Liberty, a secret brotherhood, was being formed. Concord had several members — how many, the town never knew, for no man, in these uncertain times, cared to question his neighbor too closely.

In an atmosphere tense with awareness that the rights of town and colony to govern themselves were being seriously threatened, Concord ordained its new pastor. His name was William Emerson, and he was the great-great-grandson of the Reverend Peter Bulkeley, through Peter's daughter Elizabeth, who had married Joseph Emerson.

Sunday, the first of January, 1766, was a stormy day, and very cold. In the bleak meetinghouse the people shivered, their hands and feet grown numb. Somehow they managed to sit through the lengthy prayers of the visiting clergy, the charge to the new incumbent, the giving of the right hand of fellowship. What they were really curious to hear was a parent's sermon to his child, for William's father, a clergyman too, was preaching. "Solomon, my son, whom alone God hath chosen, is yet young and tender, and the Work is great."

Very young indeed — ardent, emotional, enthusiastic, and an idealist; just twenty-three on taking over this parish so recently storm-tossed that the ground swells of faction might have frightened a more timid or less innocent youth. But for William Emerson, life was too exciting to be overshadowed by old storm clouds or threatened by new ones rising from tempestuous talk in congresses and parliaments.

The new pastor took hold at once. He enjoyed his long rides to remote farms when he made pastoral visits. He enjoyed making marriages, and his first year netted him over twenty pounds in fees. There were funerals and christenings — old Judge Minot to be laid to rest; baby Lucy Buttrick to be baptized. He liked also doing the social rounds — dinner with Josiah Melvin on the Westford road, breakfast with Colonel Cuming.

But most he enjoyed young Phoebe, daughter of his landlady, Mrs. Bliss, widow of the former minister. When he had come on trial to preach, he had stayed with the Blisses. On those Mondays, with his duty done, it had been far pleasanter to linger in Concord than make for home. With Phoebe on the pillion behind him, they used to go for long rides in the country — raising the faintest breath of scandal in the village.

Now, living at Mrs. Bliss's on the Milldam, in the hospitable dwelling made over by the late Reverend Daniel from the massive timbered garrison house of the days of Philip's War, William grew to know intimately all the members of the household. Daniel, the oldest son, a highly successful young lawyer and a persuasive, logical, witty speaker, had recently married the daughter of the wealthiest citizen of Rutland.

Six months after his ordination, William, as everyone expected, married Phoebe Bliss. They would continue to live with her mother, then he would build her a fine new manse, modeled on a style of architecture he had admired while living in Ipswich. For land, he had his eye on a tract beyond the center of the town and close beside the river at the North Bridge. Here he could pasture his horse and a couple of cows, cut hay, and grow some corn. Here, in a pleasant parlor that should look toward the stream, Phoebe and he would entertain visiting ministers and the socially inclined of his parish.

But, as it usually does, the hard present postponed for a while the anticipated future. Before William could realize all his hopes, he and his fellow townsmen were to be plunged into a torrent that was to pour even into these quiet reaches.

From England, further trouble was threatening. Parliament, it is true, had repealed the Stamp Act. But in its place she now clapped on the colonies a duty — to be gathered by commissioners of the Crown — on certain staple imports, including tea.

What — asked Boston — did her sister towns intend to do about it? The response from almost all was like that from Concord. Concord's answer, drawn up at a town meeting — William Emerson had opened the session with a prayer for guidance — was to advise a boycott of English goods. Instead, let production and manufacture be encouraged at home.

The next thing Concord knew, Governor Francis Bernard dissolved the General Court for refusing to rescind a circular letter protesting the duties. To put force behind his mandate, he brought in British soldiers, British "lobster-backs," from Halifax.

Not since the days of Andros had so startling a curtailment of freedom been attempted.

By the will of the people, a convention was called for Thursday, September 22, 1768. It would meet at four P.M. in Boston. The people of the towns did not intend to be thwarted.

By the following summer, Governor Bernard sailed in the *Rippon*, a British man-of-war, for England, the water on this side of the Atlantic having become too hot — leaving his deputy, Hutchinson, stewing.

At least Hutchinson bore an ancient name native to Massachusetts. In getting rid of Bernard, the people had the satisfaction of feeling they had driven off the foreigner from England. In Concord, as in other towns, bells were rung in celebration.

Phoebe's two younger brothers, Theodore and Sam Bliss, had slipped off to Boston. They had gone, their sister suspected, to see the fun. Theodore, just twenty-five, a husky apprentice shipwright familiar with what was stirring at the docks, was a good deal of a hothead. His family often worried lest he get his younger brother into a scrape. All through the winter there had been trouble in Boston — the red uniforms of the British soldiers on the streets, the presence of British officers in the best taverns, were a constant irritation. That winter, many a lobster-back's tricornered hat flew suddenly from his head — the snowball that did the trick like as not having a rock inside it. March, with snowballs at their best, threatened to bring the trouble to a climax.

All afternoon, the brothers, roaming the streets, watched groups of the more unruly inhabitants wandering over town — from Long Wharf to King Street, from King Street to the waterfront at Charles. But mostly they clustered before the Court House and at the Common, where grenadiers, riding gloriously in hired carriages, were trying to catch the glances of the girls.

At eight o'clock, an alarm bell started ringing. The Bliss brothers followed the crowd.

A file of soldiers, under a sergeant, backs to the wall, was facing a rapidly gathering mob. Crispus Attucks, a conspicuous big mulatto who worked at the ropewalk, was brandishing a club in the soldiers' faces and taunting them to fire.

An English captain, appearing suddenly, took command of the detail. At his order, the soldiers, in formation, charged with fixed bayonets. But the crowd would not run. It merely dodged the soldiers' rush, then let fly a shower of rocks and lumps of ice. The burly journeymen ropemakers were rushing in with their staves. The brothers from Concord saw a soldier drop. Almost instantly he was on his feet again, and fired his musket. A volley from the entire file went off point-blank. As the mob broke for cover, five of its members lay bloodying the ground.

When William Emerson heard the story, he was torn between an immense relief that his brothers-in-law had escaped and a fury at the death of fellow countrymen. On his way for a visit to Newburyport, he passed through Boston in time to see the funeral procession of the victims of the massacre. At Wenham, from Porter's Tavern that night, he described in a letter to Phoebe what he had heard and seen. "A monument," he wrote, speaking of Attucks and the others, "is to be erected over them to perpetuate their memory as martyrs in the glorious Cause of Liberty!"

A lull followed the Boston outbreak. England, the colonists learned, had a new Prime Minister. Under Lord North the Townshend duties were repealed. Parliament seemed disposed to follow a more conciliatory policy.

But the pause was soon interrupted by a bombardment of circulars from the City of Boston — letters giving long lists of British infringements of colonial liberties, some of them wrongs which the inhabitants of Concord, busy with their farming, their milling and trading and cattle-raising, had never even thought of. Read in town meeting, this correspondence was like a shower of sparks falling into an open powder barrel. But some of the steadier, more conservative men were for going slow. Among them was respected, handsome Squire Daniel Bliss, Phoebe's older brother. Lawyer Bliss, through his rich and influential acquaintances, had eyes and ears in Boston. One clever man — it was hinted — could be back of all this correspondence; could be deliberately rubbing salt into wounds he did not wish healed. That man, most likely, was Sam Adams.

* * *

From the evening of December 16, 1773, when fifty blanketed, shouting Indians, with white skin showing oddly through their war paint, dumped chest after chest of East India tea into Boston Harbor — tea on which no English tax ever would be collected — a runaway of events brought concern to numerous people. To King George the Third and his ministers; to the British Parliament; to all the colonies of the North Atlantic seaboard; to the mechanics and apprentices of Boston; to Captain James Barrett and his constituents at Concord.

The conduct of the colonies, wrote the King to Lord North, his Prime Minister, seems to call for coercive measures.

At once these began.

Governor Hutchinson left for London to report on affairs in Massachusetts. A soldier, General Thomas Gage, took his place, sailing up Boston Harbor on His Majesty's Ship *Lively*, with additional troops to garrison the town. A series of punitive acts was passed, in rapid succession, by the English Parliament. The native processes of government developing familiarly since the start — save for the brief interlude when Andros ruled — were to be throttled. Till that spilled tea be paid for, Boston must close as a port and would cease to be the Colony's capital.

Though Massachusetts was Parliament's chief target, the other colonies, perceiving the omen, rallied to her support — notably Virginia. Since the Stamp Act Congress had proved effective, let another one, a Continental Congress, be called to deal with this new emergency. Plans were laid for it to meet in Philadelphia.

Gage, having summoned the General Court of Massachusetts to gather at Salem, decided he had better call it off. But the delegates, among them Barrett from Concord, came anyway. They locked the door against the Governor's messenger arriving with the writ of dissolution. Then they passed two measures before adjournment: they elected five men as delegates to the Continental Congress; they voted to meet again, in whatever manner possible.

News of these doings presently got to England. "I am not sorry that the line of conduct seems now chalked out," wrote the King to his Prime Minister. "The New England governments are in a state of rebellion; blows must decide whether they are to be subject to this country or independent."

*   *   *

In America, far from these secret councils, Gage still hoped to keep the peace. But the soldiers under him were not very helpful. They were full of contempt for the ridiculous militia that drilled like an unruly herd of pigs. One officer, however, was more impressed. "What makes an insurrection here always more formidable than in other places," wrote Earl Percy to his father in Britain, "is that there is a law of this Province which obliges every inhabitant to be furnished with a firelock, bayonet, and pretty considerable quantity of ammunition." Each town, too — he added — has its supply of military stores. And he referred to other types of explosives as well. "I am sorry to say that no body of men are so extremely injurious to peace and tranquility as the clergy. They preach sedition openly from their pulpits."

If this able young British officer had chanced to visit Concord, he would have found in the Reverend William Emerson an excellent example.

Among the punishments meted out for spilling tea was a Parliamentary Act forbidding towns to hold any gatherings save those for annual elections. Concord not only ignored this prohibition but played host to a convention of protest composed of delegates from all Middlesex — the first of its kind in Massachusetts. Its resolutions against making payments to Crown officers and for a continued boycott of British goods — along with similar resolves from Suffolk — were to serve as a vital guide for action when brought before the Continental Congress of the colonies in Philadelphia.

In Concord the rift between Whig and Tory was growing wider, with the Tories a dwindling minority. Unlike Cambridge, with its row of stately Tory houses on Brattle Street, Concord had few attractions for the conservative rich. But though in many places the ranks were more evenly divided, Concord's Tories had one considerable advantage — in Daniel Bliss they possessed an able and popular champion. His orderly, well-schooled mind inclined Daniel to the side of precedent and established institutions. Before Hutchinson's departure for London, to report, Daniel, though only thirty-four, had served as his legal aide. With a law business that linked him closely to other Tory families, with an aristocratic wife and a wealthy father-in-law who had served as a colonel in the British Army, Squire Bliss's sympathies could scarcely have lain elsewhere.

Though the pair clung to their friendship, Daniel engaged in many an argument with his brother-in-law, Concord's fiery preacher. What was to be gained by stirring up the people? But the Reverend William Emerson kept poking the fire into a livelier blaze.

While Bliss usually disagreed with the majority, it had become Concord's habit, during this protracted crisis, to elect him to important committees, and he was among her delegates at the Middlesex Convention.

So Daniel rose to present his views.

In thwarting the policies of General Gage, did not his fellow citizens realize they were also flouting their King? This was madness; this was folly deserving nothing but scorn! Were not the colonies England's dependent children? Cut off from Britain, they would perish. They should behave obediently, and be grateful. Through compliance and through humble petition let Massachusetts win her way into the homeland's good graces. England is a mighty nation, with a fleet and powerful armies. Open rebellion will lead inevitably to crushing defeat.

For what seemed endless minutes, when Squire Bliss was through, his hearers sat in a numb and brooding silence. Who could deny these arguments? Like a lawyer who has impressively addressed the jury, Bliss sensed his victory.

Then a member of his own delegation rose. Though they all knew Squire Bliss, strangers at the convention did not all recognize this man of vigorous early middle age, with weather-beaten face and scarred, strong hands, whose homespun suit of butternut brown contrasted with the fashionable coat and waistcoat of the Concord attorney. But Hosmer was a familiar figure to his fellow townsmen. They had formerly named him, along with Daniel Bliss, to the committee that drew up Concord's replies to the inquiries of Boston's Committee of Correspondence. The militia had elected him lieutenant. As the great-great-grandson of a founder, his claims on Concord were secure. By trade he was a cabinetmaker, his graceful, substantial slant-top desks lending dignity to many a Concord home.

His words came at first slowly, with effort, as if he were handier with his tools than with his tongue. But presently he forgot himself. His convictions made him eloquent. What he said gave voice to the thoughts of many plain and simple men.

This is no time for prudence and cold logic. This is a time for a man to heed his heart. Something no one of us can set to words is being threatened, but its value is clear to every man who loves his village, the house he owns, the stock he feeds, the land he plows, his mill or cooper's shop or smithy. These are the properties of a free and happy people. Round them center our rights as human beings. To no temporal power across the sea do we owe our liberty to enjoy them, nor can we permit strangers to meddle. Our privilege to live as we choose comes through the courage and sweat of our fathers who found this unencumbered land, cleared it, then passed it on for our labor. When we drove back the Indians, and fought the French, we fought for these things. To preserve them, we must be prepared to fight again.

Bliss frowned and bit his lip. There was no doubt who had won the day. The answer shone in the faces of many men.

October, 1774 was a busy month in Concord. An idea that had been growing ever since the dissolution of the spring session of the General Court had at last found realization. In August, the Middlesex Convention had voted that a congress of the entire colony was imperative, and suggested Concord, out of Gage's reach, as the place for it. Presently Gage himself unwittingly lent a hand. He summoned the fall session of the Court to gather at Salem, then, alarmed by the bristling instructions of the people to their representatives, rescinded the order. The delegates came anyway, waiting in mock politeness for the Governor. Next, under the independent name of Provincial Congress, the group adjourned to meet at Concord. Gage promptly outlawed these proceedings.

Suppose there should be trouble? To cope with possible disorder from the Tories, the whole town constituted itself a Committee of Safety. Then it passed another resolution:

"Voted, that . . . one or more companies be raised in this town by enlistment . . . to hold themselves in readiness at a minute's warning in case of alarm."

Congress was to meet on Tuesday, October eleventh. By the night before, Concord's taverns were full, forcing many delegates to seek lodging in private homes. Next morning, Concord watched three hundred representatives begin to file into the Town House, among them dapper John Hancock. Concord had hoped to welcome both Adamses, Sam and John, but they, with three other Massachusetts delegates, were still at the sessions of the Continental Congress.

No one had anticipated such a crowd. The representatives found themselves packed together in the hall like a run of shad in springtime. Fortunately, at the other end of the square, the meetinghouse could take care of them all.

The delegates moved to the larger building. The doors closed. Congress was in session.

Most of the men who had gathered at Salem — with the exception of a few Tories — were among those present. But with so many added members, a new election of officers seemed in order. The written ballots brought no upset but merely a change of title — Hancock, President; Benjamin Lincoln, secretary.

By time-honored custom, every General Court, every town meeting, begins with a prayer. Several clergymen were among the delegates. The chaplaincy could fall to one of these. Yet why not honor Concord's energetic pastor? William Emerson's fervent, patriotic sermon that Sunday, his compelling voice, had moved not a few of those now present. A committee, headed by Concord's Captain Barrett, hurried to the new manse to tell the minister he was chosen.

Though sessions were secret, and the Congress moved, the following week, to the Lexington meetinghouse, tavern gossip and the talk of delegates kept the town posted.

As its executive body, the Congress had elected a Committee of Safety, which would continue to meet after adjournment. Its nine members, with Hancock at their head, became familiar figures in Concord where they often gathered at Jones's tavern. Should Gage's troops make a threatening move, they had instructions to call out the militia. Under their direction, the "minute men" were to organize. Theirs was the duty to collect more arms and hide them out of Gage's reach.

Before final adjournment, the Provincial Congress voted that its report on the state of the colonies be published in the newspapers and copies sent to all the towns. In the Boston *News Letter,* the citizens of Concord and every other place could read the letter of censure sent to Gage:

> It is with the utmost concern we see your hostile preparations, which have spread such alarm throughout this province and the whole continent as threatens to involve us in all the confusion and horrors of a civil war.

There, too, they could read the Governor's disavowal and his demand that established government be respected. He wanted — he protested — only unity and peace. The province itself, by its conduct — he insisted — was forcing him to these extraordinary measures.

* * *

At first, minute men were slow to enroll. Even after the exchange of accusations between the Provincial Congress and General Gage, it was hard to believe that bloodshed threatened. Besides, late fall and winter are sluggish, frozen times for soldiering.

But New Year's and the early weeks of 1775 brought a change. First, there was the weather. Even old Deacon Thomas Barrett could not recall another such January. Concord's winters are usually white, but now no snow at all lay on the ground. Day after day like April — without the mud and rain. Wonderful weather for drilling, with time aplenty before plowing could begin.

These new soldiers, unlike the compulsory militia with its haphazard trainings, were all to be volunteers. Thus Tories already in the militia could be sidestepped. But even the most patriotic men grow more eager at prospect of fair pay. So the town appointed a committee to look into the matter. The wages they fixed for every training were about what a man would be allowed in taxes for a day's work on the roads and bridges, and the oftener he drilled the more would he make. As a bounty, each volunteer would get a cartridge box.

At the first militia training of the year, the terms and inducements had been announced. Three days later, fifty to sixty men had enlisted. By the springlike end of January, a hundred minute men — two companies — were drilling on the sandy, grassless green. Each company had elected its captain; each had its lieutenants and noncoms. One captain, Charles Miles, came from a farm at Nine Acre Corner which had been in his family since Concord's first decade. David Brown, a tall, robust, fine-looking farmer, was chosen to command the second company, with a Wheeler for lieutenant and a Buttrick for fifer and drummer boy. John Buttrick, the lad's father, had been named major of minute men in the county's growing regiment.

All had set their name to the same oath — a vow devised by the local committee and voted into effect by the town:

> First, that we whose names are hereunto subscribed will to the utmost of our power defend his Majesty King George the Third, his Person, Crown, and Dignity.
>
> Second, that we will at the same time to the utmost of our power and abilities defend all and every of our Charter Rights, Liberties, and Privileges, and will hold ourselves in readiness at a minute's warning with arms and ammunition thus to do.
>
> Thirdly, that we will at all times and in all places obey our officers chosen by us.

Twice each week, for a full three hours, the common north of the Milldam shook to the tread of marching feet. Nathan Barrett, son of the colonel (formerly Captain James Barrett), lent his drum for drilling till it fell to pieces through overwork and the town bought a new one. Of the hundred men enrolled, all had guns of their own save for fifteen, whom the town supplied. Most shouldered heavy firelocks. Some carried lighter, more accurate fowling pieces, like the sporting gun borrowed from the Flint family, who had brought it from England. Muskets now borne by Melvins, Hosmers, and Wheelers had seen service against the Indians and the French. And like the guns, some of the older men had been similarly tested.

Thanks to the continuing mild weather, Concord and her sister towns, by the time the second Provincial Congress assembled in February, possessed a more proficient body of soldiers than even the most sanguine exponents of the experiment had dared to hope for.

Soldiers without supplies are of little use. Two questions worried the leaders of the Provincial Congress: Where to get arms and provisions, and where to put them. Powder was especially scarce. Since the summer of 1774, Gage's soldiers had been raiding every depot they could find. But more powder was being constantly gathered. Some came from France; some from other colonies; some from local mills. As for cannon, a few were being stolen, under Gage's very nose, from the forts at Boston Neck.

The chief depots for storage should be rallying points familiar to the countryside — places to which the minute men from every part could quickly march. Concord met these requirements. Soon innocent-looking carts covered with dung rolled up from Salem, the oxen straining at the yokes. Then out from under the steaming mass would come casks of musket shot and grape, six-pound cannon balls, candle boxes packed with cartridges. Supplies enough — figured the Provincial Committee — for an army of fifteen thousand men.

Colonel Barrett, in charge of the depot, had been warned not so much as to utter the word "powder." With one's nearest neighbor a possible Tory, Gage had no lack of informers.

But how conceal a mounted cannon? Every excited child in Concord had stared at the ten six-pounders stored at the Town House. A special detail — an alarm company of forty men under a gunnery expert — was learning how to handle them.

Besides the Town House, every building with any free space was crammed to bursting. A lot of the military stores were at Colonel Barrett's, across the fork of the rivers, north, on the Assabet — four brass cannon, two mortars, many muskets and bayonets, considerable powder and lead. Within the stockade of the county prison were three formidable twenty-four-pounders. Abishai Bond, member of the town's committee of inspection which saw to it that Concord drank no British tea, had filled his attic with supplies. Deacon Hubbard's, behind the meetinghouse, Timothy Wheeler's storage shed and mill, had been turned into arsenals and commissary deposits. The chairman of Concord's Committee of Correspondence, Samuel Whitney, who owned a trim white plastered house to the right of the road from Lexington where the ridge first begins to rise east of the town, had packed with gunpowder the shop within his fenced-in lot.

The Parliamentary Act closing the Port of Boston had killed all chance of work. Riggers, shipwrights, ropemakers, smiths — all the unemployed — wandered in the streets. Having refused to build barracks for the British, the men of Boston were running short of food.

An appeal for relief went to all the towns. In Concord, where Parson Emerson preached on the text, "Sell what ye have and give Alms," fifty pounds in bills and twenty bushels of grain were collected.

Though the workers continued idle, they did not lack purpose. Some thirty of them, North End mechanics, all members of the Sons of Liberty, their moving spirit a certain Paul Revere — an expert in silversmithing, engraving, and other matters requiring a delicate touch — met regularly at the Green Dragon Tavern, close to the wharves, to swap their findings and pass them on to Drs. Church and Warren, of the Committee of Safety. The Fourth, or King's Own Regiment, had landed at Long Wharf; the Forty-third; the Fifth; and Thirty-eighth. Admiral Graves's fleet had anchored in the Bay. Four large fieldpieces were being mounted at Boston Neck, the only approach to the town by land. Hundreds of soldiers worked there, throwing up fortifications.

But just as the provincials were watching the Governor's every move, so Gage, more and more alarmed by rumors of a phantom army that would manifest itself on every village green, kept his eyes open.

*   *   *

The town had only one expert gunsmith, Samuel Barrett, who lived across the river in a house that stood on a knoll between North Bridge and Colonel Barrett's, convenient to the supply of flintlocks there.

In the cache of guns were many broken pieces — more than a single craftsman could take care of. When a stranger, wearing the leather breeches of a mechanic, with his worldly goods tied up in a homespun checkered handkerchief, walked in and said he wished to set himself up as a gunsmith, Colonel James Barrett and the local committee on supplies welcomed him as the man they were seeking. With work so scarce in Boston, mechanics in many crafts were drifting to Concord — to their profit and the town's. This was the first new gunsmith, and a godsend.

Safer to try him first, however — his skill, his politics, his background. His name was Wood, he explained; he was a Liberty man from Pownallborough.

The committee found him a shop and some tools. Then Major Buttrick brought a couple of muskets with broken locks. Wood fixed them trimly and with dispatch.

At Wright's Tavern came further questions. Did he know Colonel Wood, also from down East?

Yes, said the gunsmith — they were distant kinsmen.

When he went to fetch his tools, would he deliver a letter to him?

Lunch over, the committee and their guest examined some of the muskets at the Town House.

Could he make guns like these?

Yes, he could make any kind they wished.

After a look at the center of the town, and a brandy at the Tavern, Wood took his leave.

That was the last Concord saw of its new gunsmith.

Gage needed a map and military intelligence as well as information thus brought by spies.

In the late afternoon of Monday, March twentieth, two men dressed in citizens' clothes, but bearing themselves like soldiers, knocked at the door of Daniel Bliss's house on the opposite side of the millpond from the Lexington road. Not sure of the way to their destination, they had asked directions from a woman they met at the edge of town. Safe at Squire Bliss's, they introduced themselves: Captain Brown and Ensign De Berniere of His Majesty's forces.

Bliss had more than half expected this visit. That very morning a deputation of his fellow citizens had called to warn him that he knew too much; that if he tried to make a break for Boston, they would kill him. From a northwest window Bliss pointed to the gentle swell of low-lying hills just vanishing in the dusk beyond the river. Some miles out of town, over the North Bridge there, then up the road to the left, lay Colonel Barrett's. Here, near at hand, at the foot of the pond, where they heard that thump and clatter, Timothy Wheeler's mill was grinding flour for the minute men. Right next door, the miller's shed was full of it. Across the pond, to the right of the church, Saddler Reuben Brown was turning out cartridge boxes.

The two officers had already taken note of the town's strategic military position. Commanded as it was by hills and ridges, it might prove formidable. But surely these provincials would not fight? Their militia was no better than a rabble, totally lacking in disciplined respect. If it came to shooting, they would break and run.

Bliss glanced out of the window toward the road where his brother Theodore happened to be passing.

"There goes a man," said Daniel soberly, "who will fight you in blood up to his knees."

As the officers were about to join their host and hostess at dinner, someone knocked timidly at the door. It was the woman they had met down the road. Several townsmen, she blubbered, were threatening to have her tarred and feathered. They had seen her directing the strangers.

There was still time to get out. If their host would come with them, urged the officers, they would welcome his company.

Daniel Bliss felt certain that his wife and children would not be molested. He could send for them later.

To avoid the patrol — ten men now were on duty — Daniel struck north across the river, then circled back with his British companions to pick up the Lexington road.

The second Provincial Congress had gathered at Cambridge early in February. Now, Wednesday, March 22, 1775, after a brief adjournment, it moved to Concord. Again meetings filled the tap-rooms and private dining halls of the taverns — the Committee on the State of the Province; the committee charged with drawing up plans for an army, with quotas from the four New England colonies;

the committee appointed to bring in a resolve recommending a day of fasting to pray for the preservation of the union of American colonies in defense of their liberties — to pray also that the peoples of Great Britain might have their eyes opened to discern what course would make for peace.

William Emerson served again as chaplain to the Congress. He had well earned the report of him brought to Gage: "A very bad subject of His Majesty." Activities rarely falling to the lot of a country parson were keeping him busy. On Monday, the week before, a regimental muster, with men from all the neighborhood, had packed the streets of the town. In his sermon to the soldiers, William Emerson, who knew how to talk to young men, had chosen for his text words that rang like a bugle call: "Behold God himself is with us for our Captain!" Never permit it to be said, he warned, that we ourselves started a civil conflict by even the smallest offensive action. Let every single step, in these momentous hours, be in defense. But if they begin a war, we will have even greater justification to fight for our rights. "Arise! my injured countrymen, and plead even with the sword, the firelock and bayonet. Plead with your arms the birthright of Englishmen, the dearly purchased legacy left you!"

On March the twenty-seventh, when the pastor returned from preaching to the militia at Acton, he found Concord settling down after a brief alarm. Twelve hundred lobster-backs had marched out of Boston. But instead of continuing up the Lexington road, they had circled back to the city. The troops needed exercise, Gage explained.

How far do soldiers march for exercise? The Provincial Congress ordered Colonel Barrett to keep teams ready, day and night, should there be need to evacuate the stores. That hour when British troops, this time with artillery and baggage, should sally again from Boston, would be the moment of danger.

By Saturday, April fifteenth, nothing had happened. "Some hopeful symptoms respecting public affairs," wrote William Emerson in his diary; "Congress adjourned for three weeks."

CHAPTER VII

The Bridge That Arched the Flood

IT had been a beautiful evening to go courting. Shortly after sunset, the yellow moon, at the full, had risen above the low ridges beyond Bedford. Past midnight now, its light silvered the fields and cast a pattern under every tree. At Lexington, young Dr. Samuel Prescott of Concord said good-night to his girl.

He had just ridden past Lexington Green when he was startled to see two horsemen. They had reined in; they were waiting for him.

The hour, the times themselves, impelled caution. Prescott moved up slowly. Yes, he recognized one of them now — Revere, the silversmith from Boston, like himself a member of the Sons of Liberty. He was a first-rate rider and the messenger of the Provincial Congress. Prescott had seen him several times in Concord. Just three days before, in fact, he had been there. Dr. Joseph Warren, of the Provincial Committee of Safety, who was lingering in Boston to watch the British, had sent him at that time with a warning that Gage was up to something — might be preparing a more ambitious raid than any thus far attempted. Colonel Barrett, using every cart he could get hold of, had been shifting the powder, cannon, arms, and supplies from the central depot to neighboring villages.

Here it was, Tuesday; no, near one o'clock and Wednesday morning — thought Prescott — with Revere abroad again. The doctor spurred forward to make himself known.

Gage's troops — he learned — were indeed on the march; about eight hundred soldiers. They had mustered quietly that evening where Boston Common touched on the muddy, reed-clogged Basin. Boats from the transports had been waiting to ferry them to the swampy shore opposite, between the Charles and Charlestown. Dr. Warren, guessing that the British plans called for a foray toward Concord, had sent Revere and William Dawes to spread the alarm. At Lexington, the Britainers might try to catch John Hancock,

President of the Provincial Congress that had just adjourned, and Sam Adams, under special disfavor because of his activities with the Committee of Correspondence and with the recent Continental Congress.

Dawes and Revere had just come from waking Hancock and Adams at the house of Pastor Jonas Clarke, close on the right-hand fork from the Green. Hearing Prescott's horse, they had hidden in the shadow of the church, not wishing to hazard capture. After a lucky escape by Boston Neck, Dawes had not been interfered with. But Revere, who started from Charlestown, very narrowly missed being taken. Right at the start, two mounted officers chased him, but he had shaken them off by a dash up the road toward Mystic. At least ten to a dozen officers — friends had warned him — had been seen along the way he must follow.

There was considerable likelihood, added Revere, that the farthest out of Gage's patrols might try to intercept them between Lexington and Concord.

Three men would have a better chance than two. Prescott joined the riders. The horsemen headed up the eight-mile stretch to Concord.

Houses were few and far between along this road. About four miles out of Lexington, at a solitary farm, Dawes and Prescott stopped to wake the householder while Revere went on ahead. In the quiet night, they could hear the *clip-clop* of his horse. Then it stopped. A call from Revere broke the stillness.

"Come up! Here are two of them!"

Not two, but four.

In the moonlight, Prescott and Dawes saw a second pair, just in front, ride out from a lane on the right, back of Revere. He was in a trap between the first and second set of patrols.

Sizing up the situation, Dawes wheeled and was off at a gallop toward Lexington. But Prescott decided to bluff it out. He was a doctor; he had a right to the highway.

As he rode up, he heard one picket shout to Revere, "God damn you, stop! if you go an inch further, you're a dead man!"

Then he was at Revere's side, using the butt end of his whip in an effort to force his way past.

But the officers, drawing their pistols, threatened to blow out the brains of the first man to move on. They ordered Revere and Prescott to ride back to the small enclosed pasture where the second pair of Britainers had hidden.

The thought flashed through Prescott's mind that this might prove less of a cage than the captors supposed — a cage with a back door to it. As the four officers closed the gap behind them, Prescott shouted to his companion, "Put on!" and dug his heels into his horse's flanks. Out into the field galloped the two, Prescott reining left, Revere right, to divide their pursuers.

Ahead, beyond the stone wall, Prescott knew, ran a rough farmway. Over the barrier flew horse and rider, then pell mell up the woodsway as fast and as far as he dared in the deceptive moonlight and treacherous footing. Then he reined in, fearing to be swept from the saddle by one of the whiplike branches which were cutting his face.

Had Revere escaped?

Impossible to tell.

The most important thing was to carry the warning to Concord.

Sure of his landmarks, the young doctor rode on — through a ravine, past a swamp, then westward till he saw before him a rocky field with houses. That would be Samuel Hartwell's, a minute man who lived on the edge of Lincoln. Near it stood the farm buildings of William Smith, captain of the Lincoln Company. The third one lay on the open road for home.

These men would carry the news to Lincoln. Prescott pounded on the door.

"The Regulars are coming!"

It was after half-past one, with the stars already a little dimmer. On guard at the center, minute man Amos Melvin, whose forebears had marched against Andros and fought many a skirmish with Indians and Frenchmen, heard the galloping hoofs. A moment later, the alarm bell was clanging in the belfry of the Town House. The east wind, freshening with the approach of day, carried the brazen uproar to every house in the immediate village.

Prescott rode west to warn Acton, five miles farther.

It was no easy thing, so early that morning, to rouse out of bed. Under Colonel Barrett's direction, almost every able-bodied man had been carting munitions to various hideaways: Stow, Littleton, and other fairly near-by places. Many of the younger men, sent on longer hauls, had not returned. Those back were tired and sleepy.

Sergeant John Barrett, of the militia, hurried from house to house, waking his complement. By ones and twos, Concord's available citi-

zen soldiers — the militia, the older men of the alarm company, the
scattering of minute men — straggled into line on the road under
the ridge before Wright's Tavern. Tall, thin men in rough homespun, most of them, with lean, long faces and lantern jaws.

Among the first to arrive was William Emerson in his black
ministerial frock. With so many men and officers still absent, it was
hard to find one's proper place and unit. But after Captain David
Brown came in, there was less confusion. A detail was sent at once
to Colonel Barrett's to hide the arms still there; another started to
carry out similar orders at the center.

Lieutenant Reuben Brown, the saddler, was directed to ride toward
Lexington to see if the British were down that way; a second horseman watched the Lincoln road.

The tread of marching men shook the bridge over the stream
at the head of the millpond. Neighbors and kinsmen from Lincoln
were coming up — the minute men led by Captain Smith, the militia
by old Abijah Pierce, with only his walking stick for a weapon.
Yes, the British were close, and arriving by the Lexington road.
Reuben Brown, just back from the outskirts of that town, confirmed
this information. He had got near enough to see a distant flash of
musket fire on the green.

Even in the gathering light, it was difficult, as the men formed
for marching, to guess their numbers, because of the hurry and
confusion. Perhaps over a hundred: the minute men, with their
drums and fifers, to the right, in the place of honor; then the militia.
The Alarm Company, under Captain Minot, was to stand fast as a
guard for the village.

As the line swung into column down the road toward Lexington,
more soldiers kept falling in. Young Sam Derby and the other boys
shrilled their fifes.

A brisk march under the lee of the long hill that still cast its
shadow westward; then out into the sun's first rays at Meriam's
Corner.

In solid ranks on the road ahead, where it ran down Brooks's Hill,
six hundred yards away, came the British. The sun played on their
bayonets with glints of fire; their uniforms glowed startlingly red. As
the Yankees halted, many a young countryman stared up the road
in unconscious admiration.

Seeming to take no notice of the heterogeneous company, the
British kept on. Three hundred yards away; one hundred and fifty.
That long red serpent must number twenty companies at least — and

behind them, the might of the British realm. The British fifes and drums now sounded fantastically loud.

"About face!" roared a Concord officer at his men. With the redcoats so close behind that it looked like a parade, the Americans and British — fifes and drums playing — covered the short distance back to Meriam's Corner.

Just where the fork to Bedford turns sharply right, and the long uneven sandy ridge rises to parallel the Concord–Lexington road, the Yankees veered from the thoroughfare and took to the slope. Along the backbone of the ridge they headed toward the town. Francis Wheeler, Jonathan Farrar, and other officers, glancing back, saw Britainers — apparently as flankers — begin clambering up the hill. Other companies continued below — close enough, from this vantage point, to be reasonably well identified. Certainly Gage had sent picked troops on this mission. These were no common regiments. Instead, the force was made up of grenadiers and light infantry — those crack companies, two to each regiment, trained especially for forays and assaults. The soldiers following on the ridge were the light infantry; the shock troops, the heavy grenadiers, in column of companies, were moving below like a blood-red river along the road.

Keeping an eye on the flankers, the Americans reached a fairly strategic spot just above the meetinghouse. Here they found Captain Minot had already posted his alarm company not far from the liberty pole, his men reinforced by late arrivals. The minister, too, was there, and members of the town's Committee of Safety.

Colonel James Barrett, after giving directions how the guns still there should be concealed, had ridden in from his farm. An old man, lame and stiff and dependent on his horse, he was urging the younger officers to take command. But the Middlesex men insisted he continue as ranking officer. So the colonel designated Joseph Hosmer as his adjutant and ordered him to form the troops.

The Americans were still outnumbered three to one. It seemed advisable to fall back a little farther. As the word was being passed along the line, the British flankers moved into sight, then halted at the liberty pole, half a gunshot away.

To the westward, beyond the hillside burying ground, lay a deepish saddle of the ridge that rose again in a more northerly direction, paralleling the road to the bridge. The Americans shifted to this second eminence.

Less than a quarter of a mile off, entering the heart of the village around the curve of the hill, swept the grenadiers, glittering in arms. In the tenseness, in the feeling that anything might happen, it was a sight to unnerve the bravest. The rumble of British drums sounded like thunder before a gathering storm.

As William Emerson passed along the line, he noticed how violently young Henry Gould was shaking. "Don't be afraid, Harry," he said; "God's on our side!"

Colonel Barrett was the center of a group debating whether they should fall back once more. "Let's stand our ground," urged Concord's parson. Several younger officers chimed in to agree. But Colonel Barrett said no; it would be a pointless sacrifice. Better move north, over the river, to the long slopes beyond. There, with the stream between, they could watch the British and at the same time be gathering strength through reinforcements sure to be coming in from still more towns.

As the Americans started across, William Emerson's glance turned anxiously toward his manse, just left of the bridge. How peaceful the countryside looked in the fresh morning light! In his field that bordered the road, the rye was already up; high enough, this morning, actually to sway with the scurrying puffs of the easterly. In his orchard, this unprecedented spring, pink apple buds were just breaking into whiter bloom.

Would Phoebe be safe, and not too frightened; Phoebe and her three young ones?

The parson noticed a group of his women parishioners at the door. They must have sought the manse for sanctuary.

As militia and minute men continued up the rise of ground on the river's opposite side, the preacher crossed the field to the house.

His wife, they told him, had fainted.

News that the Regulars were coming had swept through the houses at the center, and with it spread consternation and terror.

Here we have lived unmolested, and our people before us. This is our town; these homes are ours! My husband's father, who put up this building, was a delegate from Concord to the General Court, and helped make our laws. My brother's a selectman. This moment, my husband should be plowing; my children starting for dame school. Till we drove them off, the Indians and French were our only enemies. By what right do these British strangers invade us, to harry and threaten our lives?

Many women, grabbing up such household treasures as could be dumped into a homespun blanket gathered at the corners to make a bundle, had already fled with their children to the woods. With them shuffled a few older, decrepit men — though even grand-fathers were under arms with Colonel Barrett. But some of the townsfolk were too infirm to move, and some refused to go. Old Mrs. Robinson, alone and barricaded in her house, thought all at once of the communion silver. Quickly she unbarred the door and ran to the church. The rumble of British drums, before the brisk east wind, was swirling into the square. Gathering the sacred vessels in her apron, Mrs. Robinson hurried home. Down cellar, in an arch within the chimney foundation, stood her capacious soap barrel. She dumped her load into the gray-green mess.

The grenadiers were halting on the common. Old Martha Moulton, Dr. Timothy Minot's caretaker, left in charge of his house opposite Wright's Tavern, could see the leaders entering the building used so short a while ago as headquarters by the men of Middlesex. Now the horses of the British officers were cropping the fresh new grass not five feet from the window through which she peeped.

Soldiers began pounding on her door. Water — they said; they wanted water. For so cool a morning, they did look very hot, very sweaty and red-faced. Their boots were caked with mud as though somewhere on the march the British column had waded along a creek. As soldiers, in an endless flow, tracked in and out of the house, they muddied the broad planks till they looked like a barn-yard floor.

On the hill, among the tombstones of the burying ground, Mrs. Moulton could see two officers, one with a spyglass at his eye. One was a fat man, with his white waistcoat unbuttoned. The other — he with the spyglass — was lean and somewhat younger. They were studying the ridge and road to the north, towards the bridge. Presently they came down. A detail of soldiers hurried to her door. Chairs, they demanded; chairs for Colonel Smith and Major Pitcairn, with four or five more for the other officers.

Martha heard the *clop* of an ax. On the ridge above the meeting-house, the liberty pole with its flag dipped slowly, gathered mo-mentum, then tumbled with a crash. As it fell, a roar went up from the grenadiers in the square. Soon pieces of the well-seasoned wood were being tossed in a heap against the wall of the Town House.

Grenadiers had broken into the church and were rummaging around, but apparently found nothing. With disconcerting foreknowledge, squads of soldiers were thundering at the doors of every building which had served as a storehouse. Lucky indeed for the constitutional army planned by the Provincial Congress that its powder and many of its guns had already been moved, though five hundred pounds of musket balls splashed into the millpond.

No injury was intended any person, explained officers, but if not opened, doors would be broken down. One search party set out to ransack Ephraim Jones's tavern, on the South Bridge road, knowing that Henry Gardner, treasurer for the Provincial Congress, had boarded there during the recent session. Jones, a Louisburg veteran and the brawny keeper of the county jail, either by accident or on purpose bumped so violently into Pitcairn, commanding the detail, that he knocked the major down. As the search went on, five soldiers with fixed bayonets guarded the taverner.

Quick-witted Hannah Barron, the barmaid, had run to Gardner's quarters. This was her room, this her trunk, she told the soldiers.

Gardner's records went unmolested.

Men brave enough to stay with supplies stood sullenly by as barrels of flour were rolled out, bashed in, and scattered till the road bordering the millpond looked as though a snowsquall had hit it. The yard of Ebenezer Hubbard's malt house was white with flour. But though sixty or more barrels were stored there, less than half were smashed. The rest, shoved into the pond, refused to sink. Wet dough had sealed the cracks and saved the flour.

Next door, farther along toward Potter's Bridge, Timothy Wheeler, retired militia captain, who ran the Bulkeley mill — now owned by the Minot family — waited in his house near his three storage sheds, and hoped for better luck.

When the searchers came, he invited them in for cheese and cider with the bland remark he was happy to see them.

After food and drink, all went outside for a look at the sheds. The first door was locked. A soldier got ready to kick his foot through it.

"Wait!" said Timothy Wheeler, producing the key.

As the door swung open, many barrels were seen inside.

"I am a miller, sir," explained Wheeler to the officer in charge. "Yonder stands my mill. I get my living by it." He pointed toward the dam. "In winter I grind a great deal of grain and get it ready for market." He laid a hand on a cask that was really his. "This is *my* flour; *my* wheat, *my* rye."

"Well," said the officer, commanding his detail to move on, "we don't injure private property."

When his troops first took over the town, Lieutenant Colonel Smith, like a prudent commander, at once set his light infantry to secure both river crossings. Thus Concord, at the point of the broad elbow formed by its two streams, could be cut off from many of the neighboring villages. Already one detail had torn up the planks of the South Bridge. Through his telescope, Major Pitcairn had watched six companies of light infantry, hard on the Provincials' heels, make for the bridge north of the town, to be presently reinforced by a seventh. Three or four of these companies were to proceed beyond, to destroy supplies at Colonel Barrett's — the house was plainly marked on the map Gage had furnished. All details of the raid seemed well in hand.

The broad plateau just under Punkatasset afforded a place of observation from which to see what was happening. Here Colonel Barrett halted his people.

At least two companies of British infantry, having also crossed the bridge, were following up the first rise of the hill. But they soon halted and stacked arms — one company just beside John Buttrick's house, the second farther southwestward, overlooking the river road that led to Barrett's. The other companies, after crossing, remained below, with officers hurrying about as if prepared to give further orders. One company had remained on the opposite side. The watchers could see soldiers from it going for water to Elisha Jones's well, across the road from the manse.

"Don't expose yourselves without prospect of doing service," warned Colonel Barrett. Then he rode off along a country road above to let his household know the raiders were approaching.

Scarcely had he disappeared before a detail of the British shouldered arms and began to march along the lower road toward the Barrett farm, less than three miles up the Assabet River.

When the colonel got there, he found the job nearly done. Most of the powder, many muskets, much of the shot had been carted away. Jim, his fourteen-year-old grandson, goading the oxen to a lumbering trot, was just hiding a final load under some brush in swampy Spruce Gutter, back of the house.

There had been too little time to drag off every gun carriage. But the few cannon left could be taken care of. The bed of sage in her garden was Mrs. Barrett's pride. Every bush was now carefully lifted and the guns laid underneath in the soft, rich earth. In position again, there was nothing to give the hiding place away.

Spring plowing, this year, had its special use. Into every furrow, as the ox teams plodded along, rows of muskets were being sown. Just as the last hollow was filled, the column of British infantry swung into view.

Colonel Barrett urged his wife to hide in the woods, but she refused to budge. She was too old, she said, to worry about living much longer. She'd rather stay and see they didn't burn down the house.

With the redcoats a musket shot away, Colonel Barrett rode north, over the sandy ridge behind his farm, then headed toward the right to rejoin his men.

From her bedroom window, Mrs. Barrett watched as the soldiers halted by the well at the edge of the field. Just then one of her daughters ran into the room, in her arms a heavy pouchful of bullets that had been overlooked. Together they lugged it to the attic and dumped the musket balls into an empty barrel. Mrs. Barrett grabbed up an armful of feathers from a cask near by to spread over the top. By the time she got downstairs again, troops had surrounded the house.

He had search orders, said the officer at the door.

"Very well, sir," answered Mrs. Barrett, "I shall expect you to respect private property."

One soldier started breaking open a trunk containing some pewter plates. Those were her own, Mrs. Barrett protested. In the garret, another searcher found the barrel of feathers, but his companions guffawed as he thrust in his arms.

"What do you expect to find there, you fool?" demanded the officer.

Embarrassed, his hands all feathers, the soldier backed off.

In the shed, the gun carriages had been quickly discovered. Soldiers were dragging them out, piling them close to the building, then covering them with straw.

"If you burn those carriages there," warned Mrs. Barrett, "the barn will be destroyed."

The straw, already kindled, was put out; the carriages moved to the road for burning.

*   *   *

If their restless striding about meant anything, the officers of the British company waiting by Buttrick's farmhouse, and of the company farther along, overlooking the road to Barrett's, did not much like their exposed position.

They had good reason to feel uneasy. By entire minute man companies, by hurrying groups and individuals, reinforcements were swelling the Americans' ranks. From Bedford, from Chelmsford, Littleton, and Westfield, they came, rallying to the defense of the military stores. John Robinson, of Westford, second in command of Colonel William Prescott's minute men, came up; with him his friend the Reverend Joseph Thaxter, armed with a brace of pistols. New arrivals exclaimed over the heat of the day — though the wind still was blowing from the sea.

American lookouts by Hunt's farm on the southwest slope of Punkatasset watched a British soldier climb onto a rock beyond his lines, peer intently at the gathering forces, then jump down to report to an officer. This seemed the opportune moment to force the redcoats towards the river. Ever since halting on Punkatasset, Major John Buttrick had been eager to regain that nearer vantage point beside his farmhouse now held by a single British company. In good marching order under Adjutant Hosmer's assignment, the men of Middlesex moved forward.

Hurriedly the British lookouts fell back. Then Major Buttrick saw both companies — the one at his farm, the second which had waited above the road to Barrett's — march down the slope to join the third that now tarried just this side of the bridge.

Colonel Barrett himself came up as his men were regaining this ground. Two hundred yards below, packed close together, stood the British troops. Behind them, the narrow wooden cartway arched the stream.

Half-past nine o'clock, now. In town, the grenadiers had raided the gunshop of Sam Barrett but found no muskets — only the gunsmith's venerable father, Deacon Barrett, whom they roughed up and then released. Brown's saddlery, yielding some cartridge boxes, was set afire, but smoldered out. The lobster-backs had knocked the trunnions from three twenty-four-pounders and added the wooden gun carriages to the splinters of the liberty pole heaped near the Town House. A quantity of wooden spoons and trenchers bought by the Committee on Supplies was added.

Mrs. Moulton watched the officers seated before her door get up from time to time to wander toward Wright's Tavern. Some of the twenty barrels of rum intended for another army were whetting British throats. A whispered story was going the rounds among the few townsfolk who, like Mrs. Moulton, had stayed behind. An officer at Wright's Tavern — they say — having called for a brandy toddy, had thrust in his finger to stir his drink and remarked, with satisfaction, that thus he hoped to stir the Yankees' blood before nightfall. Had Major Pitcairn, there before her door, made the boast? Some said it was he.

Glancing from the officers at their ease on her chairs, Martha noticed with alarm that the grenadiers had set fire to the heap of spoils in the trampled square in front of the Town House. Already the wind was whipping the flames against the building. To her frightened eyes, they were leaping even higher than the ridge. Not only would the Town Hall go, with its cupola and gilded vane; the whole row of houses — Dr. Minot's itself, the school, and all the rest — would be burned to the ground. Distractedly she begged the officers to order the blaze put out. They only laughed at the flutter she was in.

"Don't be concerned, mother, we won't do you any harm!"

"Harm!" She was not worried about harm — she was thinking of all the property being threatened. Fetching a bucket of water, she began fighting the fire herself. Could she have read the thoughts of one officer there, she might have considered her effort hopeless. To his friend Lord Sandwich, Major Pitcairn had written, "I am satisfied that one active campaign, a smart action, and burning two or three of their towns, will set everything to rights." But at last another officer felt sorry for her and ordered soldiers to put out the blaze. As pailful after pailful splashed over the half-consumed, creosoted gun carriages, clouds of thick black smoke rose high above the roof trees.

Those must be the minute men from Acton. Lieutenant Joseph Hosmer watched them hurry along the back — the upper — road, toward the height of land near Buttrick's, where he was lining up the various contingents. Perhaps the British too had seen them, and the sight had hastened their retreat. Just behind came some sixteen men from Carlisle, under John Heald, lieutenant.

That would be Isaac Davis, Acton captain, striding in the lead. A good thing to choose a gunsmith for a captain. Davis himself had fitted a bayonet to the musket of each man in his company. His own gun, a beauty, he had made himself.

These men must have traveled fast; on the double some of the way. Davis's face was red as a piece of scarlet broadcloth.

If their captain was willing, the well-armed Acton men could have the head of the line. They were already in position for it, halting where the crossroad dipped at right angles toward the causeway below, where the three British companies waited — the muddy, low causeway bounded towards the water by a rough stone wall that paralleled the river over swampy ground for a brief distance before reaching the bridge.

Davis ran forward to join the little knot of officers and town officials. All eyes had turned from the redcoats toward the village in the distance. Clouds of smoke, ominous and dark, were swirling above the roofs at the common.

The heart of every Concord man rose to his throat. *What are they doing to my village? That's the courthouse there, where the smoke lies thickest. That's where we tend the business of the town. Those stores for merchandise, those shops, are where we earn our bread. That's the schoolhouse, yonder. We were slow to vote the money for it — but we're proud of it now. That church is where we pray. Why just last year, before the Congress met, we had it freshly painted.*

Joseph Hosmer — cabinetmaker, lieutenant, adjutant — broke the spell.

"Will you let them burn the town down?" he shouted.

Then Davis spoke up:

"I haven't a man that's afraid to go."

Colonel Barrett rode along the line at the order to load muskets. We must not fire first, he warned (trustworthy word from Lexington had not come through yet) — if the Britainers want a war, they must begin it.

The companies faced right in column of twos. Hosmer, having lined them up as they arrived, could only guess at the number — four hundred and fifty at the most; at the least, three hundred. Major John Buttrick was to command the advance. He had offered the post to Lieutenant Colonel Robinson, his superior, but Robinson, whose people had not come up yet, would not accept, preferring to march as Buttrick's aide.

With Captain Davis leading his Acton men, and Abner Hosmer, Acton drummer, setting the beat, they started down the hill. Captain Brown, of the minute man company from Concord, marching third in the line, felt a strange exaltation. It was almost — he thought — as if he were going to Sabbath meeting.

From their actions, the British must at last be aware they occupied an undefensible position. Close on each other's heels, the three companies marched in some confusion over the bridge and were crowding the narrow road beyond. An officer, perhaps to deploy flankers, had jumped over the wall and was trampling Parson Emerson's grain. As the last squad cleared the bridge, then faced about, the leading Americans, forty yards away, saw another officer and several men start ripping up the planks.

So they meant to block the road to the town? Major Buttrick ran forward, shouting to the redcoats to leave that bridge alone. The only answer was the crack of an officer's pistol on the opposite bank. A water spout jumped up in the middle of the river where the warning shot hit. A second and a third report followed in quick succession. Then, from the nearest British squad, a volley — point-blank over the bridge.

Buttrick saw Captain Davis, right beside him, make a convulsive jump. As the Acton captain fell, his blood spattered Sergeant David Forbush and File Leader Thomas Thorp, noncommissioned officers behind him. Abner Hosmer, the Acton drummer boy, was down, with half his face shot away. As the musket balls whistled, yells of surprise and pain, farther back, told that others were hit.

"Fire! For God's sake fire!" shouted Major Buttrick.

Like a rising gust of wind traveled the order, taken up by a hundred throats along the causeway. "Fire at will!" called officers still on the slope — "High enough not to hit our own men!"

Simultaneous with the cry, almost blending with the British volley, the muskets blazed. A wave of acrid smoke burst along the causeway and at right angles up the hill. As the breeze caught and flung it back, the Americans saw the regulars, their ranks broken, running in a panic towards the town. Behind them, close to the bridge, sprawled three redcoats. Eight or ten wounded men, looking over their shoulders to see if they were followed, hobbled painfully in the wake of the flight.

The shocking, unaccustomed sight of their own dead halted the Americans at the bridge. Davis was shot clear through the heart; the hole where the bullet came out big as your fist. The Acton men who picked his body up, and that of their drummer, saw on Hos-

mer's chest the handsome breastpin he had got that month to celebrate his twenty-first birthday.

They carried the dead to Buttrick's, where some of the Americans had returned after driving the British from the bridge. The
boy's father, Deacon Jonathan Hosmer, found his son there later
that day.

The majority of the Americans, under Major Buttrick, passed
the place where the redcoats had broken ranks and fled. But where
the road turns right on the level ground between the Jones farm
and the manse, they kept on up the little rise over Jones's field to
a good position behind his wall. Here they could watch for the
return of the British.

After something of a wait, they heard the tread of men marching. Up the road from the town came a column of grenadiers —
two or three companies at least. Behind the wall, several hundred
muskets, primed and cocked, were ready for Major Buttrick's
signal.

Just out of effective range, the grenadier column halted. Then its
commander did an incredible thing. He ordered his officers to front
and center. In one group, they went up the road toward the bridge,
right under the waiting guns.

Had the British failed to notice the muskets poking out from
among the rocks? Did they see only the Americans across the river?

Tense with excitement, finger on trigger, each militia and minute
man waited. One volley, and every officer would be dead.

Buttrick hesitated. It was hard to realize that this was war — that
something old had ended and something new begun. Firing at those
British would be an aggressive action.

To the men it seemed like an eternity of waiting, though probably
less than five minutes. Then the chance was lost. The officers rejoined their troops. The grenadiers marched back along the road.

There was quiet now — after the uproar and confusion. Ammi
White, lad of all work who served as the minister's choreboy, decided, tardily, to join the musket men at Buttrick's. His only weapon
was a hatchet. Just as he was about to step gingerly past the fallen
British, one of them stirred, then rose painfully to his knees. The
man's face — livid and ghastly — was like something in a nightmare.
Terrified, the boy smashed his little ax, again and again, into the
soldier's head.

* * *

Each man more or less his own commander, the Americans behind Jones's wall swarmed over the ridge, taking back the positions held early that morning. Others made their way east behind the ridge to intercept the British should they retreat towards Lexington.

Those on the humps of the ridge itself saw the grenadiers, evidently expecting attack, peering up from below, while at the square, severely injured men, bundled up in quilts, were being put into commandeered carriages.

While the Americans were watching the British at the center, the raiders from Barrett's managed to slip safely into town. It was late now; past noon — late for a safe escape for the grenadiers, late for General Gage to do anything, late for the policy makers in England.

Since the alarm that morning, something heard as the vaguest rumor had become an ineradicable, angering fact — the deaths of fellow citizens on Lexington Green. Rather than oppose the British column, Captain John Parker had ordered his company of about eighty minute men and militia to disperse. As they were doing so, a volley of British muskets had cut them down. Eight men died; ten more had been wounded.

Near the east end of Concord, from their posts of observation on either side of the road, the people in arms watched the British column, at last in retreat, with its flankers to the right in the meadows and left on the ridge. At Meriam's Corner, where the sandy height falls away and the road comes in from Bedford, the flankers converged to cross the small bridge over the brook. Down the Bedford road, at that moment, swelling the ranks of the victors from North Bridge, marched the Reading company, and just behind, the minute men from Billerica. Taking cover behind the walls and buildings of Meriam's farm, they poured their musket shot into the British. From the opposite side, East Sudbury's contingent added its fire.

Every young man present with a musket had heard, on winter evenings, how we licked the enemy, that year of '59, at Crown Point and Ticonderoga. Here, in one's own pastures and wood lots, behind familiar walls — the one at the *back* of each field gives the best protection — one could wait, take aim, fire; then glide like a hunting fox through the cover, again to lie in wait.

Down the road up which the grenadiers and light infantry had glittered that morning, the desperate Regulars, bleeding and dusty, fought their way back against an almost invisible enemy as minute men from Framingham, from Woburn, from Lexington itself and many other towns, took up the running fight.

At Lexington, Earl Percy, with reinforcements, saved the raiders from annihilation. Here was a sight in all his soldiering he had never seen before — a British column in utter rout.

A half-hour rest for the dog-tired men, then further retreat towards Boston.

Till this day, Earl Percy had refused to believe the provincials would fight. He was ready, now, to admit otherwise. These Yankees stinging his flanks were no purposeless mob. It stood to reason there were many among them who had served as scouts and rangers. The country, wooded and hilly, exactly suited that way of fighting. There were brave men, too, in their ranks. From the concealment of houses along the road, some came out to fire point-blank at him and his officers — though sure themselves to be killed. In his report to England, he would say that this insurrection might turn out to be no such trivial matter as the Ministry might suppose.

To smoke out men in ambush, houses beside the route of the retreat were burned — an open invitation to looting. Along with combatants, some noncombatants were killed — their bodies bayoneted, their heads smashed and brains spattered on floors and walls. Lieutenant John Barker, though wounded in the skirmish at Concord Bridge, became exasperated at the conduct of the relieving troops. Their actions were shameful — they seemed to think of nothing but plunder. Worse still, some officers encouraged them, instead of paying attention to the tactics of retreat.

Towards sundown, the supporting troops, no longer fresh, had lost all zest for pillage. Fiercer and fiercer had grown the gauntlet as new attackers filled the places of those who had started the chase.

Late that night, the last boatload of weary British soldiers, under the protecting guns of the fleet, was ferried from flaming Charlestown to Boston.

General Gage, the British, the Tories who had taken refuge with them, found themselves in a trap that opened only towards the sea.

Like a great wind along the seaboard traveled the news. Inland to the remoter settlements; over the Atlantic; across France and the Continent.

The scrawled endorsement of many a committee — "We send you momentous intelligence, this instant received" — sped the present tidings from distant place to place. From New York to Philadelphia, where Sam Adams and John Hancock were to make a full report to the second Continental Congress. Savannah, Georgia, farthest south, got the news by the tenth of May.

Sailed by her owner, Richard Derby, who would not let the Provincial Congress pay for his services, the *Quero* — light, fast schooner of sixty-two tons burden, with no lading save her ballast — had already carried the news to England through a British blockade, handily beating the Royal Navy's *Sukey,* which bore Gage's official report.

In England, Thomas Hutchinson, late Royal Governor, confided sadly to his diary: "The opposition here rejoice that the Americans fight, after it had been generally said they would not."

France, too, for reasons of her own, rejoiced. This American revolt — decided the Comte de Vergennes, astute director of Foreign Affairs — might give France a chance to turn the tables on England.

At the King's Arms Tavern of Cornhill, London, members of the Constitutional Society, in a special meeting, voted a subscription of one hundred pounds — "to be applied to the relief of the widows, orphans, and aged parents of our beloved American fellow-subjects, who, faithful to the character of Englishmen, preferring death to slavery, were, for that reason only, inhumanly murdered by the King's troops."

At his palace at Kew, King George was trying desperately to minimize the significance of what he had heard:

> *40 minutes past 4* P.M. [he noted down in his precise fashion]. It is not improbable but some detachment sent by Lieutenant-General Gage may not have been strong enough to disperse the Provincials assembled at Concord.

That same day, at thirty-seven minutes after eight, he was ready to take the news more seriously. Again he dipped his pen:

> The die is cast.

CHAPTER VIII

The American Dream

FOR the next few days after the fight, Concord found its ancient road under the hill a highway for marching men. Thus had it been in every war. Only now the tide was not flowing against the French and Indians. It was rising against the British.

On Friday the Reverend William Emerson led prayers in meeting, with seven hundred soldiers in attendance. Then he went for a look at the camp at Cambridge.

At Cobble Hill and Pisgah along the lines, with Charlestown Neck beyond, and Boston over the water, men tended watch fires, cooked mush, and swapped countless rumors. Nobody with whom Emerson talked had much notion concerning plans. Months before Lexington and Concord, six generals had been named by the Provincial Congress. Two — Artemas Ward and John Thomas — were on duty. The hard-driving, overworked Committee of Safety was serving as directive body. The Provincial Congress was to meet next day in special session at Concord.

When Emerson came home to serve as chaplain, he found most of the officers of the town's companies, along with the men, back also. In numbers almost equal to those marching east, troops were heading homeward to neighboring towns, their places haphazardly filled by contingents from farther off still rallying to the first alarm. Without blankets, with little food, they were not prepared for a longer tour of duty. Worried members of the Provincial Committee admitted finding it hard to hold enough soldiers on the watch at Boston. Each minute man from Essex, Suffolk, and Middlesex, where danger of another raid lay closest, thought first of his own town's defense. Spring planting also tugged them back.

The Barretts and other Concord officers had picked up word that a new contingent, with the sole duty of chasing Gage from Boston, was to be enlisted. Already Nathan Stow, orderly sergeant in the projected forces, was jotting down a company roster: Melvin, Prescott, Finnegan, Wheeler . . . All minute men and militia were being urged to join. Soon men of Concord were joining a second company. Both would serve in Colonel Nixon's regiment. John Nixon, from neighboring Sudbury, suited the men. They wanted no stranger for commander. John Buttrick, leader with Davis at the bridge, would be major. Yet enlistments were slow. Thirty-six shillings a month in paper, with maybe a coat and blanket, made uncertain pickings. Work on the town's roads was a better bargain.

To be nearer the center of action, the Provincial Congress moved to Watertown. Five of its ablest leaders, delegates to the Continental Congress, would be missing. Thomas Cushing had just borrowed his friend Emerson's horse for the journey to Philadelphia.

As pastor at home and a chaplain abroad, the young preacher, without his horse, found himself in difficulties. Why not petition for a replacement? Backed by Colonel Barrett, the request was granted. On a handsome sorrel taken from a British officer during the retreat to Boston, Emerson rode between the camp, Watertown, and Concord. Through him and its other travelers, the town had little trouble keeping abreast of the news.

Colonel Barrett and the many militia officers in the Massachusetts Congress were uneasy about the siege of Boston. Should not a Commander in Chief be appointed by the Continental Congress? This struggle was the concern of all the colonies; waged in defense of their common rights.

Concord fairly buzzed as a center for making supplies of war. Though Daniel Taylor was in the army, his shop near the Milldam was strewn with shavings as his apprentices shaped sixty pairs of oars for the whaleboats patrolling the Charles or scouting Boston Harbor. Reuben Brown's was busier than ever with cartridge boxes. Every shop — and the number had increased materially with the influx of mechanics from Boston — furnished goods and implements. Out on Barrett's mill road, Milly Barrett, granddaughter of the Colonel, clipped and fashioned cartridges with her mother's best scissors. Before hostilities, a young British officer, taken with her looks while she was visiting relatives at Cambridge, had shown her the newest method. Now all her friends were putting the art to use.

*   *   *

As shire town along with Cambridge, Concord had enlarged its prison. Since the fight at the bridge, this jail had been set to an un-anticipated use — crammed with prisoners of war and active Tories. "Pray keep them from any infection that may arise from putting too many in one room," cautioned General Ward, mindful of patri-ots held in Boston. "Air them when necessary, provide everything needful for their comfortable substance." Ephraim Jones perhaps was willing to oblige. But how make over the jail to put redcoats at ease? Prisoners kept coming in. Already there were well over a hundred. Jones protested he could house no more.

To any well-born British officer — and several were involuntary guests at Concord — conditions, though no worse than in any county jail, would seem vile indeed. Men were herded so close in cells double-planked and spiked on every side that there was scarcely room at night to lie in. From the low ceilings, dirty gray cobwebs hung like smoke. Every visible inch of wood was black from the touch of filthy hands. Small portholes, not glazed but barred with iron gratings, admitted a gloomy light and let out the stench from excrement that littered the floors — there were far too many prisoners for all to be let out to relieve themselves in the stockaded courtyard.

Through the town's Committee of Safety, the keeper partly solved his problem by getting paroles for war prisoners willing to work. A prisoner with whom Ephraim took no chances, however, was Josiah Jones, distant relative and neighbor. Most of Concord knew Josiah. He was the son of Elisha Jones, robust, wealthy, conserva-tive old militia colonel, father of fourteen boys and a daughter, Mary. For many years the colonel had lived in his handsome house at Weston. For ten of them, Weston had named him its representa-tive to the General Court. His sons, too, were successful men. His daughter married Asa Dunbar, young minister at Salem. But Asa, like most of the clergy, was an ardent patriot, and presently at odds with his father-in-law. When Gage closed the General Court and the towns elected their own Provincial Congress, Jones was not returned by his constituents. Fearful of the tar barrel, he had fled to Boston. There most of his sons joined him. Gage made the colonel Forage Commissioner.

Jones appointed his son Josiah supercargo on the *Polly*, a sloop from Maine commanded by a man named Smith. The skipper, a patriot, had no wish to see his vessel confiscated. When Jones and a colleague, Hicks, came aboard, with orders to fetch hay to Bos-ton, Smith showed a laudable eagerness to be off. He was breaking

out sail when the commander of the convoy stopped him. No ships
were to leave till next day.

The current was favorable, the skipper explained that evening
to his supercargo; they would do well to drift down into Boston
Roads, to be ready for the morrow. But the captain of the *Polly* did
not drop anchor in the Roads. He sailed right past Brewster's Islands at the harbor mouth, past Cape Ann, and into Arundel —
Kennebunkport — where he handed Hicks and Jones over to the
local committee. The Provincial Congress ordered both men sent to
Concord jail.

Things might have turned out worse for Josiah. At least he was getting eatable food. Everyone knew that his sister Mary, in Weston
from blockaded Salem, was making her brother frequent visits at
the prison.

Late Thursday, June 15, word flew from house to house that
danger again threatened. All militiamen must hold themselves ready
to march, completely equipped, with thirty rounds each. To this
order, the Provincial Committee added a warning: *Next Lord's
Day, go to meeting armed.* Old men like Ephraim Wheeler remembered Indian days.

Had the reinforcements arrived which Gage was expecting? Was
he scheming to break through the lines and ravage the country?
With many of her younger sons enlisted, her most energetic officers in the new army, and her militia now marching, Concord was
stripped of her last defense. Late in the afternoon of Saturday, after
anxious waiting, when a rumor reached the selectmen that at any
moment Concord's own stock of powder might be called for, the
town made ready for a hectic night. Somewhere there must be
plenty of fighting.

There had indeed been a battle. In the days that followed, details
filtered back for a completer picture. That Sunday, British General
Sir William Howe, second in command at Boston, hoping to catch
the Provincials napping, had planned a surprise attack. He meant
to land at Dorchester — across the Flats — then threaten Roxbury
with encirclement. Could he have carried out his scheme, Cambridge
itself might have been captured, the new army smashed.

Lexington and Concord had already shown that Gage could keep
no secrets. General Ward, egged on by Israel Putnam of Connecticut, had beaten Howe to the punch. If Charlestown peninsula could

be occupied by the Americans, the British command would have new worries to spoil its strategy. Late Friday afternoon, two days before Howe had intended to strike, a thousand men under Colonel William Prescott, Pepperell farmer with kinsfolk in Concord, marched silently from Cambridge to take over this no man's land. Afraid to weaken his base, Ward would not send a larger contingent. This one should be strong enough to fortify Bunker Hill. Old Put, enthusiastic backer of the plan, came along to keep his eye on the proceedings.

Cautious General Ward had thought only of a redoubt on the height just beyond the neck. Why stop at that first hill — Bunker? — argued Putnam. From Breed's Hill, further on, even small cannon could punish the British in Boston.

Colonel Richard Gridley, engineer, advised against the bolder scheme. Bunker Hill could be more readily defended. It was higher and commanded its slopes to the water's edge. A redoubt on vulnerable Breed's Hill would be a pistol aimed squarely at Gage. At any cost, he would be forced to attempt its capture. With low land on either side, it could be readily flanked.

But Putnam's eagerness prevailed. Towards midnight, work at the redoubt on Breed's Hill got under way.

In the morning, alarmed at what they saw, the British opened a noisy cannonade from the nearer warships and Copp's Hill battery across the water in Boston. Captain Prescott's persuasive courage was the only thing that kept his people at work. Seeing by broad daylight the peril of the position, officers and men from other contingents kept slipping away — though Putnam on his horse did his best to stop them and bring up support.

As the British artillery stepped up its fire, grenadiers and light infantry, the shock troops used on the nineteenth, were seen crossing to attack. Watching from his earthworks, Prescott could guess their number — fifteen hundred men at least, perhaps two thousand. He was outnumbered five to one.

But incredibly, instead of attacking, the British waited. Thankful for the respite, Prescott finished the redoubt, then added a breastwork facing east along the hill.

Though he had no means of knowing it, his left flank had been strengthened. John Stark and his New Hampshire men, with others, to the number of nearly two thousand, including Brown's company from Concord, had taken cover behind a fence that ran from the water's edge to the slope below the redoubt. As they, too, waited, they made their position stronger by throwing up ramparts of brush against the fence and piling rocks across the beach.

Well past two, when the American positions were ready, the British decided to attack.

Right up Breed's Hill, fronting it like a tremendous strand of scarlet worsted, marched the grenadiers — slowly, and in perfect order, like soldiers at a funeral. Laboriously they climbed each fence, then paused to make sure of their alignment. Prescott could scarcely believe his eyes: every soldier, that hot summer's day, still carried his hundred-pound pack. Did their commanders expect to chase him at once from his redoubt, then march inland for an easy three days' conquest? They gave no sign of loading; evidently they would attack with bayonets alone.

Behind the defenses, each American captain, in the stillness — even the cricket chorus had stopped — repeated low-voiced warnings to his people: "Don't fire till you're sure of them — wait till you see the whites of their eyes — aim low, aim at the crossings of their belts."

To his left, Prescott had seen the British light infantry, in column of companies, march down the beach, then vanish below the bulge of Breed's Hill. They were planning to flank him.

A tremendous roll of musketry — not like British volleys, but continuous and steady — broke the silence below. No shouts of a British charge, no British cheers — just that drumming American fire.

"Pick off the officers!" ran the word at Prescott's redoubt, with the grenadiers almost at point-blank range.

From the crest of the hill, from the water's edge along the brush-packed fence, stabbed a continuing sheet of flame. Men loaded and aimed and fired. It was like knocking passenger pigeons out of a tree. The red lines sagged before the fence and at the hilltop, more men dead or wounded than on their feet. Flesh and blood could not endure such fire. The blasted ranks recoiled. Somehow the dazed survivors got out of range and down the slope.

The American farmers had suffered comparatively small losses. But their powder was dwindling. On the right, Charlestown was in flames from the guns of the fleet. American snipers could no longer use it for cover.

Prescott saw Gage's light infantry, in confusion, their ranks decimated, come into sight again on the beach. They were running toward the boats.

But grenadiers and infantry — it was hard to believe men could take such punishment — reformed their ranks. Again the slow march toward the defenses. Again repulsed, the British lines rallied under the spitting muskets.

In the redoubt, Prescott's men had exhausted their powder. Like an old candle, the American fire flickered and went out.

The British tumbled over the parapet.

The Americans along the fence and with Putnam on Bunker Hill covered Prescott's retreat. The attackers, too buffeted in their triumph, could not press their advantage. The men who had fought them to a standstill fell back over Charlestown Neck to Winter Hill, where, under Putnam's directions, they dug themselves into new defenses.

The Americans had lost the peninsula. They could not know, but could guess, what the British had lost. In Boston, young Sir Harry Clinton, summing up the carnage, was writing: "a dear-bought victory, another such would have ruined us." Half the British forces involved were casualties; many of these were dead. Major Pitcairn, second in command at Concord, had fallen before the redoubt. Companies that had marched in April to Concord suffered more grievous losses than on that occasion. All but four of the grenadiers of the King's Own Regiment were dead or wounded. Men of the light infantry had been served up in droves against the brush-plugged fence.

But Sam Adams, smarting at the loss of Charlestown, refused to be elated. "To be plain it appears to me there never was more confusion and less command. No one appeared to have any but Colonel Prescott whose bravery can never be enough acknowledged and applauded." Discipline and organization at the camp and on the artillery-swept road over Charlestown Neck had indeed been slack, and men there had refused to meet danger.

Those in the actual battle had come off remarkably well, with losses not large in proportion to the two thousand, five hundred or so who had taken part in the fighting. Greatest misfortune was the death of Dr. Joseph Warren, who had fought and died as a volunteer in the redoubt. When Concord got her own returns, she learned she had lost three men. All had died at the rail fence.

The very day the British guns were hammering Breed's Hill, Mary Jones Dunbar set out from Weston to visit her brother in

Concord prison. Cherries were ripe in her father's orchard. She had brought a basket of them for Josiah. But Mary had hidden files among the fruit. It did not take many nights for Jones and Hicks to cut through the rusted bars of their cell. Once in the quiet, unguarded yard, the stockade was no problem. By prearrangement, the fugitives headed for Colonel Jones's cider mill, deserted and out of mind in the summer season. There Mary had food and clothing, and a horse and carriage to take them to "Falmouth" — Portland — whence they could sail to Nova Scotia.

Concord, red-faced at this escape, claimed the joke was mostly on the other town. The horse which Mary Dunbar filched belonged to Sheriff Baldwin of Weston. In Falmouth, Jones and his comrade sold it for a couple of bushels of Maine potatoes.

Chaplain William Emerson had missed the excitement at Bunker Hill, but few sights at the camp escaped his eager attention. He saw George Washington, Commander in Chief, soon after the general arrived in Cambridge. Easy and soldierlike in bearing, his face hard and weather-beaten, with its massive nose, high cheekbones, and firm jaw, he was still young-looking in the prime of forty-four years. Though he was a Virginian, old soldiers from Sudbury, Groton, and Concord remembered having heard Washington's name around wilderness campfires back in '55. Before many months were out Concord, supplying his hay, referred to the general as familiarly in the Town Book as if he came from Pepperell or Brookfield.

It was amazing how vigorously Washington was taking hold. "New Lords, new laws," wrote Chaplain Emerson: "new orders from his Excellency are read to the respective regiments every morning after prayers. The strictest government is taking place, and great distinction is made between officers and soldiers. Every one is made to know his place, and keep it, or to be tied up and receive thirty or forty lashes." Rough treatment and a hard lesson for men accustomed to electing their own officers. But discipline, the Massachusetts Assembly stressed, was essential. Though the courage of citizens fighting beside their neighbors had won at the Concord bridge, lack of effective discipline had lost Charlestown peninsula.

"Surprising how much work has been done," Emerson continued, describing the fortifications; "thousands are at work every day from four till eleven o'clock in the morning." Drill, the parson recorded, took up much of the rest of the day. "The lines are extended almost from Cambridge to the Mystic River; so that very soon it will be mortally impossible for the enemy to get between the works."

Yet the general was having his troubles. He was alarmed to find the army far smaller than he had expected. Far too many men were overstaying their furloughs; many, apparently, intended quitting for good. There was no telling if reinforcements from the Southern colonies would arrive in time. To escape disaster, the lines, more extensive with each day's work, must be fully manned. By the most optimistic count, only about fourteen thousand of the New England troops were fit for active duty.

Washington could not realize that he was near the peak of his strength. There were to be moments when one third that number would have been welcome.

William Emerson, from his quarters at the foot of Mount Pisgah, had no notion of the general's difficulties. "Who would have thought, twelve months past, that all Cambridge and Charlestown would be covered over with American camps, and cut up into forts and entrenchments; and all the lands, fields, and orchards layed common; horses and cattle feeding in the choicest mowing land; whole fields of corn eaten down to the ground; large parks of well-regulated locusts cut down for firewood and other public uses? This, I must say, looks a little melancholy." War was proving a devastating business. But Emerson, eager, fervent, and young, cheered up easily. " 'Tis diverting to walk among the camps. They are so different in their forms as the owners are in their dress; and every tent is a portraiture of the temper and taste of the persons that camp in it. Some are made of boards, some of sail cloth, some partly of one and partly of the other. Others are made of stone or turf, and others again of birch and other brush. Some are thrown up in a hurry and look as if they could not help it — mere necessity — others are curiously wrought with doors and windows done with wreaths and withes in the manner of a basket. Some are your proper tents and marquees, and look like the regular camp of the enemy. These are the Rhode Islanders, who are furnished with tent equipage from among ourselves and everything in the most exact English taste." But even the Rhode Islanders lacked uniforms. Only the company from Wethersfield, Connecticut, had them — bright blue, trimmed with red — but had refused to wear them at Bunker Hill, lest they make themselves targets. Most homogeneous were the ten companies of riflemen from Pennsylvania, Maryland, and Virginia, which arrived with midsummer. Why not clothe all the troops in buckskin hunting jackets? As General Washington observed the growing dread shown by the British for this new type of soldier, he was inclined to press the idea — but the Continental Congress failed to act on it.

The Southern riflemen were as great a novelty to the New Englanders as to the enemy. Back in Concord, when soldiers on furlough told old militiamen what they had seen, none would believe them. Yet surely the parson, who corroborated the stories, would be telling the truth. One rifleman, at fifty paces, when another held up a clapboard with a mark on it the size of a dollar, had plugged it through the center. With their newfangled muskets, into the grooved barrel of which you pounded a close-fitting bullet, these leatherclad hunters could splinter peeled birch poles at two hundred and fifty yards.

But though these riflemen were very effective, the British soon learned to keep under cover. The Southerners were hard as wildcats to control, and their popping at the enemy usually stirred up the devil of a cannonading in reply. Washington was compelled to issue orders that no soldier could shoot without an officer's permission.

What the Commander in Chief longed for was a Continental Army, in which all distinction between colonies would be laid aside — not this heterogeneous mass torn with contentions and jealousies. In the fall, a committee of the Continental Congress decided to reinlist the army on that basis.

Another aid was contributing strength — the thought of independence. Scarcely perceptible in the spring, by autumn it was a rising storm.

Liberty! That word meant not just the struggle to correct grievances; it meant the right to drive one's oxcart freely into Boston with hay or grain for barter; the right to follow that hankering in the blood — strong through years of town government — to make one's own rules and have as few of them as possible. Parson Emerson, at the camp, saw the mood working among the men. Through May and June patriot chaplains, perhaps through force of habit, had still prayed for King George. It was no longer popular to do so. Among the officers and soldiers, that October, word was going the rounds that the Congress was planning a league among the colonies to take the place of the King should he reject their final petition for reconciliation.

Meanwhile, at Cambridge and Roxbury, nothing much happened. Without cannon, Washington could not drive the enemy from Boston. At Fort Ticonderoga, near the foot of Champlain, big guns in plenty lay rusting. But though Ticonderoga had fallen even prior to the battle of Bunker Hill, the two American commanders, Benedict Arnold and Ethan Allen, through their bickering, failed to send the guns. As fall dragged into winter and Washington's army floundered in the mud of a stalemate siege, men wondered what was happening northward, where an invasion of Canada seemed a promising venture.

That autumn and winter, Concord had an experience of its own to distract it. With its buildings at Cambridge needed by the army, Harvard College moved to Concord, already crowded with refugees from Boston. In a way it was fortunate that the perplexities of the times had cut the number of undergraduates to about a hundred. Even so, there was a battle for lodgings. President Langdon, as was his due, found accommodation on the common at Dr. Minot's, where Smith, Pitcairn, and other officers had appropriated chairs on April nineteenth. But Edward Wigglesworth, Professor of Divinity, had to go two miles east of the center on the road to Bedford.

Gay blades among the students took lodgings at the taverns, greatly to the displeasure of the faculty. Private houses were full beyond capacity.

In short order the students captured Concord. They sought the most attractive girls and explored the rural retreats. The sylvan byway up which the colonel had dodged after his visit to his house on the nineteenth became their favorite haunt — so much so that the town took to calling it "College" or "Lovers'" Lane.

Classes met mostly in the church, the courthouse, the deserted grammar school. John Winthrop, Professor of Natural Philosophy, missed his apparatus chamber in Harvard Hall where he had ranged happily over the entire field of experimental science from electricity to sunspots. At his request, a committee fetched more of the instruments from Cambridge. They also brought the college fire engine, lest it be damaged by careless soldiers. Parson Emerson, on one of his many trips, carried up the college clock for the use of the town. On Sundays, in the crowded church, the citizenry grew accustomed to the collegians in their gowns — some black, some bright-colored.

Only when a wet snow blanketed the ground did Concord have serious cause to regret her hospitality. The many-paned windows of the church proved too tempting. Although John Hancock, college treasurer, was now absent most of the time on affairs of state, the faculty promised to pay the damages. They also had other ways of recompense. They extended to Parson Emerson, of the class of '61, and to others, the privilege of the library. That winter, men with the gift of reading were busy with a little book called *Common Sense*. Some said that Dr. Franklin had written it, though he denied the authorship. By its arguments, it was convincing more and more Americans that separation from Great Britain was their only logical course.

Now that the days were growing longer, Concord began to think of her annual meeting to transact town business. Gathered convivially at Ephraim Jones's tavern, the selectmen, following ancient custom, drew up the warrant for the first Monday in March.

But when Monday, the fourth, arrived, hardly a man was left to go to meeting. That day, at an urgent call from General Washington, each member of the militia shouldered his musket and headed towards Cambridge.

At every fork in the road, companies from other towns joined the march. By nightfall, at militia campfires, men told what they knew.

In a surprise move, Washington and his Continentals were fortifying Dorchester Heights, a position General Howe, now British commander in place of Gage, had long neglected. The cannon from Ticonderoga, at last in camp, would threaten all Boston. Howe must attack or give up the town. Another Bunker Hill was in the making.

Next morning, the banging of several cannon in Boston testified to British surprise at sight of the fortified heights. But all day the encamped militia waited in vain to be summoned; waited in vain for the crack of rifles and the popping of musket fire which would mean that the redcoats were accepting battle. Then, after nightfall, the wind from the sea rose to amazing strength. Towards morning, rain fell in a deluge.

Perhaps the waves had so battered his landing boats that Howe dared not trust them; perhaps he was thankful for an excuse. Neither next day nor the next did the British attack.

When the handful of citizens left at Concord decided to put off town meeting, their choice of date was to prove prophetic. They picked Monday, March eighteenth. On the seventeenth, Howe and all his troops, along with the Tories, abandoned Boston, heading by sea for Canada.

Harvard could go back to Cambridge. Washington, President Langdon heard, meant to march to New York, where Howe, when further reinforcements arrived from England, would be sure to strike. Its many Tories made that city a natural base for the British. If the entire province was not to be lost to the cause, the patriot army's presence was imperative.

In Concord, on April 19, to commemorate a date grown famous in the thirteen colonies, Town and Gown held a final gathering. "Britain's tyrannic power," said Emerson in his sermon, "has taught us our strength and how to live without her."

"Very bad news from Canada," wrote William Emerson in his diary on Sunday, June sixteenth. All hope that a fourteenth colony might be added to the confederation had been blasted.

During the winter, the first reports, coming by sick men and deserters from Benedict Arnold's and Richard Montgomery's little armies, had told of terrific hardships, but hardships overcome. Montgomery, on the easier route by Champlain, had taken Fort St. John at the lake's outlet, and by mid-November was in Montreal — with Guy Carleton, British governor, retreating toward Quebec.

On the route through Maine, Benedict Arnold's two hundred bateaux on the Kennebec, by which he hoped to hurry his five hundred men northward, had proved a hindrance instead. Badly made of green wood, they leaked like sieves or went to pieces in the rapids. Daunted by an early winter, Major Roger Enos backtracked with one fourth of the little army, declaring the way impassable. But Arnold kept on. Up the Dead River, already clogged with ice, the gaunt, hairy, shivering men thrust northward, their clothes in rags. Over the height of land to Lake Megantic, then down the Chaudière River with its outlet in the St. Lawrence just above Quebec. In this desolate wilderness Arnold's soldiers, their food gone, tried boiling a little nourishment from shoes and belts. While his main body, more dead than alive, scorched their frozen feet at their campfires, Arnold got through to the French village of Sertigan and sent back food which saved his starving army. They actually reached Quebec before the men from Champlain.

The combined effective force of Americans numbered scarcely a thousand. Carleton had slipped safely into the stronghold.

News of further disaster was to follow. The attack on the citadel, that last day of the year, proved futile. In the savage, confused fighting, Montgomery was killed and Arnold wounded. Worse still, the Canadian French, unimpressed, had not rallied to the cause.

Arnold, partly recovered from his injuries, clung desperately to the siege with his handful of men till heavy reinforcements from England, arriving in early May, let Carleton turn on his besiegers. American support and paltry relief had come too late. Captain Theodore Bliss, with men from Concord, was among those taken prisoner at the Cedars. By mid-June the last Americans were abandoning Fort St. John.

More help, more men to stave off invasion, were needed.

On Monday, July first, William Emerson wrote excitedly in his diary, "Colonel Cuming appointed by the General Court Brigadier General of the reënforcements raising for Canada — 3000 — Invited to go as Chaplain."

Next morning he called to offer his congratulations, but was surprised to find the newmade general very downhearted, his wife utterly against his going. Twelve days later the pastor made note of the old militia veteran's decision. "Colonel Cuming resigns his command!!!!" Well, Cuming had great responsibilities at home. Emerson himself, however, had made up his mind. As soon as his wife was delivered of the child she was expecting, he would go. Her mother, Madam Bliss, would look after her and the two small daughters — Hannah, just six, and Phoebe, not yet three. His first born, Billy, was a big boy now — seven years old. Frank, the colored man, would take care of the house, feed the stock, and see to the haying.

Already sixty-one Concord names were on the muster roll of the company recruited by Captain Miles — Charles Miles, of the fight at the bridge. Captain Asahel Wheeler's company also had men from Concord, with Samuel Hoar of Lincoln a lieutenant.

By Thursday, the twenty-fifth, the contingent was ready. Captain Miles's men paraded before the church; then, with soldiers from Lexington and Westfield, attended meeting. Emerson preached.

Farewells, and the dusty march in the summer's heat — to Ticonderoga.

*   *   *

As Washington had foreseen, Howe's army and a mighty British fleet were at New York. Barbarous foreign mercenaries, Emerson indignantly recorded, had been hired by King George against the people. "The number of troops not certain. In constant expectation of a most major Battle. The Lord God of our fathers defend our land!"

Wednesday evening, August seventh, toward nine o'clock, Mrs. Emerson was delivered of a daughter. Already the church had voted its pastor leave.

Many times, he and his wife had thought of this good-by. Now, his saddlebags packed, his valise behind him, the moment was over. At White's Tavern, Acton, where he spent the night, he scribbled a letter. "Thro' Mercy have got out of the bounds of Concord, and find my Spirits rise upon it. 'Tis harder parting with my Family and Flock than perhaps you are aware of. I don't know but you are affronted with me for leaving you so abruptly, but really 'tis too much to take a formal leave, without it be in this way. And now, *good b'ye*, that is, *God be with you*, my dear, this is my prayer."

At dusk, on Saturday the twenty-fourth, Emerson reached the camp. There, under the faded sunset, lay the fort on its peninsula jutting out from the western shore near the head of the riverlike lake. Never before, till he rode that day beside it, had he seen so large an inland body of water. He was tired from his journey, more tired than he supposed possible, for he was young yet — thirty-three that spring. But in the warmth of greeting from Captain Miles and the Concord men he forgot his weariness. They were delighted to learn of the new daughter. They plied him for news from home. The Colonel, Jonathan Reed of Littleton, welcomed him into the regiment.

Next day he had a look at the camp. General Brickett's brigade — the one Cuming would have commanded if he had chosen to — was tented together, some two or three thousand men from New England. Farther along were troops from the South: Virginia, Pennsylvania, New Jersey. Surely, thought the new chaplain, these soldiers were as well disciplined as the best of the British troops. Men like these might even retake Canada. His spirits were high at his first impression. General Horatio Gates, commander of all these forces, had invited him to sup at headquarters and received him in the friendliest fashion. He felt almost ashamed to appear among these military gentlemen in his rusty long black coat. He must beg Phoebe, if possible, to send along the blue one, shortening its skirts. He only hoped he would satisfy the expectations of these kind and patriotic friends and prove as useful as he desired to be.

Rain set in. For almost a month, Emerson saw little of the sun. The damp, cold, final week of August gave place to a colder, more dismal September. He was appalled at the spread of sickness in the camp. There had been dysentery and typhus on his arrival, but nothing like the epidemic raging now. Every day he prayed by soldiers mortally sick. Nothing done by the doctors seemed to help them. They burned with fever, shook with chills, then died by the score. The cold, soggy camp with its rivers of mud stank with sickness and death. He himself had a touch of this malady. But by nature he was hopeful, and believed it would pass.

His fever persisted. Somehow the rain and sickness transformed everything — even the soldiers in whom he so ardently wished to believe. Instead of planting a zeal for righteousness and firing them with belief in the cause, as his sermons had at home, his words were ignored by these men. In their enforced idleness, as they waited for attack from Fort St. John, veterans of the Canadian retreat — rotten with illness, underfed, ill-clothed — plied themselves with rum and taught the raw troops of the relief the tricks of their own degeneracy. The camp's profaneness and license drove the Concord chaplain to despair. News that Washington had just been driven from New York added to the demoralization of the camp.

By the third week of September, Emerson was too sick for further use. "Sir," he wrote to Benjamin Brown, his regiment's lieutenant colonel, "my ill state of health is such that I am not able to perform the duty of a chaplain, and am advised by the physicians to ask for a dismission from the army."

He got as far as Gookin's Falls on Otter Creek, near Rutland. Here he collapsed, and was taken care of by a fellow minister. As days lengthened into weeks and October winds buffeted the house, Emerson knew his strength was ebbing. Would he ever see Concord and his wife and children? Had Frank found time to cut the winter's wood? Did Billy, every morning, read a chapter from the Bible, as he had taught him? They had waved good-by, his little family, the day he left. He had turned for a final look at the end of the alley of young ash trees he had planted.

By the twentieth of October, William Emerson was dead.

*   *   *

Had he tarried a little longer before setting out for the wars, Concord's pastor might have added one more memory as the symbol of what he died for. But that experience fell to young Richard Eliot, substitute preacher.

Portents of it had been in the air. In May the General Court of Massachusetts had put the question: *If the honorable Continental Congress, assembled in Philadelphia, should, for the safety of the towns, declare them independent of Great Britain, would they, the said inhabitants, solemnly engage, with their lives and fortunes, to support them in the measure?* Along with the vast majority of the towns — the true sovereigns of the Commonwealth — Concord vowed that she would.

When Massachusetts received the Declaration, over the bold signature of her own John Hancock, President of the Congress — young Thomas Jefferson of Virginia was said to have done most of the drafting, with John Adams a powerful backer — the General Court ordered copies printed and sent to the ministers of each parish to be read to the people.

Thus Concord heard the message.

At the end of his public reading, Richard Eliot handed the copy to town clerk Ephraim Wood. In his practised script, Wood copied the resolution into the Town Book, as a perpetual memorial.

From Philadelphia, John Adams, writing to his wife Abigail at Braintree, Massachusetts, had ventured a prophecy. The day of independence would become memorable in the new nation. "I am apt to believe that it will be celebrated by succeeding generations as the great anniversary Festival. It ought to be commemorated, as the day of deliverance, by solemn acts of devotion to God Almighty. It ought to be solemnized with pomp and parade, with shows, games, sports, guns, bells, bonfires, and illuminations, from one end of this continent to the other, from this time forward, forevermore."

Perhaps it would be. Concord, where the present struggle for liberty had won its first success by battle, would not be likely to neglect its own and the new-born nation's anniversaries: April nineteenth and July the fourth. Thinking men foresaw that support of this Declaration must exact a heavy cost. But surely, though the new nation, struggling to meet the everyday problems of living, was now plunged into the midst of the unbelievable dislocations of war, the end would be worth the sacrifice.

In the immediate present, weary years of fighting. For the far future — great heroism, great sacrifice still to be rendered, before the ultimate triumph of a free and happy folk. Many times would the American dream be challenged — unwittingly or consciously by men with and without principle, by forces beyond control, by the hugeness of life. Wisdom would be desperately needed, tolerance and patience, and the will to believe in the fundamental decency of people.

CHAPTER IX

The Idea of a Constitution

AFTER more than a year's search, Concord's First Parish was positive that it had found the man to replace William Emerson, so positive that it elected him unanimously. His name was Ezra Ripley, and he came from Woodstock, Connecticut. Concord had met him briefly before — when he was a student during Harvard's winter in town. Son of a hard-pressed farmer with nineteen children, Ripley, by agricultural labor and schoolteaching, had paid every penny of his way.

When the town met to see if it would agree to the Church's invitation, only one vote was cast against the proposal, by a man so alarmed at Ripley's frail physique that he was certain the arduous business of choosing a minister would have to be soon repeated.

So Ezra Ripley was elected and the town, watching the new continental bills swoop aloft in gathering volume, voted to peg his salary to goods — so many bushels' worth of corn per year.

Ripley quickly made himself a vital part of Concord. Two years after his ordination he married his predecessor's widow — ten years his senior — and took over the children and Emerson's manse.

Since earliest beginnings, the inhabitants of Massachusetts had grown accustomed to the idea of a constitution. Citizens throughout the erstwhile province felt ill at ease under the present makeshift government of the state. With a certain desperation, a week before Bunker Hill, the Provincial Congress had appealed to Philadelphia: "The embarrassments, delays, disappointments, and obstructions, in executing every undertaking necessary for the preservation of our lives, and . . . property, are so great . . . they cannot be enumerated; and that is chiefly to be attributed to our want of a settled civil polity." Final outcome was a suggestion from the Continental Congress that each of the now sovereign states within the Federation draw up such a constitution for its self-government as should be most conducive to the happiness and safety of the constituents.

In the early autumn of 1776, the question reached the towns. In Concord, Ephraim Wood opened the long debate by reading the article setting forth the business of the meeting: "To see if the Town will by their vote give their consent that the present House of Representatives . . . enact a constitution or form of government for this State." Hours later, the people were ready to give their answer. "Voted, unanimously, that the present House of Representatives is not a proper body to form a Constitution."

To draw up an explanation of why she so emphatically opposed this method, Concord elected as committee those men whose arguments had convinced the town. Ephraim Wood, forty-three years old, former member of the Provincial Congress, a shoemaker by profession, would act as chairman. Besides holding office as town clerk, the burly, two-hundred-and-fifty-pound cobbler was head of the associated Committees of Correspondence for Middlesex County. Colonel James Barrett, still the town's representative in the legislature, was the senior of the group, sixty-six years of age. His son James was a farmer like his father. Another farmer, John Buttrick, of the fight at the bridge, was likewise chosen. Fifth and youngest was Nathan Bond, twenty-four years old, Harvard graduate, and the only college man in the lot.

While the meeting waited, the committee set the arguments on paper:

A vital function of a constitution is to serve as a bulwark against encroachment by government on the people's rights and privileges. For the acting legislative body to lay down rules covering the conduct of the state violates the principle of the Declaration of July the Fourth that power derives from the consent of the governed. The inhabitants at large, not the assembly, should attend to this business.

Having put the stamp of approval on this summary, the people of Concord were ready to propose their plan: "Resolved, that it appears to this Town highly expedient that delegates be chosen by the inhabitants of the respective towns in this state, said inhabitants to be twenty-one years of age and upward, to form a special Convention or Congress for establishing a Constitution."

But the legislature, having gained the consent of the majority of the towns, went ahead anyway. Meanwhile Concord's theory of the juster method spread with an immense persuasiveness. When the Assembly, in its spare time, by 1778 finished its version of a form of government, Concord of course voted it down. But so did five sixths of the Commonwealth. Even beyond the borders of Massachusetts, Concord had set a pattern for constitution making. The legislature, duly chastened, let the people — all men of twenty-one and upward — name delegates to a special convention.

At a meeting on the twenty-seventh of May, 1780, with one hundred and forty-seven voters present — practically all the male inhabitants not away with the armies — Concord pondered the document evolved by the procedure she had fought for.

Townsmen leaned forward — the farmer, the cobbler, the blacksmith, the preacher — old men cupped their ears, the better to hear the convention's greetings:

"Friends and Countrymen . . . In a business so universally interesting, we have endeavored to act as became the Representatives of a wise, understanding, and free People; and, as we have reason to believe you would yourselves have done, we have opened our sentiments to each other with candor, and made such mutual concessions as we could consistently, and without marring the only Plan which in our most mature Judgment we can at present offer to you."

Men nodded their heads and listened further.

"In framing a Constitution to be adapted as far as possible to the circumstances of posterity yet unborn, you will conceive it to be exceedingly difficult, if not impracticable, to succeed in every part of it to the full satisfaction of all."

Yes, Concord needed only to think of her own debates in town meeting.

"We may not expect to agree in a perfect system of government: This is not the lot of mankind. The great end of government is to promote the supreme good of human society."

Men searched their hearts at the words that followed.

"Would it not be prudent for individuals to cast out of the scale smaller considerations, and fall in with an evident majority, unless in matters in which their consciences shall constrain them to determine otherwise? Such a sacrifice, made for the sake of union, would afford a strong evidence of public affection; and union strengthened by the social feeling would promise a greater stability to any Constitution, and, in its operation, a greater degree of happiness to . . . society."

Voters weighed the next statements presented.

"A Government without power to exert itself is at best but a useless piece of machinery. It is probable, that for want of energy, it would speedily . . . sink into anarchy. . . . And a Power without *any* restraint is Tyranny. The powers of government must then be balanced: . . . Those who are to be invested with the Administration should have such powers given to them as are requisite to render them useful in their respective places; and such *checks* should be added to every branch of power as may be sufficient to prevent its becoming formidable and injurious to the Commonwealth."

Item by item, word by word, the men of Concord anatomized the charter before them. Under such scrutiny, none could fail to grasp its principles and purposes.

There were points of objection, of course. The property qualifications for voting bothered many. But the meeting had made up its mind to act in the spirit urged in the convention's greetings. With an amendment suggested here, a phrase marked there for possible alteration, each article was finally accepted.

In the majority of the towns, the same thing was happening. That June the reconvened convention declared the constitution adopted. John Hancock was elected Governor.

Because of a wish to be right, Concord had seen much water flow under her North Bridge before a state government was finally set in motion to which men might look hopefully as an omen of better days. The years of waiting, the war years, had been bitter. After one tumultuous day, active fighting had retreated from Concord, but war's blight was everywhere. Many a family, having parted with blankets for their men in the army, faced winter with not enough bedding. Food grew scarce from lack of farmers to grow it. In addition to volunteers, draft after draft from the militia were being called. Smallpox harried the weakened people. To forget their wants and the cold, men — and women also — drank rum if they had the credit. Soldiers back from the wars were especially thirsty. Blockade cut off goods from abroad; high costs of materials and labor shriveled supplies at home. No sugar. No foreign cloth. Domestic sheep, scarce and inferior, grew ragged for want of men to shear them. When meat was needed, Concord slaughtered its sheep, and looms for homespun wool stood idle. The price of things men live on soared like a kite. Two years after Ezra Ripley's settlement, when Abishai Bond, town treasurer, figured the parson's pay on the agreed on basis of fixed quantities of rye, Indian corn, and beef, his eyes almost burst from his head. A village assessment of one thousand, nine hundred and seventy-nine pounds, thirteen shillings, would be needed. By the time the second half was due, seven hundred and thirty pounds more had to be added. And at that, the parson barely managed to scrimp along. When the town bought a pair of shoes for a pauper, the cost was thirty pounds.

Concord had already tried fixing its prices, with Nathan Stow, now a lieutenant home between enlistments, as secretary of the committee for enforcement. But this inflation was like a malignant pestilence refusing to yield to measures which sought to keep it outside the bounds of the town. In desperation the inhabitants voted that something must be done to put a universal roof on prices. One hundred and seventy-four delegates, representing one hundred and twenty-one Massachusetts towns, met at Concord to devise a cure. The town unanimously resolved to adopt a table of values fixed by the convention, then appointed a committee of thirteen to keep a watchful eye over the people, particularly over the tanners, bakers, saddlers and other manufacturers — "to proceed against any who shall dare to transgress the regulated prices . . . and to treat them as enemies to their country."

As well harness the wind. Most artisans, despairing of a living — though a few grew rich — stopped making things and sold their shops. Not since the migration of 1644 had property in Concord changed hands so rapidly. Honest men went deeply into debt. If you wished to borrow money, that was easy — at ten or twenty cents interest on the dollar for a week's loan. And the lenders were quick to take advantage of the confusion in people's minds brought on by the shift from British pounds to American dollars.

Boston and many other places, Concord charged, were breaking the price compact. The towns accused returned the compliment. All that was gained by the measure was surly ill-humor. Disgusted with the experiment, Concord, like the state, sacked the agreement.

Was paper currency the primary cause of this evil? With every state and the Continental Congress issuing it, the people lacked no opportunity to make its acquaintance. At first, indeed, to the soldiers clamoring for their pay at Ticonderoga, to Reuben Brown making cartridge boxes for Washington's army, these crisp promises to pay looked just like money. Shortly after Bunker Hill the first continentals had filtered into circulation. Soon they and the several issues of the state — paper from twopence up — were plentiful in Concord. "Issued in defence of American Liberty" ran the legend above the stocky figure of a patriot, in his right hand an upraised sword, in his left a scroll marked *Magna Carta*. Hunts and Healds, looking curiously at this earliest issue, heard that Paul Revere had made it. Somehow the next series, done by another man, looked ominously shoddy. "Poverty money," people called it, soon joined by "codfish money" — its chief adornment a miraculously levitated codfish in an oval frame.

Hard money, money you can crack your teeth on, is the only sort you can trust.

Though the remedy hurt, the Massachusetts Assembly put brakes on its presses. In the war's fifth year, the Continental Congress made a gesture too — but only a hesitant half-step. Admitting its bills of credit were practically worthless, it issued fresh paper at the rate of one new tenure for forty old — but the ratio would not stick.

When rats spoiled a bin of Timothy Wheeler's flour at the mill, when casks of cider soured or apples rotted in the barrel, "Not worth a continental!" was all that needed to be said.

The overwhelming demands of the day — and the will to continue living. Through the darkness, the light of liberty, the hope, the promise. Sometimes it burned no brighter than a guttered candle; sometimes, surely, as men forgot everything but their troubles, it seemed out. Yet at gatherings of the town's Committees of Safety and Correspondence, at meetings in other towns, in the state assembly, at the Continental Congress, some voice, in the midst of defeatism, near-sightedness, and greed, some individual's voice — a Hosmer's, perhaps, a Barrett's or a Buttrick's — would recall the greater aim.

Nearly six years before, breath-taking news of Lexington and Concord had sped to the South. Now great tidings swept northeastward. Assaulted by Washington's soldiers and by the French under Rochambeau, Lafayette, and Saint-Simon, with French fleets under de Grasse and de Barras to cover the action, Cornwallis had surrendered at Yorktown. October 17, 1781, became a day to remember.

For Concord, for every village in the Confederation, surely the years of suffering had ended. In her instructions to her representative, Concord reflected this mighty hope.

Something was amiss, however, with these times slated to bring the millennium. Concord's bell, that had rung out the call to arms, had come to grief in ringing in the peace. The year after the signing of the treaty, unconscious irony marked the town's warrant: "To see what method the Town will take with the bell, that is rendered useless by reason of a crack."

The start had been propitious enough. As free and independent states, England's former colonies were now fellow members — by agreement and formal ratification — in a league of friendship; a federation for the benefit of all based on the good intentions of the sovereign members.

In Concord, the last soldiers were back. Men struggled with long neglected fields and patched their tumbled buildings. Colonel Buttrick was farmer Buttrick, cultivating his paternal acres where minute men and militia had rallied on an epochal day. Up the road toward Barrett's, Captain Brown's oxen, urged on by his mighty voice, turned furrow after furrow. At the center — in the joiners' shops, cask makers', tanners', and all the rest — there were mechanics enough and to spare. The general stores were ready for customers. Former sergeant John White, following new fashions, had painted his in gay colors, hiding the gray wood. At one end he set a jaunty weather cock, at the other a trim house for martins. He had shot off his musket many times in the running fight that chased the British from Concord, many times in the lively work that ended with Burgoyne's surrender. Now that the war was over and liberty won, he hoped his bullets had killed no one. He was a man of peace, he told his friends. So were they all.

Yet the incredulous inhabitants found themselves beset by troubles harder to cope with than fighting and more difficult to understand. Like an infection, they had stricken the country. Town taxes for current use could be held in check, but not those for state and county. And even in town, the selectmen as assessors had to make out lists to pay off old revolutionary debts of huge proportion. Taxes, but no real money with which to meet them. Soldiers of the Continental Army, returning to mortgaged farms, were forced to sell at ruinous discount the paper promises they had received in lieu of pay. No use to cart grain to Boston in hopes of a little cash. England's stoppage of the West India trade had glutted the Boston market. When inhabitants brought only produce — no money — to Concord's stores, produce which the town's merchants could no longer dispose of, even barter broke down. Town business was like a pump that needed priming.

With what little currency he had, John White had traveled all the way to Newport, Rhode Island, which unlike Massachusetts still had free trade. But the gouging rates charged by his teamsters blasted his profits. All he gained from his journey was political gossip. Each state, he saw, was attempting to solve its problems in its own peculiar way, turning confederation and a union of friendship into a very bad joke.

Concord's jail was filling up with a new sort of prisoner of war — patriot soldiers confined for debt. While bitterness and resentment spread, neighbor was hauled to court by neighbor. Townsmen, meeting on the street debtors fortunate enough to have raised funds for release, peered derisively at them through fingers crossed like a grate. Through the doors of the Court House tramped an angry, bewildered throng, short in their taxes or behind in promises to pay — the citizens of Concord, honest, hard-working farmers and craftsmen. Presently there were three times as many debtors in Concord jail as prisoners for every other cause.

It was bad enough when an old friend caught you. But when the creditor was an enemy of the country, it became intolerable. Everyone knew why Ezekial Brown, veteran of the Continental Army, had spent two years in prison. His creditor, Frederick Geyer, on the list of Tory absentees which also bore Daniel Bliss's name, had hired the lawyer who put him there. The Commonwealth's Bill of Rights, with its promise that the individual should be protected in the enjoyment of his life, liberty, and property, gave no comfort to the debtor. Farmers who had once owned land enough to give them the vote now found themselves disenfranchised and helpless to protest by ballot.

Was it for this we fought a war — to have our farms posted and sold? Everything gone — oxen, cows, pigs, sheep; my wife's spinning wheel and loom; the very food in the house!

Many gave up the struggle. New sections were opening up, men reported; land for the asking in Maine, Vermont, western New York, Kentucky, Tennessee, and a vast territory in the Northwest, where new states could be made. Pioneers moved out, as lawyers who lacked scruple, lured by the busy courts, fell like vultures on the town.

But at Davis's tavern, on the Carlisle road, at Captain Oliver Brown's near the center, and at town meeting, the talk grew loud and angry. *What are the representatives doing in the city? Squandering money and taking their ease?* "The very lengthy sessions of the General Court and the small proportion of business done there leads us to think that if the court was removed from the Town of Boston into the country, business would be dispatched with greater expedition, as the members would have little else to attend to other than that for which their constituents would have chosen them."

In Hampshire County, the rugged western region of the State, on Tuesday, August 29, in this difficult year of 1786, men's lands had been saved through halting the courts. Captain Brown's tavern buzzed with rumors of what had happened. As the judges at Northampton were about to sit, a crowd of people — fifteen hundred, said some; all agreed there were at least five hundred armed with clubs, guns, and swords, and that a captain of militia led them — had swarmed into the courthouse. Taking the hint, Court adjourned.

Who were these people, branded by Governor Bowdoin as a despicable, degenerate mob? Were they not farmers, mechanics, old soldiers like ourselves? One of the leaders, Job Shattuck, had hurried to the defense of Concord as a minute man from Groton. His bravery at Bunker Hill had won him a captaincy. Even though they would not go along with him in his present slogan — "It is time to abolish all debts and begin anew" — John Buttrick and other Concord soldiers knew him, though impetuous, to be brave and honest according to his lights. Dan Shays of Pelham, Luke Day of West Springfield, Adam Wheeler of Hubbardston, like Shattuck, had all been Liberty men and captains in the Revolution.

September Court Week at Concord was approaching. Court Week at near-by Worcester preceded it by seven days. On Tuesday, the fifth of September, as Chief Justice Artemas Ward sought to enter the Worcester county courthouse, he found his way blocked by two hundred armed men — some from the town itself, some from the surrounding country. Militia called in anticipation of trouble had refused to muster. But Ward, like many of those who stopped him, was a soldier of the Revolution. Captain Adam Wheeler of the insurgents remembered him well — General Ward, in command at Cambridge right after Lexington and Concord. Resolutely the old judge pressed forward. Unwilling to have him hurt, Wheeler let him address the crowd from the courthouse steps in a plea for the sanctity of the law and the necessity for order. Silently they heard him and in silence let him finish. But the way stayed barred.

On Friday, in special town meeting, the inhabitants of Concord faced their dilemma. The grievances of the people were far from groundless. Speaker after speaker bore witness to that. As he listened before facing his constituents and neighbors, Joseph Hosmer, now a member of the Assembly, may have thought of his tilt with Lawyer Bliss on the eve of the Revolution. Yet surely this trouble now threatening them with all the horrors of civil war differed measurably from '74. Through Concord's own insistence the delegates of the people had devised this government. The people themselves had ratified it. Surely the insurgents could be persuaded to arbitrate. Surely these present wrongs could be righted through legal, constitutional means.

Graphically it became plain to the listening citizens that this threatened Court was *their* Court. Lest the Shire Town of Concord betray a trust, they, the people, must defend the right of that Court to sit. Within half an hour, they had drafted a letter setting forth the sentiments of the meeting. Let all towns which could share these views send delegates to meet at Captain Oliver Brown's tavern early Tuesday before Court shall begin, these representatives to serve as mediators should the insurgents appear.

Leaden skies hung over Concord on Monday afternoon as the delegates sought beds at Captain Brown's, soon filled to overflowing, at Emerson Cogswell's, and at other hostelries. Following their usual practice, Justice Samuel Phillips Savage and his two associates had lodgings at Ephraim Jones's, where Major Pitcairn, eleven years before, had failed to capture treasurer Henry Gardner's trunk. Then the tense, expectant town heard the sound of men marching. The "regulators," as they called themselves, were coming — at least their vanguard: Job Shattuck with seventy men. As they moved in irregular column toward the square and courthouse, their very lack of order made them all the more ominous. Only about two thirds carried muskets, the rest were armed with clubs, swords rusted since the Revolution, knives, and hatchets. That hulking, one-eyed man bawling "Halt!" to the company, Concord recognized as Nathan Smith, from Shirley, a tough man with his fists when not too drunk. Like Shattuck, he was a Revolutionary soldier. But after the war, outlawed as a passer of counterfeit money, he had been forced into hiding, only to reappear now that trouble was brewing. With such volunteers, Job Shattuck, in spite of his declared intentions, would face a struggle keeping his men in hand.

Just as the musket butts thudded to the hard-packed common, the rain began — scattered drops at first, then a deluge. Hitching powderhorns and cartridge boxes under tattered coats, the regulators broke for cover — most for the courthouse itself, some for near-by barns and stables.

Peering through storm-streaked windowpanes, the inhabitants watched smaller contingents splash through the mud towards the square. At least three hundred in all must now be in town. The latest to come could find no room in the courthouse. They were ripping down fences to build crude shelters on the common, and making fires to dry their clothes.

By morning, for a while at least, the rain let up. As the last delegates from other towns arrived, they found the arbitration convention already started. To accommodate the crowd, the members shifted to the meetinghouse, where several of them had sat as representatives in the Provincial Congress at the outbreak of the Revolution. Less than two hundred yards away, they could see Job Shattuck's regulators mustering on the square. Two or three casks of rum had been broached near by. Wet and bedraggled from last night's storm, men were falling out of line for a nip to take the chill off the morning. Pickets blocked every approach to the courthouse. Several inhabitants, on private business in the square, hastily retreated at the bayonets' point.

At the meetinghouse, a committee, chairmanned by Dr. Josiah Bartlett, known all over Middlesex during the war as a first-rate army surgeon, and with William Prescott, defender of the redoubt at Breed's Hill, as a member, was set up to treat with Job Shattuck.

Shattuck listened to their arguments. Debate and reason, however, confused him. In an emergency, force was the thing he could understand. His lieutenants urged him not to fall back on mere petition, but to stick to the original plan. All right, he would stick to it. He would not even send representatives to the convention. He and his followers, he said, not the convention, represented the will of the people.

Dismayed and humiliated, the committee retired.

After one o'clock, as the judges waited, Dr. Bartlett and his group tried again. They had just won the slight concession that the judges could open Court, then at once adjourn till the end of November. But as luck would have it, at that moment a troop of ninety horse-

men came riding up the street. Each wore in his hat a sprig of hemlock, badge of the organized regulators from Hampshire and
Worcester. These were the men who had stopped the courts in
their own counties. Under Adam Wheeler, and Benjamin Converse
of Hardwick, they were in a tarring and feathering mood. Threaten-
ingly they halted before Jones's tavern, in their rear a noisy throng
of Shattuck's followers. Though Judge Savage and his associates
had shown themselves brave men, there was nothing they could do
but announce they would not open Court.

No sooner had Wheeler's men returned to the square than they
were back again. They wanted that message in writing.

Let them find the clerk of the court, said the judges.

While the insurgents were hunting for that officer, Ephraim Jones
brought the judges' horses to the rear of the tavern. Before the
mob's return, they mounted and were away.

Their main purpose accomplished, Wheeler's horsemen departed.
Not so the miscellany of men and boys in the wake of Nathan
Smith. The rain had again started, with resultant heavier recourse to
the rum barrel. Roaring through the streets, a drummer boy beating
tattoo, Smith went from house to house, from tavern to tavern, trying to drum up recruits. Any man who did not join to restrain the
government from tyrannical oppression, he bellowed, would be
driven out of town, let him be Court, town committee, or what else.
But even the village sots in the taprooms stayed where they were.
By five in the evening the rain had made useless the priming in most
of the muskets, the rum had sprawled many of their possessors in
the mud. By morning, hungry, tired, and cold, the last of the invaders had vanished like an evil dream.

In their instructions to their representative, the inhabitants of
Concord laid down the principles they were sure of:

> While the legislature make the Constitution their rule, they
> will ever have the cheerful support of this Town and of the
> friends of order throughout the State. As we have chosen our
> legislature, so must we put our confidence in them as well as
> watch over them, if we expect them to extract us out of our
> embarrassments. The hands of government should be strength-
> ened, not weakened. We are far from making light of the
> complaints of the people. The profits of the land are gained
> hardly and reaped slowly. A country must fail when land is
> so burdened by debt and taxes as not to be desirable property,
> and an industrious farmer is disheartened by finding that he

can lay up nothing from year to year for his family. Yet the present perplexed and embarrassed state of public affairs, the uneasiness, the difference of opinion among fellow citizens, and the consequent difficulty of adopting suitable measures to restore peace and order, is a powerful inducement to the Town to avoid an unnecessary enumeration of the grievances under which we apprehend ourselves to labor. For the well being of any people, credit must be secure, promises certain, and all proceedings governed by the principle of justice and righteousness.

Unable to win competent leaders, the rebellion in Middlesex County disintegrated. It fell apart even before Court Week in Cambridge, at the end of October. According to rumor, insurgents from Berkshire and Hampshire were on the march to join volunteers from Worcester and Middlesex. But the inhabitants of the threatened region had made up their minds to repudiate such methods. More than two thousand militiamen were now ready for duty and waiting at Cambridge. Not a regulator showed up. William Heywood, reporting with the Concord militia, was unfortunate enough to discharge his fouled musket by way of cleaning it. The barrel burst and a fragment lodged in his skull. His was the only Middlesex casualty of the rebellion.

Shattuck himself had been caught near Nashua. Half a dozen horsemen had tracked him through new-fallen snow. Instead of surrendering, he laid about him with his broadsword. Even when his leg was almost cut through at the knee by the blade of an opponent, he kept on fighting. His sword hand slashed, he was finally overpowered. Bloody, fouled with mud from the swamp through which he had waded in hopes of throwing off his pursuers, he was brought back to Concord and put in the jail.

In their western stronghold, the regulators fared no better. Soon after the first of the year, the state's militia, among them Captain Brown's company from Concord, marched under General Benjamin Lincoln, of Hingham, to the relief of Springfield, where Shays was trying to capture the arsenal. The regulators fell back across the state. But General Lincoln, at seven in the evening of February third, as a furious wind from the north drove snow and hail into the faces of his troops, set out on the thirty-mile journey between Hadley and Shays's refuge at Petersham. All night they slogged over the hills against the storm. By sun-up they surprised the rebel encampment. Shays and his men, some of them not yet dressed, fled in disorder. Lincoln took more than one hundred and fifty prisoners. The will to rebellion was crushed.

On his return to Concord, Captain Brown's first sergeant had a story to tell. He had eaten Shays's breakfast, he boasted, having found it still cooking at headquarters.

Yes, the insurrection had collapsed. But it had taught a memorable lesson to Massachusetts. The people have many voices; many ways of making themselves heard. Those comfortable men of property and commerce with their universe centered at Boston, regarding themselves as alone significant and qualified to lead, had need of listening to the full chorus. Despite restrictions that still kept many from voting, the next election was itself a revolution. Three fourths of the members of the old house failed to be returned, their seats taken by legislators more inclined to remedy abuses. Even in Concord, Militia Captain James Barrett, son of the Revolutionary colonel — Joseph Hosmer had been promoted to the state's senate — gave place to Isaac Hubbard, who cultivated a small farm near the center. A number of the new representatives had even worn Shays's sprig of hemlock.

Before the trouble, Hancock, whose political rheumatism always warned him of a storm, had refused to run again for Governor, pleading illness. Now that the people had shifted the wind, Hancock, opportunely recovered, swept into office on a pledge for reforms.

In Boston, the mills of betterment ground slowly. The burden of taxation shifted from the farms. Men without property still awaited the vote, already granted them in several states. But this, too, would come. All rebels had been forgiven, their captured leaders pardoned after a narrow escape from hanging. Shattuck, condemned at the Concord session of the Supreme Court, got off largely through the exertions of Ephraim Wood.

All along the seaboard, the thirteen bickering, debt-ridden, trouble-torn states, caught in the lashing aftermath of war, fraying the ineffectual ties of their confederation, had been vexed by storms — the one in Massachusetts so terrifying that responsible men everywhere had watched it with alarm. In this general distress, a conviction had been rising with the fervor of a religious impulse: only through stronger union can the states survive, a nation be built. Already this belief had fashioned its symbol and its plan for procedure — the work of the Constitutional Convention that began its deliberations in Philadelphia during the spring which saw the end of Shays's rebellion. Five States already had ratified. Now it was the turn of Massachusetts.

Dissection of constitutions was a familiar practice in Concord. On Monday, December 10, 1787, so many men showed up at the Town House that the assemblage had to adjourn to the church.

> We, the People of the United States, in Order to form a more perfect Union, establish Justice, insure domestic Tranquility, provide for the common defence, promote the general Welfare, and secure the Blessings of Liberty . . .

This preamble struck most listeners as in accordance with the principles of the Declaration of Independence — principles which, even before their commitment to paper, had brought the minute men to Concord Bridge. This Federal Constitution, moreover, had been devised by a method after Concord's own mind — not the work of a body of lawmakers, but of delegates chosen by each State for this special purpose.

The plan of government resembled that already adopted by the Commonwealth of Massachusetts. But what of its implications? May not this President take advantage of his four-year term — dangerously long compared with our annual elections — and make himself King? What will become of the sovereign powers of our state, thus far so jealously defended? *Where is a Bill of Rights?* men demanded from the floor.

No Bill of Rights; but the right of amendment stands secure. With exceptions shown essential by recent hard experience, this government leaves to the states their internal management.

What of the future, with its problems unanticipated by the framers at Philadelphia?

The language of the Constitution is broad, its writers wise — that must provide for the future.

Concord named Joseph Hosmer its delegate to the state convention, with instructions to favor acceptance. At five on Wednesday afternoon, the sixth of February, 1788, by a narrow margin, Massachusetts ratified.

When the news got out in Boston, torchlight processions wound through the crooked streets. It was too late in the evening for the word to spread far. But soon after sunrise next morning, like a chorus of birds, bells farther inland began ringing, Concord's among the rest.

*   *   *

Perhaps the new government had done it, with George Washington as President. Perhaps times were due for a change. Perhaps industry and frugality, so often recommended at Concord as milestones on the road to recovery, were at last bringing escape from more turbulent years. Whatever the cause, Hosmers, Buttricks, and Wheelers, when they met at the Milldam, told one another that times were better. Men began once more to get fair values for what they raised or wrought. No longer was the court calendar overweighted with cases for debt. Currency stiffened; credit was growing less limp.

Concord's brand new courthouse, long a-planning, was at last ready on the opposite side of the square from the Town House. It offered four times the capacity of the old building — plenty of room for the Supreme Court and the Court of Common Pleas, the Court of Sessions and the County Treasurer's Office. The new prison, replacing the Revolutionary jail, was one of the best in the state. Three stories high, with walls on the ground floor almost eight feet thick, it straddled the millstream below the dam, the water carrying away its sewage.

At last there was wealth enough in the town to improve the meetinghouse. Members of the old Provincial Congress, seeing again the place where they had met, could hardly believe this the same structure. At the northwest end, over a new portico, a slender spire rose above the freshly painted yellow building. Inside, thirty brand-new floor pews, with nineteen in the gallery, each auctioned to the highest bidder, went far towards paying the costs of alteration. Squire Duncan Ingraham, Concord's wealthiest citizen, who dearly loved display, already had lined his with costly cloth and cushioned it richly. Here the blasphemous Surinam sea captain and slave trader, now very much a gentleman in his retirement, loved to show off John Hancock as his friend and guest. Plain wood was good enough for almost everyone else. Captain Nathan Barrett, claiming a post obstructed his view, at first refused to make payment, and there were other objectors. But the captain gallantly rose in meeting to announce he would give his money regardless, whereupon the rest of the recalcitrants followed suit. The days of enmity and backbiting were over.

At his dedicatory sermon, Dr. Ripley spoke of the future. The progress of education and the arts, the flourishing state of agriculture and commerce, the wisdom and energy of the Federal Government, the union and harmony of the people, the natural resources and vast extent of our country — do not these all vouch for the growth and greatness of our nation? Ezra Ripley's affirmation shook the rafters.

After recent upheavals, it was good to be tidying up the town. The North Bridge was a flimsy structure. Why not give it up and build a new one farther down, where the grade toward Punkatasset was better?

Since most roads from upper Middlesex and northern New Hampshire ran to Boston through Concord, it was money in the town's pockets to keep them in order. More carters from upcountry would leave their cash at the taverns. With better highways, more upcountry farmers would do their trading in Concord. So Concord painted and ornamented its five handsome bridges, planned new ones, and built up its causeways against floods in the spring. New-fangled stagecoaches, loungers reckoned, might soon be passing through town to Leominster and Keene.

Better times, in very truth, had arrived. True, Concord's population was not greatly expanding. But that was easily accounted for. Tempted by the promise of land, adventurous young men, grown restless at home, left in a steady stream for the frontier. There was hardly a family in town without pioneer kinsmen.

John White, now a deacon, throve on the extensive trade that came from far-off Vermont, as well as New Hampshire, to his store at the northwest end of the green. Though a good man, the deacon was shrewd. Farmers, supplementing their purchases with a gill of rum on the premises, sometimes joshed him on its quality — it was too weak even to run downhill. And that cask of powder they had bought last year — someone had accidently dropped a live coal into it and more than half of it had smoldered away before it could be put out. The deacon smiled, and tended his books.

His rival, honest John Beaton, town treasurer, sold salt and molasses, almanacs and shoe buckles, snuff, spurs, and psalters, serge to make breeches, and rum. When a girl or boy was sent to his store, and John could not make change within half a penny, he would stick a row of pins in the child's sleeve to make all square.

Nearly opposite the meetinghouse, Dr. Joseph Hunt opened an apothecary store with blue pills for every manner of sickness. Lieutenant Jonathan Hildreth's cooper's shop, on land at the common leased from the town, was the most recent addition to Concord's well established barrel industry. The Munroe brothers, just moved from Roxbury, were looking for a store to set up business as makers of timepieces.

Young Peter Wheeler, son of Timothy, the miller of the Revolution, kept a store and tavern, carried on a butchering business, bought and sold cattle through his agents, barreled large quantities of beef and pork, manufactured soap and candles, and found time to manage his farm. On warm days, the smells from his slaughterhouse next to the millpond near the church mingled with the stench from John Vose's near-by tanyard and the rotten heap of scraps — an accumulation of years — before the door of Elisha Tolman's shoemaker's shop across the way. Vose had customers in most of the neighboring towns and hated to lose one of them. In anticipation of the coming of some favored buyer, he would put away a few choice sides of leather. But if another purchaser threatened to make no selection from what was left, John would dig into the special hoard, dolefully shaking his head over the necessity.

With fifty dollars he had been paid as barkeeper at the corner inn, young Francis Jarvis moved across the street and set up a bakeshop in the cellar of the old tavern which had served the British as headquarters. His route was a long one, reaching to Marlborough and Groton. He often drove the baker's bus himself to keep in touch with the customers.

Back of the meetinghouse, where he could draw water from the pond to soak his felts, Emerson Cogswell throve as a maker of hats. His napped beavers — he had learned the trick in Canada — were the first of that sort in the region, and helped set the fashion in Boston. Looking at him now, it was hard to think of him as once an agile minute man and member of Concord's Committee of Safety. He had become a symbol of prosperity — the fattest man in town, so fat that his wife had to buckle his shoes.

Four gristmills and several sawmills, Barrett's across the Assabet the most prosperous, did business in town. The thump of the fulling mill's triphammer, driven by the stream where it entered the millpond, added emphasis to the clatter of the old wheel at the wastewater. Yes, someday, perhaps, thought men like Peter Wheeler, Concord would know few rivals as a place of industry.

Success breeds sociability. Concord had its masonic lodge, the charter signed by Paul Revere, Grand Master in Massachusetts. Dr. Ripley was a loyal member, Dr. Hurd, town physician, was Master.

The town got a singing school and the church had a better choir. A Fire Society, each member equipped with two leather buckets and a bag for salvage, enrolled many citizens. A supper, paid for by fines from members who failed to turn up for a blaze, marked the end of each year.

But the happiest venture of all was the Social Circle. It grew quite naturally from the town's old Committee of Safety, adapted to fairer times. Wives privately agreed it was most helpful in checking the practice of tavern haunting. Ephraim Wood, now judge, was a charter member, and Captain David Brown, both of the original committee.

With his fondness for lavish entertainment, Duncan Ingraham had nearly wrecked the club in its infancy. None could keep up with his extravagance when his Tuesday night came round to dine his fellows, though several tried and nearly went bankrupt. A formal charter put an end to such displays — henceforth, refreshments must be moderate: a simple meal, with cider, grog, flip, or toddy, according to the tastes of the host.

Few concerns at town meeting passed without having first had an airing in the club. Few matters of national import were left out of the conversation: the national Bill of Rights, passed as the first ten amendments to the Constitution; John Adams as President, when Washington, after two terms, held it his duty to step from office; war with both France and England threatened, with protagonists for either or both courses.

Concord contributed its quota to the nation's new navy. When the frigate *Constitution* was built, some of the oak in her came from Concord, from the slopes of Nashawtuc above Willard's old farm.

Thus the century moved to its close as Concord's veterans grew older. After his Tuesday evening with the circle, sturdy David Brown, captain of minute men twenty-five years before, crossing the bridge in the darkness on the lonely way home, would burst into uproarious song. Was it to frighten the ghosts of the dead? You could hear him clear to the center of the village.

CHAPTER X

The Benefits
of a Great Political Revolution

D R. EZRA RIPLEY was to give a commemorative discourse. The
town was flattered by the good repute of its venerable minister
and the high esteem in which he was held. That very spring, on a
visit to Washington, he had preached in the Congregational Meetinghouse before President John Quincy Adams, his cabinet, and
many congressmen. The inhabitants of Concord felt sure they could
count on a good performance. In its issue of Saturday, November 15, 1828, so that no one need miss anything, the *Gazette*, weekly
newspaper of the town, reminded the inhabitants that both the
morning and afternoon services would be given over to this talk in
celebration of the fiftieth anniversary of the minister's installation.

Even if churchgoers were beginning to feel that half a day's
attendance paid their debt, most were ready, with such a subject, to
make an exception. Already the long, irregular row of sheds behind
the meetinghouse was crowded with blanketed horses. From the
Lexington road, from the highway that led north over the red bridge
toward the new mill town of Lowell, Ripley's parishioners were
coming to meeting. No longer was it necessary as in former days
for people south of the center to go out of their way around the
millpond. A wide gravel road now crossed over the dam. Along it,
the many shops almost cut off the view of the shallowing, weed-
clogged basin. Though this causeway had become the main street
of the town, the old name of Milldam persisted.

Especially to the children coming in from the frosty air the
church looked old and bleak and chilly. Its many-paned windows
rattled in the wind of late autumn, and the cracks between the
ancient floorboards gaped a fingerbreadth wide. One small boy
from each family hurried to join the throng that clustered round

the potbellied stove in the center aisle, waiting his turn to shovel a few coals into his mother's tin footwarmer, then sidled down his parents' uncarpeted, hard-seated pew, under the eyes of the four grave and grizzled deacons waiting in a row beneath the projection of the lofty pulpit, with its sounding board like a gigantic snuffer poised to extinguish a candle.

Above, at the back, the members of the Singing Society rustled their hymnals, the long free seats on either side of the gallery filled up with the poorer parishioners. Below, each in its personal enclosure, sat the principal households. Here and there — survivors of a bygone day — one could see the veterans of the fight at the bridge, venerable men with queues and knee breeches, the buckles of their old-fashioned shoes as bright and gleaming as a bride's silver spoon.

Of the parson's immediate family, only his daughter Sarah was in the minister's pew. His two boys, grown men now, had left Concord; his wife had been dead three years. Sometimes his wife's grandchildren — William, Ralph, Edward Bliss, Bulkeley, Charles Chauncy — sons of her only son by her first husband, William Emerson, the patriot minister, shared the family pew during visits to Concord. While still very young they had lost their father, rector of the First Church, Boston. Knowing their straitened circumstances, Ezra Ripley had invited the widow and her young family to stay at the manse. But Ruth Haskins Emerson presently decided to make her own way in Boston. When the children left, good Dr. Ripley sent along a Concord cow which Ralph drove daily for forage to the Common from the house on Beacon Hill where his mother took in boarders. By hard work and frugality, Mrs. Emerson had seen her children through college, though at times there was only one overcoat among them, which they wore by turns. Brilliant boys, Charles Chauncy possibly the cleverest; too brilliant, perhaps, for their own good. That very summer, Edward Bliss, studying for the law, had suffered a stroke of temporary insanity and was forced for the time being to give up his career and seek health in the West Indies. Like Edward, Charles Chauncy planned to become a lawyer. Ralph Waldo, in the family tradition, was making progress toward the ministry, plagued by feeble lungs which forced him to mend his strength in the south or seek to build it up by summers of rest and outdoor labor at his step-grandfather's manse.

The church had filled almost to capacity. At that moment, giving the cue to the assembly, the deacons rose to their feet. Concord's venerable, well-loved minister was coming up the aisle. A slight figure, a little thick at the middle, but with as quick a step as in the years of the Revolution. Like the veterans of the bridge, he clung to the dress of a previous generation. His breeches, buttoned at the knee, disappeared into long black boots of shiny leather. Great dignity, some austerity, marked his look — great kindliness also. Under his Roman nose, his strong straight mouth curled down slightly at the corners. The face, one might say, of a wise, benignant old eagle that had foresworn meat and turned vegetarian. Despite his seventy-eight years he climbed easily up the flight of stairs to the pulpit, adjusting the heavy frame of his spectacles over his ears — those same spectacles for which, in his utter conscientiousness, he had publicly thanked God when he first received them. Carefully he laid down his manuscript before him. On this occasion, before setting out from the manse, no page of it would have escaped his attention. Little Simeon, the boy who lived with Dr. Ripley and sat on Sundays in the balcony, could remember with dreadful acuteness one less fortunate time, on a day of Thanksgiving. Right in the middle of the sermon, Dr. Ripley had paused, looked up, then said in a loud voice, "Simeon, come here. Take your hat and come here." Simeon had been up to a minor mischief and was sure the Doctor had caught him. Trembling under the eyes of the congregation, he somehow climbed to the pulpit. Dr. Ripley had merely forgotten to bring the Governor's Proclamation. While Simeon scurried like a frightened rabbit to the manse, the worthy parson filled in with an immensely long prayer, snapping it to an abrupt conclusion as the lad re-entered the church.

Concord felt very close to God when Ripley prayed. He would pray for rain when rain was needed, then look modest if it came on Monday. He interceded for his people against sickness. On a sultry summer day he would pray that the lightning should not lick up their spirits. He believed, and therefore spoke.

A report like musketry rattled over the church as the people, dropping the hinged seats which they had raised while standing, settled back for Ripley's sermon. *Your present pastor is the seventh minister of this town in regular succession. It has pleased God to continue to me life and strength in this place longer than any of my predecessors.* With a twinkle, Ripley recalled the one vote against his ordination by the sceptic who distrusted his physical slightness.

Even now the town knew how readily their pastor could hold his own in the hayfield. In his prime no man could outlast him.

Full well do I remember the white locks that adorned the long seats which here stretch before me. Now the heads that are white were then on the shoulders of children.

A droll idea for the youngsters present. Could Deacon Jarvis ever have been a lad? The hot gingerbread marked off in squares, the trays of crisp rice cakes in his bakeshop, fresh from the flaming oven with its crackling bundles of faggots, were relished by every child in town. Had he not always been old, and a baker? To the girls and boys of Concord another deacon, William Parkman, was like Father Time himself. You seldom saw him now, except on Sundays. A shriveled, bent man, too feeble even to lift his feet, he would shuffle along, leaning on a staff almost as tall as he. On a quiet day you could tell his coming from the scraping noise of his shoes on the hard-packed Milldam.

Only the older children remembered the shop he used to keep in the little box of a building between his comfortable house and Nathan Brooks's on the triangle of land between the roads to Sudbury and Acton. There he had been assigned the town's first post office, a circumstance greatly abetting his trade. At his door, by way of a sign, hung a fishlike object, black and incredibly weather-beaten. Each morning the deacon would put it on its peg, then take it in at night. He had quite forgot its origin, as had everyone else, till at last a curious villager had it chemically examined and it proved indeed to be salt mackerel, so hard and deformed as quite to have lost its identity.

It sometimes fills my mind with grief, and always with solemn reflections to observe the changes that have taken place in the Town, in the neighborhood, and in families. In some instances, whole families have disappeared; in others, they have diminished. New families have risen up, or emigrated to us.

No Ingraham was now in Concord; no child of Colonel Cuming. Where they had been, were others. From Westford, Massachusetts, had come John Keyes, son of a struggling farmer, first as school-master at the grammar school — with pupils older than himself — then as citizen, lawyer, and a power in county politics. Nathan Brooks, secretary of Concord's newly incorporated Middlesex Mutual Fire Insurance Company, had moved from Lincoln to establish his family. So regular was he in his habits — going winters before daylight to his office, returning after dark, always with a lighted candle in his hand — that neighbors used his passage as their timepiece. A new doctor, Josiah Bartlett, though not new in name, had started practice in town. It was his father, from Cambridge, who had served in Concord as chairman of the committee which had tried to persuade Job Shattuck and his regulators to arbitrate their quarrel with the Courts. William Whiting, from Sterling, a grandson of the Reverend John Whiting who had once been Concord's pastor, had set up a prosperous carriage manufactory on the main street and his wares spoke for him on every road.

Those who were aged half a century ago are gone to the grave; those who then were in middle life are become old; the youth have lost their best estate; and the little children are now the citizens for business and the pillars of society.

Samuel Hoar, faithful churchgoer listening to his pastor's discourse, could attest to all of that. Before his own coming to town from Lincoln, Colonel Buttrick had died; some years after, Joseph Hosmer. Surely it was only a little while ago that he himself had hung out his lawyer's shingle — yet more than twenty years had passed, and he was fifty! At the start, his quarters had been poor enough, in the miserable little single story shack on the northeast side of the square against the ridge. The selectmen, for purposes of assessment, demanding a description of this property, sandwiched between Lawyer Jonathan Fay's and Reuben Brown's sizeable places, had been startled by the burst of lyricism brought forth by their demands:

> Between "Elm Wood" and "Button Row"
> A line of scraggy poplars grow;
> Behind these poplars may be seen
> My worn-out office — painted *green.*

After this single fling, Samuel Hoar had settled to the business of becoming head of a growing household and a pillar of strength to the town. Elizabeth, his daughter, now fourteen, his sons, Ebenezer Rockwood, twelve, Edward Sherman, five, George Frisbie, born that summer, could claim as distinguished blood on their mother's side as on their father's, since Mrs. Hoar was a daughter of Roger Sherman, of Connecticut. As for Samuel, he was a direct descendant of Leonard Hoar, third President of Harvard, and of the same blood as John Hoar, Concord's blunt-spoken protector of the Praying Indians.

Early in life Squire Hoar had declined candidacy for public office, though once Concord formed the habit of naming him moderator at town meeting it refused to let him go. No one else could be so impartial and courteous yet prompt and expeditious in the business.

Samuel Hoar had prospered famously, so much so that he now owned one of the finest houses in Concord — a large, brick-ended one with a portico supported by four Greek pillars — on the main street a little below and across the way from Deacon Parkman's. He had soon risen to be leader of the Middlesex bar. Under his guidance, many of the successful lawyers now practicing in the state had learned their profession. But Squire Hoar easily dominated the field. Indeed he appeared to be in every case, so that the only obstacle to his having a monopoly lay in the impossibility of being on both sides at once. His sense of public duty, his moral character and sound judgment, however, directed his choice. Few men were better able to brush away the rubbish and get to the bottom of a question. His directness and clarity won him the confidence of every farmer on a jury and his influence was almost unbounded. From talks round the stove and cracker barrel in Isaac Hurd's store below his second office, he knew their way of thinking. Once, when the foreman in a criminal case reported a panel unable to agree, the presiding judge enquired as to the difficulty. Was it in the law or the evidence? Neither, it lay in the plea. The law and evidence seemed to show the man was guilty, but Squire Hoar had declared his client innocent, and as the Squire always told the truth, the jury were at a loss what to do.

When Concord had needed a representative to welcome the Marquis de Lafayette to town on his triumphal tour of the nation, the choice fell naturally to Samuel Hoar. A cavalcade of forty horsemen had greeted the general at the Lexington line. They ushered him past a triumphal arch with this inscription: "In 1775 the people of Concord met the enemies of liberty. In 1824 they welcome the bold asserter of the rights of man." At the green, where the town's brass cannon volleyed a salute, Concord's prettiest girl presented the distinguished guest with a nosegay of flowers.

So successful was Lafayette's reception, so deeply did it stir the town's remembrances, that Concord determined, the following year, to celebrate in proper fashion the fiftieth anniversary of "the Fight."

Young Professor Edward Everett of Harvard, just elected to the United States Congress, was the speaker. Everyone who had heard him agreed that he deserved the reputation of orator won so early in life. Some of the things he said had struck deeply in his hearers' minds: "How is the spirit of a people to be formed and animated and cheered but out of the storehouse of its historic recollections?" Ezra Ripley himself had fully agreed to that, and was soon at work on an account of the Fight. So vividly did he see it that he half-believed he himself had watched the battle. The pamphlet had been printed the year before he gave his anniversary sermon. His step-grandson, Waldo Emerson, visiting at the time, had been amused to watch Dr. Ripley, like a keen hunter, track down the memories of old men who had been at the bridge.

Everett had said of the Fight that from the nature of the case it may be doubted whether there was an efficient order given the whole day to any body of men as large as a regiment. It was the people, in their first capacity, as citizens and farmers, starting from their beds at midnight, from their firesides and from their fields, taking their cause into their own hands. He had spoken a word, also, to the dwindling ranks of the veterans. "Honor, this day, to the venerable survivors!" At that, as if by a single impulse, Abel Davis, Thaddeus Blood, and the rest had risen to their shaky legs. "Sit, venerable friends," said the orator, "it is for us to stand in your presence." Men and women in the audience, carried away by the impromptu fitness of Everett's remark, got to their feet clapping and shouting. But after the proceedings, old Amos Baker was heard to say to somebody, "What do you suppose Squire Everett meant? He came to us before his speech and told us to stand up when he spoke to us, and when we stood up, he told us to sit down."

Concord had a good laugh over that.

Ezra Ripley had always wanted a monument to commemorate the Fight. He had almost got one in 1825, when with due masonic ceremony a cornerstone was laid at the square. But opposition had developed to the site as too far from the scene of battle. A fantastic wooden structure was raised one night over the spot by a band of hilarious objectors, to be burned down next day by their opponents, cracking the cornerstone to smithereens. There ended the scheme, at least for the time being.

We have lived to see, to suffer the evils, and enjoy the benefits of a great political revolution. Had not the people of the thirteen United

States been actuated by principles of piety and virtue, as well as the love of liberty and country, they would not have gained their freedom and independence. And let it be kept in mind that the same principles alone can preserve them.

The war Ezra Ripley was now mentioning was no longer that thought of by the younger generation. Theirs was the War of 1812, through which Andrew Jackson had won his fame. In his Concord oration, Edward Everett had declared that a pacific and friendly feeling was the duty of the nation. After two conflicts with the British, this was a stiff injunction. Yet thinking men were coming to believe it. Few citizens of New England had wanted that second war, though its profits made many of them rich. But in Concord much of the old bitter feeling had persisted, and when invasion threatened, both the town's volunteer companies — the Light Infantry and the Artillery — had mustered to guard the port of Boston. Before leaving, Captain Reuben Brown, Jr., had marched his artillerymen once around the square in hopes of winning more recruits. But none of the young men present to hear the music and watch the fun would fall in line. Brown tried it again with like results; but the third time round, four or five young fellows from Concord joined, as did Jesse Willis, of Carlisle, whose girl happened to be present. All the action they got was a two months' vigil in South Boston. The invasion struck farther south, with the British burning Washington before their defeat at New Orleans. News of the peace, signed before the final battle, had brought rejoicing to Concord. Young men and women could recall how fabulously bright and high the illuminated pinnacle of the new courthouse looked the night of the celebration. It was a small enough steeple now.

For most youngsters, in this later day, a veil had slipped between reality and war. Concord's military companies and the militia seemed to flourish for themselves alone, lifting certain men on brief occasions to heights of glory. What a brave show for the children, to see the soldiers formed in line from Deacon White's to Josiah Davis's store across the square! There was Colonel Shattuck in a splendid uniform, looking not at all like the man who sold you a jug of molasses across his counter. And Nathan Brooks, without his candle, as company paymaster. Charles Melvin's trumpet had a way of echoing clear round Meriam's Corner and across the flats towards Bedford.

Since the war, militia discipline, with each man still expected to be a soldier, presented something of a problem. Joseph Barrett, grandson of the colonel, had undertaken command partly through an ambition to perform the impossible by bringing order to this unruly local army, partly through his relish for the ludicrous. At the first parade, he had placed the most refractory under arrest — since he was sheriff as well as captain — then mollified those only slightly less troublesome by setting them to guard their fellows. Before resigning, he reduced his command to such submission that even on the coldest day of December he could march them five miles round the center with none missing when the circuit was completed.

These, to the children, were mere barnyard fowl among the military. The birds of paradise were the volunteer companies. Concord's Light Infantry was among the first in the field, incorporated in the second year of the Revolution, and veterans at Saratoga. Only the Ancient and Honorable Artillery, of Boston, was older. At the upper tavern, near Deacon Parkman's, its uniform of buff and blue, with bell-topped leather shakos, made a gorgeous showing at Concord's annual military ball among invited guests in the resplendent uniforms of the Boston companies. But the Concord Artillery, four years younger than the century, soon threatened to eclipse its rival. Its two brass fieldpieces, gift of the state, with the legend, "Concord Bridge, April 19, 1775," engraved on them, were the admiration of everybody in town. Blue coat faced with red, white vest, blue pantaloons, black cockade topped with red — its uniform caught the eye of every girl. Since the beginning, it sought the heftiest, largest volunteers and generally got them. Thomas Heald, young Concord lawyer, once the partner of Samuel Hoar, and a perfect ox of a man, had suggested at the company's formation that the smallest recruit go make the contract for the uniforms, which he negotiated at a very moderate price. When the band of giants came in to be measured, the tailor, aghast, admitted himself ruined.

We have lived to see a great and honorable improvement in the science of government, in legislation, and the administration of the laws.

Could their worthy parson by any chance mean to include Andrew Jackson, of week-before-last's election? Concord's *Gazette* still stubbornly refused to concede his victory over John Quincy Adams, President and son of the second President. Out of Concord's total vote, only four ballots had gone to Jackson. Adams, said the *Gazette*, had taken Massachusetts five to one. Yet the rumor was growing that with the help of recently admitted Western states, and of the

South, along with New York and Pennsylvania, Jackson, from the pioneers' state of Tennessee, had carried the country.

While Jefferson was living, the issue, to Concord's farmers, had seemed clear as day. They passionately supported Jefferson against Hamilton's Federalists — party of the Boston merchants, of privilege and political sanctity. Jefferson, they knew, distrusted the self-important men of commerce and culture into whose hands Hamilton wished to place the management of the nation. Jefferson believed in the common man; in the soil and its people. They, the farmers of Concord, were the citizens Jefferson and his successor, James Madison, trusted.

The Federalists, after the second British peace, had lost their hold as a nationwide party, repudiated for lack of patriotism because of their threats of New England secession and their opposition to the war. Then, after an era of good feeling under James Monroe, along had come this split of Jefferson's old Democratic-Republican Party into two factions, this pressing in of the new West — confusing New England's men of the soil and arousing their suspicions. Who now was the proper candidate, Adams of the National Republicans, as they styled themselves, or this interloper from Tennessee with his breed of Democrats, who set themselves up as Jefferson's descendants and spouted a jargon of states' rights and the leveling of political inequalities? Concord had given its answer, and it was not the nation's. Only young Stedman Buttrick and his three fellow Democrats were cheerful.

Save for its one-sidedness, this hot campaign reminded old-timers of the fierce elections of the earlier days of the Union. Federalists and Jeffersonian Democrats in town were then so equally divided that Concord's choice for representative in the Massachusetts legislature generally teetered in the balance till the final vote. Each citizen put unquestioning faith in the teachings of his party's organ — the Federalists swore by the *Centinal* (so spelled through some idiosyncrasy of the proprietor); the Democrats, by the *Patriot* or *Chronicle*. Because these Boston papers reached Concord on different days — the *Centinal* on Wednesdays and Saturdays, the trumpets of democracy on Mondays and Thursdays — the argument, as national elections neared, kept at shrillest pitch throughout the week. On the due days, these bales of public opinion would be tossed from the mail stage at the tavern doors and the children would scramble to fetch discord home.

As for town government in these tempestuous times, though Dr.

Abiel Heywood, Federalist, somehow always managed to win election as town clerk and chairman of the board of selectmen, he usually had to contend with one and sometimes two Democrats as his fellow members. Running the town was no laughing matter. When the citizens, after fierce argument, were ready for a poll of the house — *viva voce* vote nor even show of hands was to be trusted — they would file from the meeting into the common to be counted, each side lining up behind its party leader, the two rows facing each other and carrying on the angry debate till the tellers gave the score.

Ezra Ripley, in his discourse, had come to the one event difficult for him to speak of. *Lately another sect of Christians and another meetinghouse have risen up. As in its rise I devoutly committed the case to God, so I continue to leave it in his hands.* A ripple swept over the congregation. Their pastor, they knew, meant the church across the brook. It had happened a little over two years back. After communion service on a May Sunday, Parson Ripley had asked his flock to tarry. Controlling his voice with difficulty, he read them a petition from a group of fellow members. They were seeking to be dismissed to form a congregation of their own. The request had burst like a bombshell on the faithful.

Dr. Ripley, of course, had been well aware of what was going on in Congregationalist New England. He had hoped that somehow Concord would escape the trouble.

As the years passed over him, he had found it increasingly hard to visualize the complications of the Trinity or to believe in a Calvinistic God who dealt chiefly with the punishment of man for original sin. Along with the sin, surely, there was much goodness and charity in human nature — Ripley's life with his people had shown him that. As he felt, so had he taught, and his flock had seemed to agree. They were his friends, his children. He trusted them to follow his leading. First they had voted to drop the whole of the shorter catechism; finally they had abandoned the doctrine of the Trinity. Thus Concord's first Parish became Unitarian, and a part of the movement sweeping New England under the leadership of Dr. William Ellery Channing of Boston.

But the stricter Calvinists had at last protested, and emphatically.

Samuel Hoar's diplomatic motion saved the parting from the bitterness that had poisoned neighborly feelings in numerous towns. Conceding the petitioners the same right to private judgment which those remaining with the First Parish assumed for themselves, Ripley's congregation, though taking exception to the religious scruples of the objectors, granted the plea — wishing the departing members all the benefits they hoped for.

It was not so much the number of dissenters that troubled Ezra Ripley — half a dozen or so men and twice that many women. It was the fact that these, like all the rest, were his spiritual wards, his flock. He deemed himself their shepherd and the guardian of their children. In several families, the wife or husband had stayed behind, the other gone over the brook. How could these people break lifelong ties over such an issue; good people like Mercy Vose and her husband, John the Tanner — whose frugal ways of living were furnishing much of the cash to build the new meetinghouse? Also David Hubbard and Phoebe Wheeler. Eliza Stacy, wife of the keeper of the bookstore which sold the Bibles, psalters and hymnals used in town. And of the Thoreau household and family, every female member: Elizabeth, Jane, Maria — maiden sisters of John Thoreau who made the pencils, now that the Munroes, originators of the craft, had switched to clocks — also John's wife Cynthia, and her sister Louisa Dunbar. Ezra Ripley knew the antecedents and biography of every soul in Concord. Cynthia and Louisa, the vivacious Dunbar girls, when first they came to the town, had turned the thoughts of many boys from his sermons. They had lived with their mother in her second husband's house on the Virginia Road — for Mary Jones Dunbar, who during the Revolution helped her Tory brother Josiah Jones escape from Concord prison, had become the wife of Captain Jonas Minot of Concord after parson Asa Dunbar's death. Louisa Dunbar had never married, though as a younger girl she had caught the eye of no less a beau than Daniel Webster, who had taken her buggy riding at Boscawen where he was preparing for Dartmouth. Cynthia, after coming to Concord, had not done overly well, yet well enough, in marrying John Thoreau, once a clerk at Deacon White's, then absent for a while from Concord, and now turning his hand to pencils. Her older boy, named John, had been born away from Concord. The younger, David Henry, Dr. Ripley had baptized himself, entering the record in the parish register. Now his official care of these people had been stopped, though never his concern for their welfare. It was as though his own kindred had snubbed him.

The Trinitarian Church of Concord, with fire and brimstone Lyman Beecher presiding over the council, had been organized June the fifth. Daniel Southmayd, graduate of the theological seminary at Andover, had become their preacher. By December, 1826, their building was ready for dedication. "A very pretty-sounding bell in Mrs. Vose's meetinghouse," Deacon Parkman drily remarked to Mrs. Samuel Hoar. But to the First Parish, even after these two years, it made discordant music.

What almost broke Ezra Ripley's heart was Deacon White's secession. Not till after the first anniversary of the new church could the deacon — Ezra Ripley's intimate friend and an officer of the Parish through forty years — make up his mind to cross the Rubicon of the millbrook. It had hurt him as much as he knew it must be hurting his minister, but how could he deny his convictions? In the hard times after the Revolution, when Ezra Ripley feared he could not possibly wade against his difficulties, Deacon White had come silently to his help by giving him ample credit at the store.

One minor victory had lightened this major loss. Cynthia Thoreau, mother of John and David Henry, changed her mind and asked for readmittance to the fold.

November shadows were darkening at the windows. Dr. Ripley neared the end of his discourse. *I renew my request for assistance by a colleague. It seems to me that I have served my time.* Before the benediction, the parson had one more word of advice for his congregation: *My dear brethren, take all suitable care to live in love and peace. If a question of controversy should be pressed upon you, be sure to read both sides before you make up your mind upon it. Lay not stress upon human creeds. I am thoroughly convinced that vital religion does not depend on any particular creed, except the Bible.*

CHAPTER XI

The Nation's Apprenticeship
Draws to a Close

PETER BULKELEY'S blood had again entered the lifestream of
Concord. Charles Chauncy Emerson, come to try the legal pro-
fession under Samuel Hoar, had taken lodgings at the manse with
Ezra Ripley.

The town had kept posted on the progress of the Emerson boys.
When Charles was awarded the coveted Boylston prize in elocution
as Junior Sophister at Harvard, the *Gazette* had chronicled the triumph. Before him, Edward Bliss had easily been top scholar and
had won the Bowdoin premium with his senior dissertation. Ralph
Waldo, their immediate predecessor, had not done so brilliantly,
though standing in the upper half of his class. A shyer, more re-
tiring boy — yet his younger brothers always looked up to him, and
Edward, in the midst of his successes, insisted Ralph was the star
of the family. Miss Mary Moody Emerson, the boys' eccentric,
gifted aunt, who had a persevering interest in knowing what thinkers think, showed by her probing questions that she expected much
of Waldo.

Charles had graduated from Harvard with the class of '28, then
become a law student at Cambridge. Though slender and of medium
stature, he could not cross the yard without attracting attention.
He was like a young Greek in Plato's Academy — straight as an
arrow, with clear blue eyes, crisp hair, and a fair complexion. His
handsome features had that magnetic quality of inner beauty and
clear intelligence which somehow benefits even the passing stranger.

When Charles looked for a Boston law office to give him practical
experience, Senator Daniel Webster had been happy to receive him.
"Settle! Let him settle anywhere!" exclaimed that shrewd lawyer
and ambitious statesman as Charles's friends sought to give advice

on where he should hang his shingle. "Let him settle in the back woods of Maine if he chooses; the clients will throng after him." But the young lawyer, in the spring of 1834, decided for practical and sentimental reasons on the thriving County Seat of Concord. That autumn, to be near him, Ralph turned up once more at the manse.

Ralph Waldo had been through a prolonged crisis – through loss, illness, and bitter disappointment. He hoped in these quiet fields of his fathers, in his thirty-second year, to shape his life again. Five years before, he had been ordained junior pastor of the fine old Second Church, Boston. Six months later, he married Ellen Tucker of Concord, New Hampshire. She was young, talented, and beautiful. Less than two years after the wedding, she died. Ralph Waldo, never really happy within the confines of the formal church, now more than ever ill at ease and groping, resigned the pastorate. He traveled abroad; chiefly, he admitted, to ask questions of certain wise men – Walter Savage Landor in Italy, Coleridge in London, Wordsworth at Rydal Mount, Thomas Carlyle at Craigenputtock. They had been kind, especially the Scotsman, but who could solve these riddles? The answers must be found within oneself. Now, five years after Ellen's death, here he was, with Charles in Concord. He would lecture a little, perhaps write a little, perhaps edit a magazine.

Squire Hoar had just been elected to the United States House of Representatives by the anti-Jackson forces – the Whigs. During his absence, Charles was to look after his practice. But an even more important transaction was in view. Charles Emerson and Elizabeth Hoar, the congressman's daughter, were engaged and soon to be married.

With his sociable nature, his wit, his interest in persons, Charles quickly made himself essential to the town. He was especially fond of boys. Dr. Ripley's enthusiasm at the time was the Sabbath School just established in his church – one of the first attempted. In such classes, and in the schools being set up for little children, the parson insisted, lay the best hope for the future. Certainly, for the boys in Charles's group, this hour was the one bright interval in the desperately long New England Sabbath. Each counted him his friend. To one he had given just the right kind of ice skates, to another, a knife that would really cut.

The newly founded Concord Lyceum also owed much of its success, that season, to Charles. It had done pretty well thus far, save for a dearth of speakers who would give their services free. The Emerson boys, however, were proving a godsend. The lecture remembered best was Charles's on the Life and Death of Socrates. It was more than an entertainment — it was a stirring appeal to the young men present, bidding them live their lives to their utmost ideals and power. None who heard was likely to forget it — John Shepard Keyes, trying to make up his mind whether to go to college at Hanover or Cambridge; Henry David Thoreau (he had switched his name because he liked it that way better), a freshman at Harvard, who clung to his green coat because the authorities required a black one.

When the town committee had asked Ralph Waldo Emerson, instead of his younger brother, to give the historical address at the bicentenary of the founding of Concord, several inhabitants questioned their judgment. But the care with which he prepared his talk — he devoted the entire summer to it — and the success of its delivery, justified the choice.

The day following his address, Ralph Waldo drove to Plymouth, Massachusetts, where he was going to marry Lidian Jackson. Ellen belonged to a life that could be lived only in memory.

Shortly before fetching Lidian to Concord, he had bought the two-acre Coolidge place on the new Cambridge turnpike. The plain, square, modest two-story dwelling was seven years old, roomy and comfortable. The best built in town, people were saying, yet Emerson, with Yankee shrewdness, had managed to get it at a bargain. It had an excellent dry cellar — rare in low-lying Concord — and a two-story ell at the southeast corner.

When he bought his place, Emerson told himself, he had not guessed what a bargain he had in bluebirds, bobolinks, and thrushes which were not charged on the bill. Nor had he realized what sublime mornings and sunsets he was buying — what reaches of landscape, what fields and lanes for tramping. And now he was about to fulfill one hope for living — Lidian, his brother Charles, his mother, were all under his roof.

Lidian soon joined Charles as a teacher in Dr. Ripley's Sunday school. She was a devout Unitarian of the Channing type and preserved her integrity of belief — though never at odds with her husband for his greater independence. Her somewhat arrowy wit at times transfixed him, yet always with a playful quality — only the morally fake felt its sharpened barbs. Tall, slender, and very straight, with sensitive face and fine gray eyes that made up for her lack of actual beauty, she walked with a dignity that won from her husband the half-awed, half-humorous nickname of Queenie.

If Samuel Hoar kept on as Congressman, he was ready to turn over to Charles his entire thriving legal business. Charles joked about eating up the law as would a camel. What he read in the morning, he said, went into the first stomach till evening, then slid into the second, and so on till thoroughly digested. Already, at the house on the Cambridge turnpike, alterations and enlargements were under way, for his and Elizabeth's wedding day had been set.

Then, in March, riding back to Concord from Boston on the top of the stage, Charles caught a violent cold. Ralph Waldo, away at Salem for some lectures, wrote an anxious letter urging him, while ill, not to think of his office, or business, or time or cost.

Despite his seeking health in Puerto Rico, Edward had died of consumption. Now it was Charles who was threatened. Emerson broke off his tour to go with his brother to New York, whence, if needful, he could head farther south. Having returned to New England to finish his engagements, he received a letter from William, the oldest brother, at whose Staten Island home the invalid was resting. Charles was much worse. With Elizabeth Hoar, Ralph Waldo set out from Concord. They arrived too late.

"This event seems to me," declared Dr. Ripley before the gathered congregation, "loud and piercing, like thunder and lightning. Whilst many aged and burdensome are spared, this beloved youth is cut down in the morning." Dr. Channing, when he heard the news in Boston, was loath to believe it. "I think Massachusetts could not have met a greater loss," he said, "than that young man."

Ralph Waldo Emerson came home alone. In Charles he had experienced the inestimable advantage of both friend and brother. He had decided to live in Concord because of Charles. He had trusted Charles more than himself and had deferred to him on so many questions. Now he felt not only unfastened and adrift — this had happened before with Ellen and Edward — he felt a sort of shame at living at all. How much he had seen through his brother's eyes! He felt as if his own were very dim.

He must remind himself of the lesson he had learned abroad in seeking guidance from others. A man must build his fortress of reliance within himself. His little book, which he had begun in the third-story "prophet's chamber" at the manse, was nearly done. He must finish it. He would call it, simply, *Nature*.

*   *   *

Like all Concord bridegrooms, Emerson had been elected hogreeve in humorous obedience to old custom. More seriously, the town had named him to its School Committee, though he presently resigned to be free for writing his historical address. Nor having once secured him would Concord let him go as a spokesman. Ezra Ripley, after a valiant campaign for it, at last had won out in the matter of a monument to the Fight. Because with the old bridge gone there was no way of getting across, the monument stood on the Concord side of the stream, where the first British soldier had fallen. Emerson wrote a hymn for the dedication. Printed on slips of paper and distributed among the audience who formed the choir, its phrases, to the tune of "Old Hundred," echoed and re-echoed over Buttrick's hillside where the minute men had gathered, and down the quiet river that carried the words away.

More and more, with the growth of the Lyceum movement, Emerson was coming in demand, and his fees were beginning to win him a modest living. "How is the lecturing business?" George Minot would call out from his little weatherbeaten red house on the ridge across the way, and Emerson would answer that he didn't see but it was as good as ever; guessed the people would want lectures as long as the two of them lived.

Many citizens of the town and of Massachusetts felt outraged at what was happening to the Cherokee Indians. Though they held their tribal lands by treaty with the Federal Government, Georgia, feeling the westward thrust of the people, was scheming to oust them. The trouble had begun under Andrew Jackson, and now, with President Van Buren's tacit acquiescence, was reaching its climax. Refusing to leave, the Indians had been arrested and sent to hard labor. The government was planning their removal beyond the Mississippi.

In a meeting of protest, the people of Concord listened to Samuel Hoar and others attack the government's action. Emerson stated the purpose of the meeting and guided it toward the resolution it sent to Congress. Humanity, justice, and religion were at stake, and the faith of solemn treaties. But Mrs. Nathan Brooks, who had first won Emerson's active support of the cause, would not let the matter end with the meeting. Emerson must write a letter to the President, she insisted, setting forth the arguments he had used.

At first he drew back. He was a scholar, a man who had always thought of himself as living somewhat apart from the world. But his sense of morality and his sense of justice were both tugging him toward the arena. In his Phi Beta Kappa speech at Cambridge he had said that though action, with the scholar, is subordinate, it is nevertheless essential. Without it, thought can never ripen into truth.

The *Daily National Intelligencer*, Washington, May 14, 1838, carried his forthright letter. Thence it sped wide over the land. The Cherokees were sent into exile — but a new voice had troubled the conscience of the nation.

Lidian Emerson loved flowers, and soon won the reputation of being the best gardener in Concord. She had brought from Plymouth some of her finest varieties and soon peopled the village with them. Where her husband, struggling to maintain root-room for his vegetables, planted corn, it was sure to come up tulips. Indoors, after her rounds of housekeeping and of looking after her little son, Waldo, she would arrange her coral bells and larkspur, her rosemary and monkshood, and wreathe the railing of the stairway with coppery oak leaves in the fall. Each week the stage brought friends and visitors, and the door was always open. Many of these callers were strangers — young men who had been captured by something they had heard or read:

> *Trust thyself: every heart vibrates to that iron string. Nothing is at last sacred but the integrity of your own mind. Man alone can perform the impossible. That which befits us, embosomed in beauty and wonder as we are, is cheerfulness and courage, and the endeavor to realize our own aspirations. We are never tired, so long as we can see far enough.*
>
> *We will walk on our own feet; we will work with our own hands; we will speak with our own minds. Perhaps the time is already come . . . when the sluggard intellect of this continent will look from under its iron lids and fill the postponed expectation of the world with something better than the exertions of mechanical skill. Our day of dependence, our long apprenticeship to the learning of other lands, draws to a close.*

And what was that phrase he had made use of to assert an individual's right to his own judgment? Did it not run thus? *Let him not quit his belief that a popgun is a popgun, though the ancient and honorable of the earth affirm it to be the crack of doom.*

*   *   *

Emerson would sit in his chair, as the young men talked, the wise, slow, quizzical smile full of encouragement and refreshment. For those who had known his handsome brothers, Ralph Waldo had an ungainly build, his hands and feet large for his long body. He would bend slightly toward you in his chair, and he had a way, after crossing his legs, of hitching the instep of one foot under the calf of the other leg, so that he seemed braided up. Yet there was no sense of awkwardness about him. Far more than with most men, his eyes — some said they were greenish gray, others described them as violet — seemed the windows of his soul. Sometimes, to a beholder, his glance would startle like the reveille of a bugle.

Founded by a group which included William Whiting and Dr. Abiel Heywood, perennial Clerk of the Town, whose interests, as much legal as medical, had brought him to the bench as Associate Judge of the Court of Sessions, Concord Academy was supposed to furnish a better education than that publicly provided. Despite the set of rules drawn up by Dr. Ripley, the seven district schools differed little from what they had been a hundred years before. During the two- or three-month winter session, the teacher was usually an undergraduate released from college to earn money for tuition. Discipline was of greater importance than instruction, with not infrequent fights with the tougher, bigger farmboys. In the summer, under women teachers (the town could get them cheaper), ten weeks more, with mostly girls attending, the boys busy on the farm. The Grammar School at the center, with its longer terms and somewhat better paid teachers, was supposed to prepare for college. But everyone knew the school's history. Town clerk Heywood, who had scanned the records of a hundred years, was well aware that the practical inhabitants had seen little use in hiring a master save to dodge the Colony's fine. Crowding was always a major problem, so much so that girls were not permitted to attend beyond the elementary grades, in order to save the seats for the boys. All grades sat huddled together in the packed little amphitheater of wooden benches on three sides of the stuffy hall facing the teacher's elevated desk, the class reciting at the moment standing before the master.

Often a local boy just out of college was given the Grammar School. After graduation from Harvard, Henry David Thoreau had thus accepted the town's offer. But one day Deacon Cyrus Stow of the School Committee came to oversee a session. Not once did the master flog or use the ferrule. True, the pupils spoke their lessons well — but without whipping, what's to become of discipline? Deacon Stow bade the teacher mend his ways.

Was that what the town wanted? Thoreau would not take their money and not deliver. With wry humor he summoned six students — one a girl who helped in his mother's house — smacked each with his ruler, then resigned.

When the master at the Academy left for a post at Cornell, Henry and his older brother John, an experienced teacher, took over. The *Gazette* gave notice of the new arrangement: on Monday, September 10, 1838, under the Thoreau brothers, the Academy would open for a limited number of pupils of both sexes, at six dollars the quarter, with instruction in studies preparatory to a collegiate course — the sponsors: Honorable Samuel Hoar, Honorable Nathan Brooks, Honorable John Keyes, and Mr. R. W. Emerson.

From the start there was a gratifying enrollment. Those from outside the village boarded mostly with Mrs. Thoreau at the old Parkman house with its pleasant garden, its potatoes, squashes, and melons of Henry's own growing, its litter of kittens behind the stove, its box of chattering martins in the yard. Every day the children who came from Bedford covered the four miles on foot, or skated when the river was frozen.

When a pupil applied for admission, before saying yes, John would have a talk.

Why do you want to enter our school?

Because the child's father wished him to learn the subjects he understood were taught there.

Yes, but would you like *yourself* to learn these things? If you do, we will do our best to teach you what we know.

The school was a happy school, the children acquisitive. It was no rare thing, when the day was over, to see a boy or a girl catch John or Henry by the hand to hear more on the walk home.

John, the more immediately popular of the two — gay, sympathetic, and genial — taught composition, arithmetic, and other elementary subjects; Henry taught French, Greek and Latin, physics, higher mathematics, and sometimes writing. Look into the fire there, he would say, and write what you see. Go to the window, and tell what passes in the street. What your hands find to putter with, what your mind to think about, let that be the subject — not the stuffed pumpkin topics of the rhetoric book.

Instead of the usual ten minutes, recess was a full half hour, and a game of ball with the teachers. After morning prayers, one or the other would talk before the beginning of classes. When Henry spoke on why the wind blows, on what makes us live, what causes the stars to shine, you could hear a pin drop, the schoolroom was so quiet.

Such tactics were unheard of in Concord. Yet parents found their boys and girls learned more in a week than in a month at the town school. Nor was it merely what stood in the books. The brothers believed that all Concord should be partner in teaching. There would be a sail on the river in the *Red Jacket*, while Henry told how streams formed land, how water heats and cools, how bullpouts breed then guard their brood from marauding pike. Walden or White's or Bateman's Pond for swimming — and to show how vapor gathers into rain. To give a notion of the fieldwork of surveying and of the use of scientific instruments, Henry would lead a group over the farmers' fields to Fairhaven Hill — and the pupils would comprehend the earth through the geography and geology of their region. Arrowheads? The dark-complexioned, ruddy-faced teacher, stopping in his loping stride, would kick at the soil, then pick up something, clearing away the dirt to show his find.

"Do you see anything here," he might ask, "that would be likely to attract Indians to this spot?"

Yes, the river for fishing; the high bank safe from flood.

Thoreau would take a spade and start digging. Presently the blade would strike a stone, till a whole circle lay uncovered — a long disused fire-marked ring where the Indians dried their fish. These Indians — said the teacher — were the inhabitants of nature, not her guests, and wore her gracefully. But civilization, so-called, bends life from its natural course, and the white man's house, instead of providing shelter and protection, becomes his prison. All up and down this river, long ago, the Indians hunted till white men ended the hunt. They had harried the Indians from their ancient lodges — past the white hills, toward Canada, the lakes, the Mississippi. Concord boasted of its heroes of the Indian wars — the brave, exterminating forefathers! Thoreau retold the story of Jones's and Davis's adventures in Lovewell's Fight. But what of the crippled Indians? — demanded the teacher. How many musket balls lodged in them, how fared their wounds, what Berwick or Saco did they find for refuge? What pensions and what townships were granted to them? There is no journal to tell.

Henry took his spade and carefully replaced the turf over the Indian fireplace. No need to leave it thus exposed for the idly curious.

In the full tide of its success, the Academy was almost at the end of its third annual session under them when the Thoreau brothers announced they were giving up the school.

Why, asked the parents, had they not been told earlier of so important a matter?

Because, said John, had the pupils known, they might have lost heart in their studies.

John, who taught with every ounce of his brain and body, had found himself not strong enough for such energy-sapping work. Consumption, which had claimed his grandfather, three aunts, and an uncle, was the danger, and it was time to meet it. Henry refused to go on without his brother. He had discovered, as far as concerned himself, that he was teaching not so much for his own good and that of his fellow men as simply to get a living. He was still hunting a truer fulfillment, closer to what he wished to make of his life. Mr. Emerson wanted him to take a room in his house on the Cambridge turnpike as a sort of younger brother — look after the garden if he chose, help Mrs. Emerson, be companion to little Waldo. He needed just such a person as Henry, his hands strong and skillful, his mind independent, critical, and witty. He was fond of Thoreau, and enjoyed saying things just to flash his young friend's fire. With himself absent more and more to lecture, such an arrangement would be a real service, yet leave Henry master of his time.

Thoreau accepted the offer.

In the year before the Thoreau brothers gave up teaching, the children of the Academy and of the red brick schoolhouse gained an object lesson in presidential politics which they would long remember.

Perhaps a beginning had been made five or six years earlier, in the Antimasonic upheaval. When William Morgan, a Mason, following a squabble with his brethren, published the secrets of the fraternity, then mysteriously disappeared at Canandaigua, New York — kidnaping and murder the only explanation — his act and exit caused a tremor which threatened to become a national earthquake.

Before the event, no one gave much thought to Masonry politically. George Washington had been a Mason. So had Paul Revere.

The majority of men of standing in many communities were Masons. In Concord, good Dr. Ripley enjoyed the public festivals when he could wear his symbolic apron.

After the event, the fuss swelled into illogical hysteria. It took a rare person to keep his head. Former President John Quincy Adams had just published a savage attack on the Masonic Order. In Boston he chanced to meet Samuel Hoar of Concord, and asked him what he thought of the pamphlet. Both men had great respect for each other. But Samuel Hoar believed in speaking out. "It seems to me, Mr. Adams," he replied, "there is but one thing in the world sillier than Masonry. That is Antimasonry."

In Concord, as the smoke began to rise, all members of the Corinthian Lodge save one stood steadfast. Herman Atwill, third degree Mason, who owned the *Gazette*, got out, then printed a sizzling Antimasonic editorial. From that instant the shrieks of local battle blended with the din of the larger war. Atwill did not hesitate to publish the vows of the fraternity, and he was ready with his reasons. Did not Masons swear, with God for witness, to give their influence to their brethren in preference to all others? Till men threw off such obligations, announced Atwill, it was a national duty to proscribe them. He printed lampoons of Concord Masons and a list of them as a *dramatis personae* of skullduggery: John Keyes, King John of the Corinthian Chapter, a crowned king flouting the Republic! William Whiting, the carriage maker, charioteer and high priest of the powers of evil.

The Masons, of course, did their utmost to drive Atwill from town. Abel Moore, Sheriff of the County, and others, presented all outstanding bills they could gather, in the hope of breaking him. The newly founded Concord Bank called in its note, and John Keyes sought to foreclose the mortgage on the newspaper's plant and presses. But somehow Atwill managed to keep going. He used these doings to advantage by printing succinct accounts of them. He gave up the *Gazette* and founded the *Freeman* to continue the fight.

The temptation to turn out Concord's more substantial, sometimes arrogant office holders was too strong for many an average citizen. A thing almost unheard-of in Concord, it took four ballots before even a presiding officer could be chosen. Then the local Antimasonic ticket swept the field. Closest contest was for Clerk of the Town. On the first ballot the Antimasonic candidate, Phineas Allen, tied with Dr. Abiel Heywood, not a Mason but loyal in his friendships. Breaking the deadlock by seven votes, the Antimasons pushed through their man.

Samuel Hoar, moderator, called the meeting to order. Abiel Heywood, he reminded the town, had held his office for thirty-eight successive years, serving Concord with skill and diligence. Would the meeting give a vote of thanks for his fidelity? A little ashamed of itself, the town was glad to pass the motion unanimously.

The Antimasonic temblors spent themselves almost as quickly as they had risen. They represented a type of national delusion which in vanishing is presently forgotten though the cracks left behind can still cause injury. Concord settled to its accustomed ways. But a precedent for journalistic rancor and partisanship remained, ready to reappear at a moment's notice.

Young Francis Richard Gourgas took over the liabilities and assets of the bankrupt *Freeman* and soon turned it into the leading Democratic newspaper of the county. His skillful politicking contributed measurably to the local Democratic triumph and added its little push to Van Buren's national victory. Van Buren, pledged to a continuation of Andrew Jackson's political principles, took office in time to bear the brunt of the terrible depression of 1837, which even some Democrats were inclined to blame on Jackson's war on the United States Bank — which he regarded as monopolistic and catering to special privilege.

Young Gourgas was something of a prodigy. Son of a wealthy French-Swiss father and an English mother, he had first come to Concord as a student at the Academy. He was a month shy of twenty-four when he took over the *Freeman*. Very clever, very ambitious, and gifted as a rousing speaker, he reconciled the old Jeffersonian farmer Democrats in the town with the rough new laboring class Jacksonian breed. Imperious, willful, and a born aristocrat, he managed nevertheless to hold his diverse constituency. There was a haughty swing to his shoulders when he walked which annoyed those who disliked his methods. Even Emerson, who hated to criticize people, disapproved, for he admired Samuel Hoar, the village Cato, and looked with distrust on professional politicians. Regard this spruce dictator teaching his rural Jacobins their political lessons! What does he care for, save the fortunes of his ticket? Yet there is a kind of American genius, Emerson admitted, hidden in the gruff manners of these Democrats, though their leader — and here

Emerson may have done Gourgas some injustice — loved what *he* hated.

As with all things Gourgas did, he married early, and presently owned a fine house filled with the portraits of his aristocratic French ancestors. In it he installed the town's first bathroom, with tub and watercloset. Women called on his wife just to see the wonder, then plagued their husbands concerning the chilly outhouse. By 1838 Gourgas had captured the village post office held by John Keyes for twenty-five years. Like Jackson before him, Van Buren was rewarding his friends and swatting his enemies. The new postmaster moved the sanctum of the *Freeman* upstairs where it would be handy and made ready for the day when Van Buren would run for a second term.

As the star of the Democratic *Freeman* rose, the Whig *Gazette* sank almost to extinction. The best it could do was hurl the none too imaginative epithet "Locofoco!" at the opposition.

In the year of the presidential election, with General William Henry Harrison, sixty-eight-year-old Indian fighter, as Whig standard-bearer, John Keyes, Colonel Whiting, and Nathan Brooks, the latter a candidate for Congress, decided it was time to be stirring in Concord. They bought and made over to William Robinson all the property and appurtenances of the *Gazette* and set him up as editor, changing the paper's name to *Republican*.

Twenty-one years old when he took over, Robinson was seven years younger than Gourgas, but every bit his match. Unlike his rival, he was Concord born, though he had learned his newspapering as a compositor and editorial writer on the *Norfolk Advertiser*. Like his rival, he was a natural politician and did not shrink from personalities. His attacks seared all who opposed him and he fell like a fiery rain on the just and the unjust. Emerson, never reconciled to this aspect of democracy, was troubled by these pyrotechnics, though he found himself on Robinson's side.

Every Friday morning from above the post office Gourgas hurled his bolts. From the rooms over Eaton's furniture shop on the Milldam, Robinson tossed back his replies, and the campaign grew hotter with the summer. Yet Gourgas — a witty, biting controversialist — was finding himself at a strange disadvantage. Ready to defend administration measures against attack and prepared to ridicule counterproposals, he could discover among his Whig opponents no presentation of logical criticisms — even in the vulnerable matter

of the Bank — nor was there any Whig platform. During the four
days' nominating convention, though plenty of Whig orators had
ranted, not one had made a positive assertion of principle. Nothing
but blasts of hate against the Locofocos and noisy snarls against
President Van Buren. Nor did Harrison supply the lack. His plush
cushion orations said exactly nothing. And from the press across
the street, nothing more substantial than witty invective. Yet everywhere in this vacuum the Whigs, especially the young men of the
party, acclaimed Harrison and his running mate Tyler with the
wildest enthusiasm. Demonstration followed fervid demonstration,
with Harrison shouted up as the hero of Tippecanoe — a bungled
and indecisive campaign, thought Gourgas — with banners showing the old soldier downing a mug of hard cider, with coonskin caps
for emblems, and log cabins on wheels to prove to the West that the
Whigs were the party of the people. Why, for forty years the
Democrats had held that position!

"They came together for what?" Gourgas demanded, eyeing these
celebrations. "To make a declaration of their opinions on important
public questions? No! They assembled only to shout, to roll a large
ball, to drag about log cabins, to sing doggerel verse, and generally
to outvie in childishness and foolery the smallest boys who from a
congruity of mind and tastes mingle with them."

On July the Fourth, Concord held its gala day of log cabin campaigning. For weeks the local committee had been busy with arrangements, consisting chiefly of hogsheads of cider and droves of
barbecued pig. The night preceding the Fourth, the volunteer
military companies whose gay uniforms were to contribute glamor
to the parade had already captured the town. At four in the morning Thoreau, writing up his journal — he enjoyed the hours of darkness as much as the light — could hear a group of them, with muted
bugle, fife and drum, playing an old Scotch air. Some rain had fallen
and the dawn was cloudy, but the rising sun, greeted by a national
salute of twenty-six guns, put an end to that, and the bright hot day
began.

Each of the three roads into town was jammed with carriages and
people. From Lowell came twelve hundred celebrants, one hundred
and fifty of them drinking hard cider as they rode in an immense
log cabin drawn by twenty-three horses. The eastern division —
delegates from Boston and vicinity — formed a cue two miles long,
with bands of music by the dozen, the center of attraction the great
ball, striped red, white, and blue and covered with mottoes, bobbing

along in charge of the Tippecanoe Club from Cambridge. Twelve to thirteen feet in diameter, it had rolled through much of the nation and was bound farther before election. There on the Lexington road were Mr. Emerson and his friends, admiring the spectacle, some of them helping to push the ball. Since Major Barrett was about as corpulent as it was, theirs was a meeting to behold. Mr. Emerson professed interest in the ball's political symbolism — but most men showed more interest in the free food and hard cider.

The speakers' stand had been set at the river's edge near the battle monument. As the orators took their station, a majestic barge containing a bevy of fair ladies hove up from Billerica, after some difficulties with the mud below Ball's Hill, to be greeted by prolonged cheers and the waving of handkerchiefs. Daniel Webster, Rufus Choate, Robert Charles Winthrop, and others rehearsed the glories of the nation and of the party ticket. Six thousand persons — four thousand less lucky had to wait outside — ate free barbecue and drank cider in the biggest tent ever erected in Middlesex County.

> Huzza for Tip!
> Huzza for Tyler!
> With these we'll bust
> The Dutchman's biler!

chanted the throng. "With which poetical declaration of principles," sourly commented Gourgas in the next issue of the *Freeman*, "Concord's glorious Fourth ended."

At Lexington that day the Democracy — Gourgas serving as chairman of the committee — put on a rival celebration, with the meal prudently served at a dollar a head to defray campaign expenses. Governor Marcus Morton of Massachusetts spoke of the presidential record, and there were toasts to victory: "Andrew Jackson — the hero and statesman — the man of the people!" "The American Eagle — may she never stoop so low as to build her nest in a log cabin!" But not all who bought tickets could get into the tent, and outside there were discordant cries of "Hurrah for Old Tip! Let's go up to Concord and get some dinner!"

The campaign methods of the Whigs, Gourgas told his henchmen — forgetting other elections — were beneath the notice of serious-minded men. The bubble would burst before November. How could the Democrats be defeated? Through years of office holding they had built up an invincible machine — persuasive and efficient.

Yet as state after state threatened to go for Harrison, something close to desperation seized the Democratic command from the top ranks to the bottom. The populace on whom they counted were in a curious lethargy. Most of the local veterans, boasted the *Republican,* had attended the Harrison barbecue.

"Democrats!" exhorted the *Freeman* on the eve of election, "remember that last year your governor owed his election to *one vote.* Learn wisdom from this and not only see that your vote is not lost but that your neighbor's is not lost."

Gourgas was ambitious, it is true. True, he reveled in the sway he held over Middlesex County and was beginning to enjoy throughout the State. He was ready to use every trick of argument to capture the vote of the people. But he also had his beliefs — a fact ignored by most of his enemies. His demagogic Jacobism owed much to his personal rebellion against the conservatism of his family and the society in which he had been reared. This pose that Harrison stood for the common man, he felt, was an outrageous farce. "Are you for those," Gourgas demanded, "whose principles like those of their first great leader, Alexander Hamilton, advocated a President for life, a Senate for life, and an aristocracy of 'gentlemen' to ride over the 'simple men' as they call the farmers, mechanics, and laborers? Then vote the Whig ticket! Do you value the cause and the principles for which your fathers fought at Charlestown, Lexington and Concord? Vote then the Democratic ticket!"

Election day — Monday, November 9, 1840.

From the farthest farm, from houses of all degrees, the parties were getting out the vote. Towards nightfall the banging of guns — customary outlet for election celebrations — was almost continuous. The record-breaking uproar, twelve years earlier, at Jackson's first election, was beaten hollow — only this time it was the Whigs who were raising the din.

Francis Gourgas, getting out his post-election issue, sat wearily at his desk. There was one slight consolation in the landslide that had overwhelmed Van Buren. As boss in Middlesex, Gourgas could claim a small majority in Concord for every national and state office. And Parmenter had defeated Brooks for Congress, remaining the sole Democrat in the Massachusetts delegation. But "Tippecanoe and Tyler too" had swept the nation and carried Massachusetts, along with the governorship. "This is the sum and substance of last Monday's doings," wrote Gourgas, "we are essentially used up. The result of the Presidential election is very different from what we expected, and we confess ourselves disappointed and deceived."

Across the street, Robinson was also busy. "We are ready to bury the hatchet," he declared. "We shall, as far as in us lies, endeavor to assuage the spirit of party — and we wish to see all united, and a better feeling — a feeling of kindness and generosity — pervading the whole community."

One month after his inauguration, old Tippecanoe was dead, and Tyler, whom few men before the campaign had ever heard of and whose politics no one had bothered to look into, moved into the White House.

Gourgas was soon removed from office as postmaster, and a good Whig, John Stacy, who ran the bookstore, received the political football. A spoils system works in either direction.

Guests were a rule of life at the manse. Dr. Ripley loved humanity and his door was open to all men. No horse from the eastern country, from the west or north or south, would jog past the gate, so habitual was the traveler's entry.

For visiting clergy, there would be a sumptuous dinner (judged by country standards), and a chat in the parlor. Then Jeremiah, Francis, or Nicodemus — whichever lad filled the rôle of cowherd at the moment — would knock deferentially.

"What pasture shall I turn the cow into tonight, sir?"

"Into the battlefield, Nicodemus," Dr. Ripley would answer. "Into the battlefield!"

A tour of the site would naturally follow, with a lecture on its history.

But even more welcome to the parson were his sabbath evenings before dusk, when his parishioners were fond of calling. The men came with their wives and children — Deacon Francis Jarvis, Squire Hoar, John Keyes. Religion and politics, philosophy and the affairs of the village, news of the day and social gossip, with anecdotes and amusing stories, while the boys and girls sat gravely by to listen. In old age Dr. Ripley had planted fruit trees, and there were always apples for the children.

The parson loved his manse; it had helped give him a living during the hard years. His orchard, when it reached its prime, netted a hundred dollars a season. He had pear trees — just beginning to appear in that part of the country — as well as apples, a couple of quinces, two long rows of currant bushes, and several peaches. Near his barn stood his hen house, pigeon roost, and stone pigsty. He made the best of his simple living. When he packed his pork, he always put the choicest pieces at the top of the barrel. Thus, while the contents lasted, the topmost was the best all the way through.

Though strict as guardian of the village morals, his interpretation was liberal. Once, in the early days, an agitated housewife sought him, full of horrid scandal. The schoolmaster was inviting the larger girls and boys to stop for an hour after school while he taught them dancing to the tune of his fiddle. Surely Dr. Ripley would wish to put an end to such wicked frivolity. The parson listened patiently. "Yes, I have heard of this dancing," he answered, "and am pleased to notice that the children have learned a great deal better manners than they had before."

Dr. Ripley never shirked in any duty. In a winter storm, with snow drifted high as his horse's shoulders, he would brave the gusty stretch between manse and meetinghouse, preaching on the coldest days — the pulpit was far from the stove — in his greatcoat and mittens.

Following his request, the town had given him an assistant, but he had already outlived the first one, Dr. Hersey Goodwin, by nearly a decade. And Barzellai Frost, Goodwin's successor, had time on his hands to tutor young fellows like James Russell Lowell, rusticated from Harvard for minor offenses.

On Sunday, the second of May, 1841, the day following their pastor's ninetieth birthday, the ladies of the parish presented him with an elegant carpet for the church. The meetinghouse was to undergo a complete renovation. Already Dr. Ripley was at work on his dedicatory sermon. But at twenty minutes after four in the morning, on Tuesday, the twenty-first of September, death took him. Concord lost the last voice which had heartened the people through the dark years after the Revolution, while the nation was struggling to find itself. With Dr. Ripley's passing, remarked Emerson, had vanished almost the last banner of a mighty epoch.

CHAPTER XII

Principles Not Marketable or Perishable

PERHAPS the town did not realize what an interest Emerson took in its doings. Farmers he spoke to on the road never noticed anything out of the ordinary, for he was a listener and learner, concerned with the elemental things — the state of crops and the weather. If the woods caught fire, he was there with the neighbors, beating out the flames with his pine bough. On his way to the post office he would stop to hear what they were saying about the coming election, and he understood New England better than did most of her politicians. Housewives were not surprised if their new-fangled coal ranges became a topic in common, and they found it easy to talk with him about their problems with the children.

It was never only the wholesome which caught his glance — he took in also the rough and hairy, the idiots and drunkards. He observed all, helped where he could, and was tolerant. He always hoped his townsmen would do their best. He would not join associations, trusting each individual to handle the moral problem. But when some scurvy trick was done, like this outrage to Dr. Bartlett, Emerson could act swiftly and with force.

Someday, surely, Josiah Bartlett would be regarded as a hero. Since his first hour in practice, the muscular, active doctor had answered every call, defying time, distance, and the weather. Poor men got the same attention as the rich. It was unthinkable for any man to wish him harm. Yet some did.

On its founding, Concord's Total Abstinence Society had elected the doctor president. He had seen enough in practice to give him zeal for the cause. Never had there been heavier drinking. The habit would ruin the young Republic. There was need, felt Dr. Bartlett, for new lessons in living. Farmers remained convinced rum was medicine for hard labor, and fueled themselves accordingly. There was scarcely a household not cursed with a drunkard. As for notorious tipplers, the town had several — Breed the barber, lying in a stupor on the highway till hauled aside like a log lest he be run over. Once, after he had lain there longer than usual, someone discovered he was dead. As long as a man's legs could be trusted, he was judged temperate. At elections, those chosen to office treated all comers, and on Christmas holidays husky Sheriff Abel Moore, a reasonably sober citizen, gathered his cronies to tour the taverns till the last reveler staggered home. Yet no one thought the worse of the celebrants — they were, in fact, the leaders in the town. At a funeral, rum was as essential as the corpse.

Dr. Bartlett set to work on public opinion. He made the round of the half-dozen general stores that sold rum over the counter, the unrinsed, fly-specked glasses draining into a shallow pan covered with rusty wire grating. If a farmer could buy his gallon or hogshead cheap, with a treat thrown in, he would generally stop for the rest of his trading. Owners of these stores were often deacons, good men and shrewd. Why lure fish with such costly bait? Dr. Bartlett's persuasion gradually won them. But tavernkeepers were tougher. They made more money from the highway than from the town — from the drovers, prodding slobbery herds toward Peterborough, New Hampshire, toward more distant fattening pastures in Vermont and Maine; from passengers on through stages; from thirsty teamsters halting their ponderous baggage wagons drawn by eight to a dozen horses till they lined the way as far as one could see. At night, in his house near the road, Emerson could hear the rumble of the endless procession of wares from England, China, Turkey, and the Indies heading for the inland towns. Often some driver, walking beside his team after a stop at Bigelow's, would trip beneath his iron-shod wheels, his skull cracked like an eggshell. Dr. Bartlett, trying to stop this drinking, got nowhere. Short-spoken and impulsive, he began to arouse more temper than good will. So he took to the pledge as his weapon — over six hundred signatures in Concord alone — and worked for a license law.

Their livelihood threatened, the publicans struck back in the cruelest ways they knew. Well primed, their partisans girdled the apple trees in the doctor's garden. They tossed a bottle of filth through a window and ruined Mrs. Bartlett's parlor carpet. One night someone sneaked into the stable and cut the buggy top to shreds, then docked the tail of the handsome horse that was Dr. Bartlett's single vanity. Next morning, on his visits, the doctor drove his chaise about the town, streamers flying like a crusader's pennants.

Emerson watched this persecution. Rarely angry, he was angry now. On his way past the Middlesex stables he noticed on the door a broadside of doggerel verses, produce of the barroom wits, lampooning Dr. Bartlett. Watched with interest by the loafers, he raised his cane and beat it to pieces.

A caricature of the attack on the poster took its place, but presently someone tore it down.

Dr. Bartlett gained more signers in his crusade.

There was one peculiarity concerning Emerson — his habit of attracting queer visitors — which, after some puzzlement, the town decided to ascribe to an eccentricity in his habitual benevolence. This foible could be readily forgiven, even though some of Mr. Emerson's menagerie was threatening to settle in Concord. What really counted, as Sam Staples, village constable, put it, were Mr. Emerson's qualifications as a first-rate neighbor who always kept his fences in good repair. So when Putt Meriam, who owned the narrow lot opposite Emerson's between the Lexington road and the Cambridge turnpike, tried his hand at artistic blackmail, the town knew what to do. Thinking to force purchase of the triangle at an exorbitant rate, Putt dragged an unsightly shed down the road and set it directly in Emerson's view. But the quiet of that night was fractured by the groaning of timbers and a fearful crash. Putt jumped from bed to pursue the marauders escaping with their hooks, ropes, and ladders. He grabbed one invader, only to have him wriggle out of the green baize jacket he was wearing and run off with his similarly disguised fellow conspirators. Next morning Putt stormed into Reuben Rice's store near the courthouse, sure he had seen a bolt of cloth which would betray the ownership of the garment. Young Reuben's mind was a blank — so far as he knew he had never sold that kind of stuff. There was a store over to Bedford that maybe carried such material.

Emerson followed his quiet round, giving his lectures — the town's Lyceum got them free — writing his books. The presence of Henry Thoreau added a tangy zest to the household. And if one had Henry, one had John, for the Thoreaus were as close as twins. On a quiet evening one could hear John's flute, each soft note, like a subtle communication, coming with perfect distinctness from his mother's house half a mile away.

Emerson, the whole village, were shocked to the heart when suddenly John died. He had cut the index finger of his left hand while stropping a razor — very slightly, only enough to draw a little blood. Replacing the skin, he used a rag for bandage, then forgot the injury. Two days later his whole hand grew painful. Dr. Bartlett dressed the finger, but on his way home John felt strange sensations and acute pain. He went to bed and the doctor was summoned. His jaw, John said, was stiffening. The following night, as his distracted friends watched, he was seized with violent convulsions — Henry, through the psychic bond between them, suffering the same paroxysms. In his delirium, John thought he had written something which he wished his brother to read, something for his friend Robinson's paper. At two in the afternoon he was dead.

Death was in the air that winter. A couple of weeks later, Waldo, whose five-and-a half years had been seldom troubled with sickness, was down with fever. His father was holding his hand by the bedside. But the boy fled like a dream. Later, sitting mute before his journal, Emerson groped for words to encompass his loss. Death's seizure of youth was always incredible; now death had struck with a tenfold pang.

What is done and suffered in a house gives domestic life its significance. Where there had been two there was one child now, but others presently followed. Ellen Tucker, a baby when Waldo died; then, later, Edith and Edward.

Emerson never talked to children, but with them. They were as old as he. His neighbors could see him sitting by his doorstep, Edith perched on his knee, Edward galloping about the lawn on a stick with a hobby horse's head. If any child cried or was restless at table, Emerson would send the fretful member out to see if the garden gate were closed or to look at the sky and report on the clouds. A little perplexed, but with tears forgotten, the messenger would climb back into his high chair. All neighborhood children were welcome when Emerson took his own for a walk. After a glance at the sunbeam in his face they never felt bashful.

And right after Waldo's death, there was the saving distraction of work. On top of his speaking and writing, Emerson was taking over the active editorship of the *Dial*.

Since its inception two summers before, Margaret Fuller had been managing this organ of the New England transcendentalists. Emerson had known Margaret for six years now, and was getting used to her. His first impression, when she had come on a three weeks' visit right after his marriage, had been anything but reassuring. An extraordinary person, no doubt, with perhaps the most entertaining conversation in America — satiric, full of drollery, phenomenally intelligent. But Emerson, sitting before this robust, tall, very plain, very emphatic young woman, with her mass of reddish brown hair, her colorless complexion, her nasal voice, struggled against an emphatic revulsion. Margaret possessed such disconcerting mannerisms — a nervous, rapid blinking which prevented one's discovering her really fine gray eyes; a way of drawing back her lips to expose her teeth as she talked. She showed an annoying disregard for Lidian as wife and hostess. And after she left came an avalanche of letters: "Let no cold breath paralyze my hope that there will be a noble and profound understanding between us." Then, sensing his response, she added, "You need not be terrified at this prophecy nor look about for the keys of your cell."

There was nothing possible except surrender.

Though Emerson accepted Margaret, many in Concord refused to. One dark, stormy night when she was boarding in the village she fell victim to a mishap. A messenger hurried to summon the doctor.

"Who's there?" demanded Dr. Bartlett from his bedroom window.

"Doctor, how much camphor can anybody take by mistake without its killing them?"

"Who's taken it?"

"Margaret Fuller."

"A peck!" roared the doctor, going back to bed.

The *Dial*, though its first issue — Emerson admitted — contained little of consequence, at least was better in aspiration than anything of the sort thus far seen in New England. Yet almost every paper and magazine attacked it, as though transcendentalism were an infamy. Coming to the defense of the movement, Emerson essayed some definition — Mankind has ever divided into sects: the materialists thinking from the data of the senses; the idealists, or transcendentalists perceiving that the senses are not final. The idealist does not deny the sensuous fact, but he will not take the fact alone. He insists on the reality beyond appearance. He believes in ecstasy and inspiration. Society should behold this class with what charity it can. Possibly some benefit may yet accrue from them to the state. Amidst the downward tendency and proneness of things, with every voice raised for a subscription of stock, for an improvement in dress or in dentistry, for a political party or the division of an estate, will you not tolerate one or two solitary voices, speaking for thoughts and principles not marketable or perishable?

The *Dial*, poor little thing, was born to misfortune. At the outset its publishers failed, its short list of subscribers grew shorter. Its views appeared contradictory as the winds and its erratic course, with Margaret at the helm, was steered without a compass. Miss Fuller, very generous of her time, giving her services free, at last would pilot it no longer. Its life or death was up to Emerson. He had scant adroitness, he admitted, in turning away work likely to be little more than a vexation. He had not the heart to kill the *Dial*.

When this hampering literary stepchild became overly troublesome, there were always the pines to retreat to. In January the snow built sudden cathedrals with his trees; in May his grove sheltered the first rhodora. At eight dollars and ten cents the acre, he had bought his field on the northern shore of Walden, then the stand of pine beside it, later, the larger tract on the farther side. Meanwhile his house lot, with vegetable garden, orchard, and pasture, grew to a farm of nine acres. West of his study window, the young firs and pines — good friends had given them — were thriving, full of orioles, cedarbirds, and goldfinches.

But Emerson cherished larger plans for growth, and did his quiet best to cultivate the crop. He would gather in the village a community of thinkers. With such inhabitants, he told Elizabeth Hoar, Concord would add to its earlier honors. He intended to ask Henry James why he should go to Europe when America had such claims and Concord offered so good a neighborhood. Thomas Carlyle might be prevailed on to cross the ocean and settle. If people grew interested, Emerson knew what houses were for sale or rent; what rates were fair.

With Thoreau's help, he tried without success to find a house for Margaret Fuller's modest purse. They fared better with her sister Ellen, recently married to the Reverend William Channing's nephew Ellery. Ellen was as beautiful as her sister was homely; her husband, a poet, capricious and the victim of his moods — wonderful company when he sought it but the worst when it forced itself on him, capable of incredible selfishness and unexpected generosity; as naturally whimsical, said Thoreau, as a cow is brindled; a man who wanted things but would never pay the price. When Channing decided a trip to Europe would help his poetry, it was Emerson who raised the cash. His verse was in the sublimo-slipshod style, as Henry put it, but Emerson never ceased to be his backer. Perhaps he got his reward through walks with Channing. No one in Concord, save Henry, had a keener eye.

Channing had come to Concord because Emerson lived there. For fifty-five dollars a year he took the small red cottage a short distance down the Concord turnpike from his friend's house, and here Ellen set up an infant school — the oldest Emerson girl attending — while Ellery cultivated his garden if not his verse. His methods were something of a mystery to the farmboys. In his row of corn stood a tremendous weed which he carefully avoided uprooting. It had, he insisted, an equal right to live.

A year before the arrival of the Channings, another honeymooning couple had come to Concord. Nathaniel Hawthorne was the bridegroom; his bride, Sophia Peabody from Boston. Emerson had known him, very slightly, for several years. He had published several short stories, in the *New England Magazine*, that won notice, though Emerson was somewhat puzzled by these praises. Morbid romances, he saw little value in them though he liked the man. Since they were not good for anything, this reputation as a writer, he decided, was all the better — it was a tribute to the author's character. He must live in Concord; he was the kind of person wanted.

"I saw Mr. Emerson at the Atheneum yesterday," Nathaniel wrote Sophia, in May, "and he tells me that our garden, and so forth, make progress. Would that we were there!" By July they were in the manse, vacant since Dr. Ripley's death. With the passing years the exterior had faded to a weather-beaten gray. The musty rooms had never been repainted. The paneling, the plaster walls, the huge hewn crossbeams, had turned a dismal brown. The rooms were sparsely furnished with such pieces as Dr. Ripley's heirs decided not to take away — high-backed, short-legged, rheumatic chairs, small old tables, four-poster beds. Now, inside, all was bright and new again, ready for Sophia's gifts as homemaker. Sophia painted on the headboard of their maple bedstead a copy of Guido's Aurora with its flying horses, its graceful youths and maidens. For his study, Hawthorne took the small back chamber where Emerson had written *Nature*. From the single window toward the back, Hawthorne could see the tumbled western abutment of the old bridge and the gleaming new monument near it. Someday, perhaps, in a story of that battle, he would show how conscience haunted slayers of their fellow men.

In its gathered antiquity — Hawthorne reminded Sophia — this house had sheltered other newly wedded couples. Here children had been born; people grown old and died. In these dark closets the ghosts of former inmates must be hiding. Snug in bed beside her husband, Sophia heard a sound in the room such as paper would make when crumpled in hand — a sermon, perhaps, that had turned out a failure. Yet surely these were benign spirits.

Summer at the manse moved into winter, and February thaws marked spring's return. Each day Hawthorne trudged through the snow to the post office without speaking to a single soul. For exercise, he liked to skate. Sophia, in her wadded dress, muff, and tippet, admiringly watched him, wrapped in his cloak, gliding over the river, in long, sweeping curves, now shooting away, now darting back to her.

Hawthorne's business was writing, and he followed it with persistence. Now that he had begun in earnest, wearing down-at-the-heel slippers and the gorgeous purple-and-gold dressing gown she had made him, Sophia's leisure began, for she could not see him till dinner. So she busied herself about the house or called on Mrs. Prescott, her neighbor, who was perpetually doing favors for which she refused to be paid. She had papered Sophia's kitchen with her own hands. When the Hawthornes went away for a visit, George, Mrs. Prescott's friendly, handsome thirteen-year-old son, fed their dog Leo so sumptuously that he grew fat as a mealsack.

At the entrance to the manse, the gate, fallen long since from its rusty hinges, had never been rehung. But casual callers did not enter — only a limited few came in: Elizabeth Hoar, emerging briefly from the self-effacing life she led in the vibrant circle of her strong-minded family. Henry Thoreau, invited to dinner as reward for help with the garden. Ugly as sin, thought Hawthorne, botanizing him as he botanized all human beings, long-nosed, queer-mouthed, uncouth yet with courteous manners. One of the few persons with whom he could speak without restraint or embarrassment. To talk with Thoreau was like hearing the wind in a forest tree. Yet along with all this wild freedom, mixed with a certain iron-pokerishness of opinion, was a high and classic cultivation.

For seven dollars Thoreau had sold him a skiff he had used once on a river trip. The boat was associated, it seemed, with a brother who had died. Henry could no longer bear to use it.

Then there was Ellery Channing, one of those queer and clever young men whom Mr. Emerson was continually picking up by way of genius. Once Channing, as a special favor, took Hawthorne to Thoreau's favorite pool in Gowing's swamp. But Hawthorne, glancing around with great distaste, exclaimed, "Let's get out of this dreadful hole!"

And there was Emerson. Somehow Mr. Emerson, thought Sophia, represented the tutelary spirit of their paradise and came as naturally and with as little interruption as a sunset. Hawthorne had read *Nature* with enjoyment, and the essays. Nevertheless, he was disposed to question the expediency of stating truth in disembodied form — philosophy should be made incarnate through characters in a story.

Somehow Emerson got Hawthorne to come to a tea. One could never tell what strange hobgoblins of mortal flesh one might meet at Emerson's, but Hawthorne decided to risk it. They came, he knew, attracted by the powerful magnetism of an original thinker. Young visionaries sought a clue for guidance from their self-evolved bewilderment; old reformers knocked to invite Emerson's free spirit into their own thraldom. Hawthorne marveled at Emerson; so patient, so without pretension, meeting each caller as if he expected to receive more than he gave. There had been a time, he admitted, when he could gladly have sought the master word from this prophet. But now, being happy, there was no need. At the Emerson party, he sat in the shadow at the edge of the circle round the fireplace. After a while, he rose and stood quietly by the window, with his hands folded behind him, watching the dead winter landscape. No one bothered him. It was as if all knew his silence was to be respected. But one young visitor found his gaze drawn irresistibly toward the broad-shouldered, silent figure in the semidarkness. He had noticed the stranger before, with his turbulent black hair, his wide high forehead — so broad there was a shadow behind each temple. Just then he caught one glance from those dark brows, the eyes searching and unforgettable. The party was breaking up; the stranger the first to go. Emerson, who noticed everything, came over to the puzzled youngster. That was Nathaniel Hawthorne, he explained, riding his horses of the night.

Ezra Ripley's nephew Samuel, who owned the manse, was anxious to return. Ending their idyl of four summers, the Hawthornes, with Una, their little daughter, would go to Salem, where Nathaniel, while he wrote, could at least gain a living as customs collector of the port.

It would be good to have the Ripleys in town. Yet Emerson hated to see the Hawthornes go. Strange that his secretive friend's final act in Concord should be to help recover a drowned girl, a suicide, from the river. He was ever the stern but sympathetic friend of unfortunates and sinners. It was like one of his somber stories.

Amos Bronson Alcott had been name-giver of the *Dial*, which Emerson was still struggling to keep going. He had first heard of Alcott, and his school in Boston, through a mutual friend. The Temple School, Alcott called it — not just because it occupied a handsome room in the Masons' building on Tremont Street, but because that name symbolized the spirit he strove for. A Socratic method of inquiry was the basis of his teaching, to bring out those rational ethical ideas he believed innate in every child. He strove to show that study in itself is a pleasant thing.

Emerson read with approval Alcott's record of his school, edited by his assistant, Elizabeth Peabody. His invitation brought Alcott out to Concord. Greeting his guest at the gate, Emerson saw a spare, tall man with long narrow head and hair a golden brown, almost the color of cornsilk. Alcott's complexion was amazing — like a child's, the skin clear, the blood close to the surface at the cheeks. His high forehead set off features of generous proportions — a massive Roman nose, slumberous, innocent eyes under bushy eyebrows sweeping downward and outward like little horns, mouth wide, the lips not so thin as to suggest the Puritan yet thin enough to hint the ascetic. Alcott's tongue seemed to have a little trouble with his host's name, getting no closer than "Mr. Emison" — but the two men's minds met intimately.

After that, there were many visits. Emerson soon learned how uncompromising Alcott could be — refusing to bend even to the severest hurricanes of public opinion.

The Temple School, patronized by Boston's Brahmins (who really knew little of what was going on and noticed merely that the minds and bodies of their children prospered) flourished till Alcott's second and third reports — his *Conversations with Children on the Gospels* — appeared without benefit of Miss Peabody's judicious editing. What was this? How dared Alcott trifle with innocent children by prompting them to thoughts of their own about religion? Worse, what horrid blasphemy to speak, even in symbols, about the mysteries of birth! The Boston *Courier*, the *Daily Advertiser*, raised righteous shrieks, though Emerson pled with the editors to let the book be read. Attendance at the school dropped by a third. The handsome furniture, the well-stocked library, were sold to meet Alcott's debts. "I hate to have all the little dogs barking at you," wrote Emerson, "for you have something better to do than attend to them." Why not bring Alcott to Concord? True, Emerson had found Alcott at times rather taxing. Yet for his large ideas and virtues, Emerson believed Alcott deserved maintenance, even at public cost.

For two more years, Alcott struggled to save his school. But when principle compelled him to admit a colored girl, most of the parents who had remained half-heartedly loyal withdrew their children, and the Temple fell.

Why not accept the invitation to Concord? Of all his contemporaries, Emerson knew him best; was his truest friend.

A house was found for the Alcotts at fifty dollars a year (Emerson, it was whispered, paid the rent) — the tenant building across South Bridge on the farm which Joseph Hosmer of the Revolution had owned. Its sloping roof sheltered two stories in the rear and one in front. "Dove Cottage," the Alcotts called it.

They moved on April Town Meeting Day, with Concord too busy to notice. But when the town caught on that Mr. Emerson, with one of his strange whims, had added another specimen, Concord's inhabitants of the solid, rock-bound type, fearful of the good name of their village, raised their eyebrows in disapproval. Was not this the Boston schoolmaster who could not be trusted with a school? He looked harmless enough, working in the fields by his cottage, or hiring himself out for day labor. Yet it was safer to be watchful. But motherly, cheerful Mrs. Alcott, in her neat, threadbare gray cloak and unfashionable bonnet, with her brood of little girls — a fourth born that summer — soon won their good will. She was one of those women with a "Can I help you?" look, yet surely it was she who needed help. Both from principle and lack of cash, no meat, no cheese or butter for that matter, were used in Dove Cottage. The Alcotts were thinking of giving up milk till a caller persuaded them not to, for the baby's sake. Two meals a day were all they ate, so that the children could carry what was left to a widow up the road who had just lost a drunken husband and had four children to support. Alcott sawed up her wood for her.

Though this current experiment in the art of living, as Mrs. Alcott half-jokingly referred to it — manual labor to support thought — was proving reasonably successful, Alcott himself was getting restless. It fretted him not to be more in the midst of the active struggle to make a better world. In the British Isles, a group had founded a school near Richmond. They called it "Alcott House" in his honor. These Englishmen were showing a faith in his theories denied by his own countrymen. Perhaps in England he would find a base for his visions.

Quietly Emerson set to work raising money for the trip. When the fund he got was not enough, he paid for the passage, though he could ill afford to.

Alcott found little in materialistic England to encourage him, but at the school which bore his name he met a handful of enthusiasts who shared his philanthropic idealism. These good and great men he would bring to Concord — together they could work for a newer world.

Emerson heard these tidings with dismay. He scribbled a hasty note of warning, bidding Alcott show it to these Englishmen. They might safely trust Alcott's theories, said the letter, but must put no trust whatever in his statements of practical fact.

Presently the little troupe reached Concord: Charles Lane and his nine-year-old son William — the father dry and humorless as a thistle seed and equally as prickly; young Harry Wright, a nebulous mystic who had given up the headship at Alcott House to found Utopia in America.

Had they been shown the letter? Emerson demanded. They had, so his conscience was clear.

But not his time. Almost at once the Englishmen became anathema in the village. So Emerson felt he owed them his politeness. The conversations he was being forced to listen to, he admitted, served mainly to invade and injure him. In his private exasperation, he vented his spleen in his diary. Could these men not die? Or succeed? Or help themselves? Here was the dear, grand Alcott himself solemnly declaring: "You dig in my field for a day, . . . and I give you a dollar, but that does not make it a business transaction." Such mystical subterfuge made Emerson sick. As long as money is the handiest measure for material values, why disown the term?

All winter the Englishmen cluttered the Dove Cot, laying plans for a marvelous enterprise. When wind of the scheme broke loose in Concord, it raised a whirlblast of derisive laughter. No cow on this model farm — the milk belonged to the calf. No stable manure, lest nature be polluted. No hog or horse or pig or poultry, since animals must be neither enslaved nor robbed nor killed. All labor by hand, with hoe and spade and mattock. Not even the worms in the apple trees need dread disturbance, since they hold their place by natural right.

For two thousand dollars, all his savings, Lane bought a farm of one hundred acres on a northern slope, with sour soil, near the village of Harvard. Thursday, June the first — a miserable cold morning, with wind, rain and even hail — was the day of departure. The small horse the philosophers were willing to enslave for the purpose strained in the shafts of the heavy wagon. Serene as ever, Alcott was driving. Beside him sat little William Lane, clutching to his thin chest a plaster bust of Socrates. On the motley pile of goods behind rode Mrs. Alcott with her baby in her lap. There was a satiric set to her mouth, though her look was determined. She loved her husband, and his purposes were hers, though she might favor different methods. Two other children, their hands full of girlish treasures, sat under an old shawl. In front, with Wright, stalked Lane in his long blue coat, his sharp features spearing the weather. Beside him the limber-legged, tomboy member of the Alcott family, Louisa, trudged through the mud as though she liked it.

By winter, all but the half-starved Alcotts and zealous Charles Lane had deserted. By spring, Fruitlands, with its canker-bitten apple trees, had belied its name. By autumn the Alcotts were back in Concord.

Through great good fortune, at this juncture, a small legacy, left Mrs. Alcott by her father, with a little help from the usual quarter, enabled the family to buy the Cogswell place, an ancient, broken-down, dirty box of a house with a gambrel roof, located under the ridge three hundred yards east of the Emersons. Mrs. Alcott scrubbed and painted. Alcott and the carpenters put a gabled dormer window over the entrance and added wings with broad piazzas. He tidied up the gravel-strewn, hog-rooted soil and planted trees and flowering bushes. Even the crustier villagers were amazed at the transformation. Though many of the rough farmers and hard-headed merchants were slow to modify their open contempt for this fanatic, the kinder folk were sorry for him and far sorrier for Mrs. Alcott. Despite their poverty — Mr. Alcott, his wife explained, could not bring himself to work for gain but only to further his enterprises — their charity to persons poorer than themselves continued. They welcomed to their house all the children of the village. Sunday evenings, each guest was handed a little basket, covered with a red and white checked napkin. Best not expect too much — a cracker and an apple only — but there were always good times after supper. Games; or

Alcott would read from *Pilgrim's Progress*. The Alcott girls were wonderful at plays. With their mother's rag bags on their backs for burdens, they would toil from the City of Destruction in the cellar up to the housetop, where stood the Celestial City. So alluring was the sound of this City that the youngest Hosmer determined in good earnest to find it. Not till several hours later did his distracted mother recover the child, trudging along the Lexington road, an improvised pack on his shoulders.

By the brook at the foot of the field across the road Alcott planted willows and made a bathing place for his four little women. The oldest Alcott girl, Anna, was fourteen now, and threatening to be pretty, with large blue eyes, golden brown hair, and the serenity of her father. A year younger, tomboy Louisa was the liveliest, her chestnut mane flying behind her, for she ran more readily than she walked. Though he liked them all, Louisa was Emerson's favorite and he lent her books or let her sit in his study to read them. "Little Tranquility" was her father's name for Elizabeth, the ten-year-old — shy, and a dweller in a world of dreams. May, the Concord-born child, at five was charming, with a good deal of temperament, and the enslaver of her family. Mrs. Alcott's deft fingers fitted over for the girls cast-off clothing given by friends, and Alcott supervised their lessons. Henry Thoreau, too, helped with the teaching and became the children's closest grown-up friend, dropping in from Emerson's.

Henry had brought to the Emerson household almost everything hoped for, and had drawn his interest in the bargain. He had also been a help in ways not foreseen at the outset. While Emerson was away lecturing, he edited the *Dial*, thus helping keep the magazine alive, though at last it died in the fourth year of its existence. That same winter, with Emerson's warm approval, he had arranged the season's schedule for the Lyceum. By vote of the citizens, the young curator received one hundred and nine dollars and twenty cents — a bit short of the customary hundred and a quarter. With that he lined up twenty-five lectures. For a ten-dollar fee the historian George Bancroft came, and several other well-known men spoke for a like amount, the highest Henry could pay. Some came for eight, Theodore Parker for three — not enough to meet his expenses — while Horace Greeley, Wendell Phillips, Emerson, and the curator himself, spoke gratis. Henry closed his Lyceum year with the nine dollars and twenty cents left, to remind the town of its frugality.

He had bought them their hundred dollars' worth. How much more could be done with one thousand! What barbarians we are — thought Henry. Here was the town about to spend a fortune for a brand-new courthouse, not from need but because it feared Lowell would win away the remaining sessions. How little Concord did for its own culture! A half-starved Lyceum, the puny beginnings of a public library, a passable system of common schools, Henry admitted, but no uncommon school for grown-ups. Having reached a certain age, why should the inhabitants shed education and growth like a coat? New England could hire all the wise men in the world to teach her, if she wanted to. The town was rich enough, could spend money enough for such things as farmers and traders value. Why should not every American village be a university; enrich its life as a patron of the arts and learning? Why not omit an extra bridge over the river, go round a little, and throw one arch at least over the darker gulf of ignorance? There were other civic problems, Henry argued. Since collective action for common good accords with the spirit of American institutions, ought not each town have a park, or rather, a primitive forest, as common possession forever, for instruction and recreation? And roads should be of ample width, with groves for the use of travelers. Especially at springs there should be broad recesses where the citizen can rest or camp. The view, the sky above it, is by right the private property of none and should belong to mankind inalienably.

Emerson, when he listened to these extravagances, never laughed as some did in the village. Perhaps they might cease to be mere notions. Yet he was troubled about Henry. Henry was twenty-seven, still without any means for support which could give him fullest life and self-expression. With all his practical ability and energy, here he was, a loiterer in Concord, with apparently no greater ambition than to be captain of a huckleberry party.

In the moments he felt thus, Emerson was leaving out of account the book on the Concord and Merrimack Rivers which Thoreau was writing. Pastoral as Izaak Walton, spicy as flagroot, rich through vital years of study and thinking, he decided, when Henry read him some chapters.

Isaak Hecker, late of Brook Farm, Protestant turned Catholic, and a recent boarder with Henry's mother, had a proposal. Let us work our passage across the Atlantic, he suggested, and so through England, France, Germany, and Italy, earning our way as we go.

Thoreau felt strongly tempted. Yet might not these farthest Indies be reached by other modes of travel? Isaak offered Roncesvalles, Cape Finesterre, Rome, Athens. But might Roncesvalles not be found in Concord, and with finer luster? Was it so great a compliment to propose this enterprise as though he had nothing to do, with his life thus far a failure? He was not without destination at this stage of his voyage.

He would build himself a hut in Emerson's pines. He would seek the woods in order to live deliberately, to learn what life teaches. He would live so sturdily and Spartanlike as to put to rout all that was not essential. In proportion as one simplifies existence, solitude is no longer solitude, or poverty poverty. If one builds castles in the air, the work will not be lost — that is where they should be. Now put foundations under them. He had traveled a good deal in Concord. Everywhere, in shops and offices and fields, the inhabitants were doing penance in a thousand ways. Young men, his fellow townsmen, inherited farms, then found their possessions easier to come by than to get rid of. Few fathomed their trouble, though hard-working Edmund Hosmer, his friend and Emerson's, was frank to admit unnecessary labor went into care of the stock, till many a farmer became a horse's horse and a pig's pig. Even in this comparatively free country, most men, through mere mistake, become so occupied with worldly goods, factitious cares, and superfluously coarse labors, that they cannot pick life's finer fruits.

On a late March day Thoreau borrowed Emerson's ax and headed for Walden. From the hillside where he worked he could see the pond, the ice not out yet though here and there black water gleamed. He was cutting arrowy young pines for timbers. On his way homewards he could hear larks and peewees, ready to begin another year. He returned the ax sharper than he had received it.

For boards he would have to look no further than the dirt-floored shanties of the Irish, arriving in great droves from the mother country, driven from home by recent famine and age-old oppression, only to be plunged into further precarious struggle — the Irish who were building America's railroads at starvation maximum wages of sixty cents for a sixteen-hour day. Near the fill and cut by Walden, Thoreau had watched them, with indignant compassion, living miserably in hovels no better than sties, with an open door all winter for light and little or no wood for heating, since they lacked the time to gather it and would be chased from the farmer's woods if they tried.

The roadbed from Charlestown to Concord had been recently finished. Most of the pick-and-shovel men had already shifted westward where the tracks, like giant centipedes, were creeping towards Fitchburg. Only a few squatters remained, destined to become a part of Concord. From one of these, Jim Collins, ready for further wanderings if he could raise a little cash, Thoreau bought what planks he needed. Elsewhere he got old bricks, old shingles, two secondhand windows, two casks of lime, some nails, some screws and hinges.

By July he was ready for the raising. Early on the morning of Independence Day his helpers gathered. They came not from any necessity — Henry could have finished the job himself — but for the fun of it. First Edmund Hosmer shouldering his ax, with his three elder sons behind him, trudging down the turnpike toward Emerson's, picking up Bronson Alcott and Ellery Channing on the way. Two young recent Brook Farmers and Emerson himself joined them, and they set off across the fields and through the woods to the site — a small, level, open space on the side of the hill, in front the one little cove on the northern shore, with a sandspit called the Devil's Bar at the entrance.

An average house in Concord cost eight hundred dollars. Henry had his for twenty-eight, twelve cents, and a farthing; ten feet wide by fifteen long, with garret, root cellar, and closet, a large window on either side, a door at the end, and space for a fireplace opposite.

In the morning, Walden threw off its nightly cloak of mist. Evenings, he might sit in his boat, the perch, as if charmed by his flute, hovering where air and water blended and the moon traveled over the invisible surface. Yes, Concord nights could be stranger than Arabian.

Little time for reading that first summer. Henry shingled and plastered his house and hoed beans in the near-by field. There were moments which he could not sacrifice to any work, whether of head or hands. Yet by autumn the hearth and chimney were done, the bean patch harvested.

After an evening at the Lyceum or in some bright parlor of the village, he would launch toward his snug harbor with a bag of Indian meal on his shoulder. Especially if the night were dark or stormy it was pleasant knowing all would be secure within, and himself with a merry crew of thoughts under the hatches.

Sometimes, when it was raining and he knew there could be no farming, he would pass the time of day with the Hosmers. He might read to the children from the *Canterbury Tales*, stopping to think about a line. "You can sometimes catch the meaning better by listening," he would say, then continue, his voice in its skillful rhythm making strange music.

At the cabin he put the final touches on the rivers book and recorded his experiences of living. He earned readily the few dollars needed to feed him.

Henry had three chairs; one for solitude, one for a companion, one for a crowd. His friends always found him good company. If this was a first visit, their glance would take in the room: the narrow hard bed with its crude caning, the three-legged table, the desk, the tiny looking glass, the washbowl, jug for oil, the japanned lamp. Henry's spyglass for field trips; his kettle and skillet.

Sometimes he received as many as thirty people — but the second chair was best. Ellery Channing often used it. Rain, sleet or snow never deterred him. His pixylike humor accorded with Henry's till the cabin rang with boisterous laughter that fractured for the moment the murmur of sober talk. With utmost approval Channing studied what he saw: Henry was as close to his aim as the bark on a tree. This hut was a durable garment, an overcoat, convenient for shelter and meditation, belonging to nature as much as to man. Henry's life was of one fabric, cut to suit him. Not one man in a million lost so few hours. He had flung out of the window his only ornament — a paperweight — because it needed dusting.

Alcott came oftenest in winter, when his gardening was at a standstill. There was one memorable night when he trudged through snow, through darkness, till he saw Henry's lamp. Before becoming one of the last of the philosophers, Henry knew, Alcott had been a pedlar. He was a pedlar still, offering the thoughts which man to his disgrace would not receive. Disregarded now, his day would come — a friend of human kind, himself the sanest man with the fewest crotchets.

Other visitors, too — the owner of the grove, visiting his wood Gods; children berry-picking; fishermen and hunters.

"Have you see my hound?" asked the stranger, looking at the man in the rough gray-green-brown Vermont homespun, pants tucked into hobnail boots; "Why, what do you do here?"

"I live here. No, I haven't."

"Haven't you heard one in the woods anywhere?"

"Oh yes, I heard one this evening, but he was some way off."
All men are seekers. Henry sat at his homemade desk, and wrote:

I long ago lost a hound, a bay horse, and a turtle-dove, and
am still on their trail. Many are the travellers I have spoke concerning them, describing their tracks and what calls they
answered to. I have met one or two who had heard the hound,
and the tramp of the horse, and even seen the dove disappear
behind a cloud, and they seemed as anxious to recover them
as if they had lost them themselves.

The Alcott girls loved to visit; and the boys from the village.
Henry knew how to make pipes of every sort — from the leafstalk
of a pumpkin, from water reeds, from golden willow shoots when
the rising sap loosens the bark. Joe, Edmund Hosmer's youngest
child, came all alone to spend the day soon after the cabin was up and
before the chimney was finished. At his primitive fireplace, a hole
lined with stones, Henry cooked their dinner: roasted horn pout,
roasted corn, beans, bread made from dough on a thin stone for
baking. Thoreau was disappointed that one of his companions, a
wood mouse, failed to appear. It had first come one evening, he
said. Down the wall against which his shoulder was leaning it had
come, then across his sleeve to eat the cheese in his hand. He had
tried flute music on it. From its hiding place the mouse would listen,
but disappear when he tried another tune. This story did not seem
in the least strange to Joseph. Had he not seen chickadees light on
his friend's arm, watched him lift fishes in his hands from the lake,
seen him stroke a woodchuck?

Early one summer Sunday, five railroad construction engineers
came to his cabin. "I like your notions," remarked one of them,
younger than the rest, and handsome, "I think I shall live so myself."
He had traveled, he said, among the Indians near Appalachicola.
"I like your kind of life, only I should want a wilder country, where
there's more game."

Unlike some in the village, Thoreau held no grudge against the
railroad. The fill and cut southwest of the pond, a hundred rods
from his cabin, served as a beeline to town, and the men on the
freights waved to him as an old acquaintance. It interested him to
watch men shuttle their possessions — southwards, pine from the
hills, beef cattle, bleating calves and sheep from Peterborough and

the Green Mountains; northward, bailed rags for paper, salt fish, molasses, rum and brandy, shop goods for the inland traders.

Not curiosity, such as Henry's, but rage filled the hard-bitten teamsters, who for years had been driving their baggage wagons up the inland route, with that comforting stop at Concord's taverns. To them the trains were hell in harness. And the taverns, too, and the stagecoach lines, were done for. Teamster and taverner had tried in vain to stave off the inevitable, with "No monopoly!" scrawled on the carts, and "Free trade and teamsters' rights!" painted on the guide boards. Railroads were needed, railroads were the solution, argued Beacon Street bankers as the huge open maw of metropolitan New York threatened starvation for commercial Massachusetts. Without railroads, how can we get cotton for our mills? — argued Lowell's manufacturers. The Damons at West Concord could not readily ship their flannels, or the bucket factory dispose of its oaken pails. Alvah Crocker, who ran a paper mill at Fitchburg, was paying eight cents a pound for transportation where his rivals paid three. So the iron roads were run. First came the Boston and Worcester. Then Lowell got the jump on Fitchburg and Concord, but the Fitchburg route soon followed.

The company organized at Concord. By connections with Vermont, New Hampshire, and northern New York, would not this road become a trunk line to the West? All Canada would be tapped past Lake Champlain.

By December of 1843 the rails reached Waltham; by spring of the following year they were nearing Concord. Impelled by the same urge as his fellow citizens, Ralph Waldo Emerson went to inspect the depot that was building. Like a shrewd Yankee, he had purchased stock with his small capital. Already it had gone up ten per cent. The contracts for the entire line, heard investors, had been let for thirty per cent under estimated cost. And was not the town's own David Loring, lead-pipe manufacturer, a director?

On the seventeenth of June came the gala opening — four trains up and four trains down, at fifty cents for the ride, one third less than the fare by stage. About an hour's journey to the terminal at Warren's Bridge, Charlestown, where one could catch an omnibus for Boston. Concord had once been a hundred miles from the city — four hours in one direction (unless one caught the mail stage from Leominster or Keene) by crusty Deacon Brown's accommodation coach. Now Boston was part of the neighborhood. For this Emerson, mindful of his lecture schedules, was thankful. Most of his fellow citizens, he noted, were taking to this epoch-making contrivance as if it were the cradle they were born in. The departures and arrivals of the cars marked the cycles of the village day. Reuben Rice, erstwhile storekeeper, now station agent, was thinking of building Western railroads as a profession. Isaac Day, former stagecoach driver, had been wise enough to climb aboard the train and gather tickets as conductor.

But the livestock were not so readily won over. Cows and horses ran in terror as the engine snorted by with its shower of sparks. John Wheeler and his son, with a load of lumber, were nearly killed when their nag bolted and smashed the wagon on a pile of rocks.

Yes, the railroad had pulled Boston to Concord. But some fearful ones murmured lest it go the other way, lest the town be dragged to the city. Certain shopkeepers grew especially dubious. How much trade were old customers shifting to Boston? Ambitious farmers, however, soon discovered their advantage. After haggling over rates, they got a milk car to the city, and tripled their herds. The corn-and-pumpkin farming of many generations was giving way to fine fruits and special crops for the city. The rails brought out better agricultural implements: new horse-drawn rakes and kickers, Hussey and McCormick reapers, threshing machines and cultivators. Yet more than ever the farmer's son found the city or the West a temptation — and lilacs grew tall beside tumbled foundations. As farmers left, men of affairs discovered it was pleasant to do business in Boston but live in the country. Would these newcomers, with associations elsewhere, cleave to Concord?

Emerson listened to the whistle of the locomotive in his woods. The voice of the nineteenth century — he thought — interrogative, prophetic. How is real estate, it demands, here in the swamp and wilderness? Down with that forest on the side of the hill! I want ten thousand chestnut sleepers, a hundred thousand feet of boards. I will sprinkle yonder pasture with white houses like a snowbank in March. Along with their depredations, the rails were working their magic — uniting the advantages of town and country life. And for the nation, had they not come at the opportune moment? Did not the vigor of the enormous West need them? *The railroad is one arrow in our quiver, a sort of yardstick and surveyor's line, linking this continent, state on state, territory on territory, to the waves of the Pacific sea.*

* * *

As the first half of the century was thus ending, Emerson's reputation abroad, thanks to Carlyle and others, had grown. Great Britain wanted to hear him. He might be gone for a year. Would Henry come again to play older son to the household?

After twenty-six months at Walden, Thoreau closed the door of his hut.

CHAPTER XIII

A Shift in the Political Weather

TO the common man in Concord and elsewhere, the slavery issue, till at last it could be ignored no longer, had long been a scarcely discernible shift in the weather. In 1844, lean, grizzled Democrat James K. Polk of Tennessee, who had favored admission of slaveholding Texas, and, as a determined expansionist, was to add to the nation half a million square miles, beat Henry Clay of the Whigs, who straddled the issue. Four years later, with Western territories — slave and free — competing to enter the union, both old parties, cautiously dodging the vital question, lost votes to the Free-Soilers, made up of divergent groups whose only unity was refusal to compromise on the spread of slavery. In Massachusetts the new party's strength came mostly from the Whigs — "Conscience Whigs" they named themselves, pointing a finger at their fellow members who favored appeasing the South: "Cotton Whigs" they called them, dependent on the plantations for cheap raw cotton. The Massachusetts Cotton Whigs backed Zachary Taylor, Louisiana slaveholder, their party's regular nominee, forming an open entente of the lords of the loom and lash. Since President Polk had refused renomination, and Lewis Cass, a noisy nobody from Michigan, was being run in his place, the time seemed ripe to throw the Democrats out. Anecdotal and pithy, speaking in a style new to that section of the country, a lanky young congressman from Illinois — "Honorable Abram Lincoln," some of the Eastern papers called him, but had it partly wrong — pled in Massachusetts for the unity of the Whigs. But the Bay State leaders, big with their importance and their quarrel, paid him little attention.

Men of Concord had played a part in the birth of the Free-Soil Party. When the news of Taylor's nomination came, a call to bolt the ticket summoned the Conscience Whigs of Massachusetts to

Worcester. Its author was Ebenezer Rockwood Hoar, Sam's oldest son, and himself a rising lawyer. Samuel Hoar chairmanned the meeting, a gathering so large no hall would hold it. In the open square, handsome Charles Sumner, junior senator and friend of Emerson, addressed the crowd; so did Charles Francis Adams and other leaders. A motion passed to hold a national convention. But when all Free-Soil delegates met in Buffalo that August, Martin Van Buren, vote-getter and erstwhile Democrat, was named Free-Soil standard-bearer, much against the wishes of the Massachusetts contingent.

The Free-Soilers weakened both old parties, but were not yet strong enough to win.

The most dismal election, remarked Emerson, ever known to the country: three great parties voting for three candidates whom they disliked, with Taylor foisted on the nation as President.

To right-thinking men the next few years showed little improvement, certainly not in Massachusetts. Over night a fungus growth had arisen, the Know-Nothing Party, anti-Catholic, anti-Irish. It grew strong enough even to capture the governor's office, so apprehensive had the native born become, watching the sudden horde invading the country. Ever since the Commonwealth's founding, Massachusetts had dreaded the Pope, but new fears were raising new brutalities. Less than twenty years before Know-Nothingism, a looting mob had burned the Ursuline Convent at Charlestown. Tried at the Concord session, only one of the rioters had been convicted. The fires still smouldered.

Great issues and events — but immediacy makes every issue major.

Smallpox and a mad dog scare brought Concord's first Board of Health, with hard-worked Dr. Bartlett a member.

Factory Village — West Concord — making Donnets flannels, lead pipe, harness, pails, chairs, and other commodities, was also producing children — but the frugal town turned down its request for an extra school district.

Paradoxically, Henry Thoreau, lover of nature, set the woods afire one April Tuesday when all good citizens were supposed to be at town meeting, as he and Edward Hoar, younger son of the Squire, were cooking fish chowder on the north shore of Fairhaven. No rain for weeks, and the grass dry as tinder. A leaping spark started the blaze, which a warm south wind fanned into a runaway despite the frantic efforts of the culprits. Henry's shame seared him like the fire he had fought, till he comforted himself with the thought that a bolt of lightning might just as readily have caused the damage. Only the complicity of a son of the leading citizen staved off prosecution, and, at that, Henry had to face black looks from some of his fellow citizens for several years. But sparks from the railroad burned even larger tracts, and Henry's carelessness was presently forgotten. Soon Concord was hiring him, as its best surveyor, to straighten the Carlisle boundary.

In 1846 Hawthorne's *Mosses from an Old Manse* was published, making that building seem truly venerable. Three years later, at the author's expense, Thoreau's *Week on the Concord and Merrimack Rivers* was printed — the first spark, Emerson, Alcott, and Ellery Channing hoped, in a far different conflagration. To raise the cash Henry had worked hard at the family pencil business in addition to the usual jobs he did for his support. When the book would not sell, Henry took his disappointment better than did his friends. It amused him to say he now possessed a library of nine hundred volumes, over seven hundred of which he had written himself.

That same year gold turned up in California's streams, and the steady exodus to the West became a rush. For Concord it was part of an ancient trend, begun with that first exodus to Fairfield in the time of Peter Bulkeley. Now, more than ever, cartwheels lumbered along the distant trails. With a willingness to work, with a readiness to live like his ancestors, foregoing the comforts of New England, a pioneer with just enough capital to get there should soon gain more in the West with its limitless land at two dollars an acre than on an exhausted farm at home. Kentucky — so the natives boasted — bounded on the east by the rising sun, north by the aurora borealis, west by the procession of the equinoxes, and south by the Day of Judgment. The lush Ohio valley. Iowa, with corn sixteen feet tall. Missouri bottom land. Michigan territory, Kansas, Wisconsin, Minnesota. Wherever they went, hometown settlers took Concord with them — the notion of town meeting, the remembrance of churches, of schools and houses they would copy and improve on. Yet always enough spirit and vitality remained for Concord to go on being Concord.

Shortly after getting its railroad, the town was fascinated by another wonder. Through sparks along a wire you could send a message to Boston or to the universe. The telegraph was complete as far as Concord.

A great invention, said all the world. Why, snorted old Colonel Whiting, what Morse had done was no more than what that Dyar boy did right here in town a quarter of a century ago! Harrison Gray Dyar was his name. Used to work for Lemuel Curtis, clock and watch maker on the Milldam. An amazingly smart fellow, we lads thought him. I remember Curtis, who used to let him experiment in the shop, saying Dyar would some day make a noise in the world. He did, too; sooner than expected. Blew out the windows with some chemical mess. He was working on an electric storage battery; and he made it, too. Curtis knew all along that his guess was right. Dyar invented an eight-day clock with a rotary lever that cut the number of wheels from half a dozen to two, and it was a first-rate seller. The telegraph? I had a hand in that myself, along with some other boys. Asa Jarvis was there, and young Dinsmore, who taught at the Center school. The notion was to send electric impulses along a wire, spacing the sparks in combinations to form an alphabetic code. With our help he strung his line from tree to tree beside the Red Bridge road clear to Curtis's, using apothecary's glass phials for insulators. Then he hooked on his batteries. The contraption worked. He could improve the receiving apparatus, he told us, recording the sparks on a ribbon of moistened litmus paper on a spool revolved by a clockwork mechanism, the nitric acid that formed leaving red marks on the blue-test litmus. Older folks in Concord laughed when they heard of it. Dyar was too far before his time. It was just a boy's messing around to them. But he got some backers elsewhere who advanced a little cash. With that, he erected several miles of wire on Long Island, then proposed to run his line from New York to Philadelphia. But the Jersey legislature, calling him dangerous, turned him down. Then one of his backers threatened to sue him. Dyar was a shy and diffident boy, and easily frightened. He cleared out, and settled in Europe, where I hear he made a fortune in aneline dyes. Morse deserves the credit, sure enough. After all, the idea was nothing new. What counts is to bring it into practical use. But it's curious Morse came to know many of the people who had worked with Dyar, among them Charles Walker, whose sister Morse married. Walker still had many of Dyar's drawings.

Colonel Whiting and the rest of the oldsters liked to recall other bygone matters, especially the glories of Court Week which they enjoyed as boys. For years September Court Week had been the county's favorite holiday, supplanting even election. On the farms, men hurried to finish the last haying and cut the corn. It was the regular thing for mechanics and tradesmen to give their apprentices Wednesday off, though few expected much work the entire week. From all over the county the people came — for fun, for swapping horses or to race their trotters down the Lexington road, to watch wrestling matches, gossip, and talk politics. At three cents a drink, New England rum was in its glory. For the boys, old father Mayhew dispensed egg pop at a penny a glass. Whiskered, wrinkled Lazzaro Montefiore, a little Italian who had somehow wandered into town to set up a shop as candystick maker, used to hustle about, in white coat and apron, with his loaded tray, selling stomach aches to the children. "Walk up, tumble up, any way to get up!" shouted Captain Jefts from Cape Ann, dispensing raw oysters to the crowd swarming about the many booths that stretched round the square and past the church. Here were wares of every description; more drinks, more food. Roulette wheels in the tents, shell games, and other ways to part a man from his money. Towards evening, thanks to the heavy drinking, there were sure to be fights — though Colonel Whiting and other temperance men recalled their efforts to close down festivities by nightfall. If the disorder reached major proportions, Court adjourned. The sheriff and his deputies, with judges and jurors for a posse, would sally out to extinguish the riot. A great time for the people, but greater for the lawyers, whose dominion included the inns and the Middlesex Hotel. At the height of its prosperity, just before the railroad came, the hotel had burned down, only to rise like a Phoenix more resplendent than ever, with a reputation for good food and drink reaching far beyond the county. The lawyers always pre-empted the best tables, with the judge presiding at the head of the board. For the sober, whist was the standard evening diversion; for convivial souls, drinking, singing, and laughter made all men brothers. But when the bell tolled for Court in the morning, every lapse from dignity was forgotten. Led by the county's sheriff in full regalia — cocked hat, blue coat, buff breeches, and a spatter of brass buttons, with dress sword at his side — then the judges, then the members of the bar, the formal procession would march from the hotel to the courthouse, substantial citizens and solid farmers standing by with hats respectfully doffed, then crowding in to hear the arguments — each lawyer fighting not only for his client but for his professional fame among the people.

Court Week was not what it had been, mourned the patriarchs.

Judges and lawyers came by the morning train and left each night. One by one the taverns had closed, Hartwell Bigelow's among the last. Once forty through coaches a week stopped in Concord. Was the town now any better than a mere way station on the line? Once three fifths of the courts of justice in the county had sat there, Concord outranking Cambridge and aspiring to be the capital of the state. Through failure to keep pace with upstart Lowell, the little that was left would go. The river was too sluggish to drive big mills; the race for commercial and political pre-eminence seemed lost.

When at three o'clock one morning the remodeled courthouse burned to the ground, the final blow had fallen. Seizing its chance, Lowell entered a bill before the legislature to capture the last of the courts.

Soon only the district court would be left to remind old timers of the town's departed legal glory.

The usual cluster of little politicians on the porch of the Middlesex Hotel — its yellow paint already cracked and chipping — picked their teeth and shook their heads. What was going to happen to Concord? Loafers spitting tobacco juice in the dusty square where the booths and tents of Court Week used to stand growled there was no place even to enjoy a drink. Husky, tow-headed, ruddy-faced George Prescott there, the widow's son, on his way to the coal and lumber yard he ran (folks said he did a pretty good business) was in part to blame — with his teetotalling notions and his Young Men's Total Abstinence Society. There was that good-for-nothing failure, Bronson Alcott, on his way up Main Street towards Mrs. Thoreau's, to hobnob, likely, with Henry, his equal. The idlers curiously watched another crank, Ephraim Bull, once a prosperous goldbeater, trudge across the green toward his land along the sidehill on Lexington Road. Trying to play tricks on nature, was he? Thought he could make grapes better than God intended? Ripped out all of his vines each year, instead of harvesting his crop! (Charlie Bartlett, though, they say, is getting good money for his strawberries, which no one ever before thought to grow here.)

If you lolled long enough in the shade of the big oak by the Town House, you'd be likely to see most of the people passing. Tall, long-shanked young Ed Wheeler striding by — why didn't he go pioneering; head West for gold like other men? (Some folks were remarking he was doing pretty well with that part of his father's farm he'd taken over — raising asparagus and other truck along with the usual Wheeler cattle.) Rockwood Hoar, coming from the train (the Governor had just named him Judge of the Court of Common Pleas): he'd never be the great man his father was! There goes John Shepard Keyes, the big man's son (doing quite a legal practice, ain't he?). Too bad old John died! Frank Gourgas, his political enemy, gone, too — died young, while speaker of the State Assembly. What was to become of Concord, losing the best she had? There was Mr. Emerson, with a smile and nod for the swarm of boys playing ball on the square. Heading down Main Street toward the station, a bundle under his arm — some book, most likely, he'd written, to be printed in Boston.

Well, times had changed. Men weren't what they used to be. The good old days were gone.

CHAPTER XIV

Slavery Shadowing the Nation

THE long-debated Fugitive Slave Bill, with Webster's support, had become an Act. Emerson stared at the *Boston Daily Advertiser*. Under penalty of a thousand-dollar fine, no person might henceforth aid an escaping Negro. Instead, he must bring what help he could to the Federal man hunters. This filthy enactment, Emerson had to tell himself, was passed on Wednesday, September 18, 1850, in an enlightened century, by men who could read and write. By God, he would not obey it!

For years he had steered clear of Garrison and his abolitionists because he disliked the violent unreason of their assault. Now this law made abolition every man's problem. To befriend in one's own state, on one's own farm, a fugitive who had taken the risk of being burned alive, or shot, or starved to death, or suffocated in a wooden box, is an act of common decency. It is not meddling with the Southern planter; it is hindering him from meddling with us.

What added injury to insult was Webster's backing of the bill — Webster, the one man in the North fit to be president. Let him not try to run for office now! In bygone years, as an example of the best in American statesmanship, Emerson had sent Carlyle a volume of Webster's speeches; speeches eloquent in every great cause — among them his reply to Senator Hayne, of South Carolina, the nullifier: that plea for a united nation, with the ringing appeal for liberty *and* union, now and forever, one and inseparable.

Webster meant to appease the South for the sake of union. Emerson had listened to a Boston acquaintance say this compromise was the crowning work of a fine career. No! Webster had torn to the ground what he had spent years in building. His reasoning was based on despair, not leadership; all the drops of his blood had eyes that looked downward.

Some of his fellow citizens in Concord had asked Emerson to speak. He would do so. This act was poisoning even the air of his village. It had turned free, expanding, hospitable America, the refuge of the homeless, pregnant with the hopes of the world, into a jail to make safe the chattels of a few thousand Southern planters. Thus the inhabitants of Concord heard him.

Here was a special problem, he declared, which *one* man cannot solve but *all* men must.

First, abrogate the law. Like Webster, he was a unionist. But when the Constitution ordains an iniquity, it ordains disunion.

Next, confine slavery to the slave states and help them make an end of it. Why not dispassionately put the question to the South as a problem of political economy? The South itself once confessed that slavery was an economic evil. Buy the slaves as the British nation bought them to end the abuse in the West Indies! In view of the hazards, twice the price would be slight. Whilst this devilish seed of war is in the soil, there can never be peace. In the name of common sense and the good of mankind, why not bring the states shoulder to shoulder? Why not end this explosive dispute on some basis that will give fair compensation to the South, and to the North a free conscience?

When he learned of Emerson's words, Charles Sumner, junior senator from Massachusetts, exclaimed, "I have more satisfaction in this voice on our side than in that of any politician."

On previous occasions, Concord had heard the short, sharp sentences which Emerson fell into when his blood was stirred. If the cause was unpopular, his words struck all the harder. When the right of public speech on the topic of slavery became a question in Concord, Emerson had thrown his weight into the struggle. At the request of Mrs. Mary Merrick Brooks, president of Concord's Antislavery Society, he made an address to celebrate West Indian emancipation; though the selectmen wished to deny the use of the Town House, and Thoreau tolled the bell to summon the people.

The battle in Concord, in those earlier days, had resolved itself into a fight for a free Lyceum. The fiery words of Wendell Phillips, brilliant young lawyer and abolitionist, who like Garrison was ready to wreck the Union if that would further his cause, had exploded the powder. Lyceums, argued the cautious magnates of the village, had been founded for unhurtful enlightenment, not for controversy. Phillips must not be allowed again to speak. John Keyes (it was the year before his death), branding the recent talk as pernicious and abominable, moved that the orator, already engaged for the approaching season, be asked to choose another topic. But Thoreau, as curator, Emerson, and the young folk voted down the motion.

The hall was packed to the aisles for the second engagement, and word had gone round to expect a row — John Keyes was planning to answer Phillips. But Mr. Keyes, perhaps unwilling to tackle so eloquent an opponent, held his peace till after the meeting. Then he and those who sided with him gathered to censure the speaker. Phillips, with his dangerous skill — said Keyes — was bamboozling the silly, sentimental women. An arrogant young man against whom the young folk should be warned, declared Squire Hoar, who like Keyes disapproved of slavery but was unwilling to countenance an attack that laid the blame on the apathy of the church and on the Constitution. But Phillips, tipped off by Thoreau, was seated in the back row of the vestry. He now stepped quietly forward.

Would the gentlemen like an answer here and now?

That had hardly been the plan, yet there was no help for it.

So Phillips loosed his blazing oratory with a direct appeal to his supporters:

"I would say to you, my young friends, who have been cautioned against excitement and advised to fold your hands in selfish ease: Throw yourselves upon the altar of some noble cause! Enthusiasm is the life of the soul. To rise in the morning only to eat and drink and gather gold is a life not worth living."

By an overwhelming vote, the Lyceum moved to hear Phillips again.

Concord, in those times before the passage of the Fugitive Slave Law, had shared, vicariously at least, another adventure.

At town meeting, Monday, November 11, 1844, the Honorable Samuel Hoar had resigned from the School Committee. His family had at last persuaded him to take a vacation. He would spend the winter in the South.

To soothe his New England conscience and his zeal for work, Mr. Hoar bore in mind there was a little matter of business to attend to. For several years the State of South Carolina had been taking Negro sailors — free Negroes from Massachusetts — out of vessels come to fetch cotton. These black men she fined, flogged, and usually imprisoned. True, she had a statute — was such a law constitutional; did it not challenge the sovereignty of the Federal Union? — forbidding their entry, as a precaution, she said, against an uprising. But entry was far from these sailors' intention. A Bay State ship should be as good as Massachusetts soil. At last the General Court protested. An amicable settlement might strengthen the ties of commercial friendship profitable to North and South alike.

As her official agent, Massachusetts appointed Samuel Hoar of Concord. There was every reason to applaud the choice. Mr. Hoar had no connection with the abolitionists. His fame for probity and honor shone beyond the borders of his state. A conservative, a stickler for order and the law, he would ask no more than simple justice. Moreover, as his close friends knew, he had greater knowledge of the South and its ways than most of them. After graduation he had spent two years as tutor to the children of Colonel Tayloe, owner of Mount Airy, one of the largest plantations in Virginia. Sam Hoar's courtly manner, though tempered by the east wind from the Bay, was in part ascribable to this early training. He should get on well with the Southerners.

Soon after dawn on the last Thursday of November Squire Hoar and his daughter Elizabeth stepped ashore on the Charleston battery. The warm air, the green of liveoaks and bougainvilleas, were delicious. Elizabeth was eager to explore the city. But her father, mindful of his duty, first wrote a courteous note explaining his mission to Governor Hammond at Columbia.

As former congressman from Massachusetts, Mr. Hoar had several old acquaintances in Charleston. These, and the sights of the town, took care of the week end.

On Monday evening, three grim-faced men called at the hotel. Briefly they introduced themselves — the Sheriff of Charleston, the acting Mayor, and a delegate from the Board of Aldermen. Where were his credentials? Did Mr. Hoar realize that for Massachusetts to send an agent on such business was an insult to South Carolina? South Carolina must consider herself the sole judge of the laws she passes to check the danger of a rising of her slaves. Did he know that the legislature, on hearing from the Governor, at once passed resolutions ordering the expulsion of the emissary? Speaking as man to man, they must warn him of his acute personal danger. They would do all in their power to prevent a lynching, but the safest course would be to leave Charleston at once.

Mr. Hoar explained that he would not be driven out like an

incendiary or spy. He had come, he said, on strictly lawful business.

One of his friends, Dr. Whittredge, hurried in. He had just made a tour of the city. Though it was a mortification to admit it, he felt bound to say that a state of feeling existed which he had not thought possible. Already mobs were gathering. He owned a plantation twenty miles out in the country. Would Mr. Hoar accompany him there for safety?

The man from Concord would not budge. He was too old to run, he remarked with a smile. Whatever was about to happen, he must abide the result.

So great was the threat of mob action that the keeper of the hotel, fearful lest his property be burned, begged the visitors to leave. Next morning, what called itself a deputation of leading citizens began to gather. There were so many — seventy or more — that they could not all crowd into the lobby but spilled onto the piazza or remained in the street. They could hold back the angry people no longer, explained the spokesman. Either Mr. Hoar would get into the carriage waiting to take him to the north-bound ship or they would force him into it.

Samuel Hoar had done his best to carry on his mission. Further resistance would be foolish. The old man and his daughter left the hotel.

At Washington, he spoke to the congressmen from Massachusetts. He talked with Governor Briggs who had come to hear him. Then, before Concord town meeting, over which he had presided more than a hundred times, he gave his fellow citizens his story.

The Bay State took the matter hard, with a special message from the Governor and resolutions of censure and resentment passed unanimously by both houses. So South Carolina felt herself aggrieved? If ever she had intended to act with honor and justice in her intercourse with her sister states, that opportunity had been given her by Mr. Hoar's mission. This was no question of abolition; it concerned honor and the Union. If war between two states were permissible, this insult to the dignity of Massachusetts should be cause enough.

Within a year, the gulf of differences had grown enormously wider and deeper through the problem of Texas. Having fought their way to independence from Mexico at San Jacinto, most Texans wished to link their fortunes with the United States. But Texans were slaveowners; Texas almost thrice the size of all New England. Might not the South turn annexation into a conspiracy? Might she not capture Congress and the Federal Government by carving several slave states out of this territory?

The first treaty to bring in Texas was defeated in the Senate, but the second passed — and the entire nation fell heir to Sam Houston's quarrel with Mexico. War soon followed, although few in the North but the Democrats were willing to take an active part in what quickly became a crusade of aggression. As General Santa Anna's reverses opened wide the prospect of new states in the enormous Southwest and President Polk's dream of lands fronting the Pacific seemed to be coming true, even conservative Boston began to realize that slavery remained no longer an institution peculiar to the South, to be tolerated for the sake of good business; it was gathering power to challenge the North and shrink New England into insignificance.

Emerson, pondering the problem, decided it was one of those questions which the present looks at one way, the future in another. It was obvious that the strong British race, having overrun so much of the continent, must run over the Southwest territory and Oregon also, no matter what the methods and occasions. The nation was feeling its oats. But at this immediate moment, it was true to the New England character — and he was as angry as the rest — to consider the question in its temporary bearings, resisting annexation and the Mexican War with tooth and nail.

Henry Thoreau refused to entertain so dispassionate a view. He had heard some of his fellow townsmen say of the civil authorities: "I should like to have them order me out to march to Mexico; see if I would go!" Yet had not these very men, by paying taxes, furthered the government that furthered the war and slavery's spread? He would not for an instant recognize as his government a political organization which was also the slavers' government. His time had come to exercise the right of revolution.

So Henry refused to pay his tax. He had never declined to pay the highway rates or support the schools, because he was as desirous of being a good neighbor as he was now determined to be a bad subject. It was for no particular item of the tax bill. It was merely that at this moment his feelings refused to owe allegiance to the State.

Henry was on his way to the shoemaker's to get a shoe which was mended when he met Sam Staples, the constable.

"I'll pay your tax, Henry, if you're hard up."

Henry neatly explained how the matter stood.

Once before, with Bronson Alcott, Sam had found himself face to face with a similar dilemma. After hearing Alcott's confused and lengthy peroration, he had realized it was all a matter of principle. But he had not offered to pay Alcott's fine as he wished to pay Henry's.

"I'll have to shut you up then."

"One time's as good as another."

The prisoners, in their shirt sleeves, were enjoying an evening chat by the door of the jail. "Come, boys, it's time to lock up," remarked Staples.

Sam introduced Henry to his cell mate, in for burning a barn. Henry gathered he had slept there when drunk and his pipe had set it afire. He had been three months in prison awaiting trial, but did not mind since he got his board for nothing. Thoreau pumped his fellow prisoner dry, and in turn answered his questions. Then he took the bench under one grated window, his companion already having turned in on the other, and blew out the lamp.

A novel experience, and quite to be enjoyed, seeing one's native village from fairly inside it. Not just the sounds from the neighboring inn. It was as though the shadowed streets were peopled with the earliest generation; as though it were the voices of the old burghers that he heard. Plenty of time, too, for thinking. Practically speaking, the enemies of reform are not the slaveholders; the true opponents are the merchants and farmers right at home, more interested in commerce and agriculture than in humanity.

In the morning the prisoners' breakfasts, in small pans holding a pint of chocolate, some brown bread, and an iron spoon, were shoved through a hole in each door. Then locks were opened and the prisoners went out haying (it was curious that there were always more prisoners at a busy season). Henry was ready also, but Sam told him he must leave. After dark, he explained, somebody had left money with his little daughter to pay the tax. She had not recognized the giver — Squire Hoar perhaps.

There was nothing for it but to go. Thoreau was amused at the glances of his neighbors. They looked at him as if he had returned from a long journey.

Emerson, cogitating on Henry's performance, found himself not sure just what to think. His friend's quizzical humor, of course, had something to do with it. Yet it is better not to run amuck against the world. Have a good case before you try the question. Fanatics fight revolutions on the shape of a surplice, or fish on Friday. But so long as the State means you well, why refuse your pistareen? Ninety parts of it will be spent for what you yourself think good; ten parts for mischief. You cannot fight heartily for a fraction. The State is a poor good cow which means to be friendly.

But what if the cow tries to hook its horns into you when you walk the fields?

As if in answer to Henry's battle against the State, the spirit of compromise had clapped this Fugitive Slave Law on New England. Though he was a judge, Rockwood Hoar, remembering his father's experiences in Charleston, declared from the bench, "If I were giving my private opinion I might say that this statute seems to me to evince a more deliberate and settled disregard for the principles of constitutional liberty than any other enactment that has ever come under my notice." And the activities of the underground railroad diminished not one bit.

Shadrach was the first Negro seized under the new Act. His real name was Fred Wilkins and he had escaped from Norfolk, Virginia. Soon most of the facts and many rumors were current in Concord. With several other black men, Shadrach was a waiter at Cornhill Coffee-House, in Boston. There, on Saturday morning, the fifteenth of February, he had been arrested by Deputy Marshal Patrick Riley, on a warrant taken out by John Caphard, of Norfolk, hired by the owner to recapture his property. Riley at once took the fugitive to the United States Court House where he was brought before George T. Curtis, not a judge presiding over a trial by jury, since the law denied that constitutional right to the accused, but a Federal commissioner who, should he decide the black man was an escaped slave, would get a ten-dollar fee, but only five if he discharged him.

When Shadrach asked for counsel, he got as volunteer young Richard Henry Dana, who as a college student seeking health and adventure had rounded Cape Horn in the brig *Pilgrim* and sailed two years before the mast. Dana hurried after a writ of *habeas corpus* as Shadrach waited between two constables set to guard him. Patrick Riley meanwhile ordered from the courtroom all persons with no official business. The corridor and stairways were crowded with men, mostly colored, who had heard what was going on.

Towards two o'clock, as Dana, having failed to get the writ, was returning, he heard a shout from the Court House. Next thing he saw Shadrach, his clothes half torn from his body, hustled down the steps and into Court Street by a couple of Negroes. Others swarmed close behind. The little group, like a black squall, made off toward Cambridge.

Inside the courtroom, Dana found the deputy, his assistants, and the constables picking themselves up from the corners where they had been tumbled.

From the jumble of voices, the young attorney pieced together what had happened. Robert Morris, colored lawyer and a fellow counsel for the defense, in court as was his right, had decided to leave. As he opened the door — possibly wider than needed — a mob swept through the room, grabbed Shadrach, then rushed out the opposite door.

So stunned were the officials by the speed of events that pursuit had not occurred to them. It was an act of rebellion, declared the angry commissioner; he would telegraph Webster in Washington.

Outside, mixing with the passers-by, Shadrach and one of his rescuers (Lewis Hayden, free colored businessman, according to later rumor) were heading toward East Cambridge, keeping each other in sight on opposite sides of the street. As Hayden brought Shadrach to the Reverend L. C. Lovejoy's house — a post of the Abolitionists' Vigilance Committee — a carriage with drawn blinds drove up. Shadrach was put inside.

Sleet and rain, beginning to fall harder, made slow driving along the route of the underground railroad.

Toward three on Sunday morning, Francis Bigelow, Concord blacksmith, heard the clink of iron shoes on the stones of his court-yard. Peering into the storm, he recognized the team by its white horse next to the brown one.

Lest his absence cause suspicion, the driver left to be home before morning. Over the air-tight stove in the bedroom Mrs. Bigelow got ready some food. Meanwhile Francis went next door for Mrs. Brooks. Her husband Nathan had warned her that since the passage of the law he could not countenance aiding and abetting. But when he saw the frightened Negro, his ripped clothes still wet from the rain, he forgot. As Bigelow drove toward the northern star, the fugitive had on the lawyer's coat and hat.

Hayden, Morris, and several white men were arrested in Boston for complicity. Again Dana acted for the defense. And Francis Bigelow, blacksmith, of Concord, was among the good men and true drawn for the jury. Judge Rockwood Hoar, with his younger brother George Frisbie, practising as a lawyer in Worcester, was there as a character witness.

"Would Bigelow make an impartial juror?"

Judge Hoar looked at his old friend.

"He is a thoroughly honest man and will decide the case according to the law and evidence as he believes them to be, but I think it will take a good deal of evidence to convince him that one man owns another."

There were no convictions.

The Democrats nominated Franklin Pierce for President. For the needed campaign biography, Pierce appealed to a man grown nationally famous as an author, though far from wealthy — Nathaniel Hawthorne, his friend since undergraduate days at Bowdoin.

How to live while writing had remained an acute problem with Hawthorne. The customs post at Salem had gone to a deserving Whig when Zachary Taylor succeeded Democrat James K. Polk. After a couple of frugal seasons at Lenox, slightly better returns through *The Scarlet Letter* and *The House of the Seven Gables* had enabled Hawthorne, in this year of election, 1852, to purchase Hillside, where the Alcotts once lived, Emerson carrying out the negotiations for his friends and Lidian signing the title deed.

Hawthorne renamed his property "The Wayside." Here Sophia, with the Concord first-born, Una, and Julian and little Rose, had been living since early June, while Nathaniel, before tackling the biography, put final touches on *The Blithedale Romance*.

An uncongenial service which his college chum had begged of him! But Pierce had a way of putting his arm round your shoulder, of transferring a glow of warmth which his shy companion experienced from no other man. To refuse his best efforts at this crisis in his friend's career would make difficulties with his conscience. Besides, Hawthorne had been irritated by the flood of indiscriminate, ignorant abuse and aimless praise which had engulfed the candidate.

What was discouraging, once Hawthorne started, was the dearth of material. How explain the nominee's surprising national obscurity, despite opportunities for distinction that had crossed his path — congressman, then senator from New Hampshire, then a brigadier general in the Mexican war? Yet all the voters had to go by was an ingratiating manner and appealing smile. At least his honesty could be vouched for. In choosing Pierce, the nation would choose a man of practical sagacity who loved his country for what it was, not for what unrealistic reformers might dream of it. A conservative, he would do his best to bring good from things as they are. That view was easy for a man of Hawthorne's temperament to champion.

Slavery, of course, was an evil. Hawthorne could remember the queer feeling that came over him, once, at a wayside tavern, when a stranger from the South remarked of a respectably dressed Negro that he wished he owned a thousand such men in Alabama. His sympathies were revolted by slavery. Yet peace and union require compromise. Was not the Fugitive Slave Law largely a result of extremes practised by the abolitionists? Had human effort ever brought great improvement into the world? Hawthorne's answer was no; amelioration of man's lot comes through the inscrutable acts of Providence. It would be so with the slaves.

Franklin Pierce, he wrote, was not the man to adopt the cause of one section of his country against another. He had fully recognized the rights pledged to the South by the Constitution, and would continue to do so. He would never bring aid to men whose misty philanthropy left only half a country to their affections.

Hawthorne realized his words would cost him hundreds of friends. Yes, Pierce was reaching that high altitude where a man careful of his personal dignity should begin to think of dropping his acquaintance. If Pierce should win, carrying the South and much of the West, Hawthorne knew what people would be saying. Already rumors were about that he could be Ambassador to Russia or hold some other office he neither wanted nor had asked for.

On July the fifth, at the Wayside, Hawthorne, who never dreamed of giving a party, found himself host to a pre-election reception. There was Pierce, beaming at the throng, and there were the constituents — the Concord Irish who were becoming voters, but in greater numbers the rough New England farmers who through the generations had stuck to Democracy from Jefferson through Jackson.

"Don't be scar't, General, don't be scar't," cackled old James Adams, the cabinetmaker, clapping the candidate on the back. "We'll put you through, General!"

The Whig candidate, Winfield Scott, turned out to be an antagonizing speaker and a worse getter of votes, and the legs of his platform straddled the slavery question. The result was a landslide for Pierce with the Whig party smashed among the debris.

Jefferson Davis, who wanted new slave states, became the strong man of the administration as secretary of war in a proslavery cabinet. Hawthorne, settled in Concord, he supposed, for life, found himself bound for Liverpool as consul by the act of a grateful President. The United States, having imagined that compromise might settle the problem, found itself frying in the hot oil of controversy. Trouble in Kansas tossed fresh fat on the fire.

The westward surge of the people, the thrust of the railways towards transcontinental routes, had created the territories of Nebraska and Kansas. To please the South, which had an eye on Kansas as a possible slave state, Congress decided that popular sovereignty among the settlers should determine the issue. Nebraska would doubtless come in free, which should satisfy the North. But at once a howl went up from New England. Did not this measure invalidate the Missouri Compromise, good since 1820, penning slavery below 36° 30'? Were not senators from Missouri and Kentucky seeking outright revocation? Concord, in town meeting assembled, forgetting its rivalries of the last election, passed almost unanimously a resolution urging the Massachusetts representatives to oppose repeal — "not merely because it violates a solemn compact, but because it is a wicked attempt to extend and perpetuate slavery in territory now free."

Free it most certainly had been, but a deadly race was on. Up from slave Missouri swarmed "settlers" — "border ruffians," the Free-Soilers called them — to cast their votes; from the East and North came pioneers who knew that slave labor pushes out free and ruins every chance for a homestead. Each side reeled at the impact. The repeal of this bill, declared Sumner, ends all hope of compromise. "It puts freedom and slavery face to face and bids them grapple. Who can doubt the result?"

One result Sumner hardly expected followed shortly. As the Senate recessed for luncheon and Sumner lingered working at his desk, Preston Brooks of South Carolina struck him senseless with repeated blows of a heavy cane. Bloody Kansas had widened its boundaries.

"This stroke rouses the feeling of the people," exclaimed Emerson at Concord's indignation meeting, "and shows everybody where we are."

Already a party was forming for a political fight. In Concord, many Democrats joined former Whigs at its rallies. But when Emerson asked George Minot if he would go with him to cast a vote for freedom, the old man leaned on his hoe.

"No," he said, "I ain't a-goin'. It's no use a-ballotin', for it won't stay so. What you do with a gun'll stay."

As with the brief-lived Free-Soilers, the Hoar family played an important role in the national organization of these new Republicans. And when the party met for its first national convention, to nominate Frémont as challenger of Democrat James Buchanan, Ralph Waldo Emerson, named as alternate delegate, came near going to Philadelphia, since Governor Boutwell feared he himself would be too busy.

In the election, the Republicans were jubilant to win as many as one hundred and fourteen votes against the one hundred and seventy-four of the victorious Democrats. Four years hence might tell a different story.

Meanwhile there was plenty more trouble in Kansas. Emigrant Aid societies to settle Free-Soilers had sprung up all over New England. Concord had one, but Boston's was the heart of the movement. Secretary of the executive committee at its permanent office was tall, long-legged Frank Sanborn, young Harvard graduate, one of Emerson's finds, brought to Concord as head of the Academy once conducted by the Thoreaus, and now on leave of absence in Boston.

Early one January morning in 1857 Sanborn looked up from his papers to see two men — one between fifty and sixty, though his lean hard vigor made guessing difficult, the other obviously his son. A glance at that chin, aggressive as the jaw of a militant Puritan, that wind-tanned, deep-lined, smooth-shaven face with its firmly compressed slit of a mouth, drove every other thought from Sanborn's mind. He stared at his visitor — at his short and bristling hair, touched at the temples with gray, shooting back as though a prairie wind had blown it, his deep-set, steel cold, blue-gray eyes, and medium forehead with its three deep, perpendicular wrinkles to the bridge of the massive hooked nose that put the upper lip in shadow. The stranger was taking off his heavy military overcoat and coonskin cap, and the action curiously changed the first impression of a soldier to that of a rigorous, very masculine deacon in an old-fashioned brown coat, waistcoat, and trousers. Sanborn's gaze left his visitor long enough to read the letter of introduction. It was from George Walker, of Springfield, Ohio, a member of the national committee. He wished to present John Brown, and his son, Owen.

The fame of Brown's doings in Kansas — the fight at Osawatomie, where his band had terminated the careers of not a few border ruffians, his daring rescues of whole droves of Negroes — had of course preceded him. In a very few days, through Sanborn's planning, he met those men in town whom he wished to see. In Tabor, southwestern Iowa, the Boston committee had cached two hundred Sharpe's rifles — newly invented breech loaders and far better weapons than most Missourians would carry — with ammunition and equipment. If he had these, said Brown, he could arm his force to defend free Kansas. He would act on his own responsibility, not involving the organization in his immediate plans.

Brown got the guns.

Before returning, he spoke at several meetings in Massachusetts. Through Sanborn's management, February brought him to Concord. He arrived by the noon train and lunched at Mrs. Thoreau's with the boarders, Henry there too.

Shortly after the meal, Emerson called on an errand and remained to talk.

How had Brown first come to Kansas?

Four of his sons had gone there to settle. He had followed to help keep Kansas free. Ever since 1812, when he saw it face to face while a lad driving cattle in western Virginia, he had sworn eternal warfare against slavery. It was nothing, he said, to die in a good cause, but an eternal disgrace to sit still in the presence of slavery.

In the evening, at the Town House, a hundred or more people gathered to see and hear this wiry man of medium height, with nerves instead of flesh, talk in a quiet, deep, metallic voice about Kansas. All honest lovers of liberty and human rights, he said, could back his cause. Then suddenly his tone changed. He held up a tracechain and shook it. That chain, he said — and words and gesture remained long after with his hearers — had bound his son John in Kansas — his son who had been dragged to prison by mounted dragoons for no other crime than resisting slavery. He once had seven sons — till one was crazed by his ordeal, another murdered. He and the five left would never stop fighting.

Next day, at Emerson's, it was hard to remember that this modest man, diffident in company, was the wild-eyed speaker of the night before. His glance now had the gentle look of a mystic and dreamer, and twelve-year-old Eddie Emerson listened fascinated as he talked about animals.

"The children always come to me," said Brown.

He did not leave Concord empty-handed. Henry Thoreau had given money, Emerson, and many others. Already, in a speech at Cambridge, Emerson had warned that these times were full of fate for the Republic. The revolution of the century lay close at hand; it would be a far more complex war than in '75.

In this time of national tension Emerson was thankful that primal Adam in the Garden offered one constant among variables. Sure as the fall season the Cattle Show would come, the annual festival of harvest.

Wednesday, September 29, was one of those splendid autumnal mornings. Long before dawn the town was astir — the air filled with the lowing of cows, the squeal of recalcitrant pigs, the *clippity-clop* of teams and the rattle of carriages. Farmers from all Middlesex crowded the village streets and streamed through the gate of the Sleepy Hollow Fair Grounds to find stalls and benches for their exhibits. Children with something to show — if only a hutch of Belgian hares or a crook-neck squash of their own raising — could get in free. No work for the tough-palmed lads today, dressed in their best pea-jackets, their pepper-and-salt suits of homespun, their coats of corduroy or kersey. Henry Thoreau, watching them plunge in and out among the stock pens, knew that he loved these sons of earth (despite his indignant outbursts at man's folly and blindness), loved every mother's son of them. Even the plodding, sober elders walked with unusual springiness this morning, jabbering earnestly with one another — these men whose ancestors had sown the seed of national greatness.

For an hour or so the doors of the agriculture building — pumpkin hall the boys called it — would be shut during the judging. Then everyone rushed in to see who won the prizes.

As usual, John, son of former sheriff Abel Moore, who owned the magnificent farms next to Ephraim Bull's cottage below the hillside, scored for vegetables. With his up-to-date methods, new crops, and skillful marketing, Moore proved over and over that farming paid, though old-fashioned farmers faced extinction.

Mrs. Maria D. Moore, of Framingham, showed butter golden as its namesake flower and gained five dollars. George Prescott's mother won a butter premium too. Harriet Hoar's loaf of bread, victor in the class for girls under twenty, made mouths water as the time drew towards dinner. And Abby May, youngest of the Alcott girls, as talented as Louisa who wrote children's stories, received a prize for her Concord scenes drawn in crayon.

Though the season had done poorly for fruit, with storms while the blossoms set and hail just before harvest, the loaded tables exceeded the committee's expectations. Each year the varieties were increasing: Lady apples, one side green, the other red and glossy; Pumpkin Sweet, the largest apples exhibited; Ram's Horn, dark crimson. Domestic fruits formed a class highly valued by Emerson, who took pride in his orchard. But the best he got, this year, notwithstanding his Beurre Diel and Flemish pears, was a single premium, third prize for grapes. First prize, as always since the day he introduced them, went to Ephraim Wales Bull for his Concords.

The moment he bought his place in Concord, Ephraim Bull had begun his experiments. In the North, hard, sour native grapes were scarcely edible, and the Southern Catawba and its variants died. Varieties from Europe failed through mildew and rot. Late frosts that nipped the flowers, early ones that killed the fruit, made low-lying Concord fatal to grapes. Bull lost every vine brought from Boston.

Why not see what can be done with Northern wildings? Americans want results quickly. But he felt he had the patience to wait.

His first ventures with transplanted vines proved disappointing. By raising pears from seeds the Dutchman Van Mous had worked wonders, producing fruit of a size and excellence unheard of. He would try similar methods. But he kept his own counsel. Anyone hearing he was working with pits of a sour wild grape from a corner of his wood lot might consider him crazy.

His little seedlings throve in the sandy soil to the southwest of the ridge that had sheltered Concord's first settlers. In the second generation — which he nursed six years — Bull got a single vine that improved on its parent; in the third, one still better. Cautiously he offered a bunch to a neighbor.

"Why, this is finer than the Southern Isabella!"

For five more years Bull tended his newest vine, increasing it by cuttings. Boston's Horticultural Society was about to hold its annual exhibition. Despite the grower's reticence, several members of the committee had got wind of miracles in Concord. Could and would Mr. Bull exhibit?

But the day before the show, Ephraim Bull fell ill. A neighbor took in the basket for him.

At noon the next day two members of the committee appeared at the cottage. Where were the promised grapes?

He had sent them, he explained.

Sure enough, among the hothouse varieties and fancy vegetables, by mistake, stood the basket. Full of flavor, hardy, aromatic, delicious, the Concord grape achieved an instant sensation.

So incredible was the fruit, so incredulous the committee, that a deputation was sent to investigate. Perhaps the grapes had been grown under glass? Bull was not at home when the members came, but his sturdy field-grown vines won their own victory.

If a man is benefactor to the race — wrote a clergyman from Andover — who makes two blades of grass grow where but one grew before, what praise, what honor is too great for him who introduces to our soil and climate this new treasure, easy to cultivate and sure to overspread the entire globe?

Those admiring Ephraim Bull's Concords at the Cattle Show could well agree.

The Spading Match had been taken over by the Irish, with only two Yankees among the twelve competitors, though Enoch Garfield won and the four dollars for second prize went to Michael Flannery, of County Kerry. Concord still remembered the contest of several years before, when Mike's prize money was pocketed by his Yankee employer. Henry Thoreau had seen to it that a like sum was made up for Michael, and his wrathful comments singed the ears of the farmer.

This colossal, sudden Irish immigration, screamed the Knownothings, would ruin America. It was packing the slums with dirty, ignorant paupers, polluting elections, exalting the Pope, underselling American labor. Even in Concord, prejudice and exploitation hounded the newcomers.

Yet they won sympathy also. There was little Johnny Riordan, mused Thoreau, whom you could not see for five minutes without honoring. Johnny lived in Shantytown, along the deep cut, where the warmth of Irish affections made up for the firewood his family lacked. Henry often watched him, in thin, ragged clothes, with large holes at the toes of his shoes, floundering through the snow down the miles of track to the grammar school, where he sat at the head of his bench as the brightest scholar. There was a hero for you, traveling by his own brave steps! Had not the world waited for such a generation?

With farmers' daughters finding better paid, more congenial work in Lowell's mills, Concord housewives who used hired help were forced to employ Irish domestics, though most lacked skill and some were sickly from hardships they had suffered. The Alcotts, newly returned, after further wanderings, to Concord at Orchard House — closer to Emerson's than the Wayside — suffered a tragedy of their own because of the Irish. Mrs. Alcott and the girls had nursed a poverty-stricken family through scarlet fever till Elizabeth caught it and died. Three little women now, girls no longer, left to Marmee and Bronson Alcott.

But to Concord farmers, the Irish were a problem in profit and loss. At a Farmers' Club meeting at Abiel Wheeler's they threshed out the question. With their sons gone West or setting up in the cities, there had been nothing to do but hire Irish labor from the horde of applicants left behind as the railroad gangs moved toward the Pacific. These Irish, said grumblers, were unreliable, always ready to take advantage of their employers, never knowing how to do things, wasteful and squandering in their care of the stock. With their ignorance, their dirt, their foreign ways, their Popish religion, who would care to bring them into his family?

Yes, said J. B. Moore, but think of the profit! He preferred native help but got Irish cheaper, and did not have to board them. An Irishwoman he had hired, added Willard T. Farrar, was fully up to any man at binding grain. You had to pay a man a dollar a day; you could get a woman for only a quarter of that or a third.

Minot Pratt, secretary of the Club, former Brook Farmer, now owner of the fertile tract from Punkatasset Hill to the river, raised his quiet voice. He did not feel badly used, he said, by his Irish. Of course, they had their failings, but could these not be regarded with charity? He hoped to have a mantle of that same heavenly fabric on Judgment Day thrown over his own shortcomings. Even if it were not a Christian duty, besides being sound democratic doctrine, to treat these strangers well, giving them sympathy and justice — justice not merely in dollars and cents but in all relations — would not such treatment pay through service?

J. P. Brown seconded these remarks. Experience had taught him that kindliness was the better way. So he talked with his Irish help, he said, as he used to talk with his neighbors' sons working beside him, and made them his companions. They were nowhere near so backward as they seemed. They were learning his ways and he had even profited from some of theirs — one of them making a retaining bank of turf where he had expected to use expensive masonry. In the evenings, he taught them to read and write.

Thus the Irish, among the first of the new migrants, were beginning to make their way in a strange land. In due time the School Committee took notice. "The children of these uneducated parents now constitute a considerable part of our total number," wrote the chairman. "It is wise to educate them well. They are to be permanently with us, and are hereafter to have no small influence in controlling the character and destinies of the Town."

Crowning event of every Cattle Show was the annual dinner. This year the President, John S. Keyes, sheriff of Middlesex County, had invited his friend Ralph Waldo Emerson to speak. Farmers and their wives, and also men of politics and letters, marched from the Fair Grounds to the new Town House to hear him.

"Mr. President, Ladies and Gentlemen! I suppose there is no anniversary that meets from all parties a more entire good will than this rural festival. Town and country, trader and manufacturer, clerk and layman, soldier and sailor . . . all have an equal stake in the prosperity of the farmer. It is well with all when it is well with him. . . . Every wise State has favored him, and the best men have held him highest. . . . Let us look at the condition of . . . the man with the hoe, at his strength and weakness . . . at his share in the great future which opens before the people of this country."

At the end of one more harvest, in October, 1859, from Harpers Ferry, Virginia, from the South where toil had lost all dignity, came that flash of news which Emerson and other wise men knew, sooner or later, would be forerunner of the inevitable conflict that must be fought before the nation could hope to realize its destiny.

John Brown, thought by most to be still in Kansas, had stormed the Federal Arsenal at Harpers Ferry with a band of eighteen white and black men, and the Arsenal had been recaptured by United States Marines.

The first reports were that Brown was dead.

He who takes the sword must perish by it, said most of Concord, shocked at the violence of this man so recently among them on a second visit. He had grown a prophet's tremendous beard in the interval, and had looked to Concord many years older and sterner. Now he had thrown his life away; died like a fool.

Then came the news that Brown was wounded and a prisoner and would be tried for treason.

Serves him right, said Concord, the man is undoubtedly insane. Yankee-like, some asked: What did he expect to gain by it?

But not all citizens of Concord were critical, certainly not Alcott and Thoreau. This deed, thought Alcott, so surprising, so mixed, so confounding to most persons, will give impulse to freedom and humanity, whatever comes of its victim and of the states that howl over it.

Every paper had columns full of details which were avidly read.

The South was fearful of a colored insurrection.

Governor Wise, of Virginia, asked Brown his purpose.

He had tried to do his duty — Brown answered — he had tried to free the slaves from bondage.

CHAPTER XV

The Flag of the Union
Has Been Fired On

NEWS of the raid reached Sanborn in his Concord schoolroom. He was deeply, perilously implicated. What he knew as agent between Brown and the Committee, he told himself, might also be disastrous to others. And Brown's men had been armed with the Massachusetts rifles.

Plans had been made for the Academy's annual chestnuting excursion to the Estabrook grove. He would hardly be missed. That night Sanborn went over his documents, burning all possible evidence. Next morning he hurried to Boston. There he learned that a whole trunkful of letters had been captured at Brown's Harpers Ferry headquarters. John A. Andrew, Boston lawyer and a friend of Kansas Aid, gave it as his opinion that for those involved there might be sudden arrest on the charge of treason. Two of Brown's backers already were heading for Montreal.

Cramming a few belongings into a bag, Sanborn caught the night boat. At the Metropolitan hotel, Quebec, he registered under the name of Stanley.

Sanborn got himself out of the country before any of his Concord friends could know of it. He should stand his ground, felt Emerson, writing him a laconic letter to return.

Thoreau read all the newspapers he could get within a week after Harpers Ferry and could not find a single expression of sympathy for the captives. Even Garrison's *Liberator* termed the attempt ill-considered and foolhardy. The more he thought about what men were saying, the higher his indignation soared.

Had not Brown shown the courage to face his entire country when he knew she was wrong? Brown deemed slavery wholly opposed to American principles. Therefore his act had sprung from his respect for the Union, not from any shallow hatred of the Constitution. By descent and birth a New England farmer, deliberate and practical and slow to wrath, Brown, when aroused — Thoreau told himself — was like the best who had stood at Concord Bridge, on Lexington Common and Bunker Hill.

Thoreau sent a messenger from house to house in the village, notifying the neighbors that he would talk on Brown that night at the Unitarian vestry. One of the friends on whom he most counted sent a note suggesting this might be premature. "You misunderstood," Henry scribbled; "I did not ask advice."

A sizeable group, Emerson among them, gathered. "I trust you will pardon me," Thoreau began; "I do not wish to force my thoughts upon you, but I feel forced myself." He was visibly stirred, but spoke with moderation.

"The newspapers seem to ignore, or perhaps are really ignorant of the fact that there are at least as many as two or three individuals to a town throughout the North who think . . . as I do respecting the life and character and last action of John Brown. I do not hesitate to say that they are an important and growing body."

Why — demanded the speaker — did anxious politicians wish to prove that only seventeen white men and five Negroes were concerned in the raid?

"Why do they still dodge the truth? They are anxious because of a dim consciousness . . . that at least a million of the free inhabitants of the United States would have rejoiced if it had succeeded!"

Henry helped turn the tide of public feeling. This fatal blunder at Harpers Ferry, Emerson perceived, had brought out all Brown's virtues. He was that rarest of heroes, a pure idealist with no by-ends of his own — precisely the sort of man lawyers call "crazy."

Emerson hoped to the last Brown's life might be spared. He hurried to a meeting at the American House, Boston, to discuss with several men of influence the possibility of intercession with Virginia's Governor Wise. But Sanborn, back again in New England, said that Brown did not wish to escape.

Speaking on "Courage" at the Music Hall, Boston, Emerson paused in the midst of his lecture.

There was to be a new saint, he said, than whom none purer or more brave was ever led by love of men into conflict and death. "The new saint awaiting his martyrdom" — the speaker's voice, with

its thrilling quality, rang out over the hushed, shocked audience —
"if he shall suffer, will make the gallows glorious like the cross!"

On the day that Brown was hanged for treason, Concord held
memorial services. Even Rockwood Hoar, justice of the Supreme
Court of Massachusetts, took an active part, though he sided with
the selectmen when they refused Thoreau's request that the bell be
tolled, lest its ringing stir up a counter-demonstration. Thoreau, pro-
jector of the meeting, though his emotions had fevered him and
made him sick, could feel no sorrow on this day of translation. Of
all his contemporaries, it seemed to Henry that John Brown was
the only one who had not died.

Hawthorne, returning to Concord from his European missions,
listened to reverberations which grew louder and louder. He hoped
he had not heard aright the phrase attributed to Emerson, his esteemed acquaintance. Nobody had been more justly hanged than
this bloodstained fanatic Brown. There was even a certain intellectual
satisfaction in his death as requital for his preposterous miscal-
culations.

The evening after Brown's execution, Francis Jackson Meriam,
one of the raiders — with a price on his head — knocked at the door
of the house on Main Street where Sanborn lived. Sanborn was out,
but his sister Sarah took in the fugitive, gave him supper, and kept
him out of sight. Half-crazed by his adventures, he spoke wildly
of raising another insurrection. Sarah met her brother at the door
and told him who was inside. Sanborn went at once to Emerson's.
"I'd like to borrow your mare Dolly early tomorrow morning
for a drive to Acton."
"Certainly," said Emerson.
At Henry Thoreau's, Sanborn explained he was harboring a friend
who must be taken, even if he protested, to catch the Canada train
at South Acton. Would Henry drive him?
Next morning Thoreau got his passenger, tucking him into the
rear of the closed carriage.
He must see Mr. Emerson; he had important plans to lay before
him, insisted the man in the back seat.
Imperturbably Henry drove along the lonely road.
"Perhaps you are Mr. Emerson? You look like one of his por-
traits."

"No," said the driver, urging Dolly to a quicker gait.

Meriam flung himself out of the carriage.

"I'm going back to Concord!" he shouted.

But Henry was as quick as he. Skillfully, persuasively, he argued with the distraught boy. That evening he saw him off to Canada.

Sanborn was on his way to the village post office. It was almost five-thirty, and January darkness dimmed the snow-clogged streets. As the schoolmaster fumbled for his letters, he was startled by an unfamiliar voice. Next moment he felt something thrust in his hand. It was a summons, said the stranger, to appear at Washington before a Senate committee of inquiry.

"Shall I write them you will be there?"

"Make such return as you please," answered Sanborn, and walked away lest his refusal to declare himself lead to arrest.

Ephraim Bull and John S. Keyes, both just back from the Capital, had conflicting views to offer. Senator Wilson had warned Bull the investigation would be strictly and vengefully carried out; Sumner had told Keyes that the committee, not wishing to goad the North, would be lenient. Either way Sanborn would be a key witness.

Frank began arranging things at the school for a fortnight's absence — perhaps at Montreal. But Judge Hoar assured him that any attempt to take him to Washington could be prevented by a *habeas corpus*.

As a precaution, his friends lodged him in their houses: a night at Colonel Whiting's, another at the manse, at Emerson's, at Mrs. Thoreau's. But so sure had he become that the Southern senators would not give him the advantage of gaining public sympathy that he decided to spend the night of April third at home

Just past nine. He and Sarah were returning from a call. Frank lighted the lamp and was putting on his slippers when he heard a knock at the door. Two men stood in the darkness.

"Run to Colonel Whiting!" shouted Sanborn to his sister as one of the intruders began to read from a warrant.

Screaming at the top of her lungs, Sarah dodged past the pair; past two more men lurking in the street and a fifth driving up in a hack. In less than a minute she had roused the Whitings and the Bigelows next door.

Meanwhile the men clapped handcuffs on her brother and were trying to drag him into the carriage. But Sanborn had remarkably long legs — "God Almighty's tongs," an irreverent farmer had called him on first catching sight of him striding about in a theatrical performance staged by Louisa Alcott. Sanborn had always shone in these affairs, his abundant hair sweeping in a dark cascade almost to his shoulders, his romantic if slightly weak features aglow with fervor. Now those legs served a more serious purpose. Each time his captors tried to push him through the door he thrust his agile limbs this way and that, blocking the passage.

Anne Whiting began to belabor the horses with a broom so that their plunging would hinder the abductors. Brawny Francis Bigelow, the blacksmith, running up, pitched into the battle.

The First Parish bell started ringing. Soon thirty or forty excited persons gathered, blocking the road. Emerson, though his house was a half-mile away, arrived in a very few moments. Even young Mason, a Southern scholar at the Academy who once had cursed the teacher for being an abolitionist, was now on hand to help in his rescue. John S. Keyes, warned by Grace Mitchell, another of Sanborn's pupils, ran to Judge Hoar's for a writ of *habeas corpus*. Keyes had no use for the violent antislavery people — but this rape of a fellow townsman was a different matter.

The mob had swelled to over a hundred. Keyes served the writ on the kidnapers. Their carriage pounded with stones, their clothes in shreds, the would-be abductors fled toward the city.

Next day, by consent, Sanborn appeared before Chief Justice Shaw — John S. Keyes, John Andrew, and others as his counsel.

No one save an officer of the Senate, the Justice pronounced, had legal authority to make such an arrest.

His wrists still marked by the manacles, his hands a bit stiff, Sanborn returned to Concord. It was a hero's homecoming, with speeches by Grindall Reynolds, new minister of the First Parish Church, by Thomas Wentworth Higginson of the Boston Kansas Committee, by Thoreau, Alcott, and Emerson.

Right after the Sanborn fracas, John S. Keyes left for Chicago as a member of the Massachusetts delegation to the Republican National Convention. Governor Seward of New York, said the Bay State hierarchy, was sure to be nominated — their journey was a mere matter of form.

But when they got to Chicago, the aloof dignitaries from Massachusetts found themselves rudely jostled by the vigorous Westerners. Keyes, younger than the others, with a lively sense of humor and a ready wit, his sociable spirit delighting in public occasions, got on well with these wild men. Ruddy-faced, stocky, ruggedly built, popping with energy and brashness, he was all over the hall, plunging at once in the midstream of public opinion. These Westerners, he learned, had not the slightest intention of following the lead of the capitalistic seaboard. The panic of 1857, with its intolerable weight of mortgages laid on by Wall and State Street bankers, was too fresh in their memories. They had their own candidate.

Lincoln was named on the third ballot.

Keyes did not share the horror of his fellow delegates from New England. Though he stuck to Seward, he was a practical enough politician to perceive the strategy behind the nomination. In Town Meeting among Concord's rough farmers he had learned respect for the power of a man of the people. This crude, homespun rustic — with his shrewd, reliably homely face and amazing gift of gab — could carry the West, an outcome next to impossible for Seward.

Though urged to protest against the new party's antislavery fence round the Western lands, the Democratic Convention hesitated to write a proslavery plank into its platform. Promptly the Southerners bolted, and named John C. Breckinridge of Kentucky as their candidate. Douglas became the choice of the regulars, but it looked as if the split might wreck the chances of the party. Silently many men realized that the election of a Republican president would have one certain outcome — South Carolina would secede from the Union, taking with her as many sister states as she could.

With other nominees more or less out of the running, the campaign was Lincoln versus Douglas, and a resumption of those debates which had won Abe his enthusiastic Western following. Again on the eve of election, through the Concord streets, boys carried torches and transparencies. "Old North Bridge, Ever True to Freedom!" "Lincoln and Hamlin, Andrew and Goodrich!" Even Bronson Alcott, who up to this election had agreed with his friend Thoreau that no man should surrender his independence by consenting to make use of the ballot under the auspices of a government which he could not honor, cast his first vote for a president and governor. Should John A. Andrew enter the State House, a steadfast defender of the abolitionists would at last hold office.

*   *   *

"The pronunciation of the masses of America against slavery" was Emerson's comment on the Republican triumph — though to John S. Keyes it looked more like support for the principle of Union.

Soon after the victory, Keyes was opening a letter from the incoming President. It contained his appointment as United States Marshal for Massachusetts.

Several days before the inauguration, John S. Keyes was on hand in Washington to carry out his duty of protecting the President. To Keyes, the marshals thus far named from other states appeared alarmingly apathetic, so he readily and energetically assumed the burdens of his trust. Already he had sworn in a dozen Massachusetts men, had got their badges and secured good horses.

That evening, at the Willard, as he tossed in bed, he thought over the appalling dangers. South Carolina seceded in December; a Confederate Government formed that February! War was in the air. Slave territory lay on every side of Washington — and Buchanan's disintegrating cabinet, the Congress, all Washington, was a termites' nest of secessionists. An attempt on Lincoln's life seemed more than possible.

Next morning, very early, as Keyes sat in the lobby, who should walk in but Mr. Lincoln himself, looking wan and haggard after his night's train ride.

Later, the Massachusetts marshal called to confer. The long, lank, lean, ill-dressed President-elect shook hands cordially. Then Keyes explained that he had studied carefully the route of the inaugural procession. Were there any particular ceremonies Mr. Lincoln wished observed?

Lincoln threw his bony leg over the top of the table at which he was sitting.

"My only wish is to go to the Capitol, take the oath, and return to the White House as directly as possible."

Somehow Lincoln's attitude, the good stories he told, cast a happier light on the uncertainties of the morrow.

A gusty wind was blowing dust in the eyes of the procession. Keyes kept his horse abreast of the carriage, and close as possible, to shield Lincoln from possible snipers. The huge unfinished dome of the Capitol looked like a bashed-in egg up the interminable distance which they still must travel along broad and messy Pennsyl-

vania Avenue. Buchanan, the young marshal noticed, looked faint
and nervous — very tired, almost collapsed, as if riding to his execution. The man who was really facing trouble sat calm and collected,
speaking occasionally to the committeemen on the front seat, and
bowing at the faint huzzas that greeted the carriage.

At the Capitol, Keyes took his post less than ten feet from the
President, keeping his watchful eye on the crowd. They did not
seem to take very well what the awkward, ungainly man was saying,
or pay much attention, but Keyes, despite his anxiety, was impressed
by the good sense and homely strength of the phrases which began
to penetrate his concentration on duty.

"Physically speaking, we cannot separate," Lincoln declared, his
words evidently on secession. Keyes could readily agree. This nation
is too complex, too intermeshed to be torn asunder without fatal
consequences.

"I hold that, in contemplation of the universal law and of the Constitution, the Union of these States is perpetual."

Keyes glanced at the earnest speaker. Surely Lincoln was the
homeliest man he had ever laid eyes on! A cross between Jake Farmer
and Beauty Weatherbee, the two homeliest plowmen in Concord.
Like theirs, it was a friendly ugliness, but with a strange, inexplicable
dignity.

"I shall take care," Lincoln was adding, "as the Constitution itself
expressly enjoins upon me, that the laws of the Union be faithfully
executed in all the States."

On Sunday, at Concord, the inhabitants were just coming out of
church when they got the news that the flag of the Union had been
fired on. Each man wondered, and every woman, if this meant
war; if their company, the Concord Artillery, of the Fifth Regiment, Massachusetts Volunteer Militia, would be mustered to the
colors.

On Monday, April 15, 1861, using red ink, Alcott made an entry
in his diary:

"News comes of General Anderson's surrender of Fort Sumter,
and of President Lincoln's call for 75,000 volunteers."

George, son of Stedman Buttrick, was plowing in the fields which
his great-grandfather, Major John of the fight at the bridge, had
been plowing many Aprils before. His thoughts kept wandering

from the furrow, and the heavy team lurched and stumbled. Had his father brought the morning's paper from the village?

One glance at the front page, and George did not return to his oxen. The Fifth Regiment had been ordered to Washington.

At the Town House he met up with several members of the artillery company and the captain, Richard Barrett, grandson of the Revolutionary colonel. Plenty of room for volunteers, said the captain. He set the new recruit to work. Members on distant farms to be notified; others who might wish to join. It was Wednesday; they would leave on Friday.

Again the hour of national crisis had struck at a crucial farming season.

Edward Selfridge Wheeler, just out of grammar school and learning the trade of carpenter, had few problems. The high school, which met in the Town House, had just been dismissed, and many of the girls were watching from the gallery. Ed soon had on a uniform from the extra supply. When she saw him dressed as a soldier, his sister Mary streaked for home. Just as Ed and a couple of companions strutted into the square, his father arrived on the run.

"Take off that uniform!"

Edward stuck to his resolution. If he did not enlist now, he pointed out, he would have to serve later among strangers.

George Buttrick was also having difficulties. His vision was poor and the medical officer sent to examine the men was known to be tough.

"Is your eyesight good?"

"No, I'm a little nearsighted. Guess I could fire a gun though."

"Take a look at the door of that barn across the field and tell what you see."

George gave an excellent description, even to a knothole near the top. Warned that this was the doctor's method of testing, he had already made an inventory.

There was trouble as to who would be in charge. Perhaps he could go later; he could not go now, said Captain Barrett, for two decades the company's commander. There was no one he could trust with the management of his heavily mortgaged farm. His work at the Middlesex Fire Insurance office was of vital importance.

For a moment this decision threatened the wreck of the enterprise. But George Prescott, leader of the young people since the days of the Abstinence Society, came up with the answer.

"I intend to go," he said, "if I go alone."

As lieutenant in command, he mustered the men.

Toward the bottom of the roll call: Ball . . . Fitzpatrick . . . Garty . . . Hosmer — farmers, Irish farm hands, storekeepers, artisans, clerks — Lieutenant Prescott paused. "There's that young Wheeler," he remarked, "they say he isn't eighteen years old." But Judge Rockwood Hoar whispered to the lieutenant that the boy had won his father's consent.

The whole town had emptied into the square — head selectman Ephraim Bull, superintendent of schools Bronson Alcott, town clerk George Heywood, Grindall Reynolds the minister. And there was Mr. Emerson, shaking hands and speaking words of encouragement as his grandfather had done at the start of the Revolution. A five-dollar gold piece was handed each volunteer, along with Concord's promise to look after his family.

Almost noon now. The company, as guests of the town, marched to the Middlesex Hotel for dinner. Then back to the square again where Nathan Hosmer after valiant struggles had at last replaced the missing upper section of the staff so they could run up the flag. More speeches — then the whistle of the train. Blond, ruddy-cheeked, fine-looking, Lieutenant Prescott raised his sword. But before he could order forward march, his wife burst through the crowd for a farewell kiss. Then, in a swirl of yelling, laughing people — and some who wept — the column swung toward the station.

The inhabitants watched the train vanish behind Walden woods, then walked silently home.

Under a cloudy sky, with occasional showers, the company marched to improvised regimental quarters at Faneuil Hall. Saturday brought an issue of brand-new Springfield rifled muskets, each man turning in his old one, and of sky-blue overcoats, made of felt and rather cumbersome, but a fair substitute that night for the blankets which most of the men lacked. That day by ballot in the time-honored fashion, the Concord Company elected its officers: Lieutenant Prescott, Captain; Joseph Derby, Charles Bowers, Humphrey Buttrick (George's cousin), lieutenants; five sergeants, among them Cyrus Hosmer, descendant of the Revolutionary adjutant; George Buttrick himself among the corporals though he never had drilled.

Sunday, about daylight, the Fifth Massachusetts marched to the Boston and Albany station. The Massachusetts Sixth, which had gone before, had been stoned on its way through Baltimore.

Delays at the station, and at Springfield. Not till dusk that evening did the regiment reach New York. Marching by company front down Broadway, their overcoats stiff and enormous, the men grinned at admiring comments on the size of the soldiers from Massachusetts.

At the fashionable St. Nicholas Hotel — the rest of the regiment had been billeted elsewhere — the Concord Company ate their first square meal after three days of sandwiches and coffee.

Though dawn was approaching, the streets were empty and dark when the company set out, as they thought, for the station. Instead, they found themselves at the North River piers. There the whole regiment, along with the First Massachusetts Battery, their guns and horses, crowded aboard the steamer *De Soto*, so packed that most of the soldiers stood through what was left of the night.

The ship's pitching and tossing added seasickness to the general misery of the thousand or more landsmen. Two days of retching, stench, filth, cold — then smoother water in the late afternoon and the sight of Fortress Monroe dim on the hostile Virginia shore. Explosive Baltimore had been by-passed.

A downpour of rain, that night, postponed the landing at Annapolis. But Wednesday dawned clear. Before eight, Concord's Company were ashore, rifles stacked on the Naval Academy grounds and guarded by two disconsolate sentries. Men rushed in all directions in quest of food — the prodigals trading their gold pieces for a mess of pottage.

Corporal George Buttrick found a row of oyster boats just in from the Chesapeake. Soon he and the members of the squad, then most of the company, had moved aboard, eating oysters as fast as the shuckers could open them. Call again in the afternoon, remarked the oystermen; but in the afternoon came an order to fall in.

Two o'clock, three o'clock, four. Waiting for something to happen, growled newmade cynics, was soldiering's principal function. That, and swapping rumors: the Federal stores at Portsmouth had just been burned lest they fall into the hands of the rebels; Virginia Secessionists were attacking the Navy Yard at Norfolk; the way to Washington was already blocked.

Past ten, and at last the regiment moved to the station, the Concord Company seventh in the line.

Room for only the first five companies. The rest must march till a returning train could pick them up.

On the awkwardly spaced ties the column headed into the darkness. Every moment some sore-footed soldier would miss his step, clattering with his rifle to the tracks. Most had thin boots which wore through the soles. All semblance of military order soon vanished and the companies became hopelessly mixed, even the most vigorous walkers half-asleep.

A roving squad of rebels had pulled the spikes from the tracks and derailed the returning train.

The sun, next morning, shone hot on the antlike, depleted line. Tired almost to death after fifteen hours of marching, the raw recruits slumped into the grove at Annapolis Junction where the right wing of the regiment waited.

So great was the fear of attack that no unit was permitted to leave the Junction till another arrived. That night the sweaty, exhausted men slept without blankets on the open ground. By next morning the tracks had been repaired, and relieving troops had arrived at Annapolis. The Fifth rode to Washington — guards, on the lookout for sabotage, patrolling every foot of the way.

The Concord Company took over a room in the Treasury Building. The stone floor was very hard and very cold. At least, remarked Corporal George Lauriat, wrapping his overcoat about him, there was no danger of being kicked out of bed.

Captain Prescott, his ruddy face drawn with fatigue, was finishing a letter. All the way, cheerful and hearty, he had looked after his men. Now he felt free to air his opinions. "We had an awful time getting here," he wrote. "No regiment had a harder. We came before we were ready. No regiment should start until *fully equipped*."

When the baker got drunk — a chronic affliction — the company dined on iron-hard bread. Smoked pork three times a week was the principal meat. Clothing raised another crisis. At the first official review the regiment got an eyeful. Captain Wardwell's men, from Boston, were still in civilians'. Every other unit had on the garish rig which time-honored convention had draped upon it. Silliest of all was the Concord Company's. The red-trimmed blue coats with their absurd bobtails soiled and torn to tatters, the tall, hot bearskins, the red-trimmed indigo pants, made their wearers look like comic opera soldiers caught in an earthquake. When fatigue uniforms of the regular army were issued, the regiment climbed into them with relief. But only the outer layer was thus provided for. Two weeks in service and no fresh underwear. The lack was growing emphatically noticeable.

The nights stayed cool, yet only thirty blankets had been issued. One cover for every two men on those morguelike floors. Generally the more wakeful, watchful soldier, when his companion slept, managed to disengage the entire blanket and curl up in it. Corporal Buttrick, having thus filched his neighbor's, was dropping into semiconsciousness when he felt a gentle tugging. This premature attempt at robbery he greeted with a burst of curses, only to hear the voice of the captain mildly expostulating — Prescott never swore, though he never chided those who enjoyed it — "Why, George, your feet were sticking out and I was covering them to prevent your taking cold!"

Sickness in plenty — diarrhoea and sore throats. When Judge Rockwood Hoar came to Washington — he was having conferences with the President, with General Butler, and various cabinet officers — with a bundle of mail from Concord, the men felt better than at any moment since arriving. Soon boxes from Concord began to arrive — underwear, socks, handkerchiefs, tobacco, sixty-four crash towels hemmed by Miss Dillingham's pupils of the intermediate school, sixty sewing kits assembled by Miss Bean's charges.

On the first of May Colonel Lawrence's command marched to the White House grounds. There they were sworn into Union service for three months — long enough, surely, to finish the war — and the ancient and honorable Concord Artillery became G Company, Fifth Massachusetts Regiment, United States Infantry. Dressed in black, with a stovepipe hat, President Lincoln stood on the veranda. The men passed close enough to notice his extreme height, his kindly expression. Not very handsome, thought Private Brown of Lexington road, but he looks smart.

A cub West Pointer had been assigned to drill the Company. Three hours daily in the sun, in the rain, then back to quarters on the double. Colonel Lawrence — who rode a horse — had a passion for double quick, though at first the men dropped like ninepins. One day the officers of G Company had all gone to the range, and the professional from the Academy took advantage of the chance to bully and abuse the enlisted men. But Captain Prescott, learning of it, took the young man aside. These were volunteers, he explained, eager to learn, ready to die for their beliefs, but expecting their leaders to behave like gentlemen. The West Pointer caught Prescott's meaning. Soon the company was taking pride in its gathering endurance and skill.

Washington was one vast armed camp, fresh regiments arriving daily. Sixteen, twenty, twenty-five thousand troops. With government buildings crowded, the newcomers camped in the public squares or on the outskirts of the city. General Butler was opening the road to Philadelphia. With Maryland in a proper attitude, surely the compliments of the season would next be paid to Virginia.

But nothing happened. Each Concord soldier was now sure of at least one thing — waiting makes up the bulk of a soldier's life: for rations, equipment, pay. Waiting in formation. Waiting for no known reason. Waiting.

Prescott at last arranged with the colonel for passes, and things grew better.

Wandering about, Corporal George Lauriat was disappointed. He had expected a city like Boston, but so many of the streets and buildings were unfinished! Lieutenant Bowers remarked he did not mind the rain so much — it rained a lot — but hated the mud, a bilious-colored clay, sticky and horrible for walking.

Older men often stopped you on the street.

"What state you from?"

"Massachusetts."

Then a handshake, or sour looks. Plenty of Southerners still in the city.

Young Francis Buttrick, thinking of pickerel he had caught in Concord, liked to stand where the long bridge crossed the Potomac. A Federal picket paced up and down on the Washington end, a Confederate sentry at the other. On the opposite shore, some fishermen were rigging a seine. Promising to venture no farther than half across, Francis got past the Union guard. The Virginians were hauling in their nets.

Could he go buy some fish? — he asked the Confederate sentry.

That evening, Francis and his cronies held a feast on fresh shad.

Horace Greeley's *Tribune* led the Northern press in a howl for action.

Friday, May 24, toward midnight, Lieutenant Bowers was writing letters when he heard the muted tap of a drum. Hurrying to the gate he peered into the street. Silently, save for their measured tread, a multitude of soldiers was passing, the moonlight glinting on the bayonets. For an hour the steady platoons kept marching. Then the road grew still as the grave.

Bowers could get no more sleep. Before daylight he was out, but no one he met could tell what had happened. At six-thirty, while he lingered in front of Headquarters at Willard's, three mounted couriers galloped up. Fifteen thousand troops had crossed the Potomac. Alexandria, seven miles below Washington, had been captured with hardly a shot fired. The war was on.

At noon Colonel Lawrence, very excited, told the regiment to prepare immediately for action. In less than fifteen minutes, ten minutes ahead of the rest, G Company was ready in the street. Double-quick, ordered the colonel. Across the Potomac and into the green Virginia country trotted the men, their hearts pounding, their lungs ready to burst. So done-in were they when commanded to halt that, had the enemy appeared, hardly a man could have mustered strength to pull a trigger.

But this stop was not on account of the enemy. Colonel Lawrence had not studied his instructions. A mounted courier, overhauling the regiment, bore orders for them to return to quarters for the rest of their equipment. Not till ten that night did they set out again, this time in heavy marching order, with company and regimental supplies stowed in baggage wagons.

They marched till well past midnight — this time, unlike the disorganized trek from Annapolis, in orderly formation. At one-thirty on Sunday morning they reached an open meadow. On lush, foot-high grass heavy with dew, the men slept better than at any time since getting to Washington.

Later that day the regiment moved to join several others on a high point of land overlooking the river about two miles northwest of Alexandria. Here was a clear brook on either side of which to pitch their "A" tents, and a level field for drill. Pickets were posted and the kitchens set up. No one was sure how long the Fifth Massachusetts would stay, but there would be beans for dinner, already baked Saturday night.

Their chief job turned out to be guard duty in and around Alexandria. The Minnesota First Regiment had swelled the brigade's numbers — strappers, thought the men from Massachusetts, suspender-busters and as straight as arrows! When the brigade paraded through Alexandria, they made a great addition to the line.

The secessionists left in the town had not expected this march. Women with brothers, sons, husbands in the Southern army broke into tears, fearing the troops were headed for Manassas.

> Davis is a traitor, Davis is a thief,
> Davis steals from Uncle Sam
> But soon he'll come to grief . . .

sang G Company, shouting out the words invented by Asa Melvin —

> We will go to Davis' house,
> And if he hasn't fled,
> One of the Concord butcher boys
> Will chop off Davis' head!

But picket duty at night was a squeamish business. A flash; the whirr of a bullet. The first man killed in the Fifth Regiment was shot on picket duty. Corporal George Buttrick, moving in the blackness from post to post, was amazed to discover how extraordinarily scared a man can get. Daylight was a blessing though it brought five hours of drill in weather hot enough to cook bacon. Many times the boys from Concord longed for Walden and a swim.

In his Fourth of July speech, Colonel Lawrence announced there were sixty thousand troops this side of the Potomac, under command of General Irwin McDowell. But here was the morning of July sixteenth, and nothing stirring.

The boys had polished their rifles till they glistened. What they heard about the rebels was puzzling. Their chief forces — nearly thirty thousand, it was said, under an old West Pointer, General Beauregard — were at Manassas Junction, toward the southwest about twenty miles distant. But thus far, in spite of all their boasting, they kept retreating from every position and very likely would from this one.

That evening Captain Prescott got his orders. The regiment would march at ten in the morning. Three days' cooked rations for their haversacks; forty rounds of ammunition. He wished they could have shelter tents, or at least rubber blankets. Not a man, fortunately, on sick list, and all in the best spirits. They were good boys, thought the captain, fine boys. He cared a great deal for every one of them. He would do his best by each.

Back in Concord, Emerson and his friends were smiling over Lowell's witty, cheerful "Pickens-and-Stealin's Rebellion" in the June *Atlantic*. Probably Lowell was right about the Southern character — they would not put up a real battle. But Emerson refused to minimize the Confederate soldier. A Southern minority, because it knew how to fight, had dominated Congress — why should that temperament change when it turned to gunpowder? And Alcott, in place of flowers, planted a vegetable garden.

Hoeing his beans took time, but Alcott was giving even more to Concord's schools since the town, after years of neglecting his talents, had risked appointing him Superintendent — at one hundred dollars a year. He tramped from district school to school, six miles from Nine Acre Corner to Bateman's Pond. He reported so fully and faithfully every month to his School Committee that he wore them nearly to a frazzle.

The first object of a free people, declared Alcott, his gentle, kindly eyes shining, is the preservation of their liberty. But freedom is a social no less than an individual concern, and one object of the State is to protect it. The surest means, an enlightened education, is the best gift it can bestow on its children. And there should be strict equality among boys and girls for the privilege of learning.

The Superintendent pled for better-paid, permanent teachers, who would take pride in their achievements — teachers, he insisted, possessed of living minds to inform and quicken the living minds of children. Teachers' meetings, the committee agreed, were among the most important and useful novelties he had introduced. So were the occasional Sunday evening gatherings of the parents in the several districts.

A taste for books, said Alcott, and good habits of reading, are omens in times of stress of happier things to come. The town must build for that future, must collect a well selected assortment for the special use of the children. Not just old books. New ones too: Hawthorne's *Liberty Tree*, his *Wonder Book* and *Tanglewood Tales*. "I am sure the Committee," wrote the Superintendent, "have offered a good suggestion to other towns in putting into our schools copies of the *Constitution* and of the *Declaration of Independence*."

Nowadays everybody takes a newspaper. But the schools still wait for theirs. A good one, thought Alcott, would catch hold wonderfully, a magazine of people, sports, amusements, science, nature, art — and something of politics too, and of the times.

Painting and drawing became part of the studies. Perhaps few of the boys needed gymnastics, but the girls certainly did. Dancing and music also, giving zest and relieving the long day's tedium.

All this, and lots besides, Alcott put into his reports, astonishing many inhabitants by their size and doctrines. One hundred and sixty-five dollars to print his report, while the selectmen issued theirs for thirty-two dollars and ninety-two cents! At this disclosure, some of the pennywise farmers began skulking in the electioneering underbrush for the Superintendent's scalp.

Most exciting feature of Alcott's program, from the town's point of view, was the annual exhibition.

"We spend much on our Cattle and Flower Shows," said the Superintendent; "let us each spring have a show of our children and begrudge nothing for their culture."

By the brevity of his remarks, John S. Keyes, chairman of the festival and school committee, set an excellent example. Sam Staples, master of ceremonies, presented the performers. "Fresh varieties from our conservatory," said Sam, rising to the occasion; "good stock, and music hopping about from twig to twig."

The stress of war now threatened the entire program, snatching away boys like Billy Bowers, the lieutenant's son, just seventeen. Yet the three months' enlistment was nearly ended. Rumor that a battle pended had drawn several Concord elders to Washington where they hired carriages to go watch the downfall of rebellion.

The Fifth Massachusetts headed the column as the brigade marched Wednesday morning, July seventeenth, toward Fairfax Court House and Manassas Junction. G Company labored under its blanket rolls slung like boa constrictors over every right shoulder, the heavy Springfield on the left and heavier haversack on each sweating back. Camp in an open field that night after nine hours' marching — sleep fitful through intermittent exchanges between pickets and the roving enemy who let out high-pitched, bloodcurdling yells that were hard to get used to. Then up and on at half-past four. All day the column advanced into enemy country — experienced men like Gene Wright, who had fought Indians in the West during two years in the regular army, bothered because the leaders sent out neither scouts nor flankers. But such enemies as they met, save for one unwary picket of six rebels who surrendered, vanished quickly into the woods.

Sangsters Railroad Station, between Fairfax and Manassas, at 3 P.M., just too late to intercept part of the Confederate army, though the Fifth fired at their rear guard.

Rations already were running low, the boys who had loaded up with corned beef — "salt horse," as the army called it — finding it spoiled on the very first morning. While the regiment stood at attention before stacking arms, an order was read threatening punishment to all caught foraging. But so many sheep and hogs and domes-

tic fowl wandering about made the men's mouths water. While the
provost guard was not looking, members of G Company managed
to bayonet several ducks, some turkeys and chickens.

That night, the regiment's field staff, including the colonel, dined
well, along with the culprits.

Friday evening brought the Fifth, in a drizzling rain, after an
exhausting all-day march, to one of the many hills overlooking Centerville. Here they found themselves part of the largest encampment
any man of them ever had seen.

All Saturday the Northern army waited, watching the slow smoke
where the rebels were burning bridges.

Sunday morning, before the first streak of daylight, the troops
were ready to move.

"I want some holes in that flag before night," said Colonel Lawrence, pausing to inspect the regimental colors. Yes, but what about
holes under it? — thought its members, among them Corporal Buttrick.

Though reveille had blown at two, the sun was up before the
regiment threaded its way through the confusion of camp toward
Centerville, then over the bridge that crossed Cut Run — as they
called a stream in this part of the world. Ahead lay another creek
— Bull Run, someone said it was. The bridge over it was smashed.

The column turned to the right into a dense oak grove along the
stream — artillery and rifle fire somewhere fairly close at hand raising a terrific racket. Trees had been felled across the road, making
tough, slow work for the engineers. The rebels were on the run,
said occasional couriers; they must hurry or miss the fight.

Colonel Lawrence took them over the stream at a ford. After ordering them to drop all unnecessary equipment, including canteens, he
gave command for double-quick, heading past little windrows of
dead soldiers which the panting men stared at, not quite believing
what they saw. Beyond that strip of brush lay the enemy.

As they cleared the wood, then halted under the blazing Virginia
sun, an officer from the staff hurried up. Corporal Buttrick of the
Color Guard, gasping for breath, was close enough to hear.

"Colonel, can you make your regiment charge? If you can *only*
get them to charge!"

"They're too tired. Let them rest a few minutes and they'll
charge."

When the regiment got back its wind, something had evidently
happened to the battle. The mass of Confederate troops ahead had

moved to the right, toward a secure position on a near-by plateau. The chance to cut them off was lost.

The regiment now hung in a doldrum of ineffective fighting, shooting at long range at the enemy. To the left, the farthest-over companies watched with horror as the supporting Eleventh Massachusetts fired by mistake into its own advance platoons. Then came fresh orders to march toward the right along a road sheltered for some distance by the brow of a hill, though the way itself was so jammed with soldiers that the men, shuffling through the dust, were forced to halt every few moments.

Up ahead burst the sound of concentrated fire. No one seemed sure what was going on, though Colonel Lawrence, lacking a courier to keep him posted, kept shouting to find out. The men from Concord were learning a second principle of soldiering — a man can know nothing more of what is happening in battle than what he sees. Like a badly managed freight train, the column of companies bumped together and came to an absolute halt. There they stuck for what seemed hours — out of the fire but also out of the fight.

In front, as Company G learned later, there was no fighting — there was slaughter. In close formation, the head of the column, topping the hill where the road ran over, was caught in a funnel of bullets. Along with most of the guard, the colors were down till Corporal Buttrick snatched up the Union standard and brought it back to where the sergeant major was posted. No one could locate the colonel and rumor flew that he was wounded.

Hot, thirsty, not knowing what to make of it, the line fumbled in confusion with no visible sign of command.

Captain Prescott, deciding the time had come to act on his own, deployed his company along the brow of the rise, where they could perhaps make effective resistance. The other captains might follow the example.

None of them did.

G Company had gone perhaps twenty rods farther when Prescott, glancing to the left, sang out at the top of his lungs, "Get into the woods, boys, the rebels are behind us!"

To the right, in a little depression, stood a grove of trees. Already rifle fire was whistling among the ranks. Projectiles from the batteries of both armies screamed overhead. At a sprint, the men broke for cover.

*   *   *

All over the rolling country that bordered Bull Run, brigades, regiments, companies, were reverting to what they really were — untrained soldiers, mobs of men in utter bewilderment, a tide of demoralized humanity swirling in flight towards the Potomac.

During what was left of daylight, few members of the Concord Company saw each other again, caught up in the general flood — artillerymen on foot without their guns, along with infantry and an occasional citizen who had come from Washington to see the rebels whipped. Now and then the hurrying mob met some officer who exhorted them to halt and form lest the rebels cut the line of retreat. As effectively beg the wind to stop blowing.

Past an occasional field hospital moved the flight, where ambulances had driven up with their loads, blood dripping from the wagons like water from an ice-cart. What had been dust was now a red and trampled ooze.

Each bridge still standing across Cob Creek bore a solid clutter of army wagons. Every few moments a shell from a Confederate masked battery would burst in the midst of it. Men found it safer to wade and swim, tossing away their rifles if they had not already done so.

Between sundown and ten that evening, most members of G Company managed to struggle back to their camp at Centerville. No sooner had they dropped into an exhausted sleep than orders came to retreat to Alexandria. On their feet since an hour before dawn, with nothing to eat all day, and little to drink — and now they must march again. Men dropped by the roadside. It was impossible to rouse them.

Shortly after sunrise it began to rain. All that Monday, rain fell in a deluge. At Alexandria, in their sodden clothes, those of the Company who got there snatched a few hours' rest before they were again mustered. After dark, in the downpour, the regiment crossed Long Bridge into Washington.

Defeat — abject and humiliating.

On to Richmond! had reached its conclusion.

The men of the Fifth felt especially bitter. Ready to do their duty, they felt themselves victims of the blunders of untrained leadership. The regiment, though in the midst of battle, had not at any time been placed where it could perform effective service. Had they matched experiences with other units, they might have felt a little better.

Lucky for the Union that the Confederates in victory were almost as confused as the Union in defeat — their officers nearly as inept in handling masses of troops. Though its own momentum turned the Northern retreat into a rout, Beauregard could not press his advantage. Washington awaited the stroke, but it did not come.

Tidings of the battle reached Concord, with many rumors. The Company had been cut to pieces; had lost half its members! Several anguished hours passed before the arrival of kinder news. It was bad enough, at that — five men missing, either killed or prisoners. Civilians, gathered at the station to receive the rest, looked with wonderment at the men's tense faces, the torn and faded uniforms.

Concord had prepared a bountiful supper and had scheduled welcoming speeches at the Town House. What he really wanted, Corporal George Buttrick told himself, was a swim. Already the regiment had listened to its commander, with his arm in a sling, haranguing a large crowd in Boston, his words designed more for home consumption than for the soldier of the line. As the Company stood at attention in the hot square, George slipped from the ranks and went home. The house was deserted, but he found a towel, and the river was near.

CHAPTER XVI

"I Hate War"

I HATE war," said Captain Prescott. "A battle is dreadful to me." He and Grindall Reynolds were walking across the sandy strip of Concord Common. "Do you think it my duty to go back?"

"I cannot advise you," replied the minister, "this is a question whose affirmative answer may cost you your life."

By the end of October, three-and-a-half months after Bull Run, Prescott was again recruiting a company.

By mid-November, seventy men had decided to join. They would be in for three years. Defeat after defeat had at last taught the Union to expect a long conflict.

For home — businesses great or small to set in order; shops and farms to be planned for. The old cow sold, or the heifer. The little account in the Middlesex Institute for Savings to be reckoned up as a domestic nest egg.

For themselves, the inexpressible question: Why am I doing this; what am I fighting for?

Some had motives deeper than the temptation of the hundred-dollar bounty promised by the town, the desire for excitement, or the fear of staying home if their companions went.

James Baker Brown, Concord schoolmaster, impatient at the reluctance of several of his friends, scribbled his opinions into his diary: "The events of the last two weeks teach, in my judgment, that we are not yet fully alive to the magnitude of this struggle for nationality which is before us. This is the war of progressive civilization, and demands of every man the utmost sacrifice that he is able to make."

Funny, till that flag came down at Fort Sumter, I had little enough feeling about the country. The South has started this war, and by God, we'll finish it. If this Union goes, doesn't everything

*go with it? Secession, once accomplished, will be repeated till bit
by bit the United States will break into feeble little nations, mouth-
fuls for the monarchists of Europe who could kill with ease the last
survivals of liberty. Lest the whole be lost, not one shovelful of
sand on the southernmost key of Florida ought to be surrendered
by the Union.*

Older folks, like Mr. Emerson and Mr. Alcott, staying home, kept
saying slavery was the greater issue. Now was the time, men heard
Emerson say, to cut out this cancer of slavery. But Lincoln was
out to save the Union, and Lincoln was right.

Some Concord boys, visiting Boston, watched as a column of
soldiers, led by a son of Daniel Webster, came marching up State
Street. They were singing. No one knew where the catchy tune, the
queer, crude verses about old John Brown, had come from. But this
much was sure — its swing took command of your feet and its words
set your blood to tingling.

Rockwood Flint, lineal descendant of Thomas Flint, a founder
of the town, was fifteen years old and afraid the war would be over
before he could serve. So when no one was there he sneaked up
the winding stairs of the Town House to Prescott's headquarters
and put his name on the roll.

As for Prescott, though he himself could never phrase it, each
man knew that the captain was back in the war for a principle, was
again in uniform because he knew it his duty.

There was not much fuss when the Company left. They were not
going far. They were heading for garrison duty at Fort Warren,
on a bleak island in Boston Harbor. Here they became part of the
First Battalion, Major Francis J. Parker commanding.

In the next few hours B Company made the unpleasant discovery
that they were now under strictest discipline. In line with the practice of the regular army, no soldier, in the free and easy fashion of
volunteers, could sit in the presence of an officer. A failure to salute
meant the guard house. Strenuous daily drill for the six companies
— by squad, by platoon, by the whole battalion.

And always vigilant guard duty over eight hundred or so Con-
federate prisoners — soldiers from North Carolina captured by Gen-
eral Burnside. Also under lock and key were Mayor Brown of
Baltimore, Kane, his chief of police, and J. M. Mason and John
Slidell, Confederate agents taken by Captain Wilkes, of the Union
Navy, from the British steamer *Trent* — a business still raising merry

hell on both sides the Atlantic. For many a dreary night, in the bitter east wind, the soldiers of B Company patrolled that fort. It was going to be a very long winter.

In Concord and elsewhere, hard times were setting in for men of conscience — everyday business falling off or stopping entirely, though plenty of profiteers were raking in money. No new clothes for the children, few Christmas gifts, and always, everywhere, the war talk. Despair in the hearts of many Northerners about the conduct of things and Lincoln's inadequacy.

By April, 1862, B Company and the First Battalion had been drilled through the book. By May, Colonel Dimmock of the regular army, at a dress parade, complimented Major Parker on his disciplined troops, and the men of B Company — buttons gleaming (never a single pocket flapping), boots polished like an old copper pot — were heartily fed up with the course of sprouts that had developed them into soldiers.

On Sunday, May 25, one hour past midnight, as the battalion officers, feeling something was stirring, waited at headquarters, Major Parker came in. The battalion, he told them, had been activated as the Thirty-second Massachusetts Infantry Regiment, United States Army. They were to leave at once to protect Washington. McClellan's advance toward Richmond up the peninsula between the James and York Rivers had been checked by the rebel field defenses, then halted through diversion of reinforcements when the Confederate General, Stonewall Jackson, started a sudden march down the Shenandoah. Once again the Union capital was threatened.

An old stamping ground to many of the Massachusetts soldiers — but more bedraggled now. Indeed, Washington had the look of a beleaguered city and was deeper than ever in mud.

Five weeks of inaction — while the feints at Washington continued and McClellan, short of reinforcements, was retreating from his stand at Gaines's Mill where Lee, with superior forces, had expected to trap him — Gaines's Mill, only ten miles from Richmond.

While they waited, the Thirty-second, especially its officers, saw plenty of Washington. "A hornets' nest of spies and enemies" was the way the town impressed them. On the finer streets, as you walked along, elegant ladies swished away their skirts from the contaminating touch of Union blue. Children screeched and shook their fists.

Washington bumbledom had apparently forgotten them. The regiment, still numbering only half the regulation strength, remained an orphan, assigned to no brigadier, with no tents, no wagon train, no provisions except what they bought with money supplied by Massachusetts.

At last came an order to march to Alexandria. So they pitched camp, before nightfall, near that town. No higher-up having condescended to take charge of them, they invented their own countersign — they were well-trained troops — and had the pleasure of bagging half a dozen officers from neighboring outfits. Then suddenly headquarters noticed them, at least for a moment. Two new companies — one from Pennsylvania, one from Rhode Island — swelled their total to eight. But telegrams to Washington for instructions drew no further response.

They were supposed to proceed to Fortress Monroe in Chesapeake Bay, weren't they, then reinforce McClellan at Harrison's Landing? Colonel Parker decided to operate on his own hook. A ramshackle steamboat, misnamed *Hero*, was idling at the pier. The colonel, greeting the sour looks of her captain with a bland remark about military necessity, ordered the regiment aboard. At first her engineer quit, and her captain sulked in his cabin. But when the *Hero's* skipper saw the usurpers had plenty of men who enjoyed running his steamer and that it was his own rations they were eating, he decided to hurry the regiment towards its destination as the one way to get rid of them. Down the Potomac, into the Chesapeake, past the mouth of the York, past Yorktown where the ancestors of some in B Company had watched Cornwallis surrender. Then Old Point Comfort and Fortress Monroe. But no orders were waiting, so Colonel Parker ordered the sputtering skipper to proceed up the James to Harrison's Landing.

To the moment of coming ashore, the little regiment had lived practically by itself, knowing nothing of generals. At last the time had come when the Thirty-second, like a drop of water hitting the ocean, was to be absorbed into the army. As the boat hove to a landing, an officer jumped aboard, in his hand a soiled hunk of envelope. On this was scribbled in pencil: —

To commanding officer of troops on steamer. Land your men at once and move direct up the road to me at my headquarters, where you will be stopped. Come up with arms and ammunition. This order is from General McClellan.

F. J. PORTER, BRIGADIER GENERAL.

B Company, disembarking on the unlovely shore, stared curiously at the swarms of men in spattered uniforms — mud all around so deep it nearly pulled your boots off — who greeted them with derisive jibes at their cleanness and precise marching. These were the soldiers of McClellan's Army of the Potomac, who had just fought and won their most desperate battle at Malvern Hill, six miles distant, checking Lee's pursuit. They did not look like victors — yet they had decimated the enemy and had saved their self-respect and their wagon trains.

A pile of tolerably clean straw a quarter of a mile up the soggy road turned out to be headquarters. Colonel Parker, trying to report, stumbled over a dozen mud-stained, weary officers snatching a cat-nap. One roused sufficiently to admit he was General Griffin, who commanded the brigade they were being assigned to.

Would he mind addressing the new regiment, begged Colonel Parker?

Struggling to his feet, their brigadier made an effort to show interest in his reinforcements.

"We've had a tough time, men," he said, "and it isn't over yet, but we've whaled them every time and can whale them again."

Then he flopped back to the straw.

The regiment pitched its camp in a field bordering a grove. Beyond, in a marsh, vast numbers of lily-like plants were in blossom, strange to the men and very beautiful, but with a fragrance that grew sickening, soon hardly preferable to the smell of the dead — a carrion stench wafted over the encampment every time the breeze blew northeast over Malvern Hill.

For a while, nothing to relieve the monotony. Then B Company got news that further additions to the regiment were coming, among them G Company, largely from the vicinity of Concord, and commanded by Charles Bowers, lieutenant of Prescott's former outfit, with Edward Shepard, former teacher at the High School, as first lieutenant, George Lauriat, a former corporal, as top sergeant, Bowers' son, just eighteen, also a sergeant, and young Charlie Bartlett, the doctor's boy, among the Concordians in the ranks.

For some reason known perhaps to the superior powers, the regiment's camp was ordered shifted a half-mile towards the James, on ground so swampy the soldiers had to chuck in dirt and brush before they could lay their blankets. In less than a week, men began to burn and shiver with malarial fever — those still out of the improvised hospitals harassed at night by salvos from roving Confederate batteries. James Brown, now Company Clerk, was kept busy writing letters of condolence and attending the sick.

To be sent to the hospital turned out to be almost as fatal as a death warrant. By the second week of August, fourteen men of the Regiment had died. Soon a third of the command was stricken. The Thirty-second Regiment, once so brisk and military, degenerated to the shiftless, listless level of the rest. Beaten by overwork and anxiety, Captain Prescott himself was down with the fever.

Corporal Brown wrote an unauthorized letter. It was to Dr. Bartlett, at Concord.

As Dr. Bartlett came ashore at Harrison's Landing, he found three thousand sick men wrapped in blankets, awaiting transportation. They lay so close together under the open sky in the twilight that he had to pick his way with care lest he step on some of them.

After considerable searching, he found Prescott.

"I think I might do well enough," whispered the captain, so feeble had he grown, "if I could get out of this accursed hole." But that, he explained, was impossible; it would take too long to apply for a furlough.

Bartlett looked at his friend. Already he had reserved place on the return boat. Army red tape be damned; he would take Prescott with him.

On August 14, the regiment got its marching orders. They came like a reprieve from slow torture. Their fighting blood stirred at the prospect of action, with Richmond so close. Instead, Washington had ordered a piecemeal recall of the Army of the Potomac. The soldiers, who believed in him, could not know that the country had lost confidence in McClellan — he was a Democrat, too — and that Lincoln had refused to back him further.

After an exhausting trek under heavy packs down the entire dusty length of the Peninsula, the Thirty-second found itself back at Fortress Monroe where the abortive thrust at the heart of the Confederacy had started. Their next move, after Prescott rejoined them, was by boat into the Chesapeake, then back up the Potomac. At Aquia Creek, below Washington, the regiment disembarked.

A hundred miles, in depth, of Virginia had been abandoned. Now, learned the men, they were to be attached to an army under General Pope.

It was late in August. A year ago, the veterans were just returning to Concord from the rout at Bull Run. Here they were again,
headed right back for the old Manassas country.

Because men were still weak from malaria, the forced marches
were bad enough. But the manner in which they were carried out
was incredible.

Shortly after midnight, sometimes before, orders would come
down to get ready. The cursing, sleepy soldiers would fall in line,
march an hour or so, then the march would stall. Expecting each
moment that the column would move, no one dared fall out till
at last one man, then another, would sit by the roadside. Two hours,
three hours. Then, just as the climbing sun grew hot (no rain for
weeks — dust ankle-deep underfoot and a cloud of it over your
head), without warning the army would lurch into motion. No
time out for breakfast; no time for a snack at noon.

Often, ahead, they heard distant firing.

Sick, exhausted men, gray faces pinched, tortured bodies cramped
like mummies', would drop as the column passed, though Prescott,
as long as his horse lasted, managed to put one or two on its back
while he took to the road. Usually these derelicts hung onto their
rifles, but many of them were never heard from — dying either in
the parched fields or caught by the enemy.

At the very few wells, the shoving men, without any such intention, barred out the weakest who were most in need. Then the
straggling would begin — men in little groups stopping to light
fires and brew coffee. At ten or eleven at night, after twenty-five
miles, sometimes less than thirty soldiers — less than half a company
— would arrive at the designated camp site with the leading captain;
none of these, like as not, members of his own command. All night
long the men would come toiling in — all, that is, who would ever
get there.

In the last week of August, after criss-cross marches and skirmishes
with no discernible objective, the brigade found itself close to
Bull Run.

On the Orange and Alexandria Railroad, near Manassas Junction,
they passed a long train loaded with casualties, the cars packed so
full that many wounded had been laid on the roofs. There had been
a repetition of the first battle. For a third time, Washington was
threatened.

Though they had not fired a shot in this final action, the Thirty-
second Regiment was as badly decimated as some that had. A

week's rest was imperative. The regiment got it at Upton's Hill, on the outskirts of the Capital, where it also received a thorough overhauling. Captain Prescott found himself advanced to lieutenant colonel, and Cyrus Tay took over B Company. Three freshly recruited companies were assigned to the regiment, their numbers exceeding those of the shrunken eight companies they reinforced.

But the new men, looking somewhat apprehensively at the sun-tanned, wiry complement they were joining, got little time to ask questions. The Confederate Army of Northern Virginia had crossed the Potomac by the shallow fords above Washington. Stonewall Jackson was again on the rampage down the Shenandoah. Lee would march right up Capitol Hill, wailed the politicians. He was aiming to win Maryland for the Confederacy. He would go north to the railroad junction on the Susquehanna at Harrisburg, Pennsylvania! From there he could carve up the Union.

Lincoln, after a private talk with McClellan, put him back in command. To the troops, this news was as good as a victory.

For once, McClellan moved fast. The Thirty-second Regiment found itself part of the army that was marching, not to protect Washington as the politicians demanded, but if possible to intercept the Confederates' northern advance.

The thirteenth of September found them in the valley to the east of a smoky blue ridge. From its summit, scouts could watch a ribbon of dust westward — the track of the Confederate Army.

On the fourteenth, the Thirty-second saw Little Mac himself, erect on his charger, pointing the way to Crampton's and Turner's Gaps through the ridge of South Mountain — intersecting hollows he was planning to get hold of. As they passed, the men cheered him in a frenzy, some breaking ranks to touch his horse for luck.

By nightfall, they crossed the ridge from east to west. Lee's army, up ahead, might thus be cut off from Stonewall Jackson's, which was following.

But McClellan, with a return of his habitual caution, lost a couple of days in reconnaissance, and Lee, hurrying back along Antietam Creek from Hagerstown, barely managed, near Sharpsburg, to join forces with Jackson. There, on the seventeenth, he awaited.

McClellan held the Fifth Brigade among the reserves while Fighting Joe Hooker, on the right, opened the battle. All that morning, a cool and sunshiny one, B and G companies, with the rest of the regiment, waited — their view of the fighting cut off by the knoll from which Porter's battery was lambasting the enemy. But Colonel Parker, Lieutenant Colonel Prescott, and the other officers, freer to move about, had climbed the hill and were standing among the guns watching the action.

In front and below them, Antietam Creek washed the base of the rise. Beyond lay fields of ripening grain. And further on, they guessed, was the enemy's center. Just across the creek, Prescott could see Union skirmishers advancing. He watched little puffs of smoke float from their rifles, though the sound of firing was lost in the battery's thunder. In front was a ragged line of men running for their lives — Jackson's advance brigade, most likely. Every now and then one would jerk his arms, falter, then lie still.

Suddenly, far off, on the western edge of the fields, the whole of Jackson's corps burst from the woods, with Hooker's men striding to meet them. Though the smoke of battle partly obscured their view, the watchers, when a light breeze moved it, saw that neither side was yielding. Instead, their ranks thinned perceptibly — and a fringe of wounded and their helpers, behind each line, struggled towards the nearest shelter.

You could not mark the moment when the fighting ended. Little by little the lines melted together, then melted away, and the dead lay thicker. By evening, all life at the center was gone, while from the hills and edge of the woods on either side belched the smoke and flame of the batteries.

That day's fighting at Antietam was too nearly a draw. It aroused all of McClellan's reluctance to expend his men. Next day, despite the reserves he had left untouched, he refused to renew the battle. Lee, happy to get out of it, stole across the Potomac and back safe into Virginia.

McClellan, ordered to chase Lee's decimated forces, temporized for the rest of September and through October. At last the North's impatience exploded. Though grateful for Antietam, Lincoln put General Ambrose B. Burnside in command of the Army of the Potomac.

After helping chase Lee's army through Northern Virginia — the Union forces keeping to the east of the Blue Ridge, the Confederates to the west — the Thirty-second Regiment went into winter quarters with its brigade at Stoneman's Switch, about five miles north of Fredericksburg.

There Corporal James Baker Brown, now a company supply sergeant, was detached to Washington on official business. Had the members of the Company seen him, they would have got over their envy. After passing through the hell of Harrison's Landing and living through the forced marches, Brown fell suddenly ill. Men from the sanitary corps, burdened beyond endurance by sick and wounded, dumped him at the Columbia College Hospital, which of course was crowded to bursting. No room within, so they put him in a gloomy, cavernous tent.

At first it was good just to have a place to lie in. But the doctors were too busy to come his way, and the only man he saw for days was a dirty attendant who brought him what passed for meals. He could get no real nourishment from them. One evening he struggled to his feet, staggered out and found a shop which sold him a cup of milk. Night and morning he made this perilous journey.

A later evening, thinking to do a good turn to the man in a cot near by, he brought back some milk in a bucket. But Brown could get no answer. He touched the man's hand. It was as cold and dank as a knuckle of pork from the brine barrel. The day before, another soldier, on that same cot, had struggled up, got to the street, then died there.

Days passed, with Brown too weak to move. Towards evening, there was a stir in the tent. Jim opened his eyes. He could not make up his mind if he were alive or dead. There were his father and Dr. Bartlett.

"I've come all the way from Concord to see you," said the doctor, "and I'll take you home if I have to apply to the Secretary of War!"

Now that Lee had been driven off, the men of the Middlesex companies at Stoneman's Switch, guessing they might stay camped some time, set to work making themselves comfortable. They built wooden floors, boarded up the sides of their tents for warmth, tinkered wood burners out of sheet metal, and constructed a fantastic miscellany of tables, chairs, and improvised bedsteads.

But General Lee had other plans. With Jackson, he dashed across Virginia, and from the wooded heights of the south bank above the city of Fredericksburg took command of the crossings and bridges of the Rappahannock before his opponent could secure them.

Now that it was too late, fringe-whiskered Burnside got into violent motion. He had already botched his supply system. His soldiers were hungry. Even as they advanced into action under intensive fire from the heights, the men of the Thirty-second stooped to pick the frost-bitten leaves of cabbages in the field over which their battle line was sweeping.

There followed a nightmare of terrible hours. The Army of the Potomac, exposed to devastating fire from the Confederate batteries and from the riflemen entrenched on the heights, flung itself again and again over the open plain, to be hurled back at last at the stone wall by the foot of Marye's Heights.

Seven thousand killed and wounded lay in bloody heaps, in a fight without plan or strategic outcome.

That night an icy rain began driving. The exhausted men of the Thirty-second Regiment slept on the wet sidewalks of Fredericksburg, to which city the survivors of the repeated charge had fallen back. Next day they were once more at Stoneman's Switch. Fortunately Lee, like McClellan at Antietam, dared not press his advantage.

To the folks back home it had been a breathless year yet an infernally long one. Kept in general touch with armies and battles through the press, their most poignant contact came from their soldiers' letters — on wrapping paper, on the backs of old bills, on strips of newsprint (all regular sheets for correspondence long since ruined by mud and the rains): written by campfire light, or on the knee during short rests along the march.

Concord had been fortunate enough to welcome back all five men reported lost at the first battle of Bull Run. War prisoners at Libby Prison, then New Orleans, then crowded, brutal Salisbury, they at last had been exchanged.

A great many Concord men, learned the prisoners, had joined various other units. And there was another familiar face gone from the village. Henry Thoreau had died that spring. Louisa Alcott, absent for a while as an army nurse in Washington, came back with her hair cropped short after an attack of camp fever.

The slaughter at Fredericksburg had chilled every heart. This war, if it did not end in disaster, would drag on and on, pulling everyone into it.

The one thing that encouraged thoughtful stay-at-homes was Lincoln's issuance of an Emancipation Proclamation — January 1, 1863, to be the day of fulfillment.

"Emancipation is the demand of civilization," declared Emerson, lecturing, before the passage of the act, at the Smithsonian, with several cabinet officers in his audience. Emancipation is the one moral power, though the army fail, possessing legs long enough and strong enough to cross the Potomac. Suppose England, looking to the South's cotton, and France, looking to a New World Empire, recognize the Confederacy on condition of the promise to free its slaves? Instantly the North is thrown into the falsest position. If the Union, as by right it should, proclaims itself the champion of liberty, no power on Earth would dare back the Confederacy against this humane issue.

After the post-lecture discussion, Senator Sumner took his friend to the White House.

The President shook hands cordially. "Mr. Emerson, I heard you give a lecture in the West" — and Lincoln quoted a phrase or two with relish.

The Yankee from Concord found himself far more congenial with the Yankee from Illinois than he had expected. He had always admired the hairy strength of the West. Lincoln reminded him of his honored friend Samuel Hoar, whose death five years before still left its void. Like Hoar, he loved a lawyer's good clear statement. He liked to work out the sum for himself, and had what farmers call a long head. Emerson, an advocate of compensated emancipation, could only hope that Lincoln would keep his eye on this same policy should it prove the best means to further his great objective — that of preserving the Union.

By the end of the summer, things had gone so far from bad to worse in the fields of military and diplomatic operations that Lincoln knew the government must try new tactics. Seizing McClellan's check of Lee at Antietam, Lincoln had issued his Proclamation.

With this spiritual victory, affirmed Emerson, the North, if it has to, can stand further military disaster. Through it, the Government works even when the army goes into winter quarters or generals turn imbecile. It works at home among the women, down South among the planters, in the Negro cabins, in France and England overseas.

And in the Northern army, many a young soldier, hitherto distressed and confused, caught the hope that his was the cause of Liberty — liberty not alone for the blacks, but for all men, for all races, for all of the time.

*   *   *

It was tough, thought Private Rockwood Flint, B Company, Captain Tay commanding — Prescott had been raised from lieutenant colonel to colonel of the regiment — to be called out of snug quarters in the dead of winter. Whatever it portended, this movement probably was more to please the civilians in the North who hated to see the Army of the Potomac lying idle than for any military or strategic good that fuzzy Burnside might hope to squeeze out of it. Rockwood had passed his seventeenth birthday attacking the Heights of Fredericksburg — but in the army you learn quick and grow old fast.

Orders had come down the afternoon of January 30, 1863: they would march at three next morning. Nothing must be left for the possible solace of Johnny Reb — the camp must be wrecked completely.

So into huge bonfires went all the tables and chairs they had built laboriously, the bedsteads, the platforms and sidings. Even tent cloths and extra clothing were chucked in the flames. At least, in the bitter cold, this destruction offered some comfort.

By 3 A.M. the Thirty-second was shivering in line, a bitter northeaster blowing, the air filled with sleet and snow. By nearly four, when the column started moving, the storm had changed to rain, but plenty cold.

At first the pace was fast — which helped get the circulation going — but blockages up ahead soon slowed it, with frequent halts. The regiment drew off the road after dark that night and bivouacked, icy rain still falling, so that repeated attempts failed to get fires going. But at last the men were hunched round sputtering blazes, in the dripping woods, unwilling to try the experiment of stretching out to sleep.

By morning the wind had changed. It was blowing out of the south, the air bland and mild as April in Concord. Lead-colored clouds rolled close overhead, and in the gathering light the men could see vaporous, steamy masses swirling over the fields and woods. All the snow which had lingered from the day before was changed to pools and puddles. As the column moved, rain set in again — first a drizzle, then a tepid downpour. Men, mules, horses, began to smoke as though each contained a hidden boiler. The thermometer rose incredibly — to fifty, then seventy, then eighty degrees. As the day advanced, no vestige of frost was left in the heaving soil and the road became a river. The wagon trains and mounted officers took to the fields, and the foot soldiers slogged after them.

This brought scant improvement. Beneath the rank grass, the yellow, bilious Virginia mud had no bottom to it. Men leaped from hummock to hummock, sinking to their thighs where other jumpers had missed. Here and there a supply wagon stuck, completely mired — the mules, up to their ears, braying in fright.

Just three miles covered that entire day, and mud for a bed that night. Impossible to go further.

Next morning, the Army of the Potomac began to struggle back to the winter quarters they had wrecked and abandoned.

Following the tactics of the year before, Lee was making another thrust down the Shenandoah for the heart of the Union. By the first of July, from their stopping place at Hanover Postoffice, the Thirty-second heard that he was well past Antietam; was up in the Cumberland Valley at Chambersburg, southern Pennsylvania. There was another bit of news. Meade, for some reason, had replaced Hooker as Union commander.

In the past sixteen days the regiment had been steadily on the move. They hoped for at least a night at Hanover, but barely had they swallowed some coffee when they were on the march again, to halt, late that night, near a hill named Round Top (there seemed to be two of them), just south of a place called Gettysburg.

Already, on the day the Thirty-second pulled into Hanover, there had been heavy fighting at Gettysburg as unit after unit of both armies came up. Things had gone badly for the Union. Meade's First Army Corps had been driven from Gettysburg — to make a stand, however, along a fishhook-shaped ridge a little to the south of the town, with Round Top at the opposite end from the barb.

Before dawn, Colonel Prescott led the Thirty-second up the slopes of Round Top. Here they got orders to wait.

Hours went by, hours shattered by the roar of cannon, by shells bursting beyond the ledge which gave the regiment shelter. Oblivious, the tired men slept.

Not till three o'clock in the afternoon were they summoned. The Confederates had just broken the Union lines at a salient held by General Sickles, a vulnerable bulge into more or less open farming and orchard country between fishhook-shaped Cemetery Ridge, held by Meade, and caterpillar-shaped Seminary Ridge, opposite, held by General Lee. The Fifth Corps must plug the gap.

Colonel Prescott drew up his line of battle on the westerly downward slope of a little rise just below and beyond Round Top, where stone walls and rocky ledges made excellent cover. Hardly was the

Thirty-second in position before the enemy came piling down the gentle descent toward a brook at the bottom, to be met by a galling fire that was driving them back.

But the new formed Union lines to the right were breaking, and a command from the brigadier pulled the Thirty-second to another position. Picking up their dead and injured — young Rockwood Flint, lucky to be alive, had seen Lieutenant Bowers killed at his shoulder, Lieutenant Lauriat wounded — the regiment fell towards the rear in tolerable order.

The Brigade now formed to the left of its furthest thrust, in a piece of woods bordering a wheat field — the Thirty-second Massachusetts on the flank, the Sixty-second Pennsylvania in the center, and on the right the Fourth Michigan. Then began a cautious advance into the open. Farther right lay a deep ravine, covered, supposedly, by a neighboring division.

At the very moment that the commander of the Michigan regiment saw that his counted-on support was missing, a cloud of men in gray burst from the hollow. Beset in front, spattered by fiery hail from the ravine, the Fourth Michigan, then the Pennsylvanians, curled up like a worm at the touch of flame. The men of the Thirty-second, advancing across the wheat field, saw what was coming. Soon they too were dropping like shot ducks at Fairhaven. Young Francis Buttrick fell; many others. Soldiers close by saw Colonel Prescott helped to the rear, Lieutenant Colonel Stephenson's face change to a red smear as a bullet hit him. The regimental colors were riddled, the staff shattered in Color-sergeant Davis's hand.

Next moment the enemy had them practically surrounded, pouring in a deadly fire. Just then Colonel Prescott, hastily bandaged, took command again though three bullets had nicked him. By now blue and gray were inextricably mingled, trampling the bloody wheat.

As each side was reaching the limit of physical and moral endurance, a reserve regiment turned the tide. What was left of the attacking Confederates fell back toward Seminary Ridge.

The Thirty-second had begun the day with two hundred and twenty-seven men waiting for action. Now eighty-one were casualties; twenty-two killed or mortally wounded.

All next morning they held the wall on the western slope where Prescott first had placed them. But the tide of battle had shifted to the right and center. A little past one, an uncanny silence fell, then terrific artillery fire at the center. High-pitched yells of many rebels charging — then a return to silence.

Late in the afternoon, the news filtered down to the ranks. Pickett's Division was wiped out. The Union had won a victory.

One gloomy November evening four months after the battle, John S. Keyes, along with marshals from other states, rode into Gettysburg. Next morning, among the dirt-covered graves, a national cemetery was to be dedicated.

Lincoln's close friend, big, swashbuckling, noisy Colonel Lamon, was in charge — but everything was a mess, the little town offering atrocious facilities. Sitting up all night with the colonel's staff, the marshals fashioned a semblance of order out of the chaos.

An unlovely morning, dank and threatening, met their tired, bloodshot gaze. Under an occasional shower of rain, they got a straggling procession going from the courthouse to Cemetery Hill — the President and his cabinet, various dignitaries, an escort of United States soldiers. Bullet-shattered trees, splintered gun-carriages, rusted bayonets, marked the way; and the stench of dead horses was everywhere.

Intent on saving his voice and his dignity, Edward Everett, speaker of the day, had not joined the parade. When at last the orator arrived, Marshal Keyes escorted his fellow citizen from Massachusetts to the place of honor in the grandstand. Soon the rounded periods of the address were rolling out over the graves. For two hours Keyes sat his restless horse. It was now the President's turn to end the meeting.

Lincoln had aged immensely since that inaugural morning. He looked bedraggled, for his umbrella had not shielded him from the rain. Despite the victory whose dead were being honored, things were still going badly for the Union. Conscription, full of corruption and injustice, had not filled the depleted ranks. Draft riots raged in New York. Only in the West, perhaps, were things better, where Grant was struggling to hold the river city of Chattanooga on the Tennessee, gateway to either North or South.

"Fourscore and seven years ago," began the President, "our fathers brought forth upon this continent a new nation, conceived in liberty and dedicated to the proposition that all men are created equal." Lincoln paused, in that way of his, his glance, under his bushy eyebrows, raised toward the crowd.

"Now we are engaged in a great civil war, testing whether that nation — or any nation, so conceived and so dedicated — can long endure. We are met on a great battlefield of that war. We are met to dedicate a portion of it as the final resting place of those who have given their lives that that nation might live. It is altogether fitting and proper that we should do this." The President's slack left arm bent sharply upward at the elbow, the left hand, from old habit, grasping the lapel of his coat.

"But, in a larger sense," the high, sharp voice continued, "we cannot dedicate, we cannot consecrate, we cannot hallow, this ground. The brave men, living and dead, who struggled here, have consecrated it, far above our power to add or to detract. The world will very little note nor long remember what we say here; but it can never forget what they did here. It is for us, the living, rather, to be dedicated, here, to the unfinished work that they have thus far so nobly carried on. It is rather for us to be here dedicated to the great task remaining before us; that from these honored dead we take increased devotion to that cause for which they here gave the last full measure of devotion; that we here highly resolve that these dead shall not have died in vain; that the nation shall, under God, have a new birth of freedom, and that government of the people, by the people, for the people, shall not perish from the earth."

It was over in less than three minutes.

The specially called winter town meeting had been going from bad to worse. Major item of business — how to raise more soldiers — had been stalled by a squabble over the liquor question: shall Concord, this year, go wet or dry?

In the turmoil, Mr. Emerson rose. He brought up no argument for either side. Instead, he looked at his fellow townsmen. "Is *this* Concord?" he asked. The meeting settled to business.

Judge Rockwood Hoar plunged right into the turbulent waters of the quota question. Marvelous — thought Emerson, watching his friend — to face that jaded, almost malignant little assembly with such courage, where prudence surely suggested silence. All eyes seemed to say, "We have sent our best men, haven't we? What more is expected?" But the speaker took no counsel of things past. He relied on the inspiration of his feelings, surprising his hearers with his larger view, his better knowledge, and gained the victory by talk of the future. All their hostility melting, the judge's fellow citizens applauded.

When supplies at home ceased, Concord filled its allotments, like other towns, with "bounty-bought men." One day, at the district draft station in the courthouse, a group of strangers appeared, ready to be hired, they said, in place of family men and others just called up. Uniforms were quickly issued, and bounties paid. Constable John B. Moore, however, grew suspicious. These were not the workmen they claimed to be. He had glanced at their hands; they were white and unroughened. So that night, with his deputies, he guarded old Pumpkin Hall where the recruits were sleeping. Sundry whistles and signals were heard, but next morning the would-be "bounty-jumpers" were marched off to Boston. Their civilian clothes, carefully hidden, turned up later in Hudson's lumber yard.

During this third year, Mr. Emerson had been appointed to the Board of Visitors at West Point by War Secretary Stanton. His recommendation for competitive examinations to bring in the best cadets was being carefully considered. Letters from the front told Concord that Colonel Prescott's regiment was in winter quarters at Liberty, tiny hamlet on the Orange and Alexandria Railroad.

In March, 1864, Lincoln appointed Ulysses S. Grant General in Chief.

On April thirtieth, as part of Grant's army, Prescott's men entered the second Wilderness campaign for a frontal attack on the Confederacy.

From Chattanooga, Sherman was to try a march through Georgia that would cut rebellion in two.

On the morning of May 11, Grant sent a report to Washington: "We have ended the sixth day of heavy fighting and expect to fight it out on this line if it takes all summer." The Thirty-second knew nothing of this dispatch, but plenty about the fighting. Day-long treks through God-forsaken country; marches at night through darkness so black you could cut it. Then the crash of twelve-pounders and spat of rifle fire. If you were to charge, you charged. If you were to hold, you dug yourself a burrow. Rifle pits, the officers called them, though they looked more like a hound dog's work. No tools but your hands and a bayonet. Sometimes a Confederate mortar shell would end you; sometimes, with the Rebs only a couple of rods away, it was your own battery that killed you.

The day after Grant's dispatch, the Thirty-second obeyed orders for a charge up Laurel Hill. Colonel Prescott led them forward till they overran the enemy pickets; next, the first enemy lines of defense. The blast of lead grew unbelievable. The regiment on the right faltered and was breaking. Prescott waved to his men to retire. Five color-bearers had already fallen. Of one hundred and ninety men who advanced, eighty-seven regained the breastworks. George Lauriat, though wounded, had won his captaincy.

Grant, with Lee for opponent, had expended the spring.

Spotsylvania Court House — thirty-one thousand Union soldiers lost. Cold Harbor, with a direct assault on Lee's entrenchments, and nine thousand soldiers slaughtered — papers pinned to their backs before the charge, with names and addresses for identification, so sure were they of death. Then the siege of Petersburg, Virginia, which threatened to gobble up all summer, and fall and winter as well.

Day after day the Thirty-second had faced intensive fire. One morning, the eighteenth of June, they were to take from the rebels the deep gash through which ran the railroad to Norfolk — a gully very useful to the Confederate outposts before Petersburg.

As the advance tumbled into the gulch, the defenders fled and the men of the Thirty-second started climbing the opposite side to pursue them. "Come on, men," Colonel Prescott was shouting beyond the top, "form our line here!" When they reached him, he had just been hit.

They carried him to the division's hospital. He was conscious but rapidly failing.

"Have I done my duty?" he asked General Griffin.

The division's commander nodded. "Always," he said.

Early next morning, Prescott signaled he wanted a sheet of paper. Charles Tyler, regimental chaplain, leaned over to help him. "*Sabbath Morning*," wrote Prescott, "*June 19, 1864*." It was to his wife.

MY DEAREST SALLIE,

I am lying upon my back to write you a few last lines. Mr. Tyler will send you the particulars of my wound. God Bless you all.

Yours,

GEORGE

"Add these names, please," asked the wounded man, after a pause: "Alice, Charlie, Willie, Mother." The chaplain did so. Colonel Prescott was dead.

*   *   *

New England weather had been atrocious, and for many people times were very bad. Specie was not to be had in Concord, though scrip issued by the Lyceum circulated in town as a handy medium. Lincoln had beaten General McClellan, standard-bearer of the regular Democrats and their Copperhead friends — the Copperheads including all those with faults to find because of petty privations — but for a while the election looked like a narrow squeak, with perhaps a compromise peace and the finish of the Union. Only Lincoln's insistence, said shrewd politicians, that Andrew Johnson, once a Democrat but a supporter of the war, be placed as Vice President on the ticket saved the day by winning the border states. "I give you joy of the election," wrote Emerson to a friend, "seldom in history was so much staked on a popular vote."

Somehow, in spite of acute shortage of labor, farmers were making out — thanks to McCormick's reapers. Invention showed a knack for keeping up with need. And Concord, in town meeting, dared at least to look toward peace. The town voted to put up a high school building as soon as possible.

Through the four long years the faithful in the women's Soldiers' Aid Society had done their bit for the men — in every branch of the service and on the sea. Once a week or oftener they met at the Town Hall or Fire Station. There would be Parson Reynolds, in shirt sleeves, packing the boxes which Mr. Bigelow, the blacksmith, secured with iron bands. Martha Keyes, Colonel Prescott's sister, glancing up from her work, thought how fine it was to see everybody gathered, united in the same good cause — Rebekah Barrett, Lizzie Bartlett with her sewing machine, Mrs. Mike Murray, mother of the wildest Irish boy in town, who had died a hero at Fredericksburg.

Old sheets, for bandages, were at a premium. Ellen Emerson, foraging in a neighboring town, got the same refusal from every household: "We ain't goin' to send our rags for Concord women to talk over." She had better luck in the next village.

The Society fell into the practise of stenciling its goods. When Fredericksburg overflowed with wounded from the Wilderness — men in rows on the sidewalks, their heads toward the buildings, feet toward the curb — dressings grew as scarce as space. Lieutenant Bartlett, the doctor's son, helping in an improvised hospital, opened a last packet. It was marked "Soldiers' Aid Society, Concord, Mass." In the midst of catastrophe and suffering, a wave of homesickness surged through him.

All day the women, dropping their usual chatter, found them-selves talking about the struggle (old men, lounging at the Union Club, Boston, complained the war had murdered conversation), then dreamed about it and their men at night. Yet looking out, in the morning, on the quiet town, it was hard to realize war's existence.

Not hard, though, when the dead came home — the young, the hope of the country. Grindall Reynolds, that beautiful day in June when he laid his friend Prescott to rest — the grass green as emerald, the foliage all new and fresh — could not keep his voice steady.

Lieutenant Ezra Ripley, grandson and namesake of Reynolds's famous predecessor, receiving burial. Besides his mother, still living at the manse, he left a young wife. "Remember," Grindall Reynolds had preached to the boys as they were going, "in a few months or years you will come back, not officers, not privates, but sons and husbands and brothers. Never forget that your true home is not that fort, that tented field, but that it nestles beneath yonder hill, or stands in sunshine on the fertile plain. Remember you are a citizen yet, with every instinct, every sympathy, every interest, every duty of a citizen."

But not for these.

With many dying, Nathaniel Hawthorne's passing, at Plymouth, New Hampshire, while on a journey in quest of health with his old friend Franklin Pierce, seemed just another death. Over thirty soldiers dead from Concord, and no telling where the list might end.

Spring in Virginia felt very different from March in New Eng-land. Somehow, in this blessed warmth, the whole army could not banish the crazy hope this campaign might be the last.

Grant had lost many men, but his tactics in the Wilderness had pinned down the Confederates and prevented their stopping Sher-man's march to the sea. Hatcher's Run, Dinwiddie Court House, Five Forks — the Thirty-second losing men in each engagement. But the rebels were losing more than men; they were losing heart. Lee, fearing Grant would envelop him, pulled out of Petersburg. Soon the Thirty-second was marching through Richmond, then into the country beyond. It looked like the beginning of a chase. Once, Captain Lauriat, in charge of four companies, crept through the woods to the rear of the enemy skirmishers and stampeded not merely them but their support. For this exploit he was made a major. The regiment, hurrying in, ate the rebel dinner of bacon, and their own besides — the Confederates' was so shockingly lean.

Sunday morning, April 9, 1865.

Each soldier, as a veteran campaigner, had a notion something was pending. Surely Lee was in a trap. Sheridan, they say, has brought up an army behind him. Lee must break through or fight.

The Thirty-second was assigned that day to the head of the column, marching into open, rolling country. Leaving the road, they turned into pasture land — a gentle slope rising before them. No towns here, though somewhere near by lay Appomattox Court House. The Regiment formed column of companies, then deployed, the others of the Brigade following in order. Save for the grimness of the men, it looked like a dress parade on that ideal ground. Ahead, on a slightly higher level, they could see the enemy's infantry with artillery support, drawn up in line of battle.

The Union forces pressed steadily forward. At any moment would come the order to charge. Already they were under heavy-caliber punishment, with now and then a rifle ball droning by.

Then an amazing thing happened. The enemy's firing ceased. Lieutenant Colonel Cunningham, commanding the regiment, ordered a halt. His field glasses were sweeping the hill. Men in the advance thought they saw something white waving.

Cunningham and his adjutant spurred forward. Near the enemy lines, soldiers could see two gray-clad officers join them. Then the adjutant was back, riding at a gallop toward Grant's headquarters. Soon every man in the Regiment had the news — Lee was proposing to surrender.

Blue and gray were again intermingling — this time not in battle.

Because of the rapid advance, the Union Army was shy on rations. But when the men saw the shape their enemies were in, they split the contents of their haversacks. Some of the hungry Southerners offered to pay with Confederate money, which they had by the bushel, but the Yankees laughed it off.

Wednesday, the twelfth, was designated for the surrender of weapons. General Chamberlain, in charge, detailed the Fifth Brigade to receive the arms of the infantry. By nine that morning the Thirty-second was in regimental front at the right of the line. At route step, arms trailing, the Confederates approached. Some regiments carried their colors furled tight to the staff; some flourished them bravely. When the nearest unit drew abreast, Colonel Cunningham relayed orders to the Thirty-second:

Dress ranks! Shoulder arms! Eyes front!

The Confederate brigadier, seeing this courtesy, closed up the straggling line. Proudly, with arms at the shoulder, the Confederates marched past.

Till four o'clock the ceremony lasted — each brigade halting, stacking arms, then laying their colors across them.

That same week Lincoln was speaking in Washington. There were to be no persecutions, no hangings. This rebellion must be forgotten through a just and lasting peace. As soon as one tenth of her white inhabitants have taken an oath of allegiance, each seceded state should be admitted to her rightful place and all her privileges in the Union.

In the Yankee North, farther from the fighting, Emerson, shutting his eyes to his old abhorrence of force, was revolving his doubts. Somehow Grant's terms looked a little too easy. The problems ahead, certainly, would prove intricate and perplexing. Suppose we let the Southern states into Congress — will they not join with the Northern Democrats, who so nearly defeated Lincoln, to thwart the righteous victor's will? What will become of the humanitarian gains for which the North has done battle? Should not the rebels be taught they are conquered?

CHAPTER XVII

One Hundredth Anniversary
of Independence

ANTICIPATING the year 1875, the town of Concord was already busy with plans to commemorate the one hundredth anniversary of Independence. By virtue of its fight at the bridge, Concord would be called on to lead off with the very first of the many celebrations over the length and breadth of the land.

Ebby Hubbard, long irritated by the monument on the British side of the river, had bequeathed sums for a new one and for a footwalk to it where the North Bridge used to stand. Stedman Buttrick was ready to present enough of his ancestral land for a site. This was a starter, so the town's committee, with John S. Keyes as chairman, soon had ready its recommendation: "That the Town procure a statue of a Continental Minute Man, cut in granite, and erect it on a proper foundation on the American side of the river, with the lines of Emerson, that are 'household words,' . . . enduringly graven for an inscription on the base."

But in the South, ten years after Appomattox, Independence was a mockery. Lincoln's dream of a reunion with malice towards none had vanished with Lincoln — and the word "Reconstruction" stood for perversion of the vision.

At Concord's memorial service for the President, in the midst of a mourning nation — April nineteenth the day at Concord, heretofore a day of rejoicing — Emerson had told how he came at last to recognize the greatness of Lincoln. This man, said Emerson, represented the best instincts of the American people. Step by step he had walked before them, slow with their slowness, quickening his march to theirs, with the pulse of the nation's millions throbbing in his heart, the thoughts of its millions articulate on his tongue. "Because of the mysterious hopes and fears which, in the present day, are connected with the name and institutions of America, I doubt if any death has caused so much pain to mankind."

Emerson, thrusting aside his Northern rancor, sat down, in that first summer of peace, to write a letter. He sent it to South Carolina, to the late Secession's birthplace, to Robert Barnwell, once United States Senator, then a signer of the ordinance of severance from the Union, then Confederate Senator, advisor and close friend of President Jefferson Davis. Would Barnwell come to the forty-fifth reunion of Harvard '21, at Cambridge? "I wish you to know that distance, politics, war," wrote his old classmate, "have not been able to efface in any manner the high affectionate exceptional regard in which I, in common I believe with all your old contemporaries, have firmly held you." Barnwell could not come, but he valued the gesture.

The Radical Republicans of the North harbored no such sentiments. They mustered sufficient strength to refuse seats to the Southern senators and representatives elected under Lincoln's liberal program. Then they sponsored an amendment forbidding former leaders of the Confederacy to hold office. When Andrew Johnson tried faithfully to carry out Lincoln's aims, the Radical conservatives, led by swashbuckling Ben Butler of Massachusetts and demigogue Thaddeus Stevens of Pennsylvania, who thirsted for Southern blood, sought to impeach him. But though this pair vied with each other in their appeals to prejudice and bigotry, doing their damnedest to trample justice, they had failed to win a conviction.

So in the first postwar election, Ulysses S. Grant, a great, once magnanimous soldier — who understood the commanding officer's necessary trick of delegating authority, and was not much interested in politics — became the Republicans' successful candidate. Only three men of ability found place in his cabinet: Hamilton Fish of New York, Secretary of State, Jacob Dolson Cox, Secretary of the Interior, and Judge Ebenezer Rockwood Hoar, of Concord, Attorney General. But Cox and Hoar were soon forced out — disgusted with the course of events, and glad to quit.

Henry Wheeler, veteran of Bull Run, once an involuntary visitor to the South as an inmate of Libby Prison, had moved to Alabama as a mining engineer. He became a citizen of Birmingham and married a Southern girl. Slowly he came to understand with what amazing endurance and courage the South had fought for what it believed in. But how give any insight to the North?

The Radical conservatives had their rope around the old Confederacy's neck and were gaining the sort of peace that was bound to follow. Their beloved soil treated like that of a subjugated enemy nation and divided into five army districts policed by Federal troops, the Southern members of a former union writhed under the metal foot of despotism. Only after protracted sojourn in the valley of humiliation — with carpetbagger, scalawag legislatures passing the amendments required for readmission, at the same time squandering in stupidity and ignorance the few resources left — could the still unregenerate South at last emerge.

During the decade or more of Radical reconstruction, Concord, far away from it all, fared tolerably well, though she long felt the pang of her losses. The once dirty little common, crisscrossed by ill-defined roads, had become a handsome unbroken green, with the granite obelisk of the war memorial at its center. Farmers, forced to drive round, had protested at first. Then they and their nags forgot that things ever had been different.

Concord's war deficit, large for the size of the town, was reduced by a happy circumstance of compensation. The town had felt deeply grieved when the last session of the County Court was snatched away. But presently the County bought out its share in the handsome, deserted courthouse — and the frugal selectmen shrank the debt.

Bit by bit, men and women learned to speak of rebels as Confederates — and an enlightened few, traveling in the South, caught on that one referred there to the tragedy as "The War between the States." But Concord, raising its eyebrows at the Ku Klux Klan, found some obstructions in its own vision. On the Milldam, a dozen or so white men fell upon two Negroes and beat them up. On the principle of locking the stable door, the town voted itself a permanent police force.

During and right after the war many marriages took place. None stirred greater excitement than Edith Emerson's to good-looking Lieutenant Colonel William Hathaway Forbes — not quite twenty-five. With the house empty of young folk — Eddie away in Europe studying medicine, Ellen absent on a visit — tragedy almost overtook old Mr. and Mrs. Emerson. One July night, John S. Keyes, who added the function of town watchdog to his multiform activities, woke up with a start. The First Parish bell was ringing for fire. Up and out before the alarm had stopped, Keyes saw by the glow on the low-hanging clouds that the blaze was near Lexington Road. Running toward the trouble, he was dismayed to see Mr. Emerson's house with the roof and whole upper story burning. First he made sure that the Emersons were safe — yes, there was Mrs. Emerson, there was her husband, somebody's coat thrown over him, all dripping with rain — then he hurried inside.

The inhabitants, from long practice in such matters, had learned how to work like a team. While the firemen kept down the blaze, the men of the village lugged out furniture; women and girls ransacked closets to save household stuff and clothing. Mr. Emerson, member of the volunteer brigade in earlier, more primitive days, wished to help, too. Somebody had just saved the ancient leather bucket that was his badge of office.

Already the rooms of the lower floor were filled with choking black smoke. Then someone remembered Mr. Emerson's books and manuscripts in the downstairs study. Impossible to see them — men and boys felt where they were. They dumped their loads on the lawn, then ran back for the rest. Already the upper timbers were falling.

After hours of labor, in the wan, rainy day, the village gazed at the ruin. The new steam pump-engine, from which the horses had been unhitched lest they take fright and bolt, had mastered the blaze. But the place looked a wreck — only the walls of the lower floor left standing.

John Keyes took the Emersons to his house, lent them dry clothes, and gave them breakfast. Old Mr. Emerson smiled his thanks, but his mind seemed confused — it was clear he was suffering both from shock and exposure. For a householder — as he said — who had hoarded in fixed corners all his papers, his books, his habits and labors, this whirlwind struck with terrific force.

The Emersons decided to spend that night at the manse. Mrs. Sarah Bradford Ripley had died shortly after her son's death in the war, and the place was empty save for Elizabeth, her daughter, who was glad to welcome them.

Taking stock was like toiling at a giant jigsaw puzzle. Articles were everywhere — in people's houses, in barns, even dumped in carriages. But as far as Mr. Emerson could see, the books and manuscripts had all been saved. Volunteers helped carry them into the courthouse, which now belonged to the insurance company. Here Emerson sought to arrange his treasures. His own insurance, by the way, covered less than half his loss.

Then, as Emerson believed, a miracle happened.

Tactfully his friends told him they had deposited ten thousand dollars to his account. And the fund was still growing. He must use part for a trip abroad. During his absence, he must permit the neighbors to rebuild the house.

With Ellen, he visited Italy and Egypt, traveled through Switzerland and France, saw England again where he once had lectured and where his books, especially *English Traits*, had made him famous. Then he came home.

The inhabitants, not quite sure which train he might be taking, had asked the engineers to signal with their whistles as the cars rolled along the downgrade from Walden. A blast from the 3:30 set the bells to ringing and swept the townsfolk toward the depot. When the train pulled in, there was Judge Hoar, the Alcotts, Mr. and Mrs. Frank Sanborn, waiting in carriages, and an open barouche for the returning hero.

"Is today a public holiday?" asked Emerson, looking in amazement at the crowd. Then he heard their cheers for him, and the band played "Home, Sweet Home."

Up Main Street and Lexington Road moved the triumphal procession, where stood an arch garlanded with apple blossoms, the town's schoolchildren singing beside it.

There was his gate, there his front door, there his house just as he had known it. Inside, in the study, each book, each paper, in its accustomed place. Tears welled into Emerson's eyes as he tried to thank his friends and neighbors. Surely this was not just a tribute — he wished to say — to an old man and his daughter returning home. This was a tribute to the blood and spirit common to them all — one family — in Concord. But the words failed him.

Concord could no more dream of a public occasion without Emerson than it could think of ignoring the memory of its famous fight at the bridge. So when the town was ready, that summer, to dedicate a fine new public library, Emerson, who had served on the committee for forty years, of course was speaker.

In due time an industrialist named Andrew Carnegie, who in this age of mammoth corporations had made a fortune in steel, was to scatter libraries with a lavish hand on many cities and towns. But Concord would not need his bounty. Already she had public-spirited citizens of sufficient wealth to look after such needs — men like John W. Brooks who set the great Chicago, Burlington & Quincy

Railroad System in running order; like Reuben N. Rice, starting as clerk in the Green Store, becoming Concord's first agent at the depot, then going West to help build the Michigan Central, in the management of which he employed so many men from his home town that it became known as "Concord's railroad." Rice now lived in retirement in the fine house he had built on Main Street. When the loafers on the Milldam spoke of him under their breath as Old Moneybags, Reuben smiled, remembering his beginnings. But the town's greatest present benefactor was William Munroe — wealthy through his commercial ventures in Boston and elsewhere — whose father once had pioneered in the making of pencils.

Not content to give merely a building, Munroe let it be known that his will would provide the wherewithal for maintenance and extension. Another half-century of industrial prosperity, he declared, would make enlargement essential.

All that fine autumn day of the opening, the town dropped by to admire the structure. A dramatic growth since the days of Colonial Concord's first semi-public collection, which consisted of the Bible and the *Book of Martyrs;* or those three shelves belonging to the town at the turn of the century, with Stephen Brown keeping watch over them in his dingy shop on the Milldam, the stench from his tanyard flavoring the reading. Here, in this model library, were innovations which would have delighted Henry Thoreau as they delighted Bronson Alcott: a reference department to unravel questions, the beginnings of a card index for the rapid finding of books, a children's collection.

Many persons had brought gifts to help celebrate the occasion: three trunkfuls of Thoreau's unpublished diaries, the selectmen's reports from the year the town had started printing them, files of all its newspapers, many documents. And now, as the venerable sage of Concord, Emerson was once more sharing his thoughts with his neighbors. He and his fellow townsmen, he was saying, knew how to prize the simple political arrangements of New England villages — each independent in its local government, electing its own officers, assessing its taxes, caring for its schools, its charities, its highways. Fortunate the town with a healthy site, good lands, good roads, good sidewalks. More fortunate if it had good churches and good schools. But doubly blessed to share the benefits of a collection of good books.

I know, Emerson went on, the word "literature" has in many ears a hollow sound. It is thought the harmless entertainment of a few fanciful persons and not at all to be the interest of the multitude. To these objections, which proceed on the cheap notion that nothing but what grinds corn, roasts mutton, and weaves cotton, is anything worth, I have little to say. There are utilitarians — he added, as though the notion were an afterthought — who prefer that Jesus should have wrought as a carpenter, and Saint Paul as a tentmaker. But literature, Emerson continued, is the record of man's best. Every attainment and discipline which increases his acquaintance with the invisible world, lifts his being. Everything that gives him a new perception of beauty, multiplies his pure enjoyments. A river of thought is always running out of the invisible world into the mind of man. Shall not they who receive the largest streams, he asked, spread abroad the healing waters?

Secure, established, venerable, yet ever renewing its youth through the generations, Concord was ready to move on to its centenary of Liberty. The statue of the Continental Minute Man had been contracted for. Dan French, Judge French's son, was to make it. Dan had drawn up a sketch and shown it to Mr. Emerson, who had talked with the committee.

Dan agreed that any pay be left entirely to the town's discretion. All the committee need do would be to pay for materials and incidentals — the whole not to exceed three hundred and fifty dollars.

An awful risk, muttered certain members. Dan was a fine young fellow, but what had he done, what did he know about this kind of statue? One month's work in the shop of a New York sculptor, some drawing lessons with a professor in Brookline, a premium at the Concord Cattle Show! Only twenty-three, wasn't he; where was the time for experience?

Dan himself was none too certain — though he shared his doubts only with his father. Anyhow, he told himself, another year would furnish the answer. An optimist by nature, he expected his schemes and the world to work out well.

Young French was a native of Exeter, New Hampshire, but Concord had grown to regard him as a son of her own. Ever since the judge, who carried on a modest practice in Boston, bought the farm down Sudbury Road toward Nine Acre Corner — the asparagus he grew was the best roundabout — he and his likeable family were part of the town. Like the Alcotts' Orchard House at the other end, Judge French's became a gathering place for the numerous young folk.

One evening, at an impromptu party, the guests were all seated round the open fire, playing cards, telling stories, munching raw turnips. Dan got out his jackknife. Presently his turnip developed a goggle-eyed head, bow legs in front, and behind, legs for jumping. Not an ordinary frog, at that, but dressed in a frock coat like a dandy — clearly the frog who would a-wooing go, just mentioned in a story. Dan modestly held it up. Attracted by the squeals of delight and the laughter, Mrs. French came over to see.

"Why, Dan," she exclaimed, "you're a genius!"

Perhaps, thought the judge — he was a wide reader, had contributed to the *Atlantic*, and liked to encourage his boys toward broad interests — perhaps this is Dan's career. Next evening, on his way back from the office, he stopped at an art shop and bought twenty pounds of clay.

Mrs. French tied an apron on her husband, on Dan's older brother Will, and on Dan himself. Then, like ducks headed for a puddle, the whole family plunged into the clay. Will and the rest made various little objects. But Dan stayed with the one large lump he was modeling. It was turning into a dog's head — a very recognizable dog's head. Then the clay got hard and crumbly. Nobody had the vaguest notion how to keep it soft.

Judge French, the first chance he got, talked to May Alcott about Daniel. May had studied art during two years in Paris. She had started a drawing class for girls and it was her ambition to set up an art center in Concord.

"If he will come down to see me," said May when the judge inquired, "I'll lend him some tools."

Dan harnessed up old Bucephalus, their sway-backed horse, and drove to the Alcotts. He got not only tools, but instructions, and sufficient clay for work.

With the Minute Man contract safe in his wallet, Dan started a small working model. For thirty days, ten hours daily, he stayed with the job. Under his hands a youthful Continental soldier was emerging, throat bare, shirt sleeves rolled up, in his right hand a musket, his left resting on a plow. He was stepping forward to defend the bridge.

On the day Dan planned to cast the plaster, Judge French stayed home from the office. Four hands would be needed. Even so Dan and he nearly boggled it. They had stood the mold on its head and were ladling the wet stuff into the base when a sudden hole burst through the hair and the whole mess ran out on the floor. Because the clay model had been lost in shaping the cast, this looked like the Minute Man's finish. But they patched the gap, then scraped up and poured back the plaster.

When the shell came off, there was the Minute Man, ready for inspection.

The committee nodded their approval. Dan got from them enough money to rent a tiny, poorly lit cell — you could hardly call it a workroom — on the third floor of Boston's Studio Building on Tremont Street. There he began a seven-foot model in clay for the final statue. He had persuaded the committee it should be cast in bronze.

For the figure, since its anatomical structure must be right, Dan borrowed a cast of the Belvedere Apollo. Athletic friends like Charlie Baird and young Charles Hoar were impressed as occasional models, while the Minute-Man's husky forearm — typical of a plowman's — was copied from Irish Patrick Harrington's, farmer and coachman at the Frenchs'. Dan got the loan of a full-length mirror in which he could also study his well-built self.

Friends, coming to survey progress, were amused at more than a faint resemblance between the sculptor and the handsome statue. Why not? Dan was Yankee to the bone — with an ancestor who, on a famous occasion, had helped flavor Boston Harbor with tea.

Almost three years of work, and the final model was finished. It was too perishable, agreed the committee, to take chances in casting. The Ames Foundry, at Chicopee, Massachusetts, best in the country, would convert it to bronze. Judge Hoar, now a member of the House after resigning from Grant's cabinet, got an act through Congress authorizing the gift of ten historic brass cannon. The metal left over paid the expenses.

Two days before the unveiling, the town was already abuzz. On Saturday President Grant's party rolled up Main Street to be settled as Rockwood Hoar's guests in the stately Georgian mansion built by the present chief of Concord's royal family. In front of the dignified columns in relief stood an iron dog, the only thing of its kind in Concord, so lifelike that folks said it attracted fleas. Cabinet members, senators, potentates of all descriptions were housed by other dignitaries of the village — James Russell Lowell at Mr. Emerson's; a brace of governors with John Keyes; judges, congressmen and mere mortals at Reuben Rice's.

The April weather was none too good that Saturday — more like March or November. But Monday, the nineteenth, was forty-eight hours away, the bluebirds had returned, and robins were building.

Church in the morning on Sunday, then the rattle of carriages all afternoon as the swelling throng was whisked to inspect the various sites where history had happened. That evening, houses glittered with the splendor of receptions for governors and their military staffs.

The great day dawned — but only after a struggle. A bitter northwest wind was blowing — the sky clear to start off with, then screened by itinerant snow squalls. People who had thought to avoid the push by using their rowboats as points of vantage for the unveiling found themselves chopping a path through ice before they could leave the shore.

Up early today as marshal of the show, John S. Keyes herded the governors — blue-nosed and shivering — to Judge Hoar's, where they would join the procession. Then the parade to the footbridge and monument — a cumbersome, unwieldy host of all the New England governors with their escorting regiments, not to mention Grant and his cabinet, the members of the Massachusetts General Court, distinguished men of letters, the clergy, and an immense concourse of people watching. Mere animal heat should have warmed the air had the odds not been so against it. More persons, remarked a wag, were likely to catch their death that day than had perished in the battle they were celebrating.

At the unveiling, Emerson, standing by the pedestal that bore his verses, made a mercifully brief speech. Then there was an unseemly dash for the tent which was to shelter the crowd during the oration — a bigger tent had not been seen in the Northeast since the July 4, when Concord had held its mammoth barbecue for Tippecanoe and Tyler. Even so, only about six thousand could squeeze in, while many times that number milled round outside.

Supposed to attend to the amenities and introduce the speakers, Judge Hoar, usually so calm, was for once in his life distracted. It was quite too evident that there would not be enough chairs on the platform for this throng of dignitaries.

Just as President Grant and most of the others had been seated and Parson Reynolds was rising to lead in prayer, the judge noticed some disturbance at the entrance. The women! Good God, he had forgotten all about them!

According to ancient custom, on this day of masculine glory, the women had been assigned no place in the procession. But when many said they wished to hear the oration, they were told to meet in the Town House at half-past nine, whence they would be led to the tent, where a limited number of seats would be saved. For an hour the women waited. No one paid them the slightest attention. The Marine Band long since had marched past. If they wished to hear the speeches, they decided, they must shift for themselves. So with veils close-reefed and skirts kilted up, they walked to the tent.

On one corner of the platform Louisa Alcott spied several chairs, the only ones vacant. She had in tow a granddaughter of Dr. Ripley, descendants of Colonel Prescott of Bunker Hill, of William Emerson and John Hancock. Some were old and tired. Could they occupy those seats, asked Louisa?

"They can sit or stand anywhere in the town," burst out the harassed judge, "except on this platform, and the quicker they get down the better, for gentlemen are coming in to take these places."

Seething within, Louisa led her cohorts directly below the stand, where the chairs originally reserved were now filled by the press and other male spectators. A few, a very few, made room. The rest of the women perched like disgruntled doves along the sharp edge of the platform.

Louisa felt ashamed of Concord. Soon, she vowed, there would come a day of reckoning. The town would not be allowed to forget its politically exiled, tax-paying women.

As Parson Reynolds began his prayer, the weighted stand, with an ominous groan, slipped and settled several inches. The preacher gulped, then went on.

George William Curtis, once a Brook Farmer, once a boy in Concord, now editor of *Harper's Magazine*, was orator. At it for a solid hour already, he seemed good for at least one more. All the little warmth of their early brief exertion vanished, his listeners, chilled to the marrow, sat helpless. Finally Grant could stand it no longer. Taking another shift of the platform for excuse, he rose abruptly, set his blood in circulation by a vigorous shake, then took a vacant chair among the ladies. Poor man, thought Louisa, he looked so bored she longed to offer him a black cigar.

But not all in that audience watched Ulysses S. Grant with looks of kindliness. Some stared with a jaundiced and fish-cold eye at the soldier-turned-President. Right after his second election — less than two years ago, wasn't it? — the worst financial panic in America's history had flattened the banks and most business. Four years before that, those robbers Jim Fisk and Jay Gould, with cronies right in the cabinet, had almost cornered the nation's gold. With the cities full of bread lines, with a horde of unemployed tramps flocking through Concord, what had been done to improve conditions? Nothing save further government scandals, with the riches of the United States in the octopus clutch of giant corporations, which, leagued with bought officials, were proving what unhampered money could do.

They should remove their shoes — thundered the incandescent orator, still warm at the conclusion of his address — since they stood on hallowed ground! No one seemed eager to comply.

That night, after a mammoth banquet of five thousand places, there was a splendid military ball, at which the girls, dressed in colonial costumes, danced in the somewhat trying splendor of the gas jets. Louisa Alcott, chaperoning the youngsters, grinned sardonically to herself. Now five chairs were rushed forward for each possible occupant, and the gallants swept the dust with their courtesy.

Not till four in the morning did the lights go out. Almost the last in bed, John Keyes tried to reckon up the totals. Concord could afford to be proud, and Lexington's nose must be quite out of joint. What other town could furnish not only the occasion, but a statue and poet? A great day, a most successful affair, with from thirty-five to fifty thousand persons present.

CHAPTER XVIII

Like Athens and Alexandria

WITH all that fuss over the Minute Man and the shot heard round the world, ·the women had to hold their fire. But they opened battle as close to Concord's day of liberty as possible — with a rally of all Middlesex on the nineteenth of May.

Louisa, of course, got up the meeting. Days beforehand the town noticed her busily driving about in her wicker pony cart pulled by its patient white horse. She was rounding up not only speakers but an audience.

The lethargy of the women, she complained, was appalling. They let servants and the baking of cakes fill their minds and their days. Yet Louisa was no rabid feminist. She liked and respected men who did things and she wanted also to respect women. She knew the history of her cause back to the times when Ann Hutchinson attempted to exercise the rights of free speech and assembly only to be banished by the Puritan fathers as an upstart Jezebel. Bitter experience had taught her what was sure to happen today, in this man-managed world, if a woman tried to exercise every capability. At mid-century, when the Boston *Saturday Evening Gazette* first published her stories, the editor, when he found his star contributor was a woman, tried to beat down the price agreed on. Men, declared Louisa, sought to monopolize every interesting and profitable employment, then had the effrontery to talk of "protecting" woman, forcing her to submit to laws in the making of which she could have no voice, and denying rights given even to the most degraded and ignorant of their own sex.

Were women not people? Had they not proved they could play an honorable part? For examples, no need to search beyond Concord. Look at Goodwife Pellit, in early colonial days, who swept the meeting house and rang the bell — though her husband collected the fee, as likewise did the husbands or fathers of many of the teachers. Look at Margaret Fuller. Or Mrs. Sarah Bradford Ripley, who, the town was fond of remarking, could tutor a Harvard student in Greek and at the same time rock the baby's cradle and shell the peas. And there was Ellen Emerson, product of her father's teaching and of Sanborn's and Dr. Agassiz's schools, who could translate Greek, Latin, French, and Italian.

Unless one first recognized this fundamental problem of the rights of half the human beings in the world, how discuss logically the hot question of the status of Negroes? Louisa could remember when antislavery, long a prohibited question, stood exactly where equal suffrage stood now.

To address her meeting, she would have liked to get the Judge's younger brother, George Frisbie Hoar, now a member of Congress, knowing that he considered the nation's political attitude toward women false to the principles of the Constitution. He advocated equality of rights with as great a vigor as the judge employed in heaping sarcasm on the question. But the Congressman was away in Washington.

Louisa's father would be a speaker, Julia Ward Howe, Mrs. Lucy Stone, Garrison, and Mr. Emerson.

Emerson remained Louisa's idol. Every year she found greater reason. Had he not always valued women? At mid-century, he had spoken before the first women's rights convention to be held in Boston — urging that the laws be purged of every barbarous impediment: statutes denying parity in ownership; blocks in the path of education and preferment. He was quick to declare he was still not sure women in general really wished to enter the political arena. He was opposed, she knew, to aggressive campaigning. But when they asked for the vote, he said, it must be given them.

The selectmen, who formerly placed barriers in the way of abolitionist meetings in which she had been interested, raised no objections when she asked for the hall. Instead, they smiled in tolerant indulgence, like men humoring a wife's raptures over a new bonnet.

Why did masculinity persist in regarding woman's efforts at self-improvement as so irresistibly funny? Such a cheap, provoking trait, like sudden softness in a bully! Even the reporter for the *Journal* sought the humorous twist, though he took no liberties with Mr. Emerson's remarks at the meeting.

Certainly, declared that speaker, legislation for human betterment would be sooner carried if women voted. And — he concluded — if we refuse them a vote on their demanding it, we shall, of course, refuse to tax them.

Yet five more years went by before any direct advantage came out of that meeting. Indirect progress, of course, continued, as it had ever since the mid-century gathering at Seneca Falls, New York, which began the movement. Many reforms, sponsored by women, had seen at least partial realization. No longer did the law permit West Concord's mills or other factories to squeeze sixteen hours of labor out of little boys and girls. Massachusetts was first in the Union to pass a minimum wage law for women and children. But children still were broken in the mills. Factory work, once looked on by farmers' daughters as a way toward independence, had sunk to drudgery carried on mostly by immigrants. The greed of the owners saw to that. Four looms to tend instead of two; then six. Work mounting in intensity of effort while kept at the lowest possible minimum of pay. Only legislation could curb exploitation amounting at times to downright murder. There was little Johnnie Ahern, eleven years old, of West Concord, with his hand mangled in the machinery. Dr. Bartlett had done what he could to save it.

As long as the factories employed children, and parents stayed ignorant and very poor, West Concord's school was sure to be empty. Concord, where going to school had become a habit, definitely did not like this state of affairs. That was one reason the men had elected Ellen Emerson to the School Committee. Perhaps Concord, in public matters, never thought of Emersons as having sex, though Ellen, with her poised small head, serene, radiant expression, abundant chestnut hair arranged in classic Grecian fashion, was certainly feminine.

That was in 1875. Four years later, thanks to an act of the General Court, women were enfranchised to help make choice of School Committees. Thus far they could go; no further.

Wishing to be the first woman to qualify as a voter, Louisa entered the Town Hall early on the day of registration.

"Have you brought your receipt for this year's tax?" asked head selectman Charles Thompson.

Miss Alcott was vexed. She had just held a meeting at Orchard House to explain the requirements. Somehow this item had escaped her.

"Won't last year's tax receipt do just as well?"

"Oh yes, but you have not paid it!"

Louisa got angry, then laughed. So did the selectman.

Monday, March 29, 1880, women attended town meeting for the first time since Captain Willard, Parson Bulkeley and the rest met in the primitive hillside shelters. Twenty-four had registered, noted Louisa with pride, and the number should increase with the years.

For several weeks, rumors had flown that this would be a lively session. There was a move on foot to block the election of Abby Hosmer, second of her sex thus far named to the Committee. Yet the meeting got under way with phenomenal decorum. "We will have to behave," remarked one gentleman, "now that you ladies are here."

As the men walked up to the moderator's desk to cast their votes for the several town offices, the women waited, the eager expectancy of their faces shadowed by a vague alarm. Two dozen of them before ten times that number of men! It would be a good deal like running the gauntlet.

The slate was almost filled. Now for the School Committee. Hands crept up to tidy a bonnet string, pat a rebellious strand of hair, adjust a collar.

The women — chivalrously announced the moderator — would please vote first. Under that battery of masculine eyes, they cast their ballots.

In the momentary silence, Judge Hoar's voice boomed out: "I move that the polls be closed!"

Confused laughter swept through the meeting. Was this one of the judge's jokes? Then someone seconded. So voted.

Those opposing Abby Hosmer's election jumped to their feet, calling for reconsideration. But Town Clerk George Heywood — who had held office as long as his father before him — remarked, with the faintest smile, it would make no difference, the ladies doubtless had voted for the very candidates favored by the men.

Abby Hosmer was found unanimously re-elected.

What's more, the women had been taught a political lesson. The following year they held a preliminary caucus, submitting a slate which the regular caucus did not dare to reject.

Thanks to Ellen Emerson, who read a paper on the mysteries of parliamentary procedure, the women were gaining competence at

their meetings, whether those of the local Women's Suffrage League
or of the various social, philanthropic and church associations.

They had won their fight at the bridge.

But ahead lay the rest of the Revolution.

"Be ye one of them phy-loss-er-fers?" Penny, the hackman, would
ask every stranger at the depot. To accommodate the rush, Old
Penniman had bought a brand-new bus, painted cerulian blue, instead of the hearse-like black of the original barge in which Penny
for years had hauled drummers and tradesmen to the decrepit Middlesex Hotel.

Penny was none too sure — and here he had something in common
with the wisest — as to just what the Concord School of Philosophy
was all about. "I went in the hall the other day just a-purpose to
hear 'em," he told the village. "I'd just like to see one of 'em grub-
bin' stumps out of an old timber patch!" Penny laughed as he
jingled the change in his pocket.

Forty years before, Emerson had written to Margaret Fuller,
"Alcott and I projected the other day a whole university" — a university in a country town, preferably Concord. The teachers must
be those most qualified in all the world — Daniel Webster for politics;
Carlyle; Washington Irving. No rules, no limitations, no formal
organization. Since a faculty must live, each pupil shall understand
that fees are acceptable and shall pay according to his means and
his sense of benefits received. The sessions to be like Plato's Academy,
with each teacher announcing his own topic, to be dealt with as he
pleases. History, of course, and the History of Opinion. Then
Modern Literature, Psychology, Ethics, the Modern Crisis, the
Ideal Life. "Do you not see that if such a thing were well and
happily done for twenty or thirty students — it would anticipate by
years the education of New England?"

At that point nebular thought rested for the time being — while
formalized education hardened within its self-imposed limits.

Then Alcott, peddling his "Conversations" in the West where he
had gained a following, met kindred spirits full of prairie vigor. Men
like William Torrey Harris, superintendent of the public schools
of St. Louis, and founder and editor of the *Journal of Speculative
Philosophy*. Before Alcott quite realized what was happening, his
Western friends were materializing the early vision as the Concord
School of Philosophy, of which they made him Dean. Frank Sanborn, back from his successful editing of the *Springfield Republican*,

and now in energetic early middle age, became secretary and treasurer. In its issue for Thursday, July the third, 1879, the *Freeman* announced that the school was about to open as the colleges closed.

Because the world was in its summer pause, it was possible to gather a distinguished faculty and special lecturers — Ralph Waldo Emerson among the latter. The opening session met in the old brown house, standing in its roadside orchard, where the little women had played. So great became the appetite for discussion that various homes, in the evenings, were thrown open for informal symposia.

Hopes ran high for a second season. "The Summer School is certainly a success," announced the *Freeman*, launching the rumor that a benefactor had been found. Already a little peak-roofed, gable-ended chapel of butter-colored hemlock and spruce was rising on the grassy slope to the left of Orchard House, just where the largest vine from an old grape arbor could be trained across the portal. The gift of Mrs. Elizabeth Thompson, of New York, it would seat one hundred and fifty persons.

When the Philosophers arrived for the second summer, all was ready for their use.

Louisa Alcott, with the kindly irreverence she displayed toward her father's works — though she would fight for them to the last drop of her blood — was moved to the fringe of verse one August afternoon.

> Philosophers sit in their sylvan hall
> And talk of the duties of man,
> Of chaos and cosmos, Hegel and Kant,
> With the Oversoul well in the van.
>
> All on their hobbies they amble away
> And a terrible dust they make;
> Disciples devout both gaze and adore
> As daily they listen and bake.

Louisa's response and Concord's had something in common. The town's first impulse was not merely towards mirth but towards animosity. What was this new horror of Alcott's — filling the village with long-haired men and short-haired women? The innkeeper of the tottering Middlesex took an especially dismal view. Alcott's present doings would drive from the town what little business was left. "The best thing he ever did was his daughters," grumped the host when Henry Beers of Yale inquired about Alcott and the others. Now Mr. Emerson was different — the smartest writing man in the country, and a gentleman, too! . . . But the host lost his audience, for the young professor left the gloomy hotel with its bar black from tobacco juice — none of these new visitors seemed willing to stay — and took lodgings with Miss Barrett, Concord's esteemed landlady, whom her boarders spoke of as Aunt Emmy.

For several seasons, the rest of the town refused to welcome the strangers. Then at last it caught on and tumbled over itself to gather this heaven-sent harvest. "The price of philosophic board," announced the *Freeman*, "ranges from $6 to $15 per week, according to circumstances." Even the washerwomen throve. What brings money to the town, said the Milldam, is a success. It noted the social doings, too — Mr. and Mrs. Emerson inviting lecturers to tea, Miss Ripley giving a party at the manse, Judge Hoar holding an evening reception. When the judge bestowed his civilities, it was a sure sign he considered the guests of the highest standing.

Alcott, of course, was spiraling happily toward the seventh heaven. His friends and admirers loved to watch the old man, his figure tall and spare, his fine head crowned with snow-white locks, his kindly face with the pink-and-white complexion of a little child. He would move about benignly among the visitors, his rich deep voice bidding them welcome.

"Friendship, my friends, is spheroidal, but love is globular!"

Later, on being asked what he meant, he looked surprised.

"Did I say that?"

"Undoubtedly you did."

"Well" — with hesitation — "perhaps I did!"

But all honored him as the spiritual founder. Some unknown donor had commissioned Daniel Chester French to make a bust of the Dean. It stood now, in the chapel, along with Plato and a goodly company. This flattered him, but he was chiefly thankful over the school's success. Who could tell how far these humble beginnings might spread? Even should they fade, like his other projects, a creditable work would have been done. Men and women were learning that philosophy is really a practical thing; is the doctrine of living nobly and well. Not just light and inspiration were here, but the joys of harmony and sociability. Yes, this was a triumph beyond all calculation.

At first the women who came were in prints and plain ginghams, till with the school's social success a more worldly air prevailed.

Some of the ladies, moreover, were young and pretty, especially the intermittent attendants who regarded the picnics and evening parties as wisdom's greatest boon. A few college boys came, but males were mostly of the scholar, journalist, writer or teacher type, with a sprinkling of men of business. Before the audience stood the faculty's low platform and speaker's desk, where a bowlful of water lilies, fresh from the river, scented the hall. If the mind wandered, one could watch the haze over the orchard, the apple boughs heavy with small green fruit. Next door, farmer Moore's chickens scratched in the dust, his old red rooster at times challenging the speakers.

Aside from deeper matters, perhaps the chief concern of the young folk of the village was Miss Peabody — Hawthorne's sister-in-law Elizabeth Peabody, whom all knew — famous throughout New England for her good works and her total absent-mindedness. Each girl tried to defend Miss Peabody from serious lapses — straightening her bonnet for her before the session, fastening buttons, letting her know she had forgotten her collar, retrieving the gloves she was always dropping. There she would sit, day after day, with the learned members of the faculty, munching peppermints out of a pound package and washing them down with drafts of water from the speaker's pitcher. Always a good deal of speculation arose as to how many bonbons she would consume. Generally she dozed through a formal lecture, then plunged with amazing prescience into the discussion, snatching the threads of debate from disputants and weaving them into patterns of her own choosing.

Ten years of these pleasant summer sessions. Death had laid claim to several older faculty members. Others had left. Dr. Harris, appointed United States Commissioner of Education, moved to Washington. Sanborn, with many irons in the fire, was anxious to be released from the administrative burden. So, quietly as it began, the school was closed. Not that it was in any sense a failure. An old man's dream come to life, it perforce had ended. Winding up the finances, Sanborn pocketed the thirty-one cents left in the balance, as his rightful fee. Many theories had been aired; much done to counteract the materialistic tendency of thought in America. Many books would be born from these sessions. And, Sanborn told himself, the idea started in Concord would be sure to spread. The school should lead the way for similar gatherings — education, musical, literary, political — for American summers.

*   *   *

"Gentlemen," remarked Judge Hoar to the twenty-four celebrants at the one hundredth birthday of the Social Circle, "our senior member and respected friend, Ralph Waldo Emerson, whom no Concord meeting or gathering ever failed to delight to hear, I am told must not be asked to speak to us tonight. His presence, which fills our number, is itself a source of happiness to all of you." Knowing how Mr. Emerson's memory was fading — he was nearly seventy-nine — the guests regretfully acquiesced.

Four years before, at the fiftieth anniversary celebration of the Lyceum, Judge Hoar had paid Concord's public tribute. Since then, Emerson had made his hundredth Lyceum appearance. He had also given his valedictory address — "The Fortunes of the Republic" — before the nation, at the Old South Church in Boston. Beware, he warned, of rabid partisanship, of too great love of ease and wealth, of lack of idealism. Guarding against these shortcomings, the nation is assured of a triumphant destiny. He knew, for he had seen the breadth of the land, peddling his lectures — state by state, territory by territory, to the Western sea, by stagecoach, by horse and buggy, by sleigh through winter snowdrifts, by the arterial rails which were the lifestreams of the continent. *The genius of this country, through its pioneers, has coined a vital slogan — opportunity. Take in also the immigrant, for the good that is in him; open the doors of the ocean.* "I see in all directions the light breaking. Trade and government will not alone be the favored aims of mankind, but every useful, every elegant art, every exercise of the imagination, the height of reason, the noblest affection, the purest religion will find their home in our institutions and write our laws for the benefit of man."

Since his settlement among them, Concord's inhabitants had watched a once unconvinced and heedless world come to Emerson's door. Even Harvard, after twenty-nine years, recovered sufficiently from the shock of the Divinity School Address to confer on him an honorary degree, then make him an Overseer. On Main Street, watching his bent figure pass, enveloped in its cloak, Mary French, the sculptor's vivacious, pretty cousin from Washington — Concord gossip whispered she and Dan would make a match — thought how much Mr. Emerson must resemble Dante on the streets of Florence. Though he did not relish the role, he had been a helpful sitter for the bust on which Dan was working.

"Yes," Emerson remarked, gazing quizzically at it when the job was done, "yes, that is the face I shave."

April 27, 1882, a month after the centennial gathering of the Social Circle, the senior member was dead. But Ralph Waldo Emerson had long since become part and parcel of the sinews and body and blood and soul and life of his village and nation.

A unanimous vote — even Judge Keyes had agreed. At this meeting of March 30, 1891, Concord was authorizing its selectmen to sell the last of the one-room schoolhouses, standing empty and desolate in the rural sections. Education had finally moved to the center.

Soon after the Civil War, when the town built its brand new high school, the inhabitants felt sure their educational problems were settled. To celebrate the occasion, recompense for teachers was upped all around — salaries for schoolmarms in the rural districts moving from six to seven dollars weekly for the thirty-nine week year. As the Committee pointed out, here was the town, after deductions through twelve months for board and keep, paying perhaps its most useful and refined class of women less than half what it gave for domestic service or for labor in West Concord's mills.

With his one or two assistants, energetic, near-sighted, talkative Charles Almy — his pupils, like all through immemorial time, abetting his digressions — presided over the school's four grades, the highest sending its occasional clots of cream to college, the lowest filled in erratic fashion by the thin skimmings from the district schools which bumbled along as they had bumbled for a hundred and fifty years.

But hardly had the block-shaped high school with its Georgian portal like a gaping mouth, its vacant brick face broken by four staring, eyelike windows, become familiar, than a second problem clamored for attention. Like shoes on a growing child, some of the one-room schools used by the elementary pupils were also becoming overcrowded. At least at its center, Concord's population, rising from three towards four thousand, was rapidly increasing, the Irish citizenry especially prolific in the flimsy houses they tenanted near the station and in the hivelike Yellow Block on Lexington Road — glamorous with paint outside but disgraceful within, which the venerable Clerk of the Town and another respected citizen ran with profit highly satisfactory to themselves.

After a survey, the School Committee was ready with its proposal. Why not erect for the younger children a large, central, well ventilated, adequately heated building, grading the pupils like those in the high school, only in eight divisions instead of four, with a separate room and teacher for every grade? Various cities were successfully using this system, advocated by Horace Mann, former Concord resident and first Massachusetts Commissioner of Education — then why not a country town?

The older and more conservative citizens were not so sure. Through many generations each district had developed a sentimental attachment for its little school. Old Judge Keyes, forgetting his receptiveness to new ideas, turned especially bitter. The very fact that young Sam, eldest son of Justice Ebenezer Rockwood Hoar, favored this departure, was enough to rouse his fighting instincts. Sam's ironic smile, the twinkle in his shrewd, good-natured, keen gray eyes, had a way of infuriating the choleric old judge and United States Marshal, making him say things he never meant to. Preposterous, he now thundered, to crowd three hundred children into a single building, endangering life and limb! This newfangled grading system would inflict on education a sort of railroad timetable — everything so rigidly scheduled that the youngsters would lose all individuality and freedom. It would prove a disgrace to the town.

How, asked Superintendent John B. Tileston, can a teacher in an old-fashioned one-room school bridge the gap between the child of five and the numbskull or hard-worked, undertaught farmboy of twenty? She must flit from one little group to the next, from one item of instruction to another, without a chance to prepare herself or collect her equanimity and senses. Tall, slight Sam Hoar — he had never recovered the weight lost campaigning in the Civil War — summed up the argument by declaring it was useless to look to the districts for even mediocre results.

Judge Keyes not only lost the fight. He was forced to sit idly by while the town elected Sam chairman of the construction committee. Presently the new building, named in honor of Mr. Emerson, was finished.

Specially built horse-drawn barges, curtained all round against stormy weather, with parallel facing seats from front to rear, moved the children daily to and from the center. The farmer or farmer's wife from the furthest house usually served as driver — the Committee frowned on using the hired man — and plenty of blankets kept the children warm during the five-mile ride.

Once it had voted to come into the scheme, no district willingly would have gone back to its past. Judge Keyes's dire prophecy that land values would tumble proved mistaken. Now that people could be sure of better schooling, they flowed back in a perceptible movement toward the abandoned farms. Miracle of miracles, attendance rose, after having declined to a shocking level. Parents found their children less exposed to sleet and snow than when they trudged to the neighborhood schools. Soon it was impossible to tell which boys and girls came from the rural districts — children usually slower and more bashful. Concord's plan was bringing not only improvement in instruction; it was furthering unity and friendship.

Education — the town had learned — like childhood, is never static. In the old days, especially in the farm districts, boys and girls took as little schooling as legally possible. Now more and more children moved from the eighth grade into the high school — which presently took up its quarters in a bigger, finer building. More got to college.

The Emerson family, remembering Mr. Emerson's dictum — no police force so effective as a place where boys can play — gave the town a four-acre field east of Schoolhouse Row. This raised an unexpected issue: the boys wanted teams, whereas some of their elders held such sports idle and dangerous. William L. Eaton, Almy's successor, recalled his undergraduate days at Harvard and the faculty's hostility to football, baseball, rowing and track. At last, through Alumni subscription, the college boys got Soldiers' Field for their sports. Surely these games which the boys themselves started had come to stay. Why discourage them? Far better to provide adequate, supervised playing fields. A well-equipped gymnasium, urged the Superintendent, must come next.

After seventeen years in the Parish he had watched over since its infancy, Father Michael McCall was leaving St. Bernard's. This was his flock, these his people, this the Church, through God's guidance, he had worked to establish. But as he told Eddie McKenna, whose mother raised chickens at the abandoned farm where Thoreau was born, how could he refuse the request of the Bishop? The priest had noticed the tears in Ed's eyes after the service at which he announced his going — enough water was shed in church that day, said Ed, to float a ship.

Before his coming, the Concord flock, starved in its poverty, beset in an alien, suspicious land, had wandered in stony places. Very poor people — farm hands and house servants — far from the green island of their birth, pitifully lacking in life's physical needs, the promise that is America a fading mirage before them, they relied mainly on that spiritual comfort they had always found in their Church.

Not till 1863, the second year of the war, did the local Irish win a permanent place of worship, when Father Bernard Flood, of St. Mary's, Waltham, with Concord as a mission, bought the deserted Universalist Church on Bedford Street, making over the deed, as was the practice, to the Archbishop at Boston. Efforts had been made to block the purchase, but the patriotism and sacrifices of Concord's Irish soldiers helped reconcile the town to this innovation of a church with a crucifix — startling indeed to men of Puritan stock whose fathers still read Foxe's *Book of Martyrs* and thought of Rome as the Scarlet Woman.

Before the purchase, the faithful — many of them walking because they could not afford the carfare — made each week the eleven-mile journey to Waltham, save on those occasions when Father Flood, busy with a dozen villages in his parish, could arrange to come to Concord, celebrating Mass at first in the Town Hall — till the selectmen withdrew permission — then at Ann Carney's beside the green, so many attending that worshipers, to the amazement of Protestant Concord, knelt outside in the square.

Ten years after the war, Father McCall himself had come as Concord's fourth resident pastor, the others having passed in rapid succession. It was Archbishop John J. Williams's policy to break in his young men in the smaller, difficult parishes and missions.

His predecessors, Father McCall could see, had made a brave beginning. They had patched the broken-down building which housed the church. By grant of the selectmen, they had founded a cemetery in time to bury some of their Civil War dead in consecrated soil. They had bought a rectory on the square through purchase of the empty, rattletrap County House of Concord's shire town days — a building nobody else wanted, though John S. Keyes, when he sold it to the financial advantage of the town, had his misgivings.

While farmers driving in from outlying districts still stared as if catching sight of an apparition, Concord got accustomed to Father McCall's black-robed, heavy-set, broad-shouldered figure hurrying across the square from the rectory to celebrate Mass, and to the concourse of people whose numbers seemed ever to be growing. But inevitably, there were difficulties in this commonwealth the founders of which had stood for the very dissidence of dissent, with a statute once on its books forbidding even the presence of Catholic priests. Father McCall knew all about the burning of the Ursuline Convent by an anti-Catholic mob. He was aware of all the arguments. How the Irish, living on potatoes, working for next to no wages at all, would thrust the native born from their jobs. But the Know-Nothing Party had lost its hold with the war. New attacks might follow. But young Father McCall, like the ancient Church he served, was patient, and could wait.

First serious problem had been that of schooling. As in all of Massachusetts, the atmosphere of the village schools, quite naturally, was Protestant. It was also, as Father McCall well knew, anti-Catholic. As the Boston *Pilot*, Catholic newspaper, put it, "We venture to say there is hardly one Catholic child educated in the public schools who has not heard a teacher sneer at 'Romanists' and their priests. This is habitually done by a large percentage of teachers." Bible readings, hymns, and prayers were a regular part of the curriculum, and school committees, through their inborn fear of Jesuitism, intended they should remain so. But the Catholics, too, had their convictions. The Church forbade them to take part in any religious services not their own. And the brunt of the struggle fell on the Irish children. They knew they must not read from the Protestant version. Yet when the Bible was used in class, no Protestant teacher would dream of letting them substitute their own Douai version for that of King James.

For the Catholics, one solution was to set up parochial schools. In Boston, where parishes were better established, this was possible, though the few lay Catholics well enough off to pay taxes had to help support the public schools as well. In Concord, where even purchase and redecoration of the Church had been sacrificial, this was not to be thought of. Father O'Brien, Father McCall's predecessor, hoped that Catholics and Protestants would get to understand one another so well that they would iron out their difficulties, making one school system serve. Father McCall clung to Father O'Brien's hope. Yet when the Catholics tried to get a member of their faith on the School Committee, pandemonium threatened.

But Father McCall found help where he least expected it: from fair-minded Protestants themselves — just as in Boston, when the question grew heated, men like President Eliot of Harvard testified against a law aimed directly at the Catholics — Adams Tolman, member of an old Concord family, dared to remark in the local press it was hardly exceptional, since the greater part of the town's public-school children were Catholics, that the members of that faith should seek representation on the Committee.

But I am not apprehensive, he continued, the spirit and tendency of the age is more and more in the direction of the secularization of the public schools. Catholic and Protestant, Calvinist and Socinian, Jew and Agnostic, have equal rights in the community, and no one of them will long succeed in crowding his religious convictions upon the children of the rest. Then he turned to the immediate issue: I find that the Boston excitement over the school question and the ill-advised attempt to make a political matter of it have penetrated even to our quiet village, and in many quarters I hear the same unreasoning panic has seized upon some of our timid souls, who imagine our public schools in danger of being converted into nurseries of Jesuitism. Not that they understand in the least what Jesuitism is, or could give any definition that would not be ridiculous. When I hear a clergyman in a meeting called for the purpose of furthering this agitation advising the Protestant women in his audience to register their names as voters, and to notify their Catholic house servants that if *they* dare to do the same thing they shall be turned out of their places, I am justified in considering him an impudent tyrant, and his hearers, who take his advice, neither intelligent nor unprejudiced.

Through many an election, no Catholic was named to the Concord School Board — but thanks to Tolman, democracy itself was not openly flouted.

Father McCall could see better understanding, indeed, in the making. Both the *Enterprise* and the *Freeman* were beginning to print news about St. Bernard's along with that of the Protestant parishes. The fine-toned organ installed in the church came in for praise, and the trees set out at the cemetery.

Within five years of his taking charge, his flock had outgrown their fold. They raised enough money to buy the next-door property, facing the common. Like wildfire, rumors spread that soon a church made of brick or stone would rise to dominate the square. Father McCall remembered how Judge Keyes came privately to ask him not thus to destroy the architectural characteristics of the village. He had not done so. Instead, he moved forward the old meeting-house used by his congregation, adding a new vestibule to face the common, with a new sanctuary and additional seating room at the other end. "The new steeple on the Catholic Church is rising higher every day and promises to be on a level with the gilded dome of its

Unitarian neighbor," remarked the *Enterprise;* "our Catholic fellow citizens and their indefatigable rector, Father McCall, have good reason to take honest pride."

At St. Bernard's rededication, Archbishop Williams officiated before a congregation of over six hundred people. The selectmen — Prescott Keyes, son of the Marshal, chairman — attended in a body. And Justice Rockwood Hoar, Judge George M. Brooks, Honorable George Heywood, the clerk of the town, led the other prominent non-Catholics who lent their presence to the occasion.

Father McCall's task was done, with all bills paid. Father Moriarty, recently ordained at St. Joseph's Seminary, would take his place. Whereas Father McCall had first seen the light of day in the old country, the new priest was American-born. There were conversions, too, among old American families, among them Rose Hawthorne, born at the manse, destined to become founder of a hospice for sufferers from incurable cancer.

From his bigger, debt-ridden parish at Salem, with new work to do, Father McCall could look back on the early days. He had seen many of his people become useful, self-respecting citizens, drawers of water and hewers of wood no longer, but owners of their own land.

In his dedicatory sermon, the Right Reverend Dennis Bradley, Bishop of Manchester, taking his text from Kings, had spoken of the church not as a thing of wood and stone, but built of the spirit. Father McCall, in all humility, felt God had helped him do as much in Concord.

An old, infirm, nearly forgotten citizen was going home to his little cottage from the poorhouse, where he had passed the winter. That spring, March 7, 1895, the *Enterprise* had remembered long enough to wish him a happy anniversary on his eighty-ninth birthday, then switched its attention to a generation which knew him not. Most of his friends and compatriots were dead — Sam Staples; the Alcotts; their daughters Louisa and Mrs. Pratt, last of the little women; Dr. Bartlett; Mrs. Ralph Waldo Emerson in her ninetieth year; caustic Justice Rockwood Hoar; his sister Elizabeth. Extreme old age is a lonely thing.

Town selectman through the Civil War, moderator, member of the School Committee, beautifier of the village through his love of trees, his services to Concord spanned several lifetimes. Member of the legislature, enthusiast on its pioneering Agricultural Board, he had extended his services all over the state. But wider, farther still, through his seedling grape, he had spread the name of Concord over the world, to places where even its battleground and its authors had never been heard of.

Always, he had asked little in return. In upstate New York, on New Hampshire's hills with their early frosts, growers were seeking a grape with the qualities of his first production, but ripening earlier. Neglecting his business dealings with those who were marketing his Concord vines, he spent further patient years to fill the need.

After the Civil War, new processes made unprofitable the craftsman's trade of goldbeating which had supported him while his major energies were devoted elsewhere. He had sunk into his new experiments the little capital left. Working among his seedlings, with his ruddy, benign face, his bushy hair and jungle beard, his deft, gnarled hands, he looked like a prophet of ancient times tending God's vineyard in the land of Canaan.

Then, by a strange coincidence, right next door, on the side of Bull's cottage opposite Hawthorne's Wayside, prosperous Captain John B. Moore, who specialized in strawberries and other small fruit, began selling a seedling which he called the Earliana, possessing the very qualities for which Bull had striven.

"I have no jealousy of the rival seedlings which are annually being brought into notice by gentlemen of skill and leisure," said Ephraim Bull, but with a bitterness unusual to his nature. His acquaintances noticed a change coming over the simple, friendly old man. Withdrawn, suspicious of his fellows, he was becoming a hermit, pottering among the roses he now was growing. Various misfortunes, neighbors heard, were plaguing him. His brother, who long ago had joined the gold rush to California, had gone insane. His only sister, married to a drunkard, looked to him for support. He had sought the poorhouse as a refuge when a fall from a ladder crippled him. Private charity he would not accept.

In any country of the Old World, Judge Hoar had always insisted, a public benefactor like Ephraim Bull would receive government acclaim and a pension. What he sowed, others reaped. By autumn he was dead.

Picnickers' debris all over the lawns. No use to put up warnings: KEEP OFF THE GRASS! As far as the great American public was concerned, Concord was national property. Ten thousand or more tourists came annually to see where the well-known shot was fired, to gawk at the philosophers' houses, to goop at the home of the little women.

But if householders had to look to their defense, the local merchants began reaping a copper harvest through postcards and souvenirs, and boardinghouse keepers throve, having learned about the rewards of hospitality through the School of Philosophy.

Horace Tuttle, Penniman's successor, sent carriages to meet all trains and announced in the Boston papers that he had installed one of the newly introduced telephones to help visitors hire sightseeing barges. Irish lads, conducting rubberneck parties, were the town's impresarios, drawing on their Celtic imaginations for details of the famous day at Concord Bridge, where most had convinced themselves their own forefathers had played a valiant part. Saturnine, enormously fat John Tarlton, keeper of Wright's Tavern, set up view-blocking, hideous signs extolling the historic glories of Concord and the high quality of his refreshments, till everything from tallyhos to bicycles crowded his yard.

Wheels, indeed, were all over. On the sidewalks from which the constables tried to shoo them, in the streets, in the store windows — and sometimes through them. Concord, like all the world, had the craze. It began with wheels as a young man's dangerous plaything — giant hoops higher than one's head, with a tiny sphere for a rudder. Presently, having developed sex and a more reasonable pattern, bicycles were in universal use, and moonlit summer nights as well as sunny days brought shoals of riders to Concord.

Very few visitors, few citizens in the town itself, bothered to turn their attention to less agreeable manifestations of the spirit of this plush-upholstered final quarter of the nineteenth century. Unless brought home to them by direct collision, they took only passing notice of a newer Revolution, costing far more blood than was shed at the bridge, and for as vital issues. Its battles were fought mostly in America's hugely expanding industrial centers. It was a modern variant of civil war — capital on one side, labor on the other. The easy explanation that foreign agitators were to blame for these disorders was beginning to manifest a sievelike quality. After all, demands for an eight-hour day, a living wage, and tolerable working conditions made reasonable sense. And Samuel Gompers's American Federation of Labor was beginning to gain what looked like permanence and power in the American scheme — though it lost the

Homestead Strike against Andrew Carnegie's titan of steel, and the Pullman strike on the railroads. Closer to Concord was Massachusetts's pioneering Labor Arbitration Board, with Charles Hosmer Walcott, of the town, as its chairman — and closer still a brief internecine labor war, a local flare-up, between the secret society calling itself the American Protective Association and Irish Catholic labor.

One Tuesday evening, in September, twelve hundred A. P. A. members from Boston, arriving in an eight-car special train, invaded Concord, proposing to hold an organization meeting. Along Main Street and the Milldam they marched — apprehensive shopkeepers having closed their doors — while the Irish inhabitants of Concord and neighboring towns lined either side, hooting and jeering the transparencies — "The A. P. A. Has Come to Stay," "No Home Rule for America." Soon a volley of stones smashed the signs, and the fight was on. That no one died was a miracle. Bricks four inches square were flying, and bullets whined over the heads of the crowd. The line of march turned to a gantlet of retreat toward the station, but with each side about equally matched. When the invaders at last took refuge in the departing cars, rocks were still crashing through the windows.

The A. P. A. tried no further marches on Concord. Presently, denounced by George Frisbie Hoar in the halls of Congress as malicious and un-American, it had died out in Massachusetts, its former stronghold.

But the tourist invasion kept on, and with embellishments. The Fitchburg Railroad, quick to profit from a natural bonanza, set up a picnic station near Thoreau's cove, on what was becoming known as "Lake Walden," with pavilions for food and drink, with swings and seesaws, with shacks for bathing, and a pier with boats for hire.

Concord itself used its unspoiled places: Sudbury River, Fairhaven Bay. The Assabet, after long quiet, was again alive, with shoals of gaily painted, brightly cushioned canoes taking the place of the skiffs used by the earlier, select, Thoreauian brotherhood of the streams.

For social Concord, the greatest river event was the annual carnival. On the Fourth of July, with forty or fifty floats and decorated barges, Concord would turn its sluggish stream into a river from Fairyland, with myriads of paper lanterns rivaling the fireflies. Elaborate superstructures would rise like miracles to conceal leaky scows for a moment of glory. Perfect in papier-mâché, with a hinge in its neck for passage under the bridges, Lohengrin's swan would quit the Rhine for the Concord. Rowed with a giant oar in Venetian fashion, a gondola served as a setting for pretty Beth Hoar, the judge's daughter, and pretty Marian Keyes, dressed in costumes brought home after tours in Italy. "Youth at the Prow, Pleasure at the Helm" would pass — handsome Sted Buttrick plying the sweep, Mary French looking charming at the tiller. All Dan's marble maidens, people said, had a way of catching some look of her face.

Summers for outdoors; winters for entertainment, dances, and organizations. Years before, an eccentric citizen, Cummings Davis, had bought, for next to nothing, ancient mahogany highboys, banister and splat-back chairs, glistening, delicate spode, rusted muskets, even one of the lanterns hung for Paul Revere at the Old North Church. Eager to modernize, householders were glad to get rid of such trash. Davis stored it in the equally timeworn house once used by saddler Brown during the Revolution. Then, at last, Concord woke up to the worth of its treasure. An Antiquarian Society was formed, which took over Davis's collection and old Davis too, grown as rickety as some of his chairs. Once again, by rushlight and candle-light, the fine house shone in antique splendor, as ladies, dressed in ancient costumes, hair powdered and piled high round handsome combs, poured tea and chocolate at annual gatherings. Adams Tol-man, secretary — so fearful was he of fire — used often to visit the house late at night, to make sure all was safe.

May Alcott's dream of an art center was also realized, though May did not live to see it in the full tide of its success, with her *protégé* Daniel Chester French serving as honorary president. Dra-matics, likewise, flourished anew, even more ambitiously than in Louisa Alcott's day. Under the leadership of Thomas Whitney Surette, gifted son of a Concord selectman, came an unheard-of in-novation — an amateur stringed orchestra which played Mozart and Haydn and Bach.

Whist for the old folk; dances for the young. Ellen Emerson, un-official chairman of an unappointed committee to keep village cus-toms active and sweet, gave old-fashioned parties for all who would come. In the last quarter-century she had watched dancing move from the stately quadrille through the waltz to the polka and two-step. February's *Bal Masque*, at the new armory, became the event of the season, with three hundred guests in costume swaying to the airs of Carter's six-piece band from Boston — Anne Bartlett attending

as a Daughter of the Regiment; Beth Hoar as a Fairy Princess; and
Louis Surette, as George Washington, talking with Sitting Bull,
Uncle Sam, and the Man from the Moon.

With picnics and pageants, dances and celebrations, in this age of
self-satisfaction, there was little to attract one's eye toward history's
current dull show. At the White House, Presidential mediocrities
came and went. The disputed national contest — Governor Ruther-
ford B. Hayes, Republican, of Ohio, declared winner by an Electoral
Commission over Governor Tilden of New York — caused less excitement in Concord than George Frisbie Hoar's elevation from
the House to the Senate. Though Judge Hoar's younger brother
had his official residence in Worcester, his native town still claimed
him as her own. "Mr. Hoar," pontificated the *Freeman*, "comes into
very close personal relations with the administration, and will doubtless be the most influential man in Washington outside the cabinet."
Hayes's fellow Republican successor, President Garfield, caused
more excitement through getting assassinated than in being elected,
for Americans liked him as a kindly man. His Vice President, Chester
A. Arthur, a petty New York boss, surprised skeptics by giving distinction to his administration through passage of the Pendleton Act,
which set up the Civil Service Commission, knocking some slats
out of the bottom of the iniquitous pork-barrel by putting fifteen
thousand federal employees on a merit system — a reform for which
George William Curtis, once of Concord, had worked so hard and
so long.
Then Democrat Grover Cleveland in again, out again, in again,
for a couple of terms, with Republican Benjamin Harrison sandwiched between — Cleveland far more able than his immediate fellow Presidents; almost great, yet with his policies too often ham-
strung by the partisan tactics of a Republican majority, though he
kept on fighting for what he believed in: a better civil service, a
lower tariff, a check on Treasury raids by the veterans' lobby. Here,
in this legacy of war, was tragedy and shortsightedness too, whichever way one looked at it. Ignored and denied the right to work,
through depression and unemployment, young soldiers who had
saved the Union had become gaffers now, loaded too late with pensions by a Congress which had discovered they were not too old to
organize or vote.
In Concord, Stedman Buttrick, a Democrat like his grandfather
before him, and Sherman Hoar, young Republican liberal, fought

side by side for Grover Cleveland. Cleveland probably owed his victories, indeed, to Republicans like Carl Shurtz, George William Curtis, and young Hoar, nicknamed "mugwumps" by shocked stalwarts, to whom crossing the Party line was a cardinal sin. Mugwumps, said a local wit, are birds with their mugs on one side of the fence, their wumps on the other.

For the most part, however, Concord, like the rest of New England, took sides according to definite pattern. Gone were the Jeffersonian, Jacksonian Democrats — men like farmer Edmund Hosmer and James Adams the cabinetmaker — and their descendants joined the rest of the old stock in supporting the straight Republican ticket, usually outvoting the Irish newcomers whom the Democrats had been quick to win to their standards.

In '96, William McKinley's campaign was colorful in the unsuccessful opposition of Democrat William Jennings Bryan, who spoke passionately of the cross of gold on which the Republicans would crucify the nation should free coinage of silver be denied — a speech read even by Republicans in Concord. Saner, though less popular, was his later warning, that America must not turn covetous eyes toward the Caribbean, toward Spain's Cuba, toward the Pacific. In the 'fifties, Manifest Destiny had condoned the acquisition of much of northern Mexico, bringing many new states into the Union. Now that the continent was secure as far as the Pacific, said the Republicans, Manifest Destiny should take on a wider meaning. *Our factories, grown tremendously since the Civil War, are turning out mountains of goods that search for markets. Shall we deny ourselves an outlet other nations are seeking? Is not Britain again on the prowl, with her lion's paw in South Africa? France also; Germany too? Lucky indeed that the Monroe Doctrine holds like a trustworthy dike, keeping out Europe's acquisitive tides! But what of that tranquil ocean that washes Oregon's shores, and California's? Whose sea, if not America's? Already Europe is snatching at the pieces of China's disintegrated Empire, smashed by Japan's victory in '94. Through the ancient prowess of her clipper captains, does not New England hold first claim to the China trade?*

Yet even the clamor of the imperialists came but faintly and intermittently to Concord — as to most American citizens — mixed with several resolute voices that refused to join the chorus. Staunch Republican George Frisbie Hoar, up from Washington to visit the Concord members of his family, his sandy hair touched with senatorial gray, had joined such political opposites as ex-President

Cleveland in warning the Republic against hidden perils behind the songs of the new order of sirens. The ideals of the founders of the nation, the Constitution itself, declared the Senator, demand that America hold aloof from the imperialistic scramble. Giving way to possessiveness, he insisted, can end only in catastrophe.

CHAPTER XIX

Imperialistic Scramble

THE blast that sank the *Maine* in Havana Harbor on the night of February 15, 1898, echoed like sudden thunder through the country — as loud in Concord as though it had gone off right on the Milldam. Two hundred and sixty American sailors killed in what a Naval Court of Inquiry announced could have been nothing else than an external explosion.

Little Cuba's uprising against Spain's exploitation — a rebellion three years old now — had already given United States custodians of America for Americans something definite to shout about. Banner headlines over accounts of Spanish atrocities — stories in the flamboyant yellow journals that worked wonders in boosting circulation — had conditioned American thinking so that a catastrophe like that which destroyed the battleship was all that was needed to touch off a crusade in behalf of humanity. *Remember the Maine* became a nation-wide slogan — though informed realists also remembered that fifty million American dollars lay invested in Cuba's sugar cane, with an island trade well past one hundred million.

A regular army of less than thirty thousand was far too small for a war. Massachusetts, full of pride in her traditional Militia, was ready when McKinley, that April, asked the nation for two hundred thousand men.

True, Concord's Company, like those in many other New England towns right after the Civil War, when soldiers and soldiering became a nuisance, had almost died of neglect. *There will be no more wars for America.* But Concord's militia, its venerable flags garlanded with honorable tradition, hung on largely through its social value till the town's pride gave it a good armory and restored it to life.

In a special gathering at which patriotism could not quite extinguish Yankee caution, the town voted that none of the Company's married men should be allowed to muster into active service. But when Cyrus Cook, captain, and a married man himself, told the militia that he would take only bachelors, such a howl went up that he was forced to wink at several personal histories. Most of the noncoms, the best shots in the outfit, were married. Without them, how could he drill the company? Just filling the ranks looked like a problem. But the unexpected news of Admiral Dewey's victory — he had led an American squadron past the batteries into Manila Bay — did wonders for recruiting. Cook was assured of a reasonably full company — seventy-four men, and a first and second lieutenant.

No telling how long the fighting might last. Spain was an adversary with a formidable reputation. The almost fatal miscalculation of the Civil War — short enlistments — must not be repeated. The venerable Concord Artillery, veteran of three wars, would be mustered into the Federal service for two years — unless circumstances shortened this period — as I Company, Sixth Massachusetts Regiment of Infantry, United States Volunteers.

Concord's recruits would become not only the defenders but in a sense the wards of the National Government. Yet the town remembered that during the War between the States it had been able to furnish its soldiers with much vitally needed comfort and help. To play safe, the citizens elected a sizable War Committee, with Dr. Edward Emerson as general chairman.

There was little the group could do at present save show that the town was proud of its soldiers. So a farewell banquet was planned: the Ladies' Committee — soon busy making bandages — taking over its management.

Members of Old Concord Post, Grand Army of the Republic, felt the twinges of memory. The same flags and decorations. The same pretty girls serving at the tables — only, instead of wives or sweethearts, these were their daughters. And these were their sons, departing.

Next day, May sixth, a bright and beautiful morning, the same assembly on the green; almost the same farewell speeches.

This is a war, said Edward Emerson, into which generous youths may go with motives of humanity and devotion. This is another war for human freedom, against the assassin among nations.

In high places, certain men rejoiced at the chance to bring the nation into a "wider sphere of influence," as they euphemistically phrased it. But in the towns and villages, all was patriotism and high principle.

"We have confidence in you, sir," continued the chairman, turning to Captain Cyrus Cook. "We see with pleasure a Lincoln Officer" — nodding to Joseph Hart — "with this contingent, as Eleazer Brooks came with the Lincoln minute men. We see too, with pride, not merely the descendants of the old settlers, but some of Irish and Norwegian fathers and mothers, all gallant Americans, shoulder to shoulder. Lastly, we gladly remember that England is now our best friend among nations."

The day after I Company left to join the regiment at Camp Dewey, South Framingham, Massachusetts, the selectmen got a cable from across the Pacific:

CRUISER CONCORD, TO TOWN OF CONCORD, THROUGH NEW YORK HERALD, SENDS NEWS OF VICTORY.

Back in '89, while the nation was building its iron-clad Navy, the town had been proud to sponsor one of the cruisers. Concord had sent John S. Keyes as spokesman to the christening, and a bronze three-foot replica of the Minute Man, which was permanently mounted on the quarter-deck, facing the bow.

Now, through Captain Asa Walker's excerpts from the cruiser's log, the town got first-hand details from Manila Bay. How, at 12:25 A.M., the *Concord* took her place in Dewey's column as it entered silent, mine-strewn Boca Grande. How the startled batteries ashore awoke, then one by one were silenced. How a Spanish torpedo boat, running out from Cavite, had been sunk by the *Olympia*, just ahead of the *Concord*. How the Spanish Fleet, soon after dawn, off Sangley Point, was seen in array of battle, soon opening fire — though most shots fell short. Each American vessel, as it steamed past the enemy's line, had replied with a broadside from its port battery — the Spaniards burning, the *Reina Cristina* in flames when hit from the *Concord*. Soon after noon, all enemy ships had been destroyed, not a Spanish flag flying save from the staff of the battered, grounded, abandoned *Don Antonio*.

Two days later, with the U.S.S. *Raleigh*, the *Concord* had helped to silence the batteries on the island fortress of Corregidor.

"We are all very proud of this little ship, which bears such an historic name," wrote her captain, "and trust that her sponsors may never have cause to blush for any of her exploits."

Some Concord citizens, unaware what a bundle of energy, what capacity for foresight and planning, the nation possessed in Theodore Roosevelt, Assistant Secretary of the Navy, may have wondered how Dewey happened to be near Manila, ready to strike so quickly. But success allowed scant time for reflection — if any one cares to reflect during victory. Triumph after triumph was announced in such rapid order that the nation grew delirious with excitement and pride.

Meantime, first at Framingham, then at Camp Alger, Virginia, the Massachusetts Sixth went on preparing, fearing lest the fun be over before a dilatory War Department should decide to send them. Over a hundred thousand Spanish soldiers, however, they heard, were still to be chased from the Caribbean.

Two days after the American naval victory off Cuba, the long awaited orders came. The regiment would embark from Charleston.

A big time, that Friday night — perhaps their last in God's Own Country for quite some months — with the first pay they had seen since enlistment, in the now friendly South Carolina port where Concord's Samuel Hoar once ran into plenty of trouble. Then, on Saturday, off for Cuba in the *Yale*, a decrepit, reconverted cruiser.

If the *Yale* was past her fighting years, it was equally certain she was no good now as a transport. Five times as many men aboard as she was ever meant to carry, with only General Miles and his staff getting halfway decent quarters. Rotten food, literally rotten — "embalmed beef," the Volunteers called it — but on that rough passage toward the Gulf Stream nothing much mattered. Then warm blue waters, clear skies, new interest in life.

Cuba sighted on July eleventh. By noon they lay off Santiago. The guns of Sampson's fleet were pounding the town's defenses. Fascinated, the troops aboard the *Yale* watched puffs of what looked like dust, then columns of black smoke, rise from the heart of the city.

A moment of excitement when General Miles went ashore: for a talk, the grapevine telegraph reported, with General Shafter besieging Santiago. Then, aboard the *Yale*, nothing to do but sweat.

Heavy blue uniforms had been issued — no khaki available, explained the quartermaster. I Company could hear the officers grousing that the army's supply and commissary must have plummeted into total collapse — everything that could go wrong with the moving of troops had done so.

More days of idleness. The *Yale*, under the tropic sun, grew rich in smells. Inadequately equipped for so many men, the whole ship soon stank like a privy.

At last General Miles returned aboard and the enlisted men's grapevine again got busy. Santiago had just surrendered. Yellow fever — whatever that might be — had broken out on shore, a reason they had not been landed. Eleven weeks of war, and Spain's island empire, like a cluster of luscious grapes, was ready for harvest. But it was felt necessary to have American troops in Puerto Rico, to secure that island before the signing of peace. General Miles was to command the expedition. So the *Yale*, with twelve other vessels, sailed for Fort Guanica, Puerto Rico.

For the most part the natives welcomed the soldiers, greeting them as deliverers. But when his company sought to protect a town, Captain Cook had his difficulties. Every night, fires would break out. Then the natives would casually remark not to bother — it was only the house of a wicked Spaniard.

Mists lay heavy in the valleys on the inland march. The rainy season had set in. Weighted down by their blanket rolls, by the old-fashioned black powder cartridges they were carrying, by their ancient Springfields — modern Krag breechloaders did not catch up with them till later — many men, as the line probed toward the interior, collapsed exhausted. Problems of supply became acute — the trails too narrow for oxcarts, too few pack mules to take over the burden.

A final, disheartening, sodden stretch — then the outskirts of Utuado. Here, learned the men, they would make at least a semi-permanent camp.

They pitched their pup tents by the banks of a stream on what had once been a cane field and now was a wallow of mud. In the ten days of incessant rain that set in, their shelters proved of little value. The Spaniards were withdrawing from Utuado. No enemy to fight — except swarms of mosquitoes and runnels of rain. A few soldiers wished to ditch their tents to draw off the water but were warned that stirring up the mud might produce more sickness.

If rations had been bad before, they became incredible now. Maggots in the beef, the bread solid with mildew. Pay continued to come in driblets, till only the best-off could buy food from the natives. And — worst of all — the fever.

Sergeant Francis Jackson found himself recording in the sickbook more than a quarter of the names of all the company, Captain Cook's among them. Presently, out of a regiment of thirteen hundred, only seven hundred and eighty-two could report for duty. And many of these, unwilling to risk the hospitals, could scarcely stand on their legs.

The small medical personnel was soon hopelessly swamped, and volunteers had been called for. Already nine members of I Company were serving as orderlies and nurses.

Corporal Hosmer's was the first Concord death, casting a gloom over the company. Then Charlie Hart, who had enlisted while a senior at the high school. Private George Adams next, who caught the fever while nursing a companion.

Why are we being kept in this pest hole? men began asking. "We enlisted for the war," Lieutenant Joseph Hart wrote to his folks, "and the war and our duties are over. Now let us return." Spain had capitulated; a preliminary peace had been signed. That news, indeed, was a month stale now.

Colonel Edmund Rice, Civil War veteran, did his best to cheer the regiment. They were the bravest soldiers he had ever commanded; braver than many who had experienced battle — and his voice shook as he said it. But most heartening of all, for the men of I Company, was an unexpected visit from Parson Loren Macdonald, bringing news and gifts from Concord.

"This is the sickliest place," he wrote home, "that one could imagine. The whole business of this camp seems to be to take care of the ailing." Some of the boys, he reported, looked like living skeletons. "I go through three hospitals every day," he continued, "and it does me good to see the men's faces brighten up at the mention of home. The desire to go home is universal, and the intense longing on the part of some seems to produce a sort of melancholia."

Concord had a chance to see for herself when Sergeant Ted Smith and Private Johnny Flannery were shipped back. They had left home healthy and strong. They returned as shadows of their former selves — listless, emaciated, burnt-out by fever.

"Whether it is the heat or the unsatisfactory sanitary conditions of the place, or the miserable rations," wrote Parson Macdonald from Utuado, "it certainly seems that if the men remain here two months longer, there will not be a well man in the whole regiment."

Would the list of dead end with Ralph Hosmer, George Adams, and Charlie Hart? Concord recalled Charlie, the previous autumn, playing football against Lexington High School. Ralph Hosmer, son of a wounded veteran who died soon after the Civil War, had carried in his veins the blood of Concord's founders.

No women nurses at all in Puerto Rico, the war committee learned. Wrapped in the web of red tape it was endlessly spinning, the War Department had forbidden their passage. According to regulations, female nurses could not be sent out of the country.

Had not Florence Nightingale, and her volunteers, in the Crimea, traveled a distance to prove their worth and courage? Concord's Committee joined forces with representatives from other towns, presenting a strong petition that pay, supplies, medicines and nurses be not only ordered sent; it was up to the Administration to see that they actually *got* there.

Sherman Hoar managed to pull enough wires for Concord's convalescents to be sent home with as little delay as possible. As a volunteer inspector of army hospitals, he had seen at first hand what the sick were putting up with. Together with a recommendation for the troops' recall, he sent his report to his uncle, who immediately addressed the President. Senator George Frisbie Hoar knew just where the shoe could be made to pinch.

> My nephew, late a member of Congress [he wrote], has devoted the whole summer to the relief of sick and wounded soldiers. He is a man of absolute honesty, good judgment — though somewhat liable to be influenced by his emotions — and has no political or selfish desire which would affect the accuracy of his statements. Enclosed is a copy of a letter just received from him. I concur in his recommendations. Public confidence in you is undiminished. But it will take only a very little addition to the popular complaint, fostered by the press of all parties here without exception, to make a political revolution this fall.

When the Sixth Regiment, with Concord's Company, got back to Boston that October (election day still one week distant), though Edward Emerson and others were at Rowe's Wharf to greet them, Sherman Hoar was not with the committee. He had died from fever caught while inspecting the camps.

That autumn, Americans totted up the score. Cuba in Washington's charge, till the people should prove themselves ready to take over their own affairs. Puerto Rico America's by official secession. The Philippines and Guam in American hands, pending final disposition in the treaty being negotiated at Paris. Those steppingstones to the far Pacific, the Hawaiian Islands, had already been annexed in midsummer by Act of Congress.

On the fourth of January, in obedience to the second article of the Constitution, the President submitted to the Senate for ratification the final treaty — and struck snags, both in the Senate and out of it.

Was not the nation launching itself on those very seas of imperialism from which it had driven Spain and warned other nations? Would we not have to conquer those islanders — expecting freedom and resenting America's rule as they had resented rule by Spaniards?

In Boston, Charles Francis Adams was organizing an Anti-imperialist League, with chapters in various towns, including Concord. On Capitol Hill, a few Republicans, notably Senator Hoar, had the courage to cross the party line and join the opposition — where some Democrats were opposing the treaty from conviction, many as a partisan measure.

As Congress reassembled for the great debate, Senator Hoar called dutifully at the White House.

"How are you feeling this winter?" the President asked his ruddy-faced, stocky, white-haired friend.

Mr. Hoar was determined there should be no misunderstanding. "Pretty pugnacious, I confess, Mr. President!"

There were tears in McKinley's eyes — he was a soft, good-natured man — as he and the Senator parted.

Yet through the bitter controversy, George Frisbie Hoar respected the principles of friendship. It was the President's policy, not the President, that both his conscience and his honor compelled him to fight.

So the Administration claimed inherent privilege to govern as it pleased these islands in the Atlantic and Pacific? Unequivocally Senator Hoar challenged that right.

Annex the Philippines when the Filipinos themselves had won their independence by the time that Spain, without a foot of ground to stand on, claimed the power to hand them over? No wonder Aguinaldo's men had fired on American soldiers — an act which Administration leaders were twisting into a treasonous assault on a friendly nation.

The ideals of our Constitution, our moral duty, call on us to withdraw from these archipelagoes in distant seas. "If we are to enter into competition with the great powers of Europe in the plundering of China, in the division of Africa; if we are to quit our own to stand on foreign lands; if our commerce is hereafter to be forced upon unwilling people at the cannon's mouth; . . . if we are to govern subject and vassal States, trampling as we do it on our own great Charter which recognizes alike the liberty and the dignity of individual manhood, then let us resist this thing in the beginning, and let us resist it to the death!"

But Senator Hoar found little support through the length and breadth of a victorious country.

Clearly, America's duty lies just in the opposite direction. America must uplift and civilize these barbarous people, not throw them back on their heathen ways.

Besides, have we not paid Spain twenty million dollars for these islands?

So the treaty won the two-thirds majority needed.

Even then, Senator Hoar would not be silenced, though he put his chances for re-election into jeopardy.

Imperialism, he warned, is not a question of a day, or of a year, or of an Administration, or of a century. It will affect and largely determine the whole future of the nation. There is still time for modification. "I appeal from the Present, bloated with material prosperity, drunk with the lust of empire, to another and better age. I appeal from the Present to the Future and the Past!"

But the people, in their first response, gave McKinley a thumping endorsement, with Teddy Roosevelt — late Governor of New York, late Assistant Secretary of the Navy, hero of San Juan Hill and impressario of Manifest Destiny — as the new Vice President.

Secretary of State John Hay, Roosevelt's friend — good friend, also, of Henry Cabot Lodge, junior senator from Massachusetts — using the Navy as a club with which to threaten, and backed by the British Fleet, too, since England, dismayed to find so many entering the old game, now saw in the United States policy a better chance to score, was showing commendable zeal in securing international adherence to an open door policy in China, blocking the private spheres of influence which France, Germany, and Japan, following Britain's earlier lead, were now intending. Strangely, the Chinese themselves seemed scarcely to appreciate Hay's efforts. But the bloody Boxer Rebellion's eventual outcome was to make Peking safe for the alien powers.

A war and an epoch which, for most Americans, had begun with altruism was ending in a scramble for power.

CHAPTER XX

The Thunder of Guns in Europe

IT was hardly generous of the departing century, by way of final gesture in Concord, to burn to the ground the ancient First Parish Church which had housed the Provincial Congress. Nor was it fair of the incoming one to horrify the nation through the death of President McKinley, struck down by an assassin's bullet. But the town soon built a replica of the lost building, and in young Teddy Roosevelt, McKinley's running mate in the recent election, the country got a far more energetic President, who had no intention of letting the Union drowse in the enervating air of its domestic prosperity.

In Concord, during the final year, the new incandescent street lights had been turned on with a flip of the switch. Out for good were the thirty-one flickering kerosene lamps along the Milldam, each perched like a bird cage on a post. The clutter of electric and telephone wires, tacked like giant spider webs every which way to poles and buildings along Main Street, were gradually disappearing underground. Right at the start of the past quarter-century, the town had gained the luxury of running water. Gone was the ancient well — neighboring the cesspool. With water piped into low-lying Concord, it became imperative to let it out, so a public sewerage system presently followed. A malaria epidemic during construction was blamed on the Italians who dug the ditches — new immigrants, who were beginning to settle in town, crowding St. Bernard's till Father Moriarty had to warn the older parishioners of his polyglot flock that God bade mankind love one another. But the town's young doctor, Theodore Chamberlin, blamed the mosquitoes that bred in the stagnant ditchwater, and poured in oil.

Concord was jealous of all it had, both good and bad, and wore its civic pride like a chip on its shoulder. When the long arm of the Commonwealth reached in to control Main Street, with intent to make it a part of the state highway, the town gathered its forces at an indignation meeting. "We think ourselves fully competent," ran Concord's resolution, "to take proper care of our streets, nor do we wish to give control to state commissioners, who are unknown to us and naturally cannot be expected to look after our interests in preference to their own." This proved to be a solitary victory in a war setting powerfully in the opposite direction. Bit by bit, in matters concerning general welfare, the towns were finding themselves surrendering their initiative, while the Commonwealth too, in its relations with the Federal Government, was buffeted by the selfsame tide. Yet — as Moderator Richard Barrett remarked — surely a way could be found to safeguard the interests of both parties.

In the nation, Theodore Roosevelt's orders for the day were progressivism, the strenuous life, and a square deal for labor. Though parts of the program he outlined — *I'll smash monopoly; I'll bust the predatory trusts; I'll put claws on the Interstate Commerce Commission; I'll set up a Federal Department of Commerce to enforce fair practices* — caused the Old Guard to shiver in its comfortable boots, Teddy's hint that now was the time to build that canal across the Isthmus, his plea that we must save the natural resources of our country, his air of taking the average citizen into his confidence as a partner in civic responsibility, won for the President a host of new friends. The nation — even the solid South, though it reserved its privilege of voting against him — liked the big-toothed grin the cartoonists gave Teddy, the Rough Rider hat, the big stick he carried.

One man in Concord was especially delighted — jovial, hearty John Maynard Keyes, owner of the town's highly successful sporting goods and automobile accessories emporium. Not only was Keyes a staunch Republican. His looks so closely resembled those of the new President that strangers were forever mistaking him for Teddy, an error it was John's delight not to correct too quickly. This, and John's flamboyant notions of advertising, brought considerable pain to his staider relatives, a situation which prompted John mischievously to accentuate matters. "Don't Forget — Keyes Has Everything!" proclaimed his ad in the *Enterprise*. Soon his slogan became a byword, publicized far afield by John's hail-fellow-well-met affability. But John's greatest moments came at the annual outings of the New England Fat Men's Club, where he was always in demand for impersonations of Teddy. Clad in khaki, he roared up an imaginary San Juan Hill. Posed as The Peacemaker, he reminded his laughing audience of the Treaty of Portsmouth, when the President's big stick had threatened the groggy Russian bear and warned off greedy European powers looking longingly at China, though the Japanese, victors at Port Arthur, were not permitted to gobble up all the spoils they hoped for. But John's funniest act, sure to bring down any convention picnic, was Teddy as The Big Game Hunter, after 1909, when Theodore, having handed the White House over to his good friend Big Bill Taft, sailed away to terrorize the African jungles. With a live lamb for a lion, with his huntsman's garb festooned by cartridge belts, an enormous blunderbuss on his shoulder, John, his teeth gleaming in an expansive grin, could bring howls of delight even from an undertaker's picnic, to which, as chairman of Concord's Board of Health — one of his numerous civic functions — he always rated an invitation.

It was just as well that the old marshal had died, though probably he was revolving in his grave at his cousin's shenanigans. As a retaliatory measure, the marshal's son, Judge Prescott Keyes, who succeeded his father on the District Bench, took a special satisfaction in soaking the motorists who were John's best customers. "Any person driving faster than ten miles an hour in the thickly settled parts of the Town," ruled the selectmen, "will be summoned to court." This edict brought in unexpected profit — a thousand dollars in the first year of enforcement. Best day for the constables was that of the Groton–Saint Mark's football game, with Concord on the main route north. Over two hundred dollars flowed into the municipal till, and the victims included a Vanderbilt.

Meanwhile, as John's mimicry brought laughs in Massachusetts, the actual Teddy's outspoken assertion of the rights of Americans in the Pacific gave notice that anti-imperialism was as dead as its champion, Senator Hoar, now at rest in Concord's Sleepy Hollow cemetery. True, the near-sighted Filipinos, forgetting to be grateful for their rescue from Spain, had resisted America's benevolent intentions — preferring liberty. But their insurrection had been crushed before the end of the second Rooseveltian year. Presently William Howard Taft, as first Governor General, a sympathetic and understanding administrator, had created at least a measure of confidence among America's little brown brothers, as he called them. In Boston, Colonel Richard Barrett, of Concord, with many of his townsmen sharing a financial interest, became director of one of several companies to further the expected Philippine trade. They launched a twin-screw merchantman, the *Concord,* and sent her, with a cargo of canned goods and sheet-iron, on her maiden voyage by way of the Mediterranean and Suez. When the Panama Canal should at last be finished, the enterprise would be bound to thrive. The directors considered themselves fortunate in securing the services of their Concord fellow citizen, Captain John Bordman, veteran of the Spanish–American War in the Philippines, as resident manager.

When Taft resigned as Governor General — to become Roosevelt's Secretary of War, chief trouble shooter, and eventually handpicked successor — a man with Concord antecedents, William Cameron Forbes, Ralph Waldo Emerson's grandson, filled his place. The United States Pacific sphere was becoming firmly established.

In their local paper, the *Enterprise,* Concord's citizenry read with interest how Baron Takahira, soldier of Japan, and Thomas J. O'Brien, American Ambassador, speaking at a dinner in New York, predicted lasting friendship, peace, and amicable trade-relations between their two nations, ridiculing the notion that all possible misunderstandings in the Pacific could not be settled without talk of war.

To the average American, war with anyone, for that matter, was unthinkable. Did not broad oceans protect the Republic? Had not President Roosevelt received the Nobel award for his efforts towards universal peace? Concord's clergymen — for the Unitarians, for the Trinitarians, for the Catholics, for the Episcopalians, for the Union Church at West Concord, for the Scandinavian Methodists — had each set his name to a petition to Congress, protesting against increased military and naval expenses, since plans drawn up at the Hague Convention should prove effective instruments for arbitrating international problems without recourse to war.

Portly John Keyes, in his jocular moments playing Teddy, proved a better physical amalgam of the presidential friends than the actual pair. Before the conventions of 1912, with Keyes himself a G.O.P. delegate from Massachusetts, reports of a breach between Roosevelt and Taft, who was by nature conservative, had gone fatally beyond the stage of rumor. Fresh from shooting lions in Africa, Teddy was searching for bigger game in the American jungle. His ardor for reform was stronger than ever — ready to make Big Business behave, through the threat of public ownership of the railroads; ready to curb the courts, for voiding acts of social justice. Though he had said he would not seek it, Teddy announced he felt himself compelled to accept the Party's nomination should it be offered him.

At once an undignified scramble resulted, with Roosevelt bent on cutting out Robert La Follette, candidate of the progressives, as well as his former friend and present enemy, Taft.

In Concord, as in many towns and cities, nominating petitions were set in motion. Walter Carr, town clerk, sought signatures for Taft; John M. Keyes urged them for Roosevelt. Shortly before the Republican Convention got under way, the two Roosevelts — original and facsimile — met face to face.

"Delighted!" said Teddy, peering over his glasses and thrusting out his hand.

"Delighted!" said Keyes, shaking it, and showing his teeth.

"Well, Mr. Keyes," said the former President, "I'm a trifle disappointed. I had always considered myself the finest-looking man in the country, but, by Jove, here I find another fellow who looks just like me!"

"Never mind, Colonel," replied Keyes with a grin, "out my way the people say that is the only good thing about you!"

"What do you think about Taft, Mr. Keyes?"

"Why, only Saturday I ordered John W. Raymond out of my store," replied Roosevelt's double, "because he looks like him!"

"So you have a man in Concord who resembles Taft, have you?"

"Oh, yes, we have lots of resemblances in Concord. I look like you, Mr. Raymond looks like Taft, and Billy Cross looks like Jim Jeffries."

Here, unfortunately, the Colonel mistook Concord, Massachusetts, for Concord, New Hampshire, but the Bay State's delegate quickly set him right.

"Well, Mr. Keyes," concluded Roosevelt, "tell the good people of your town that I am pleased to know they have an eloquent and able representative of my policies. Tell all those who agree with me that they are bright, progressive citizens, a credit to the town and state. Tell those that are opposed that they are reactionaries, dead ones, and members of the Ananias Club!"

At the Convention, John M. Keyes was a stand-out die-hard for Teddy. But not enough of the delegates voted as he did, despite Roosevelt's great personal popularity, so Taft headed the ticket.

Keyes was presently among Roosevelt's supporters who attended a launching of the Progressive Party, at Boston — meetings of Roosevelt enthusiasts were taking place all over the land — but he held off voting for a Party split, preferring, along with many of the big fellows, to mark time and keep an eye on Baltimore, to see what sort of candidate the Democrats would produce.

They produced Thomas Woodrow Wilson — governor of New Jersey, late President of Princeton — on the forty-sixth ballot. "A progressive with the brakes on," Wilson called himself, though in boss-ridden New Jersey he had smashed the political ring which hoped to use him as a front, and had fed more liberal legislation through the legal hopper of the state than any previous governor.

Young Roger Sherman Hoar, of Concord, a delegate from Massachusetts, was elated at the choice. He had not taken kindly to Speaker Champ Clark, the chief contender, whom Bryan, switching to Wilson, branded a minion of the house of Morgan. Like Wilson, young Hoar was an intellectual. Like the new party leader, he believed in enlightened reform, including a gradual lowering of tariff barriers. Like Roger's great-uncle, Senator George Frisbie Hoar, Wilson was anti-imperialistic. The Democratic Party put a plank in its platform, very welcome to the delegate from Concord, pledging independence to the Filipinos as soon as they proved themselves ready.

John M. Keyes, always a staunch Republican, could not bring himself, that August, to attend the Progressive Party's Chicago convention which pitched the hat of his idol so exuberantly into the ring. "I'm feeling like a bull moose!" exclaimed Teddy, and gave his party a mascot for the race with the donkey and elephant.

Since the hour was late, Concord lost little time in forming its Bull Moose organization. Keyes was elected to the local committee, along with another erstwhile member of the G.O.P., Frank Pierce, shoe manufacturer, who had voted the straight Republican ticket for the past forty-two years. Daniel Potter, who way back in '56 had cast his ballot for Frémont, at the Republican Party's first appearance on the national stage, also became a Bull Mooser, and proudly displayed on his lapel the new party's badge — a large shipment of buttons having just come in.

"No fear of Concord," local followers of Taft and the G.O.P. said reassuringly to one another, though a few privately expressed alarm at the Democrats' cool appeal to reason and at the vociferous antics of the Bull Moose faction. Word that John Keyes had resigned from Progressive Party activity, and would support only the head of the ticket, brought considerable satisfaction to the town's conservatives.

Meanwhile, the Wilson Club got off to a rousing meeting, with one hundred and twenty-nine charter members, and more added daily. Charles Francis Adams, believing the Republican ranks too disunited for effective rule, crossed the Party line and was named a member of the Club's Board of Directors. Old Frank Sanborn — abolitionist, friend of John Brown, and supporter of Lincoln — was willingly hauled out of retirement, in this his eightieth year, to reverse all precedent by declaring for the Democrats. Not since the days when Grover Cleveland was running, old-timers assured all who would listen, had there been such goings-on in Concord and the nation.

November fifth found Wilson victor, Roosevelt far behind, Taft out of sight. Even rock-ribbed Republican Massachusetts had been carried by the Democratic presidential candidate. Concord, with little in the way of mill-hand population to balance its shopkeepers, businessmen, and conservative farmers, had clung to Taft, with Wilson fairly close, and Roosevelt trailing.

Woodrow Wilson — enemy of privilege and seer of a better world, high-minded teacher and scholar yet shrewd student of the game of politics which he could not stoop to play basely, aloof aristocrat yet lover and leader of the common man, obstinate as a mule, confident of his way — was ready to press forward toward domestic reform.

The month before the election, the *Enterprise* had brought news of a novelty: "The straw ballot, in vogue at present, will have an exemplification in this town on October twenty-ninth." Only not for the men, who would make their choice in real earnest that November. "The plan is to allow the women of Precinct One to vote on the presidency just as if the election was a regular one."

"Allow" was perhaps not quite the diplomatic word, since women who headed the suffrage cause in town had conceived the notion. But at least the town's officials let themselves be persuaded to open the polling places from two to six so the ladies could make-believe to their hearts' content. By way of dress rehearsal, automobiles went out to bring in the voters, and watchers were alert at the polls. Though the antisuffragists — strong in town, as in much of the nation — boycotted proceedings, one hundred and sixty-three women were actively interested. Not a single faulty ballot was cast —

unheard-of in regular voting. The day after the actual election, when results were compared, though Taft also led among the women, Wilson proved a stronger contender than among the men.

Now that this make-believe was over, Concord's Equal Suffrage League, under the presidency of Mrs. Robertson James, sister-in-law of William and Henry, had no intention of letting matters rest. A minor but significant incident, on the day of Wilson's inauguration, brought fresh impetus to the cause. Staging a duly permitted parade of their own, with floats, banners, and handsome costumes, eight thousand women marchers in Washington had found themselves beset by gangs of hoodlums, many of them obviously primed with rum and whisky. As women were pulled off floats, slapped, spit at, and variously insulted, police stood by and took no action. Shocked masculine spectators plunged in and gave battle till soldiers called from Fort Meyer quelled the uproar. Indignant editorials all over the country, even in papers hitherto opposed to equal suffrage, drew the issue to attention. True, leaders like Alice Paul, warned some papers, had brought reprisal by resorting to such militant methods as the picket line — many women who favored the cause disapproved of such tactics — but this barbarism in Washington was offensive to fair-minded America. In Massachusetts and other Eastern States, leaders felt the time was ripe once more to try for state amendments.

Should enough states grant the vote, women could no longer be brushed aside as a negligible political factor. Congress might more readily be persuaded to set a national amendment before the voters. When there is so much talk about the question, remarked the *Enterprise*, it may be interesting to know that in Wyoming, Colorado, Utah, Washington, California, Kansas, Arizona, and Oregon women enjoy full suffrage. The pioneering West, added the paper, has the jump on us. Even the Southern States may beat New England.

Under the heading "Woman Suffrage Notes," the local paper began an occasional column. It told how Margaret Foley, well-known suffragist and lawyer from Boston, speaking at a rally in Concord, had made a hit. Where were these sexless, fanatical harridans one heard about? Thus far, the national leaders seen in Concord had been college-bred women who conducted themselves with dignity and decorum. Nor, the *Enterprise* noted, did all meetings deal just with "the cause." A local program had been arranged at which the chairman of the Civic League for Immigrants had spoken; also the president of the Minimum Wage Commission. Thus, organizers explained, they hoped to show why women wanted the ballot and to what advantage they would use it.

Not to be outdone, the Concord Branch of the Massachusetts Association Opposed to Further Extension of Suffrage to Women — despite its cumbersome name, it contained able and conscientious women who feared that descent into the common arena would jeopardize that influence through which their sex had furthered reforms in the past — held a meeting at which five members read papers analyzing the platforms of the five parties in the recent election. If they were that interested, wondered some suffragists, why dodge the responsibility of playing an even more active part?

November elections came, with no amendment offered, December vanished; the year 1914 slipped in.

In January, Concord people flocked to Boston's Majestic Theater to see *Little Women* come to life on the stage. March brought its town meeting. In April, the Fleet seized Vera Cruz in a quarrel with President Huerta over Mexico's arrest, at Tampico, of some United States Marines. In May, citizens stood admiringly around as Daniel Chester French's marble Emerson, benignly seated in familiar pose, was unveiled at the Concord public library. Early in June, Cyrus Cook, Captain of the Concord Company in the Spanish–American War, died and was given an impressive funeral. Then Boston and Maine commuters, settling down to their morning papers on the 7:55, read, on an inside page of their *Globe, Transcript,* or *Herald*, how the heir presumptive (whatever that meant) to the Austro–Hungarian throne had been shot to death in the town of Serajevo (wherever that might be) by a Serb named Princip.

While Americans looked on in puzzled wonderment, nation fell on nation as Europe's "balance of power," which one's high school teachers had spoken of as a preserver of peace, collapsed like a house of cards. Germany threatening Russia for challenging Austria, declaring war on France for not promising to be neutral; next, Belgium overrun by German armies, with England, as Belgium's protector, soon part of the whirlwind.

Up to that summer, most Americans, including the President, had kept their eyes pretty much at home. Lively internal politics attended to that, while south of the border, Mexico, in a ferment, with presidents coming and going like will-o'-the-wisps, had called for watchful waiting. True, a few inquisitive citizens tried to understand what the Old World was up to; but its ancient capitals, far over the Atlantic, had long been shrouded by the fogs of secret diplomacy. In the Balkan cockpit, recent disturbances looked to most Americans like a pack of little Christian countries breaking loose from Mohammedan Turkey — not without aid, perhaps, from the several large European powers, each, probably, with an eye on desirable chestnuts in the fire. America also had got used to Europe's race for bigger and better armies. England and Germany, one gathered, in the navies they were building, had a special rivalry. Each Continental nation was forever holding summer reviews, inviting neighboring statesmen to attend and be impressed. Rotogravure sections at home had shown America's own Teddy Roosevelt as the Kaiser's guest, reviewing the *Vaterland's* goose-stepping legions.

Now the arsenal was exploding.

Belgian neutrality, felt Americans, ought not to have been violated, and rumors of what was happening in that unhappy land strengthened the sympathy of most for the Allied cause. But in Concord, as in towns and villages all over the nation, spectators watched in fascination as the Germans rolled efficiently toward Paris. The Five and Tens sold all their pins and thumbtacks as citizens played the game of keeping tabs on the front. Clearly Wilson's proclamation of neutrality was the proper move. At the outset, most Americans wished to live up to it. An Irish school superintendent in Cambridge, seeing a chance both to be neutral and get in a dig at the English, forbade the town's children even to whistle "Tipperary."

Boston commuters, reading their *Heralds*, could ponder Hugo Münsterberg's public letter. The professor, graduate of the Universities of Danzig, Leipzig, and Heidelberg, personal friend and adviser of the Kaiser, and now a member of the Harvard faculty, had been invited by the editor, for the sake of fair play, to state Germany's view. Germany, complained the professor, was misunderstood. "Is it really possible to doubt that Emperor William desires nothing but honorable peace with all the world? For twenty-five years he has been the most efficient power for European peace." At any cost, however, because it represented the State, German *Kultur*, when threatened, must be preserved. "For the German, the state is not for the individuals, but the individuals for the State."

As the titanic war roared onwards, the wide, the free Atlantic, so long regarded by Americans as a broad avenue of commerce as well as natural barrier, was inexorably changing to a sea of contention.

First England was the chief offender. Britain's enforcement of the blockade through which she hoped to starve the German Powers into submission, complained William Jennings Bryan's Department of State, was violating the principles of international law.

Next Germany, by submarine warfare against vessels bound for England, roused America to anger. Without observing the rule of visit and search, U-boats were sending American ships to the bottom — *spurlos versenkt* — with, of course, a wreath of diplomatic apologies.

May first, 1915, the American tanker *Gulflight*.

Next, shocked readers, staring at black, bold headlines, learned almost unbelievable news. *LUSITANIA IS TORPEDOED BY THE GERMANS*, screamed the *Boston Post*. Eyes hurried to the rest of the story.

> *Queenstown*, May 8 — Germany made good her covert boast yesterday afternoon. Two of her torpedoes sent the splendid giant *Lusitania* to the bottom, a tangled mass of wreckage carrying with her to their deaths more than 1400 men, women and children.

New Englanders read how Charles G. Lauriat, of the Boston book firm, finding himself alive in the water after the vessel sank, saved many by his courage and sea-craft. Two recent sojourners in Concord, Elizabeth and Percy Secombe, brother and sister, who had rented the Wayside, were among the dead.

> What the outcome is to be no man dares state tonight [concluded the *Globe*], but Washington is moved as never before since the war began.

Washington, and all the nation as well.

The citizens waited for their President to speak. Passionately they wished to keep out of this war they had not asked for, in a quarrel that first seemed so far from their shores. But passionately they demanded justice.

Two days after the disaster, and before sending an official note, Wilson, in a speech at Philadelphia before four thousand naturalized Americans representing former inhabitants of every belligerent land, referred obliquely to the issue. There is such a thing, said the President, as a man being too proud to fight. There is such a thing as being so right on a question that one does not need to convince others, by force, of that rightness.

These remarks, guessed the press, meant that while the United States would strive to continue at peace, it would seek to convince Germany how unjust to mankind was the tragedy of Friday.

Wilson's note, when it came, was stronger than the nation expected. Germany must stop her unlawful acts. Unrestricted submarine warfare, disregarding reason and humanity, must be brought to an end.

PRESIDENT IS BACKED UP BY ALL CITIZENS, headlined the *Boston Post* along with most of the Country's press; *GREAT WAVE OF PATRIOTISM AND PRAISE FOR NOTE DEEPLY AFFECTS PRESIDENT.*

Dapper Count von Bernstorff, German Ambassador, assured the State Department that liners would henceforth not be sunk without protection of the lives of noncombatants.

Yes, but with U-boats as the instruments of attack, how was that to be managed?

For the time being, however, no more Americans were drowning. *Perhaps Wilson, by the strength of moral suasion, can keep us out of war.*

Though Europe's battles claimed the major headlines, the nation, its breath still tense, went about its daily business. Massachusetts, with an Equal Suffrage Amendment up at last for masculine consideration, was finding considerable warlike distraction in its homes.

The Concord Equal Suffrage League had opened its campaign by a vigorous rally, with a brass band from Boston, and Margaret Foley once more as chief speaker. Men who ventured to attend announced themselves favorably impressed, and several signed pledge cards to support the amendment by their vote in November. But the *Enterprise*, which thus far had been impartial, now began running a series of readymade articles obtained through a syndicated service.

Do you know that 1,000,000 socialists are working for women's suffrage? If you are prepared to help the socialist cause, then work for suffrage. If not, then work against it.

Assuming that canvassing the men and getting pledges was the way to win, Concord's suffragists, in September, opened local headquarters on the Milldam, over Anderson's grocery. This room they decorated with the league's canary yellow, and here distributed literature, buttons, badges, and symbolic paper bluebirds. Perhaps, since several attractive daughters of the village served tea, it was not so very amazing that every afternoon quite a few men, on their way home from business, formed the habit of dropping in.

One windy Monday toward the end of the month, idlers on the Milldam gaped at workmen from the municipal light plant struggling to put up a huge yellow banner over the street where, three years before, Taft and Roosevelt and Wilson standards had been flaunted — where, through the presidential generations, the campaign slogans of the nation had flapped in the breeze.

But no sooner was it up than the crew took it down — on orders, according to rumor, of John M. Keyes, chairman of the road commission, backed by his cousin the judge.

The party leaders, who had obtained permission from head selectman Murray Ballou, sought an explanation. A State law, announced Commissioner Keyes, gave him control over advertising matter on public highways. And, chimed in the judge, who did the municipal light plant men think they were working for, anyway?

The suffragists knew an answer for that. In the presidential year, had not these very men put up the banner for the judge's esteemed Mr. Taft, and done it *gratis?* The suffragists at least had paid for the work. Of course, if this action marked the beginnings of a campaign to banish political banners entirely, the League would be glad to comply.

When these matters were aired at a public hearing, Commissioner Keyes hastened to withdraw his ruling; the judge, withholding further comment, grunted assent.

With covert amusement, the Milldam watched the yellow standard flung once more to the skies — though who paid the municipal light plant men on this final occasion remained a secret. It was hardly up to the League, explained its officials.

As for John M. Keyes, he soon was busy with more important matters — presenting, at a town Republican rally, the President of the Massachusetts Senate, Honorable Calvin Coolidge, whom he introduced as "our next Lieutenant Governor."

Climactic event of the state suffrage campaign was a monster parade staged in Boston. The blue-and-gold banner which had belonged to Louisa May Alcott's league, in '87, was again on the march. Young Mrs. Roger Sherman Hoar with her husband — men who took part risked an unmerciful razzing — served as decorations on a float labeled "Together at Home." In a crowd for the most part well-behaved, the yellow roses of universal suffrage vied with the American Beauties and crimson badges of the opposition.

While the Allies were driven from the Dardanelles, while Ludendorff, then von Mackensen, was turning Russian retreat into a slaughter, while the British clung with desperation to their trenches near Ypres and the French braced to meet a second assault on Paris, America, busy with fall elections, turned her eyes from the vexed Continent and troubled seas. Some newspaper editors were still writing of men's wives and mothers as "unsexed women," while others prophesied an eventual Federal Amendment.

But the cause in Massachusetts was still doomed to failure — beaten by over one hundred thousand votes. It was the same in New Jersey, Pennsylvania, and New York. Prejudice, along with honest conviction, inertia in the path of change, the opposition of party machines unwilling to run the risk of hanging on to a doubled electorate, had again prevailed.

Within twenty-four hours, new campaigns in each state were under way.

Even the presidential year, 1916, with its electoral din, could not wholly drown out the thunder of the guns in Europe, though the Democrats' slogan, *He kept us out of War*, helped keep Wilson, by the narrowest of margins, in the White House for a second term.

Then, before the second inauguration, Germany served notice that total submarine warfare would again begin. Wilson ordered von Bernstorff to leave. Diplomatic relations were ended.

> *Resolved*, that we, the citizens of Concord, Massachusetts, in annual Town Meeting assembled, commend and endorse the action of the President of the United States in his attempts to protect the lives and property of our citizens upon the high seas, and to uphold the rights of this nation to conduct its commerce unmolested; and we urge that the President use all the power and authority at his disposal to that end.

Already — by sanction of the National Defense Act — Company I, Sixth Massachusetts Regiment, United States National Guard, had been recruited from sixty-five to the peacetime maximum of one hundred.

Fathers and mothers — urged Captain Michael J. Dee — let your son enlist. He will be taught respect for authority. He will know how to take care of himself in emergencies. Through acquiring habits of obedience, discipline, self-control, order, and command, his value as a son, a workman, a citizen, will increase.

Join the Company — was the captain's message to young men — and the drills and tours of camp duty will bring you comradeship and health. Uncle Sam pays you while serving. And the experience will fit you to discharge your duty should your country call.

Already, down on the border, during the summer, nearly half the Company, under Captain Dee — with George Prescott, son of the Civil War colonel, as lieutenant — had sampled soldiering. Pancho Villa, of the fierce mustachios, who disliked Gringoes, had raided Columbus, New Mexico. The United States, with President Carranza's reluctant consent — remembering the fleet's brief seizure of Vera Cruz, there was little else Mexico could do — had sent an expeditionary force, under Pershing, to chase Pancho through the rugged Mexican state of Chihuahua.

Thinking of Memorial Day, in these tense times, an editor of the *New York Tribune* permitted his mind to wander to a little New England town.

In Sleepy Hollow cemetery [he wrote], where are buried so many whose names live in American literature, the visitor will find the hillside bright with flags that a beautiful custom prescribes shall mark the graves of those who served in war. Row on row, climbing the curving slopes he will see the family plots bearing the names so familiar in the simple and not wholly insignificant history of the village.

But such a visitor will see still more. In the broad avenue at the foot of the hill, . . . he will see a new Concord company, a new gathering of young men, not alone acting as a guard of honor, . . . but preparing for the service which may yet be asked of them. The Spirit of Concord is not merely a glorious memory — it is a living fact. Of five generations that separate April 1775 from May 1898, three have marched. From father to son there has been handed down not a tradition but an example, there has been transmitted the lesson that life, liberty, and the pursuit of happiness, are not easy inheritances . . . but rather that they are fruits of an ancient sacrifice, to preserve which there is demanded of Concord boys a service, and there may be demanded a future sacrifice as well.

This is the true spirit of Concord, and it lives.

CHAPTER XXI

Boom and Collapse
During an Inconclusive Peace

SO many ships of every description, their decks loaded to the rails with state and city officials, with delegates from hundreds of towns, with plain dads and mothers, crowded Boston Harbor that the flag-dressed, bunting-clad, puffing little steamer *Ossipee*, with Concord's committee aboard, was lost in the scramble, though third in line of the twelve official vessels — among innumerable volunteers packed together like an erratic school of herring — which chugged out to meet the *Mount Vernon*, six thousand men aboard, first of the troop ships bringing back New England's Own, the veteran Twenty-sixth, from the war to make the world safe for democracy.

Eighteen months before, the Yankee Division of close to thirty thousand national guardsmen had slipped quietly, furtively, from Hoboken, in the strange silence that is part of war, into a submarine infested sea. In record time, surpassing the expectations of the War Department, it had got in fighting trim. Earliest of American troops, other than regulars and Marine Corps, to reach France, it had been first of the citizen army in actual battle.

Clouds and a spat of rain threatened the day of greeting. Now, near noon, the skies were clearing before a stiff breeze which kicked up whitecaps and whipped eastward the plumes of dirty black smoke mingled with puffs of steam from the shrieking, welcoming, grunting, roaring whistles. There, ahead, off quarantine, with her four rakish stacks, with Old Glory snapping above her stern, lay the *Mount Vernon*. Her two decks, parts of her superstructure, swarmed with khaki. Khaki-clad figures climbed even on the elongated, tire-shaped life-rafts lashed to her rail; men who craved each sight in the bay, all that meant home.

A growl from the transport's siren warned the onrushing fleet not to draw too close in the choppy sea. Even the city-owned *Monitor* with Mayor Peters and six New England governors aboard, a band blaring on her afterdeck, found the going rough. Governor Coolidge's first attempt to bellow through a megaphone the official greetings of Massachusetts was lost in the general hubbub of whistles, of seaplane motors overhead, of yells and shouts from the troopship. Many doughnuts, packs of gum, rolls of newspapers, chunks of candy with which the passengers of the smaller vessels pelted the troopship fell short, but some landed, dexterously caught by the men. *MIGHTY WELCOME AWAITS THE MT. VERNON* ran the banner headlines of these first American papers, April 4, 1919, that the men had seen since leaving; in the left-hand column, an account of Wilson, Clemenceau, Lloyd George and Orlando conferring in Paris — "Peace Plans at Deadlock; Sweeping Character of French Claims Renders Situation Difficult."

Aboard the *Ossipee*, selectman Murray Ballou, Judge Prescott Keyes, and his cousin John, hoping to catch the attention of some local boy, took turns waving their large banner, "Welcome Home, Concord!" But the warmth and uproar of the general greeting made up for the hindrances of wind and wave.

As the doctors who had come aboard at quarantine began checking for typhus, cholera, yellow fever, the *Mount Vernon* resumed her course up the bay, the official boats in a line behind her. Past Castle Island, black with people, moved the motley fleet. Every craft in the inner harbor that had a whistle, from the puniest tug to the rusted tramps and the ocean liners, carried a feather of steam at its stack.

"We are proud of you, we are proud of New England" — those whistles, those shouts, those tears also, seemed to be saying — "Nor do we forget men once of these shores who sleep now by the winding Marne; in Picardy where poppies bloom near your year-old graves; or within the shell-torn forests of Argonne. God bless you, Boys, and welcome home!"

As a national health precaution, no civilian was allowed on Commonwealth Pier when the transport docked shortly after four. Next morning, in nine troop trains, the soldiers were to proceed to Devens for one more delousing. But though the men must wait a little longer for final dismissal, women's reception committees had already arranged for a giant pie-fest at the camp.

But that Friday afternoon, as the *Ossipee* tied up at the wharf again, John Keyes made up his mind not to leave without personally greeting the boys. Spotting a rowboat at the dock, he hired it. Gunwales awash, the little craft pulled toward the open flank of the troopship. A yell from her deck. Leo Hurley, of West Concord, Headquarters Detachment cook, had spotted John's ample figure. Soon the railing was a solid mass of home-town boys, eager for a sight of familiar faces. Forgetting their imminent danger of swamping, selectman Ballou and his delegation craned their heads upward. There stood Mike Dee himself, Captain of Company I two years before when mustered into Federal Service. Waving, shouting, yelling, twenty or thirty other soldiers from Concord were almost smashing down the rail.

The exigencies of war had not permitted the Concord men, despite their wishes, to fight as a unit. Plattsburg and officers' training had drawn away a number. Then Captain Dee had been assigned command of the Division's contingent of military police, taking more of the old crowd with him. But wherever they served, Concord was proud of her sons. The Yankee Division's One Hundred and First Field Artillery — nicknamed "the lucky 101st" on account of its moderate losses — veterans of Château-Thierry and St.-Mihiel, had been commanded by Robert Goodwin of Concord. "It's because we played the game every minute," explained the colonel, refusing to take the credit; "the men were foxy in switching batteries that had been observed." So skillful had the cannoneers become that they fed their seventy-fives on the recoil — forty-four shots a minute — a feat their French instructors had declared impossible.

All through the war, letters had brought word to the folks back home. "Here I am up at the American front," wrote Olga Olsen, Concord High School graduate, now an army nurse. "Day before yesterday the C. O. presented us with our new spring hats — steel helmets." Black Jack Pershing himself had inspected the unit; had spoken to her. "Just now we have Captain Archie Roosevelt and several of his men as patients." Pretty badly hurt, she hinted, but he ought to recover. "There isn't a nurse with the A.E.F. who'll be willing to go home until this thing is over."

"Too bad about Lieutenant Mansfield," Private Feehan, of the Concord Company, had written — Lieutenant Mansfield, killed at Château-Thierry. "The boys showed up wonderfully going over the top. We are after the Boche left and right, and hope to be in Berlin by Christmas."

For three years, from somewhere in France, Joe Keyes scribbled home his experiences as driver of the Field Service ambulance Concord had given. Back with a Croix de Guerre and two French citations, he was luckier than Gordon MacKenzie, another Concord driver, who died at Verdun.

"I know what gas smells like," Private Henry Bergeron wrote, "but I am not dead yet and do not expect to be." Two days later came the War Department's notification.

The slain and the decorated, in that distant war. . . .

To Major Joseph D. Murray, with the first contingent of Marines, a Croix de Guerre — the same to Walter Lovell of the Lafayette Escadrille. To Private Edmund Coolidge, a Distinguished Service Cross — "for extraordinary heroism in action near Belleau Bois." To Percy A. Rideout — at Concord High School he had written the words of the class song, and, besides his Bible, he had carried to France the *Oxford Book of English Verse* — the same award, *posthumous*, for his bravery at Cierges.

Before that Monday morning, November 11, 1918, when Concord was awakened at 4 A.M. by the fire siren, and by the ringing of bells — thus, long ago, the bells rang in the peace at the Revolution's ending — Concord's home front had carried on, while people learned to go easy on sugar, and butter got scarce. During the summer — America's first at war — as more volunteers left and men twenty-one to thirty-one registered for the draft, even very young children helped on the farms. With the coming of winter, the suggestion had been made that the schools be closed to save coal for production. But Superintendent Hall objected. "There is every reason to believe that one of the greatest struggles in the world's history will come in the reconstruction period. It is the inalienable right of every boy and girl to be prepared as well as possible for his part in it. Until clubhouses have shut their doors; until theaters and movies have curtailed their activities; even until churches have learned to combine and consume less fuel, the schools must not be touched. All that schooling can give to strengthen the intellectual, moral, and industrial fiber of our people will be needed in the coming period of trial."

The townsfolk heeded.

Twenty-five names in gold letters, among close to five hundred, appeared on the Honor Roll panels that the town set up facing east on the common. Lance Corporal Gordon Mortimer Channell, Princess Pat Regiment, Canadian Army, killed at Cambrai. Private Clemente Napoletano, of the Italian Army. These, beside Concord's familiar names.

But town clerk Billy Cross, compiling vital statistics, knew that more citizens died in the town itself, during the influenza epidemic in the war's last year; more children were crippled by infantile paralysis, two years before, than soldiers maimed in battle.

At last the boys were back, save for five in Germany with the Army of Occupation, and two others with an expeditionary force against the Bolsheviki — though just what that was all about nobody seemed to know.

They had returned, the soldiers found, to a changing America. After a brief pause and depression, the nation was busy with the blueprints of industrial expansion. Prohibition had become the law of the land. Women had at last got the vote.

For their mothers, sisters, wives and sweethearts to be fellow citizens struck most veterans as fair enough. But many were bitter about prohibition — put over, they felt, while their backs were turned.

It had been exciting to read about Wilson's triumphal European progress — how vast crowds hailed the President for his fourteen points on which to base a just and honorable peace. Open covenants openly arrived at — self-determination of peoples — removal of economic barriers between nations — freedom of the seas.

But by the time the Treaty of Versailles and the Covenant for a League of Nations which formed part of it had been submitted to the Senate, attention was beginning to wander. Concord guardsmen helping in Boston's police strike, the James J. Mansfield Post of the Legion getting organized, the British dirigible R–34 skirting New England's coastline after crossing from Scotland, made more exciting news. Few bothered to study the text of the Covenant. That was the Senate's job. But when its Committee of Foreign Relations, chairmanned by Lodge of Massachusetts, refused to recommend ratification, people took another look. Yes, Article X was clear enough — a pledge by each member of the proposed League to protect against external aggression the territorial integrity and political independence of every other. *If we sign we shall be sucked into war again before we know it. If we keep out of Europe's affairs, we'll be let alone.*

"I can predict with absolute certainty that within another generation," cautioned Wilson, "there will be another world war if the nations of the world do not concert the method to prevent it." Sure that the vision and altruism which had sustained the nation through the fighting would again respond, Wilson — tired and ill though he was after his struggles in Paris — decided to go before the people. From his special train, members of the press covered his crusade.

Through the West and Middle West he pleaded for his league. He would never, he told them, abandon the cause of the mothers who believed their sons had died to save liberty. It was for the sake of peace that American soldiers had fought; it was to see to it that there would never be such a war again, that their children need not be sent, twenty years hence, on a similar errand. If the next war comes, he warned, its weapons will make those of the last seem puny.

Then the speaking stopped.

The President had overtaxed his strength, the papers announced: he was ill. He had suffered a stroke — the whisperers hinted — he would never get well.

When the Senate failed by a narrow margin to give the Treaty and the Covenant the necessary two-thirds majority for ratification, people shrugged their shoulders with a sigh of relief. For what had America been founded, anyway, if not to be free of Europe's past mistakes and perpetual quarrels? *Let's forget the war and the Old World; it's high time to get down to the business and pleasure of the New.*

May's Memorial Day Banquet of the veteran groups, with impromptu speeches from the floor, turned into an uneasy feast. Disturbing news had been brought from Boston. Did the veterans realize that the Fellowship of Youth for Peace, planning to hold a week's session in Concord, was an un-American, subversive organization — a wolf in sheep's clothing?

A personal friend of mine — declared Edward B. Caiger, Judge Advocate of the James J. Mansfield Post, American Legion — has attended the Fellowship's meetings. Not one good word spoken for our government or the army and navy. Nothing but knocks. What's more, they are known to welcome speakers with bolshevist leanings. Some members, it is reported, have even sworn what they call the absolutist oath — never to bear arms in defense of their country. Slackers' oath would be a better name for it!

The Legion — all the veterans — wanted peace, but not peace by methods which would render the country defenseless. Were not even the disarmament conferences going too far? Shouldn't something be done? Might it not be fitting for Concord's veterans, for citizens of the town which had seen the beginnings of America's liberty, to sound the alarm that, under innocent names, organizations were scheming to overthrow the American government?

Then and there, by unanimous vote, the gathering passed a resolution condemning the conference. As the best means of spreading the warning, this resolve was to be sent to the papers. Next, a Concord Veterans' Committee for World Peace was nominated, to take whatever other steps might seem needed.

The committee mailed letters to the local churches, to the managements of public halls, requesting them not to rent space for the conference. To their dismay, they found the selectmen had already promised the Town House for two public addresses. An announced speech on the League of Nations, another on Adams and Jefferson as preservers of peace, had failed to awaken their suspicions. But Wright's Tavern, named as headquarters, was persuaded to withdraw its offer. Nothing could be done about the vestry of Trinity Episcopal Church, pledged some time before for the general use of the conference. In fact, the Reverend Smith O. Dexter, heretofore regarded as a mild and kindly man, proved to be peculiarly obstinate. Though some members of his church, alarmed by rumors about the Fellowship, were resigning in protest at the minister's stand, he refused to budge.

By now, indeed, in an atmosphere of increasing tension, the murmur of doubt, loosed on Decoration Day, had swelled into a threatening tornado — so much so that responsible veterans were becoming apprehensive. "The executive committee of the Legion would urge all members of the Post to observe the utmost discretion in this whole matter" — the basic rights of free speech and free assembly guaranteed to all citizens by the Constitution, cautioned these officers, must not be overlooked.

On Saturday, June 19, the radicals arrived — some forty college students, two thirds of them girls. From Wellesley, from Radcliffe, from Simmons and Mt. Holyoke, from Harvard, Boston University, Tufts, M. I. T., Yale. Such few dispassionate observers as were left in the excited town, looking over the male representatives, decided they were, some of them, modern counterparts of those earnest, longhaired youths who used to wait on patient Mr. Emerson. Others appeared to be youngsters whose anticipations centered as much on swims at Walden, on folk-dancing promised for each afternoon, on tennis and canoeing, as on the discussions scheduled to delve into the economic, political and psychological causes of war.

That evening, joined by two hundred or so townsmen, the delegates trooped into Trinity Parish House for the initial meeting. "Nothing shall warp me from the belief that every man is a lover of truth" — ran the program's motto, from Emerson. When Professor Henry R. Mussey, of Wellesley, rose to speak on "The World Bequeathed Us," a few catcalls from the back of the hall caused necks to crane, but nothing untoward marred the rest of the lecture and the delegates returned to Homeworth, on Sudbury Road, their new headquarters, for a "get-acquainted" dance.

On Sunday, coming back from preaching, Parson Dexter found Legion Commander Elmer Joslin, tense-lipped and serious, waiting for him.

Would Mr. Dexter please see to it that the American flag, thus far absent, be displayed in the vestry at the next meeting?

Get the flag right now, suggested the minister, and we'll place it in the Hall. The members of the conference, he explained, were more than willing to meet any reasonable demands of the Legion.

So Concord watched ex-soldier and preacher march together up Main Street with the national standard.

That evening, while Dr. Auer, pastor of the Unitarian Church, was introducing Professor Carl S. Skinner, of Tufts, to talk about "The New Pacifism," a motley array, about fifty in all — teen-age boys, some local veterans, some outsiders — poured into the vestry. Noisily they took over the empty seats at the back. As Professor Skinner began, he was greeted by such a jeering and hooting that he could scarcely make himself heard. Several citizens, come to listen, faced about to beg for quiet — but with indifferent results.

Somehow the speaker finished, then asked for questions.

What about Russia? shouted objectors. What about the Reds poking their noses into America's business? What about the slackers' oath? What about this Fellowship?

One question at a time, please — pleaded the lecturer.

From the rear of the hall, an egg flattened itself, near the flag, in a greenish mess on the wall back of the speaker. Another, then another followed. As the chairman hastily adjourned the meeting, stink bombs added their stench to the eggs.

After an impromptu gathering of its own, outside, broken up by the tardy arrival of a couple of town policemen, the mob split up, some following home Dr. Auer and his wife, shying an occasional egg at them till the victims escaped by locking and bolting their door. Others, using similar tactics, strung along behind Mr. and Mrs. Edward James, hosts to Norman Thomas, another speaker. For several hours — nor did the police seem to make much of an effort to catch them — the disturbers continued a sporadic bombardment of Homeworth, of the Jameses, the Dexters' house, the Auers'.

A lot of irresponsible young men — said Mr. Dexter, next day. "I am certain," he added, "the Legion was not behind the mob nor had anything to do with the disturbance."

Concord hoped not. It was proud of the Post and its record. Under one commander, Captain Whittemore Brown, had not the James J. Mansfield Post been the only one in Massachusetts to take a stand against bonus legislation as an unjustifiable raid on the national treasury — and almost lost its charter for its pains? What's more, if individual veterans were to blame for Sunday's disturbance, was there not a measure of justification? Some of the topics announced for the conference clearly were harmless: "The Anti-Militarism of the Japanese" — to be illustrated with stereopticon slides; "The Internal Organization of the League of Nations." But others, certainly, had a peculiar ring: "American Imperialism: Fact or Fancy?" "Can a Nation Go Insane?"

When a citizens' meeting was organized for the express purpose of exposing the real objectives of the Fellowship, Concord trusted to hear the lowdown. A slate of gifted speakers from outside, announced the local committee, would deliver the goods. Judge Prescott Keyes, noted for his firm hand as moderator, would be there to preside.

It was scarcely necessary for portly, solemn, bespectacled Thomas E. Crawley, bent on imitating the days of '76, to don the ancient garb of town crier and clang a bell through the streets. A capacity crowd was already waiting.

Judge Keyes, rapping for order, fixed his fellow citizens from under his bushy eyebrows. "Some public expression," he rumbled, "should be made of the indignation and shame which all thoughtful Concord citizens feel that unlawful acts of violence and disorder should have been allowed to occur." Eggs and stink bombs as an answer to the Fellowship were hardly appropriate for the birthplace of liberty. Yet, he added, it is the obvious duty of the town to scrutinize the purpose of this conference. That's why this meeting is called. He was himself, he announced, not responsible for arranging it, nor for the sentiments of the speakers. He was there to preside.

Fred R. Marvin, of the *New York Commercial*, spoke first. Though a son of Minnesota, he explained, Middlesex, because of his forebears, could claim him as her own. "I am proud of my ancestors who settled in this section two hundred and fifty years ago; I am proud of being a citizen of the greatest country the world has ever known, the cleanest nation God ever gazed on!"

Here Marvin's voice sank to a dramatic whisper.

Did his patriotic listeners know that this Fellowship was a lineal descendant of the secret order of the *Illuminati*, founded in Austria over a century ago? Not that the present members are aware of it! He was not accusing them of that! What he was accusing them of was being dupes of this wicked order. Did his hearers know why the *Illuminati* had been founded? To overthrow all government and religion!

The speaker paused for a moment to let this truth sink in. "It is hard for Americans to realize," he boomed suddenly, "that a great international conspiracy is attempting to destroy their nation; but it is so!"

Fascinated, the victims of this coming disaster sat transfixed.

Everything not marked *Made in America*, everything not one hundred per cent American, had better stay out. To protect America's industries — while Americans complained that Europe seemed unwilling to pay her debts — tariff walls soared, checking the revival of international trade favored by Wilson. To protect her thinking, a tariff wall, too. In Massachusetts, the Daughters of the American Revolution published the names of nonconformists whose ideas — in the opinion of its leaders — were un-American. But this omniscience did not pass without rebuke. "When the level-headed Regent of Old Concord Chapter, D.A.R., received the so-called 'black list' and saw on it the name of a former Concord woman who had been dead four years, she sensibly discounted the value of the list," wrote Mrs. Herbert Hosmer, in the *Journal*. "Others of us would go still further, and actively protest against the unwarranted attempt to influence, if no stronger word may be used, an organization whose very existence harks back to liberty of thought, word, and action, and resistance to tyranny in its every form." Now I'm not in any sense a pacifist — continued the writer — but I went through the last war with my two closest men-folk in the Army, and my nephew graduates from West Point in June, and the prayer that I join in most fervently in church is "Give us peace in our time, oh Lord!" Moreover, I spent the greater part of two years in Germany not long before the war, and I know that it is as short a step from adequate national defense (in which I believe, as I believe in police protection) to aggressive militarism, as it is to extreme pacifism, for which I personally do not believe the world is ready. But I do think there is room for those who think the first an evil, and the last an ideal to be striven for. "I'm content to live my life as best I may, in the world as I find it, but I do want others, more idealistic than I, to work for universal peace, to talk peace, and to have others have the chance to hear them."

Meantime, Harding, handsome, kind-hearted, weak, distinguished-looking presidential figurehead, died in office, his passing hastened by worry over corruptions that threatened to blacken his administration, abuses he felt powerless to stop — Secretary of the Interior Albert B. Fall scheming to hand over government oil fields at Elk Hills and Teapot Dome for private exploitation; Attorney General Harry M. Daugherty suspected of collusion with big-time bootleggers fattening on prohibition. But most of America, making plenty of money, did not bother itself over national scandals.

Ranging far beyond John M. Keyes's prophecy, Calvin Coolidge filled Harding's place for a year, then was duly elected President, and, in the midst of a citizens' spending spree, practiced federal frugality as the people applauded. Concord's soldiers, the soldiers of all the states, felt they had come back to a land of limitless opportunity. Anderson's Meat Market, Mr. Peterson's Concord Clothing, all the shops, shared in the nation's well-being — Concord's farmers, saved by their local trade, unlike those in the Middle West, thriving too. Plenty of well-paid jobs for the asking. Plenty of fun and flappers and jazz and dancing; great stadiums for football; expensive tracks for racing. Plenty to drink, with the bootleggers' help, for the Country Club younger set or the boys in the know at the center. On the Milldam, more pleasure cars, more heavy trucks than ever. Concord, with most of America, was enjoying its play and its work.

In accord with the Navy's time-honored requirements, though thumbing its nose at legal prohibition, the town gave a three-hundred-dollar silver Paul Revere punchbowl to its newest namesake, the cruiser *Concord*, which Helen Buttrick, great-great-great-granddaughter of the Revolutionary major, christened with a bottle of grapejuice. In 1925, the one hundred and fiftieth anniversary of Concord Fight offered a chance for a lively blow-out, with Concord's Own and other military companies, dressed as minute men, militia, and the redcoat British, locked in epic sham battle. As leader of the patriots, a lineal descendant of Major Buttrick was to give the historic command, "Fire, fellow soldiers, for God's sake, fire!" Confused by the contents of a jug of hard cider (a necessity, considering the traditional frigidness of the day) and the enemy's sudden approach, he yelled instead, "Hey, you guys! For Christ's sake, shoot!"

By nullification, legal prohibition seemed a doomed experiment. In Concord, honest Chief of Police William Ryan's efforts, like those everywhere else, were proving less effective than those of the proverbial Dutch boy stopping the leak in the dyke. Sam Barbo's, on Main Street, raided; one hundred and twenty-five gallons of mash confiscated at Bottini's still on Old Bridge Road. All you did was change your bootlegger.

But those responsible for a people's point of view felt they had cause for alarm. "There has been in the High School," reported Superintendent Wells A. Hall, "a rather unusual manifestation of the spirit which is so marked in many adults of our day — namely, a disregard for law and order."

Through metropolitan dailies, through the syndicated columns in its weekly, through gossip, presently through new-fangled radios, Concord kept reasonably abreast of the times — though what the Boston Red Sox were doing was just as important. In the Pacific, it seemed, the Japanese were charging breach of a gentlemen's agreement because Congress passed an exclusion law. Congress is right, thought most Americans who happened to notice the distant fuss. Why should California be expected to assimilate the Japanese?

In Nicaragua, Marines chasing Sandino who had turned out the conservative government which favored America's commercial interests. Before West Concord's Woman's Club, at Odd Fellows' Hall, Captain John Bordman, who had run for Congress, emphasized the necessity of furthering interdependence and friendship between the United States and Central and South America — but to most citizens, Pan-Americanism was of slight enough interest.

Not till something very like a miracle shrank the distance between continents did the nation's interest shift suddenly outward.

"He hopped off early this morning, alone, in the *Spirit of Saint Louis*," announced the air waves, with a crackling of static, in Main Street's houses, on Sudbury Road, at Nine Acre Corner. All day, at intervals, while men stayed home from work to listen, the radios reported. Lindbergh's monoplane has vanished over a mist-shrouded Atlantic. It has been sighted near the coast of Ireland. It is over France. It has safely landed at Le Bourget, airport of Paris. Never guessing that all America, the whole continent, had breathlessly, prayerfully, exultantly, followed his flight, Charles A. Lindbergh, stepping from his plane, had tried to explain who he was. France opened wide her arms; hailed him as the New World's ambassador of good will.

In Concord, in every American town, pictures of Slim with his friendly smile, were tacked on the wall by the children of the family — at the Hosmers on Elm Street; at Mrs. Harlow's on Stow, opposite the new high school.

Was not Lindbergh, asked the prophets, a forerunner of an aviators' age — an age that would draw mankind together, shrink the earth, make the world one?

During the summer of twenty-nine, people who heretofore never thought of looking at a chart watched stocks soar higher and higher. Why not put that nest-egg into Ahumada Lead, Ajax Rubber, or United States Steel? If you already own securities, you can buy on margin. Concord's new weekly, the *Journal*, by way of a filler, printed a cheery item from the Department of Labor: "Employment in July at Highest Level." An entranced citizenry read that stocks had climbed to the loftiest pinnacle on record.

Mr. A. Y. Gowan, millionaire maker of cement, who had recently bought an estate on Sudbury Road, was struck with a splendid notion. Why not make Concord the embodiment, physically, of all that is characteristic of New England? Tear down the aimless conglomeration of business blocks and shops along the Milldam — built, many of them, within the past fifty years and of no sentimental value. Put in their stead harmonious replicas of fine old Colonial buildings. For elbow room at this new commercial center, add fifteen feet to the right of way. Behind the stores, to relieve traffic congestion, lay out wide driveways and parking places from which all deliveries and collections shall be made — so that pedestrians on the Milldam can move freely from shop to shop without peril to life and limb.

In Virginia, John D. Rockefeller, Jr., Mr. Gowan learned, was about to rescue crumbling Williamsburg. Equally stirring events had taken place in New England's Concord. Why not make it also a shrine? Not that Concord was crumbling. In his brief residence there, he had found it lively enough. Surely it would welcome the proposal.

Much to Mr. Gowan's puzzled amazement, the town, instead, got its back up. Would not this be a step to the rear, instead of ahead, asked some of the townsfolk, turning Concord into a synthetic antique; destroying, along with some homely ugliness, its living spirit and charm? What check would there be on rents, since Mr. Gowan proposed to control the entire section? What of the rights, privileges and incentives of individual ownership? No man, no matter how well-intentioned, should be allowed so much power over his fellows!

Had the shades of Peter Bulkeley, Simon Willard, and other wealthy proprietors of the township's earliest days drawn close in hopes of again walking the streets of a colonial Concord, they would have recognized that final argument.

In late September, preoccupied brokers, commuting home from Boston on the 5:15, told their wives that something queer was coming off in New York. In this protracted Bull market there had been breaks before, but these had been quick to repair, as sharp investors, jumping in at the bottom, made tidy fast profits before jumping off at the top. But despite the familiar chorus of assurance from most of the experts, this present recession seemed more ominous. Hard to be sure what portended.

"Powerful Aid Checks Selling Flood," ran Tuesday's headlines, October twenty-second; "Many Leading Issues Show Gains for Day." Dartmouth's Big Green, according to the sporting page, was nearing its peak to tackle Harvard. President Hoover was on a trip to the Middle West. Work on East Boston's traffic tunnel was about to begin. A grateful nation was honoring Edison at its Light Jubilee.

Then on Wednesday, shocking headlines:

STOCK CRASH WIPES OUT BILLIONS

In Concord, Massachusetts; in Concordia, California; in all the land between — farmers, little businessmen, shopkeepers, and clerks watched their handsome paper profits vanish, taking with them their modest savings.

Uneasy in an inconclusive peace, denied the self-help of co-operation, a world still sick with the infections of war, its debts unpaid and unpayable through the costs of rearmament and the strangulation of trade, its nerves on edge from hates and fears, was caving into collapse. The United States, long lulled into security, was in for a rude awakening. The soaring palaces raised by business on the edges of this abyss were tumbling in. Private enterprise lay flat throughout the nation. No town could escape.

"Mr. A. Y. Gowan," announced the *Concord Journal*, in December, "has withdrawn from his undertaking to improve the Milldam."

CHAPTER XXII

New Deal

THE year following the crash, it became clear that even more
drastic steps must be taken to relieve distress. Thus far, work
had been found with the Water, Sewer, and Highway Departments
for most of the jobless in Concord. Tree Warden Thomas McPhillips, that winter, set men to cutting brush along neglected byways
like Seven Star Lane and Virginia Road.

National economics, however, refused to mend. By 1931, the
Town Fathers found it necessary to name a special Unemployment
Committee to look after Concord's neediest cases. By January, 1932,
things became so critical that the selectmen decided to appeal directly
to the inhabitants for assistance, either through cash contributions
or by providing jobs.

Men would not work for such pay as they could offer, complained
some, or else loafed on the job. But Roger C. Fenn, who used help
round the grounds at the school where he was headmaster, came to
the workers' defense in the *Journal*. Perhaps employers with unfortunate experiences, he suggested, had talked too loudly. "Perhaps I
have been lucky, but if others with good reports to make would
gossip as freely as those with bad reports, we would run less risk of
discrediting the whole group of jobless men, to the serious hardship
of some of our most deserving and innocent fellow citizens."

People would not or could not keep up with their taxes. With
no other way open, the selectmen announced a salary cut for all
under their immediate jurisdiction.

"Our teachers, for years notoriously underpaid," declared the
School Committee, "now receive fair compensation. To meet present
conditions wisely, to maintain the high morale of the teaching force,
to retain our best teachers, we feel that we should cut salaries only
as a last resort and after other Massachusetts towns of the size, char-

acter, and financial condition of Concord have made this move. Concord was first to fight; let it be last to retreat."

Yet was not this protracted, terrifying crisis past remedy through local action? How meet last month's rent? How pay for food? Even the better off could not borrow money. Buffeted by a tidal wave of withdrawals, nearly every bank in the country was closing its doors, or having its power to do business frozen, as a rescue measure, by State proclamation. A sea of despair was engulfing the land.

Inaugural Day, March 4, 1933, found the usual crowd assembled at the Concord Lunch on the Milldam this side of Wright's Tavern. Standing before the white-tiled, indifferently wiped counter, men unenthusiastically studied the list of offerings overhead — *Sandwiches, Today's Specials, Suggestions*. Others sat in the walnut-stained stalls on either side the dingy but companionable long narrow room with its dirty plate-glass front; at the row of stalls, with claw-like hat racks, down the center. They were dipping up food from thick white bowls or heavy plates rimmed with a half-obliterated border pattern. Some, with only a glass of palish near-beer before them (at least Pete called it by that name) had come in mostly for a little human warmth on a blustery day. Almost all had workmen's clothes on, frayed and greasy, or were dressed like farmers, for Pete Handrakis catered to no high-flying trade.

The babble of talk scarcely diminished as the rich, familiar voice of the man about to be sworn in as President boomed over the radio which fat Mike, the sweaty, Bible-reading Greek cook, who was a little deaf, kept tuned high for his benefit. That autumn, they had heard Roosevelt promise to remember the forgotten man, promise to make a new deal in America. Dan, hairy and wheezing, who gathered the soiled dishes out front, like most of the customers had been for Roosevelt (though Roosevelt lost Concord). But like the others, he was cynical about general prospects and showed it in his present indifference.

"I am certain that my fellow Americans expect that on my induction into the Presidency," echoed the voice, "I will address them with a candor and a decision which the present situation of our Nation impels."

The hubbub rose again, then, in spite of itself, subsided. Unconsciously, men laid down their bent tin forks and battered spoons.

"Let me assert my firm belief," Roosevelt was saying, "that the only thing we have to fear is fear itself — nameless, unreasoning, unjustified terror which paralyzes needed efforts to convert retreat into advance." None in that room, probably, had the faintest notion of the genesis of that philosophy, uttered by a fellow citizen, Henry David Thoreau. But all were paying attention. "In every dark hour of our national life," added the voice, "a leadership of frankness and vigor has met with that understanding and support of the people themselves which is essential to victory."

He was castigating the money-changers, the self-seekers, as he uttered the fine old Biblical phrase — "where there is no vision, the people perish" — which Emerson, too, had loved.

The President now was getting down to brass tacks; talking of the job ahead, of the need for quick, decisive action.

Through the campaign, he had described his objectives. Was he really going to carry them out? Men and women, he had said, must be given a chance to work, in industry and elsewhere, for decent wages and at reasonable hours. Farmers have a right to farm at a decent return. Business has its claim to a reasonable profit, free both from monopoly and unfair competition, though not free to gouge the public by uncontrolled prices. Savings must be kept safe; speculation curbed. Better housing, adequate recreation, sounder health, security in old age and from unexpected and seasonal unemployment.

Should Congress fail to act, warned the President, and the national emergency remain critical, he stood ready to ask for broad executive power — "as great as the power that would be given me if we were in fact invaded by a foreign foe."

"In the field of world policy," he had said, and the characterization stuck in men's minds, "I would dedicate this Nation to the policy of the good neighbor — the neighbor who resolutely respects himself and, because he does so, respects the rights of others."

In that dingy Concord lunchroom with its fly-specked opaque lights dangling from the corrugated tin ceiling, in rooms all over the land, men listened. Something of surprise, something of new faith and conviction, was in their faces. Everyone felt somehow better. Maybe F. D. R., with his program for action, would revive and realize America's promises.

Throughout its long history, Concord had sent forth its inhabitants to do battle on many occasions, but none quite like this one. At the request of General Hugh Johnson, head of the National Recovery Administration, Concord's selectmen appointed an organizing committee to see that Concord did its part. In a place where each inhabitant knows his neighbor, most have a pretty fair notion of neighborly duty. Already, in his third fireside chat over the radio, President Roosevelt had explained the gist of the program. "If all employers in each competitive group agree to pay their workers the same wages" — here the President's voice bore down for emphasis — "*reasonable* wages — and require the same hours — *reasonable* hours — then higher wages and shorter hours will hurt no employer. Moreover, such action is better for the employer than unemployment and low wages, because it makes more buyers for his product. That is the simple idea which is the very heart of the Industrial Recovery Act." It will succeed — added the President — if our people understand it, in the big industries, in the little shops, in the great cities, and in the small villages.

Through its own representatives, each trade and industry was to draw up its national code of fair practices. Locally, merchants and manufacturers must agree to co-operate. "Only a very few employers in the town," announced the *Concord Journal* at the end of the week, "have not signed."

Elizabeth Brennan, secretary to the Board of Selectmen, chairmanned the canvassers' committee to secure consumers' pledges. "Every man and woman," argued her twenty volunteers, "owes it to himself and his community and to the nation to buy only from those employers who have taken the increased burden of increasing payrolls to bring back prosperity."

By mid-September, Concord found itself one of the first one hundred per cent towns in the state. In every house, factory and store, the blue eagle — a somewhat militant fowl, in the artist's conception, fronting the world, wings outspread, in his right claw a cogwheel, three jagged electric arrows in his left — found a perch. "The plan is already proving its effectiveness," declared the *Journal*, citing a local survey as proof. Nearly every building contractor, announced Fred Boyd, secretary of the local committee, is now working at capacity, with added labor, putting up new houses or repairing old ones. Drive about Concord, he suggested, and see for yourself.

But rugged, independent, individual New England — perhaps even more than the rest of the nation — squirmed at the compulsion hinted at by the eagle's claws. Editor Wentworth Stewart's reassurance, in the *Journal*, that F. D. R.'s methods called for teamwork, not dictation, sounded to some readers a bit like whistling in the dark.

Through radios in nearly every house on Main Street, the President's reports on progress reached the neighbors. Roosevelt's knack for simple exposition, his intimate, confidential manner, his magnificent voice, made listening a habit.

I have no faith in "cure-alls" but I believe that we can greatly influence economic forces. I have no sympathy with the professional economists who insist that things must run their course and that human agencies can have no influence. . . .

It is your problem no less than mine. Together we cannot fail.

Exercising New England caution, the town at first was slow to accept government bounty, especially since, with each outright grant, there was an accompanying loan that must be repaid. Concord had no intention of biting off more than she could chew. Many projects were talked over in town meeting only to be rejected. But almost always, through three hundred years of democratic experience, Concord had found that discussion cleared away obstructing debris. It turned out so now.

Men dug into Bradford and Maple Streets to replace inadequate pipes. A knitting and sewing group gave employment — the dresses, blouses, rompers, socks, and sweaters made by these women being distributed among the needy, along with coal, smoked pork, canned beef, butter and cheese, flour, rice, and potatoes from the government's surplus commodity purchases. Up Spencer Brook, on Strawberry Hill, at Hat Mill Pond, men cleared brush and creosoted trees in battle against the gypsy moth and depression. And a number of the town's inhabitants were among the thousands of federally employed laborers on the new Concord bypass, Route 2, the main route northwest from Boston.

We are proud of the spirit shown — declared Chilton Cabot, local Civic Works Administrator — we are indebted to many townspeople for their aid. "Your town officers," reported the selectmen, "have striven to provide projects of a worthwhile nature — projects, in the long run, to be of benefit to all the citizens in some degree commensurate with the cost."

One type of outright Federal relief with which Concord grew familiar was the Civilian Conservation Corps. The town's Board of Public Welfare was sending young men to camps on public lands and in national forests — boys who otherwise could have found no employment.

But as times grew better and the urgency for making work diminished, the derisive word "boondoggling" fixed itself to many an enterprise — not without a degree of justification — while people, most of whom had never tried swinging a pick, complained of the "shovel-leaners" along Route 2.

Les Anderson, Concord's affable dean of the grocery trade, was chatting at a public dinner in Boston with Frank Fay, Federal Director for Massachusetts of the National Emergency Council. Naturally the talk swung round to Welfare. Yes, thanks to the Emerson family, Concord had ample playgrounds, grounds now being graded and set in order. But it still lacked an adequate gymnasium. Year before the collapse, William Hunt, former resident, had given $25,000 as a starter, but before the town could vote to raise the rest, along came the depression. Fortunately, watched over by Concord's cautious Board of Trustees of Town Donations, Hunt's fund had been added to by several thousand dollars in interest.

Would a Federal grant, to make up the sixty thousand needed for a gym, be possible?

Absolutely, said Mr. Fay; such a project was the very type to fulfill the requirements asked for by the President.

"Get plans drawn at once, submit them to the P.W.A., and I'll recommend them to Washington."

So Concord, without expense to the town, got a fine new gym.

Throughout the prolonged crisis, the town's knack for self-government, its neighborliness and civic pride, were proving a godsend. Back in 1921, Concord had availed itself of the new state law allowing towns to elect Finance Committees. Now it could thank its lucky stars for the vigilance of these volunteer watchdogs over its budget.

Every article in the warrant which involved an appropriation received the Committee's scrutiny. When Town Meeting Day came, the inhabitants usually, but not always, followed its recommendations aimed at keeping local government efficient yet at minimum cost. "Ability to pay," warned the Committee, "is the obvious yardstick. These are times when appropriations must be based not on what the town might like, but on what it can afford."

Uncontrolled in its growth, a town sprawls like a cluttered wood lot. Concord's geography — the Milldam and brook, the higher ground bordering the swamps — had determined its expansion, along with the whims of the citizenry. To control these whims, at about the time it voted for a finance committee, the town adopted a zoning law to set off residential and business districts. Mechanical rules and regulations, however, proved not enough. To supply foresight and artistic judgment, Concord decided it needed a Planning Board. Thoreau's theory that each town should appoint a guardian of its beauty thus drew closer to fulfillment.

The ambitious plans of the Playground Committee, predecessor and now partner of the Planning Board, had been stalled by depression. Its chairman, Edward F. Loughlin, Clerk of the District Court, once captain of the local High School nine, then Harvard shortstop and center-fielder, had seen the fine diamond at the Emerson playground completed before the crash. But the finishing touches on the football field, the new cinder track, the basketball and tennis courts, had been forced to wait. Now that both town and nation seemed to be recovering confidence, work could be started again.

For summers, a recreational instruction committee was in prospect, with volunteers and paid instructors, to coach the children in sports. Someday, hoped farsighted citizens, the town should have a youth center, with rooms for dancing, for shopwork and sociability, to keep children occupied and out of mischief.

In one respect, the girls — often short-changed in early educational history — were more fortunate than the boys. At the very depth of the depression, through private gifts, an old barn next the First Parish Parsonage had been converted into a Scout house for their use.

Both boys and girls fared equally well through the programs of the Middlesex County Agricultural Bureau. For the farmers and their wives, the staff of eleven members carried out experiments in Concord and ran courses in dairying, home management, asparagus growing, and other matters of rural interest. For the children, there was the 4–H program. "My Head to clearer thinking," pledged its members, "my Heart to greater loyalty; my Hands to larger service; and my Health to better living for my club, my community and my country." Fred R. Jones, local director, liked to point out that Middlesex could boast a 4–H membership larger than that of any other county in the United States. Concord's junior citizens, he reported, keep themselves busy and happy raising poultry and pigs, gardening, canning, sewing, and doing handicraft work.

Depression, with its unemployment and shorter hours, posed adults with a similar problem — how best use one's leisure?

Why not organize the talents of the town in an impromptu university? Many years before, Thoreau had entertained such a notion.

With the aid of an enthusiastic committee, Mrs. Leslie Moore of the Woman's Club bent her energies towards organizing the scheme. On an October Sunday afternoon, a surprisingly large number of inhabitants showed up at the High School auditorium to go over plans. Seventeen classes were presently arranged for, each with ten or more takers and a volunteer instructor. All through the difficult winter of '33, the classes functioned — courses in nearly everything under the sun, through many months of discovery and enjoyment.

Then gradually, almost imperceptibly, Concord was finding itself again too busy for serious heed of Thoreau's injunction. Almost the only group still devoted to abstract study, along with action, was the League of Women Voters, with classes on foreign affairs and domestic politics, with pamphlets for study of the pros and cons of suggested measures, with searching questionnaires mailed to candidates for state and federal office.

Life once more was becoming crowded with the concerns and pleasures of the immediate moment.

Concord's venerable Social Circle, having witnessed the flow of the nation's history and weathered many an economic crisis, refused to bend its head to the present depression. Three years before the town's tercentenary in 1935, the Social Circle, at its sesquicentennial, had already linked the present with the past.

"Will you stand up?" asked Judge Prescott Keyes, toastmaster, turning to Edward J. Bartlett, sixteen years old, too young for membership. "Your father," remarked the judge, "is a member; your grandfather, Edward J. Bartlett, was a member; your great-grandfather, Dr. Josiah Bartlett, was a member." Here the judge paused to remark that without the Civil War doctor's assistance at birth, he himself might not be present.

"Next is David Emerson," continued the judge. "David, will you stand up?"

Fifteen-year-old David did so.

"Your father, Raymond Emerson, is a member; we all remember your grandfather, Dr. Edward Emerson, as a member; your great-grandfather, Ralph Waldo Emerson, was a member."

Thus, through the list of youngsters present, till the judge stopped at Samuel Hoar, five years old.

"Won't you stand up, Sammy? Your father, Samuel Hoar, is a member; your grandfather, Samuel Hoar, was a member; your great-grandfather, Judge Ebenezer Rockwood Hoar, was a member;

your great-great-grandfather, the Honorable Samuel Hoar was a member."

As the judge proposed a toast, "To the Ladies!" Mrs. William Bartlett — unconsciously serving as spokesman for her sex in its contribution to similar, younger organizations all over the land — rose in response.

"In olden days, woman's place was in the home, and therefore the place for a woman at a meeting of the Social Circle was in the kitchen," she reminded the gentlemen. "Did you ever stop to think of the barrels of oysters that have been eaten raw and escalloped; the flocks of chickens that have appeared à la king or in patties; of the thousand bricks and bombes of ice cream and frozen pudding?

"We, the ladies," she continued with a twinkle, "are proud to think we have marshalled this array for one hundred and fifty years. We are proud and grateful that you appreciate our efforts enough to invite us to be with you on this Sesquicentennial. We thank you for your appreciation, and assure you that we are only too willing to carry on."

The toast was pledged with a will.

Two years after this celebration, another took place, when a few friends of Thomas Whitney Surette traveled with him to the University of Pennsylvania, Philadelphia, to see him given an honorary degree.

"Potent exponent of the power of music to enrich our daily lives," declaimed President Thomas Sovereign Gates, "with rare scholarship and unerring taste you have culled out the musical treasures of the past and made them readily available to the youth of today. The scores of teachers who have absorbed your wisdom and been kindled by your enthusiasm are spreading your doctrines far and wide throughout the land."

In war, peace, prosperity, depression, through many summers, Concord had watched its School of Music hold its sessions. Its founder had seen his hobby become a mission. The pleasure which as a youngster he had drawn from the impromptu Surette family concerts in the house on Lexington Road was becoming part of the way of life of the nation. It was pleasant on mild evenings to catch the sound of young folks strolling home with a song after their day of informal lectures and music. But few townsfolk realized how the gospel had traveled; how the *Concord Home and Community Song Book*, put together with the help of Dr. Archibald Davison of Harvard; how the Concord series on the teaching of every type of music, had spread to the schools and colleges, to the cities, to the little towns. Once Thomas Surette had remarked that America was still in its musical infancy — so few of its citizens knew how to listen or what to listen to; still fewer, how or what to sing or play. Now every amateur chorus, every orchestra playing for the fun of it, directly or indirectly owed him a debt.

Like leaves of oak, maple, and willow on Concord's familiar stream, events great and small kept drifting past on time's invisible river.

Flood waters, alas, had doused Hans Miller's diminutive lighthouse, west of Nashawtuc bridge — a fifteen-foot pillar for fire which had cast its little gleam of humor athwart the dark waters of depression. Made of cast-off tinware from the village dump, its beam had pierced far beyond Boston after an editorial writer on the *Traveler* had given it space. "On behalf of the staff of the Carlisle Navy Yard," wrote a wag from that village, "I wish to take this opportunity to express my appreciation of this excellent waterways improvement." Papers all over the nation took notice. Even the *Shreveport Journal*, in far-off Louisiana, printed a solemn story.

Concord went on welcoming its annual quota of distinguished visitors. Prince Takamatsu, younger brother of the Japanese Emperor, with his Princess, visited the honorable Minute Man statue and called at the Emerson house, where a brother of Cameron Forbes, American Ambassador to the Emperor's Court, bade him welcome. A season or so later, young Eddie Loughlin, like his father a first-rate player, pitched for the Harvard baseball team, which he captained, against Keio University, then presented a copy of Emerson's *Essays*, with Concord's compliments, to Tokyo's Mayor. "This interesting gift," wrote Mayor Ushizuka, "is to be sent to the Municipal Reference Library to be kept there forever, and it will be to the lasting memory of the good will of the town of Concord."

Good will, perhaps, was needed. That year, Japan declared herself dissatisfied with the 5–5–3 ratio agreed to at the London Naval Conference. She would henceforth build as big a fleet as she pleased.

Concord's Wallace B. Conant, engineer and world traveler, spoke before the Parent-Teachers' Association on the touchy subject of Bolshevist Russia. He and Mrs. Conant had also toured the Tennessee Valley. Many enthusiastic, able, hardworking engineers, several of them friends from Boston, he explained, had shown him round and pointed out the expected benefits of this Federal project, through hydro-electric power, to develop the entire region. Surely it would be tragic, he declared, to heed the advice of certain critics and shut it down.

Of his six trips to Russia, said Mr. Conant, the last had turned out the most reassuring. It was not true, for instance, that religion was being stamped out; many churches were flourishing. He had left with a happier feeling about Russia. Its leaders — he affirmed — impressed him as alert, intelligent people who believed in their aims. The socialization of farms and other collective measures were raising the standards of living. Factories were becoming increasingly efficient. Though the lot of the older folk, Mr. Conant concluded, was often pitiable, youth seemed ready to have its day.

In Concord, after listening to Wallace Conant's little exposition, some of his hearers, when they read of President Roosevelt's query to President Kalinin of the Soviet Union — Is it not time to resume diplomatic relations? — felt disposed to agree.

On Election Day, 1936 — Roosevelt against Landon — the Republican majority in Concord, which since Cleveland's time had apparently become a fixture, found itself threatened by an enthusiastic and convinced minority for the first time since the Hoover–Smith campaign.

As an afterthought on the election, the *Concord Journal*, though a conservative paper, had this to say:

> The magnitude of the Roosevelt victory has amazed not only the Republicans but the Democrats themselves. Those who would account for the landslide by pointing to the multitude of citizens directly or indirectly receiving cash from the Federal treasury do not by any means catch the significance of the entire picture. Many thoughtful citizens are naturally appalled by the threat that an ever-increasing host of New Deal retainers may permit the Democratic party to keep itself in power perpetually. Yet the real significance of the emphatic decision of the voters is that the great mass of Americans believe in the President's sincerity, his sympathy with the average citizen, and his desire to help.

And Samuel Eliot Morison, Harvard Professor who had made his home, like several of his colleagues, in Concord, offered his own analysis. This New Deal program, he explained, is not un-American. It should acknowledge kinship not only with the attitude of an earlier, Republican Roosevelt who crusaded for what he called a Square Deal for labor; it rises directly from other reformers in the

American past. We have always been a forward-looking nation. Franklin Roosevelt — Morison contended — is merely catching up on twelve years of social do-nothing which has characterized three postwar administrations. What is business complaining about? While want and depression are bringing dictatorships to Europe, the New Deal is saving the American system of free enterprise by ridding it of its grosser abuses — by insisting on its obligations to larger public interest than individual gain.

Yet despite improvement, and the people's mandate, the strain of the long battle against depression was telling on the nation's nerves. A snappish mood of irritation and cynicism, belying the town's name, showed a tendency to break out even in Concord. "Hurray for What?" brayed the current hit over the radio. Concord's World War honor roll, dilapidated and in need of paint, drew hardly a glance from passers-by on the common. Despite its centuries of history, the National Guard Company, ten years after the war, was at lowest ebb, so shrunken in its enrollment as to put it on the suspended list of the War Department.

The town had plenty of other troubles, too — among them a little T.V.A. row of its own. The rock-bottom prices at which Concord's municipally owned light plant, in the pioneering days of electrification, had sold current, making the town's rate one of the lowest in the Commonwealth, were a thing of the past. Small, independent plants, reported the town's investigating committee, simply could not compete on an equal basis with the titanic private corporations, the enormous installations, which had since sprung up. So the town voted to buy current wholesale from the Edison Company, while continuing to distribute it over its own lines.

Why not sell lines and equipment outright, urged several citizens, and get out of the business? Why not accept the handsome offer of the Edison Company?

At this proposal, another group of townsmen balked. So vehement, in fact, became Democrat Ed McKenna's opposition; so strenuous his defense of municipal ownership in repeated town meetings, that adjournment rarely came before midnight.

True, there has been waste and mismanagement. But with the plant in our hands, we've the means to check that. Would you kill the goose that lays the golden egg if occasionally it acts like a goose? Is the Edison Company running those full-page ads in the *Enterprise*, urging the sale, just by way of philanthropy? Why hand over control to outsiders? What's more, haven't we an obligation to our employees — who are also our neighbors? If we sell, we turn them out.

Finally, at a crowded town meeting, with six votes to spare, municipal ownership won.

There were other, perhaps less edifying spectacles of Democracy. From West Concord, Boss Charley Moulton marched his cohorts to meeting, sat stolidly without bothering to vote as Moderator Marvin C. Taylor steered the citizenry through earlier articles of the warrant, then signaled his followers to rise as one man and smash the zoning law that stood in the way of erecting a roadside restaurant he wanted.

Barring such misadventures, Democracy is all very well — yet, is it efficient? What blunders it makes; what time it can waste! A fraction, a very small fraction, of the town's inhabitants, like the nation's, took a second look at Europe. *In Germany and Italy, how neatly, how smoothly things seem to be run! Of course, Hitler's Jew-baiting is unfortunate — but most of those rumors about concentration camps must be propaganda worked up by persons hunting for trouble. Mussolini's aggressions in Abyssinia, too; a nasty business. But see what he has been able to do at home.*

An infinitely greater number of citizens, their attention at last caught by events crowding pellmell on one another abroad, did not like what they saw.

> Though the vast numbers of the people [wrote Sam Kent, new editor of the *Journal*] are no longer sympathetic with "rugged" individualism, they still value those individual prerogatives guaranteed them by the Constitution and the Bill of Rights.

One should always keep in mind two pictures, he added — one, the huge, carefully staged collectivist herdings of German Nazis; the other, a meeting of the free citizens of a sovereign town, gathered to handle their own affairs. Democracy is yet to be proved a failure. In the long run — continued the editorial — the democratic method is no more inefficient, and it safeguards precious human values.

> The record of the collectivist countries is a record of blood and suppression. The American mind is not yet receptive to the return of that from which men struggled to escape. Liberty is not a theory, but a blazing fact!

After a final vain appeal to the emasculated, well-nigh helpless League of Nations, Emperor Haile Selassie forced to flee from Addis

Ababa before new Rome's conquering legions. Two years earlier, Japanese marines landing at Shanghai to begin the "China Incident." In Hitler's Reich, Jews shorn of their citizenship; shorn by the master race of their very right to be human beings. The Rhineland taken over, in violation of the Locarno agreement. After exchanges of visits by strutting dictators, a Rome–Berlin Axis formed. In Spain, General Franco, with German and Italian aid, bombing the daylights out of elected government. Hitler's tanks rolling down the Ring Strasse, Vienna, to make Austria safe for the Greater Germany promised in *Mein Kampf*. More demands; more threats of aggression. A screaming dictator forcing England's Chamberlain, France's Daladier, to agree to the sacrifice of Czechoslovakia for the sake of "peace in our time."

Back in 1931, Frank Simonds, born in Concord and the founder of its High School paper, who later won renown as the nation's best-informed correspondent on European affairs, had published a book, *Can Europe Keep the Peace?* Concord was proud of this native son. But hadn't Frank always inclined toward the sardonic?

Almost anything can happen in Europe – he had written – none of the causes that started the World War has been removed.

This did not sound too pessimistic, now.

Maybe, along with the world, the nation, too, is skidding toward destruction – moaned men and women of little faith; groaned the poets who had preached peace without comprehension, the muddled professional teachers and preachers, the punch-drunk veterans of the jazz age, prohibition, lawlessness, the crash, and what came after. *Take these soft, irresponsible boys and girls we have reared* – moaned the feeble-hearted, beating their breasts in self-righteous penitence *– surely, through our own misjudgments, they can have been given no ideals, no standards, no sense of obligation! What can we expect from them – this feckless, misdirected younger generation to whom nothing seems sacred?*

Isn't Concord, also, slipping, having lost much of its fine old stock? No great men, anywhere, any longer.

Thus the elders wrangled over the alarming condition of the children; wrangled over patriotism; over various doubts and puzzlements. *Is it silly, or isn't it, to fly the flag over Concord?*

*   *   *

In the High School and around town, the children — as inevitably they must — tended to the business of growing up. And average parents, not taking too seriously, if they noticed it, this mood of despair in the hearts of many puzzled, semiofficial preceptors, went on trying to do their human best, according to their ability, to raise their girls and boys — trying not to worry too much when the girls stayed out late; when the younger boys, as they had done, probably, since the town's first settling, rode cakes of ice downstream in the river's February break-up. At the Peter Bulkeley Grammar School, at the Harvey Wheeler in West Concord, at C.H.S., schoolteachers who knew their charges well — like red-haired, energetic Miss Emma Clahane — nourished no neurotic misgivings.

Miss Clahane's almost overwhelming vigor, her faith in folk, helped keep her thoughts straight. Though her classes in the eighth grade and her playground work claimed her by day, evenings found her occupied with her Americanization courses — the success of which, for the past fifteen years, was due largely to her enthusiasm and tact. Italians, Greeks, the Chinese laundryman on the Milldam, Canadians, Poles, Finns, Scandinavians, Germans, Belgians, their ages ranging all the way to sixty, earned their citizen's papers with the help of her teaching. As she grew older, she watched many of their children enter the High School. Mrs. Horton Edmands, Mrs. Wallace Conant, regents of Old Concord Chapter of the D.A.R., carried on as a tradition the practice of giving each successful new citizen an American flag as a keepsake — with graduation day long remembered as a great occasion. Recitals, tableaux and readings; even a play, once, written and acted by Velina Bregoli, Sabatino Finocchio, Pietro de Savatore, depicting the advantages of learning to speak and write English. In earlier years, there had been an annual party at Mrs. Edward James's brown house near the mill brook on Lexington Road. "With the natives of so many lands living peaceably in Concord — not fighting much of the time," she would remark to her guests, "might it not someday be also possible for the nations of the world to bury their differences and dwell in peace and good will?"

As for the children of the old and new settlers who make America, a certain hard-headedness, an I-want-to-find-out-for-myself attitude characterized most of them. But where, thought teachers like Gertrude Rideout and Camella Moses, lay the harm in that? Without much articulate thought, perhaps, most of them were evolving sturdy, realistic codes of their own. Underneath, as always, lay youth's inborn courage and hope, its capacity for joy, for idealism. Were not these young realists the children of depression — who know life can be tough? Boys like Mert Sanborn, running paper routes, expertly flipping, from their battered bikes, a neatly folded Boston *Globe* to land thumping on one's porch. Boys like Caleb Wheeler driving the Fordson tractor on Mom and Pop's three-acre field. Waitress and other jobs for the girls in summer, with pocket money for their clothes.

If the elders, many of them, having mislaid faith and vision, did not know their children, the youngsters pretty much knew themselves. During that June morning of Commencement, perhaps, they become most aware. Stocktaking time comes at Commencement.

Here we all are, almost one hundred strong — Albano, Anderson, Antognoni — *perhaps never all to meet together again.* Arthur and Frances Berry, Doris Jean Boyd, Mary DeRuzzo. How amazingly American all look to Charles Francis Adams, the speaker, whose ancestry recalls Anglo-Saxondom, as each comes up to receive a diploma from Leon Foss, chairman of the School Committee. Mary Harlow, Helen Kaveski, Joseph Mara. Mansfield, O'Brien, Myette, Schaal, Thoresen, Wood . . .

Why, some of us tomorrow are going to leave this town we were born in — leave home, leave it, perhaps, for good!

When I think about my living in Concord, I somehow feel so very safe. I can't exactly explain the feeling, but there it is. I want the familiar arrangement of stores and houses, and everything peculiar to my home town. I sort of wish that I could do something so that other persons in other towns could feel this way, too. But maybe they do. Yet many people envy me because I live in such a historic place. Of course, sometimes, Concord seems very dull and uninteresting. Perhaps I don't really appreciate home until I'm away. When I'm out of town, I'm always proud to say "I come from Concord." Every time I go by the Minute Man, a chill runs up my backbone and a sense of pride bursts in my head just to think that here, in the town where I was born, in this quiet village where I've made my friends, America won her first battle for freedom.

The future, immediate and distant, possesses these listeners.

For the girls:

I want to be a laboratory technician.

I want to be a psychologist.

I haven't worked very hard in school, but I want to learn all I can, and this is the time in my life to do it.

I want to travel; see the world. Then I shall enter some field of nursing or medicine.

I'm not sure I know what I want to do, except that it should be something beneficial to other people. This isn't due to any great desire to help my fellow men, because I'm afraid I'm not made that way, but being a stenog or secretary sounds pretty humdrum.

For the boys: doctor, lawyer, farmer, aviator.

Aviation's in its first steps still, but it's bound to become America's leading industry.

I want to do something worth while; something I'll enjoy doing. Money's not so important — I want a steady job, a lifetime career.

I want adventure, then I'll come home with a lot of experience and turn into a writer.

I'm lucky to have that scholarship at Amherst Aggie.

I'll enter government service.

I'll be an engineer.

Girls and boys alike, subconsciously they image each other, and think of ultimate marriage.

I'll have my career, then, if I'm not too old, get married. I'd like to have a kind, but rather dominant husband, and — let's see — four children, a comfortable home, and sufficient means. Now I think it over, I guess a woman who has raised a family deserves as much praise as anyone else.

It may sound silly now, but one of my chief desires is marriage. It's just a feeling inside me, but when the time comes, I'll find the right girl, raise a family and live peacefully — that's something worth plugging for.

And life itself, and its mysteries.

I hope to find out just why I am, and what I'm here for. To this moment I've had much enjoyment, and I'd like it to continue. I don't feel, of course, that life owes me any more than I myself go out and work for. But I'd like its full richness. Life is meant to be lived, not suffered, and one's work should be a joy, not a duty.

CHAPTER XXIII

Main Street, U. S. A.

THERE are things about Concord to which no other town in the land, or in the world for that matter, can lay claim. There is its corporate seal with two dates on it, one locally famous, the other internationally — Founders' Day, September 12, 1635; Patriots' Day, April 19, 1775. *Quam Firma Res Concordia.* And for the center of the seal, the figure of the Minute Man. Americans visit Concord from all quarters of the land to refresh their unconscious faith in the nation as set forth in the Minute Man, just as they visit the heroic, brooding Lincoln — Daniel Chester French's second great symbol — in the Memorial at Washington.

In the battleground parking place stand America's chariots — sleek cars with the palm tree and red and white of Florida; broken-down, asthmatic jalopies with the enormous white and black license plate of Tennessee. The deep blue and ochre of Pennsylvania, Wyoming's bucking bronco, Louisiana's pelican. Most visitors come to the battlefield in idle holiday spirit. But the quiet river, the green hillside where the citizen soldiers gathered, the classic repose of that resolute young face, weave their spell, and the most raucous adult voices are lowered, even as the kodaks click and insistent children needle in with questions.

The whole nation knows that figure, but only Concord possesses the original. There it stands, by the winding river, on the historic place of battle, and below the statue the famous lines by Emerson.

Yet in 1941 — as in any year — Concord's Main Street bears a marked resemblance to countless Main Streets of America. Here is the active business center — not a center at all but an attenuated double file of shops and public buildings stemming from the square. On the Milldam — as the business portion of Main Street is still referred to — crowd the cars of the township, diagonally parked for economy of space — the beach wagons of the outdwellers; the slightly dented Fords and Chevrolets of the farmers and of the little tradesmen, with name of shop and trade in gilt letters on the door; the chainstore supply truck delivering goods enough to feed a nation; the shiny, neat coupes, sedans, and touring cars of the substantial citizenry. White and red buses, too, for the limited class of the carless — maids, some workmen, teachers — are threading their way through the traffic on their beat to and from points east and west; the evening and morning buses dumping large bundles of the latest papers at the corner of Main, to be picked up for the news venders by the obliging traffic cop.

Along Main Street, America's artery of life, courses the vital blood that flows to the extremities of the nation.

At eight in the morning two short, sharp blasts like an ocean liner's foghorn irrevocably rouse Concord's citizens not already awake. Two blasts announce midday. And when there is a fire, interrupting the stirrings of day or the quiet of night, the anxious householder, counting the toots, can learn what district is involved.

Before nine in the morning, week days, occurs the purposeful visit to the post office by citizens about to begin business in the town or more distant places. Concord has her bankers and bakers and cabinetmakers; her carpenters and corporation presidents; her professors, plumbers, and gas inspectors; garneters and gardeners; stenographers, welders, and weavers. There are laborers, mill hands, and linotype operators; mechanics and meatcutters, tradesmen, and train conductors. Beauticians and bus drivers, financiers and farmers; and journalists, lawyers and reformatory officers. All can read about themselves and one another in Concord's three weekly papers, the *Enterprise, Herald,* and *Journal.*

A moment's chat with Emil Thorpe, the cop at the corner, to decide such vital matters as the state of the weather, and away to work — automobiles providing the means of transportation for the great majority of daytime absentees. In winter, spring and fall, the school buses, shuttling in from various outer stations of the township, deposit their loads before the doors of the high and elementary public schools, while boys and girls who walk are protected at crucial street corners by Officers Fred Nolan, William McCarthy, and other members of the force. All year round the street sweepers — big, burly, red-necked men — give Main and Walden Streets and the square a matutinal going-over. Billy the postman and his fellow carriers be-

gin their rounds. The garbage truck, with its congregation of wor-
shipful dogs, passes from house to house. Concord, like many a
moderate-sized American town, is a paradise of dogs, with a dog
population in the seven hundreds. Contented dogs and happy, noisy
children — symbols of a wholesome communal life.

Main Street's day belongs to the shoppers and those who tend the
shops. Food is Concord's vital commodity — and much of what it
eats it grows itself. After three hundred years, farming remains a
major industry. In the truck garden country off Lexington Road and
Cambridge Turnpike, along Bedford Street and Barrett's Mill Road,
and at Nine Acre Corner, flourish acres of asparagus and solid fields
of rhubarb, the plants almost muscular in their exuberance. On Virginia Road, and elsewhere, are dairy farms with blooded cattle. Here
may be observed the majestic waddle of a fallow sow — one vast
mass of dirty pinkness and fecundity. The marvels of agriculture
on occasion make wide-eyed the passing citizen as he walks by the
window of the Concord Fruit Company on Main Street. Perhaps
it is a two-and-a-half-pound potato grown by Joseph Dee on his
Peter Spring Farm, or a fifty-four-pound pumpkin.

Few shoppers miss a stop at one of the rival drugstores facing
each other across parallel corners of Main Street. Each has its devo-
tees, each its ardent partisans of the soda counter, each its little
group of gossip swappers. Each displays assorted stacks of periodi-
cals, and deals in candies, perfumes, alarm clocks, rubber goods private and public, writing paper, postcards, trusses, and tobacco. Each,
tucked away somewhere, in an inner holy of holies, has its drugs for
dispensation. And both, as juvenile free public libraries, have at intervals their queues of youngsters poring over the comics.

The town has no need to go unshorn and beautyless. Genteelly,
on a conspicuous side street, catering to the select trade, is one most
prophylactic, antiseptic barbershop. On the central thoroughfare,
ready to greet its patrons, stands another — conversational, convivial,
with the air and manners of a workman's club: hale and hearty,
equipped to shear the toughest whiskers and shave the reddest necks.
Over the corner drugstore is a third, the favorite haunt of the youngsters from the High School, thanks to the tolerance of the philosophic, easygoing proprietor. Women may take their pick in matters
of local improvement among the beauty shoppes — New Mode,
Rosegray, Silhouette, or just plain Tracy's Hairdressing Establishment.

Reflecting, in their window displays, the changing seasons, the town hardware stores remind the passer-by of life's necessities and temptations. In summer, lawn sprinklers and hose. In the fall, bamboo rakes. In winter, snow shovels, seed mixtures for the wild birds, skates and hockey sticks for boys and girls. In the spring, an unbelievable paradise of flowers — in facsimile only — on little magic envelopes.

The Five and Ten makes every village a city, brings to each the wares of all the world, renders every town equal. On side streets — Walden, Thoreau, Lowell — stand the garages that keep the wheels of America turning. Here, in salesrooms with enormous windows, gleam the latest, shiny models. In a moment's time, for next to nothing, one can arrange installment payments, and drive off. Eleven filling stations furnish lifeblood for the mechanized community, and there is little need to use one's legs. The children have Peanut Macone's Bicycle shop — a heaven of tempting gadgets — and Peanut himself, diagnostic, efficient, who knows every bike in town.

No need to go from town for clothing. "Shop at home" say the tempting windows. As for laundry, one can patronize the Chinaman, with his hieroglyphic bookkeeping, who apparently keeps open twenty-four hours a day till one discovers there are two of him; or send out to the steam laundry, with its witch's puzzle of pins, and its narrow paper bindings cheerily labeled in bright blue letters, "Good Morning, Sir, your shirt for today."

Liquor to take home may be bought at the package store. To its Walden Street entrance comes the hostess about to entertain her husband's friends of the sacrosanct Social Circle; here enters, clad in overalls — America's national costume — the workman at Allen's Chair Factory for his pint of cheap rye.

Business, too, flourishes along Main Street. Insurance of all sorts is sold in town. At the Co-operative Bank, at the other banks, one can draw out one's money or put it in. Twenty-one carpenters stand prepared to build one's house, with contractors and architects enough to direct them. Doctors, dentists and embalmers are ready for every need.

Very necessary, too, are the restaurants, the tearooms and taverns, the café for a quick snack at noon, the lunchroom for conversation.

Up the street from the Chinese laundry is the florist shop — witness to the town's necrology, its funerals and festivals. Tucked away mostly on second floors are the tailor shops, apt to close at unexpected times which turn out to be Jewish holidays. Radio service and repairs, gas appliances, pastry, a bookstore, gift shops, cleaners

and dyers, through the list of luxuries and essentials: Main Street,
U. S. A., can supply them all.

In a community of close to eight thousand persons it takes active
management to protect the citizenry's life and limb from traffic acci-
dents, burglary, and sudden death; to keep it free from oppressive
taxation and unjust laws; to insure its pursuit of reasonable happiness. The town fathers, when they place their annual report in the
hands of the people at town meeting, may well feel proud, for they
have presented to their fellow citizens a packed and meaty book of
facts and figures, covering from two to three hundred pages. Concord's voting inhabitants gather on the broad wide floor of the
armory. Five hundred to a thousand strong — with children as spectators in the gallery — sometimes even a greater crowd if vital
issues are at stake, they sit on camp chairs hired for the occasion,
in a wide, deep semi-circle around the moderator's desk, with aisles
like rays from this central point of illumination dividing the voters
into segments so that standing votes may be quickly counted by the
tellers. No citizen but can feel that he has had a hand in the government of his town and may open the doors to its secrets. Before town
meeting ends, the people have reported to the people — Assessors,
Board of Health, the Constabulary, the Firemen, Bureau of Old Age
Assistance, School Committee, Road Commissioners, Agent for
Suppression of Moths, Tree Warden, Water and Sewer Commissioners, Town Treasurer, and all. There, in the Town Book, are
the vital statistics: the accomplishments — the failures too — the
diary of the town, in an unbroken series through the centuries. And
the citizenry votes — approving, disapproving, pondering every measure, every appropriation.

Such is Main Street, and such its normal activities.

But like every year, 1941 cannot be called average — an average
year has never yet existed.

Since that Friday, September first, two years before, when Hitler's
legions swarmed into Poland, Concord's Red Cross chapter has
been cutting, sewing, knitting for Europe's refugees. By August
1941, two thousand two hundred and fifty separate articles have
been sent over. Before the winter sets in, Concord's branch of the
British War Relief Society has raised enough money to purchase
and equip four rolling kitchens for bomb-pocked Britain — units
already giving service in devastated areas. Ever since it became ap-
parent that Hitler meant to destroy England from the air, there

have been British children in Concord homes and schools — a very different invasion from that of April 19, 1775.

If you wish to sew for British Relief, go to Trinity Parish Hall on Mondays, weekly. If you wish to knit for British soldiers, sailors, and airmen, get wool from headquarters. If you have spare clothing, donate it. If you have only money to give, give money. Do these things if you believe Britain's stand against the Nazis deserves support.

Help for England — but also war materials, tanks, and planes, from the Arsenal of Democracy. Gossip along the Milldam, reporting that Ralph Wickford, of Lowell Road, is among the American aviators, flying as civilians, who are piloting American-made bombers from Montreal to Newfoundland, from the fogbound, granite coast to Greenland, then over the black waters to the airfields of Great Britain. . . .

Appeals, appeals, appeals . . .

China relief, relief for Czechs and Poles — all these causes hold out hands for alms from three corners of the world.

Meanwhile, at home, in the earth's fourth quarter, amid the din of debate on entanglement and nonentanglement, warnings tell how war is striding in seven-league boots.

Concord had long been filled with rumors that Company H, National Guard, might be called for a year's active service. Then President Roosevelt signed the Burke-Wadsworth Military Conscription Bill, first peacetime draft in the nation's history. It would take a while to set up the machinery of administration, but with National Guard units already trained in arms, these citizen soldiers could at once be ordered out to support the regular army.

On Sunday, January sixteenth, 1941, early in the cold, windy morning, Concord's citizenry was at the railroad station to watch its Company depart. Forty-three years before, the company had gone to the war with Spain; twenty-three years ago, to make a world safe for democracy. In 1861, on April 19, under George Prescott, the men had left to defend the Union. Now, under Captain Hagerty, with John Hutchinson next in command, what are the stakes, the risks?

Even before the departure of H Company, Concord had been watching other young men go. There were new matters, also, to think about and work for — aluminum pots and pans to be collected: essential if there was to be enough metal for promised swarms of planes. Gasoline, too, was at a premium, and Concord reconciled it-self to a seven-o'clock curfew for filling stations, and, later, gasless Sundays, though the town had already limited itself of its own free will through the operation of a Gasoline Conservation Committee.

One use for gasoline was presently shown. Some five hundred vehicles of a mechanized unit — trucks, scout cars, jeeps, ambulances — swept through the town on maneuvers: a two-hour passage that drew sober thoughts from onlookers on Main Street. Gray, grim battle-carts; tanned, sinewy men; despatch riders on snorting motor-cycles. Was this a cavalcade from the planet Mars, missent to peace-ful Concord? Many watchers cheered, but some by the roadside felt a painful confusion of emotions. Who are these men at arms? Are these like the boys we sent off to the camps and the ships? Strange to face that realization!

CHAPTER XXIV

Armageddon

FAIRHAVEN Road had a queer look to it. Its unpaved, churned surface wandered among trees with mottled bark and gimcrack branches — not at all like the elms and maples which ought to be there. Instead of a juniper-covered rise of ground, you saw tawny, unfenced fields of juiceless grass, browsed by lean cattle. For this was New Caledonia, not Concord, with the start of the road some fifteen thousand miles away. Twenty-one months had passed since Company H was sworn into Federal service. Some member of the outfit, half as a joke, half in homesickness, had set up Concord here on this threatened Southwest Pacific Island by nailing that crudely lettered sign to a Niouli tree on the company street in front of the bleached, dun-colored pyramidal tent of the officers. It was on Fairhaven Road that John Hutchinson, acting captain, lived back home. Though Company H, of the Second Battalion, 182nd Infantry, included men from Lexington, Carlisle, and Lincoln, from Littleton, from the Actons, from all the towns that long ago had rallied to the bridge, more than half, as usual, came from Concord.

For most men in service, those months before Pearl Harbor had been a chore. South, on maneuvers, members of H Company had told themselves there was a fair chance of being home for Christmas. The regiment, in fact, returned to Edwards Saturday afternoon, December sixth. Next day came the news that changed everything. This was our war now.

The next month-and-a-half had been pretty confusing. Along with the rest of the regiment, H Company presently found itself detached from the Yankee Division for immediate embarkation. From a gangplank at the Brooklyn Navy Yard, the second battalion, commanded by Captain Otis Whitney, got their first look at the

Santa Elena. In the January dusk she resembled a huge hunk of stale wedding cake dropped in the mud. Her none too white paint, badge of her peacetime assignment to the South American trade, was disappearing under battleship gray. Inside, a thumping and banging gave proof that the tiers of bunks converting her into a transport were still going in place. As each man checked aboard he took care of himself, so that the battalion officers, trying to pierce through the confusion, spent the night on deck because there was no room below. Next day and the next found them still at the pier. The ship's mess, unequipped for handling so many, kept the men queued-up for hours.

At mid-morning on the twenty-third of January the tugs began nosing the *Santa Elena* into the East River. No one aboard knew where she was bound. With some twenty-four hundred passengers — the entire Second Battalion, along with elements of the 101st Quartermaster Corps, the 101st Medics, the 200th Coast Artillery who would man the newly installed guns (though they had never seen that type before) — the *Santa Elena* headed for the narrows to join the convoy carrying the rest of the regiment.

It was rough off Hatteras. Everyone was too miserable to take much notice. But by the fifth day out, in calmer waters, it was obvious that the seven transports and the naval vessels shepherding them were headed south. Under the bright warm sun, the men watched destroyers weave in and out, then leave the convoy to scout ahead.

Hot nights in the total blackout set everybody on edge. All the whistles of the convoy would blare suddenly, then fall silent. As the engines throbbed and heaved, you could feel the *Santa Elena* list from side to side with each zigzag she was taking. Sometimes there was distant gunfire. Sometimes the vessel's creaking and groaning sides pushed inward at the muffled thud of a depth charge. According to scuttlebutt, torpedoes from enemy subs had passed right through the convoy. Yet one night the men were amazed to see bright lights close by. Some of the Coast Artillery, who had lived there, recognized the place — Miami, Florida. You could see the traffic lights flash red and green.

Then came Panama. Returning from a hush-hush meeting, Captain Whitney brought the lowdown about Pearl Harbor: the worst naval defeat in the nation's history. On Bataan, the Filipino-American forces could not hold out much longer.

The Battalion's officers tried to figure out the convoy's destination. John Hutchinson guessed Java. Whitney broke out a bunch of maps he had been given. Where's New Caledonia? he asked. Nobody knew.

On that crowded transport, Lieutenant Hutchinson found it next to impossible to carry on a satisfactory program of training — a few schools on tactics and weapons was about the best one could do. Even exercise was out of the question. Father Dumford, chaplain of one of the outfits, managed to get band concerts going. The shows he staged, with rehearsals two-thirds of the fun, furnished about the only real break. Then, on the thirty-eighth day, after a mean storm, land sighted. They were entering the long narrow passage to Melbourne.

The greeting the soldiers received as they set foot on Victoria Pier was almost frenzied. Australia was mighty glad to see these Americans. Japanese amphibious forces, striking from carefully prepared bases in the Marianas and Carolinas, and now also from Davao, in the Philippines, had the South Pacific at their mercy. They were threatening the very supply line over which the convoy had come. Even as the Second Battalion was mustering in the dusk, an air alert sounded. With ack-ack bursting overhead, Captain Whitney lost no time in getting the men away. Planes droned over Melbourne as the battalion headed for a little park on the outskirts. Here, under their shelter halves, they spent what was left of the night. Next morning, at the railroad station, they entrained in odd little open cars for Ballarat, a small town about the size of Waltham, Massachusetts.

As the train pulled in, each citizen who had agreed to play host stepped up to claim his group of two or three, stowing the soldiers' duffle in every type of conveyance from old-fashioned farm wagons to American Fords. Lieutenant Hutchinson found himself assigned to the Reverend Horace Brady, chairman of the local committee. The town's young men were away fighting in Syria, beleaguered in Singapore, or prisoners of the Japanese. The people of Ballarat, grateful for a token of America's help, welcomed their first Yanks as if they were their own sons. The morning after arrival, they brought them breakfast in bed, and protested that drill call at eight was too early.

Less than a week later, on the night of March fifth, Lieutenant Hutchinson hurried back from an officers' meeting. The battalion, he told his host, was to move at once for a theater of action. How could they gather the men, scattered about in so many houses? No need to worry, said Mr. Brady, everybody in town had the news.

At 1 A.M., as the train pulled out, all Ballarat was at the station. As they waved good-by, the women, even some of the men, were crying. Wonderful people — Company H would never forget them.

Thanks to the Navy's holding the line in the Coral Sea, the defense of New Caledonia, though the troops manned the beaches, remained purely tactical. Through the next six months, Hitler's legions in North Africa, matching the *Wehrmacht's* thrust towards Moscow, rolled further along the road toward Cairo. In the Philippines, Corregidor had fallen.

A. P. O. 502, care of Postmaster, San Francisco, was bringing the mail to the Second Battalion's camp at Qua Tom. "According to the latest Massachusetts casualty list," home town papers reported, "Navy Lieutenant Whitney M. Cook, of 12 Garland Road, is missing in action." Every man in H company had read Whitney's letter from Bataan. "If you wish to quote me in the *Journal*, tell the folks back home that war is a twenty-four-hour job, seven days a week, with no double pay for overtime, and no Saturday or Sunday off. Send us the materials and we'll do the fighting." It was hard, he wrote his father, to say anything without risk of giving information to the enemy. "I am well, but sunburned; happy as one can be in such an affair; cheerful, almost always; confident, in both myself and the ultimate outcome, and, above all, grateful to the Almighty for still being here. I have an overpowering faith in what is right, and what I'm fighting for, and an overpowering faith that I'll come through." A man so full of living, hoped his friends in H Company, could not really be dead.

Other news told of Concord itself. The Players had put on *The Torch Bearers*, sending the proceeds to Captain Hutchinson for the company fund. Chief Air Raid Warden Roger Swaim was cooking up blackout incidents for his corps of deputies and first aiders. Air raid spotters were manning an observation tower on Nashawtuc Hill. Red Cross Gray Ladies and Nurses' Aides were busy in volunteer work at the hospitals.

Corporal Mikey Lombardo, in a way, got closer to home than any other member. In Nouméa, the island's seaport, he ran smack into his best friend, George Heyliger. George was with a contingent of Marines commanded by Lieutenant Colonel Carlson. It remained in New Caledonia only a little while, then moved out, nobody knew where, until wounded men began coming back from a place called Guadalcanal. The Marines had made a landing on August seventh, and were hanging onto a tiny beachhead, including a landing field nearly completed by the Japs.

Studying maps of the Southwest Pacific, Otis Whitney, just named lieutenant colonel and executive officer of the regiment, could see the tremendous strategic importance of those islands. Everyone felt sure the Solomons would be next on their list. Greens for jungle fighting had just been issued. The automobile hub cap helmets of World War I had been swapped for deeper new ones. This, guessed the men, would be it.

Chow, that morning of November 12 aboard the transport *McCawley*, came hard on the heels of midnight. Now the Second Battalion, Lieutenant Colonel Bernard B. Twombley, of Medford, commanding, waited in battle gear at its stations. In the luminous darkness under the tropic stars the men could feel the thrust of the vessel's engines and sense the tenseness of her crew. This was the *McCawley's* fourth shuttle to "the 'Canal," and her luck, felt the seamen, could not last forever. Each time, she had been pounded.

Though the course lay almost directly towards the equator, the early morning air was chilly, and soldiers shivered. Not even Corporal Bill Delaney's low-voiced joking served to keep his squad in its usual easy humor. Official talks on the nature of the enemy had not been cheery. How tricky the Japanese are, how unbeatable at jungle warfare — that had been their general tenor, with mighty little useful advice. A rumor persisted on the ship that George Heyliger, Mikey Lombardo's friend, had died on the island they were nearing. Though his fellow townsmen in the Concord Company did not know it, Lieutenant Commander Edmund Billings had been killed off Savo Island, eight miles from Guadalcanal, the day after the Marines had gone ashore, in a naval engagement during which the Japanese not only had been successful in landing crack jungle troops but also had sunk the United States cruisers *Quincy*, *Vincennes*, and *Astoria*, along with Australia's *Canberra*. For Admiral King, in Washington, that was the blackest day of the war. Unwilling to believe the dispatch, he sent it back for another decoding.

After what seemed like a month of darkness, the sun burst straight from the sea to show land less than five hundred yards from the

McCawley — a strip of very white beach, then coconut palms, then inland, catching the early light, high mountains. A drift of warm, moist air, sweet with the smell of earth, brought a reminder of Concord in late June.

The *McCawley* lay farthest west in the line of transports and cargo vessels. Already her giant cranes had swung the Higgins boats outward. Each landing craft was describing eccentric circles in the calm, clear water, waiting to take the men from the nets. Farther out, towards Florida Island and Tulagi, the guardian shapes of battleships and destroyers were weaving back and forth, with a screen of planes overhead. No signs of an enemy anywhere. This might have been a rehearsal thousands of miles from the fighting.

It was the first time Company H had gone over the side. How to get yourself, and your heavy pack, not to mention your M-1 rifle, into a landing boat without a ducking looked like a tough problem till advice on how to manage was passed along the line by some convalescent Marines just taken aboard.

The men were getting ashore faster than the company commanders dared hope for. Thirty-five men to a Higgins boat, and you scarcely wet your feet when she clanked down her nose to let you off, then turned back for another load. F Company was staying aboard to unload the heavy stuff — the guns, the trucks, the battalion baggage. H Company already had its eight machine guns set up to cover the grove and beach, as Corporal Ed Hurley looked over each of the Company's trucks as it rolled ashore. Loaded under all it could carry, each headed for the bivouac area, some three hundred yards inland, under Lever Brothers' coconut palms, where the battalion dump was rapidly growing.

It was getting along towards midmorning. Captain Hutchinson, checking supplies, happened to glance toward the *McCawley*. A sudden geyser of water was leaping skyward just beyond her. From somewhere back in the hills came a single heavy report. A second later, Rear Admiral Callaghan's cruisers and destroyers were throwing everything they had in that direction, while from inland came the roar of artillery. None too sure this was not the enemy replying, the men of the second battalion dove for cover. No shells were falling. The racket inland must be coming from friendly batteries. After one deafening minute it was over, with never another peep from the hills.

That one shot certainly stirred things up. Beforehand, the men of Company H, stripped to the waist in the mounting heat, had been working like beavers. After it, slit trenches and foxholes in the bivouac area multiplied like magic.

"It's about time for Tojo to show up," remarked the few Marines wandering about. Tojo had a way of flying over, they said, almost every afternoon. These Marines were mostly rear-echelon, but on Guadalcanal the rear-echelon got its bellyful of fighting. They were looking for a chance windfall from the Army. It was hard to yell at a couple of skinny men making off with a case of grapefruit juice or tomatoes. They had seen nothing worth eating since their day of landing. All were glassy-eyed, gaunt as scarecrows, and jumpy in the way men get who have been too long in combat. The tales they told were far from reassuring. In small contingents, nearly every night, the Japs were landing reinforcements. Tonight, after dark, enemy warships might be plastering this grove. There is something about the explosion of a fourteen-inch Japanese naval shell, warned the Marines, that no thousand-pound bomb can equal. Less than a month ago, when the enemy was trying to bring in a large convoy, the defenders had been on the receiving end for nearly three hours that had left them dazed and shaken. It was just before, men of H Company learned, that George Heyliger had been killed, when Colonel Carlson's Second Marine Raider Battalion was holding back the Japs at the Matanikau River, west of Henderson Field.

With Guadalcanal such a little island, it was astonishing to find so many men there from home. If they could all get together at once, it would be like town meeting. Emery Whipple, with the Marines, had been there from the start. The story got around how Joe Sheehan, the selectman's son, a corporal with the Marine Combat Engineers, had lost the watch he won back home in a ten-mile road race. When the enemy broke through on Bloody Ridge to the bivouac area, one of them had helped himself to Joe's trophy. Joe was still looking for that Jap.

It was the McCarthy brothers who provided the afternoon's sensation. Hefty Bill McCarthy of H Company glanced up as a slim Marine came towards him. It was Joe. Both were close to tears as they met.

Shortly after two, there was a stir at the communications phones. "Condition Red!" men started yelling. From somewhere inland came the wail of a siren. Moments later, defending aircraft roared above the palms that screened the battalion's bivouac area. On the beach itself, the machine-gunners of H Company, in the sharp, hot sunlight, could see the enemy formation — twenty to twenty-five bombers with Zero escort — grow from glistening specks to seagull size. Then the American fighters were among them. In the next few seconds, over a dozen planes, as the rest came steadily on, were caught by bursts from the interceptors. It was the first time members of the Concord company had seen planes go down in action. In their excitement they forgot all about keeping cover as the seven or eight surviving bombers, very close now, began their runs. The warships and transports under attack let loose. Planes vanished like hit clay pigeons. Debris spattered into the water, or fell on the beach. One bomber that had not disintegrated came wavering in, directly towards a Company H emplacement. Twice, fore and aft, the machine guns raked the plane. It sheered away, then hit the water. In less than ten minutes the fight was over.

Late that afternoon, as the transports and cargo vessels, restless to be off, moved out of sight, Company H was still lugging the last of its stuff inland. When it grew too dark to see, the tired, sweaty men bedded down where they were working.

But not for long. Most thought they had just fallen asleep when they found themselves staring up at a flare so bright that it lighted the entire bivouac area. In the stillness, the laboring drone of a plane was the only sound. If men looked at their watches, they could see it was past one-thirty. It was Friday morning, November thirteenth. Next moment a tremendous rolling crash broke from the bay. Crouched in their foxholes, men waited for the shells. For what seemed hours, though less than thirty minutes, the uproar continued, the sky through the palm fronds intermittently bright.

On the shore, the men of H Company's machine-gun platoons gained a somewhat clearer notion of what was happening. Admiral Callaghan's cruisers and destroyers must have returned, just in the nick of time to prevent a Japanese task force from giving the beachhead a going-over. On Tulagi Sound, out to the left, toward Savo Island, only a few miles from where the transports had waited, searchlights from what seemed to be oncoming enemy ships, probing the darkness for a clew to this sudden attack, blinked out instantly, shattered by our Navy marksmen. You could see the muzzle flashes of opposing guns. The slow, deliberate parabola of red-hot large-caliber projectiles looked like giant rockets on the Fourth of July. Every few seconds, star shells flaring overhead illuminated the confused action till the next salvo, and more flares, put the prospect out of focus. Aircraft — you could not tell whose — betrayed their presence only as they burst to smithereens. At two or three places on the water, now, orange-colored flames poured skywards, with streamers of exploding shells darting this way and that beyond the mass — apparently some hit ship's magazine, with the inferno extinguished as the vessel went down. The sea, calm as a millpond all day, was throwing long swells ashore, kicked up by the wake and wash of the plunging ships. You could feel the sand shake from the detonations. Like men in a dream, Lieutenant Jack Algeo and the others of H Company's machine-gun platoons watched the action diminish and drop away over the water.

Back at the battalion bivouac, soldiers were asking one another if every night would be like this one. Later they found it had been a very special affair. They had witnessed the beginning of a three-day naval battle which would go down in history as the greatest since Jutland. Throwing his cruisers and destroyers between two advancing columns of enemy battleships, Admiral Callaghan had won victory by a daring gamble, though it cost him his life.

A rickety-looking footbridge, but if the infantry of the Second Battalion were going to make it, H Company, with its heavy weapons, could too. From there on, all the lugging would be piggy-back, single file. Trucks could go no farther than the Matanikau's east bank. They had come only a short way, this morning, their sixth ashore, from their second deployment on the narrow coastal plain. No assault had come their way, though during the nights there had been a good deal of jittery shooting, and continued heavy fighting at sea. Elsewhere, Japs must have got ashore. Up toward Cape Esperance you could see what looked like several good-sized Japanese liners — the kind that, painted white, used to sail up Boston Harbor — lying with their noses tilted toward the beach, their sterns under water. Closer at hand, the Japs had run barges in, camouflaged with palm fronds like little islands. From a sandspit by the machine-gun emplacements, Captain Hutchinson had watched dive-bombers from Henderson Field go to work on the transports.

As far as any man of H Company could remember, this advance beyond the western periphery was the first maneuver for which the higher echelon had not routed them out in the darkness and made them stand around before getting started. Instead, leaving the rear installations in charge of Sergeant Pappy Brooks, they had moved up in leisurely fashion between eight and nine, and now, near ten in the morning, were crossing the Matanikau, having dropped off their four artillery pieces on the east bank to cover the battalion's position.

Swift, deep, grayish green, and probably cool, the Matanikau looked very inviting. Several Marines were swimming in it, oblivious of an occasional shell from enemy mortars somewhere behind the ridges beyond the river's swampy further side.

Come on in, the water's fine! — yelled the bathers derisively.

They were members of the Eighth Regiment, Second Marine Division — by nickname "the Hollywood Marines," because they helped make a picture before leaving the States, though what they had been through since was a far different business.

Once over the river, the men, strung out single file, advanced along a dark, tunnel-like, mucky, stinking jungle trail which unexpectedly ended in blinding sunlight on the flank of an abrupt, nearly vegetationless slope. With every soldier carrying such a heavy pack, this open side-hill made no better going than the jungle's sucking mud, now beginning to cake on each soldier's legs. Yellow grass, sickly and poor, struggled to cover the jagged coral hulk of the island which humped up so steeply that men scrambling on all fours could scarcely make it. Soon almost everybody's hands were torn and bleeding. The sun, screened off in the jungle, beat down so intensely that every back became black with sweat. To lighten their loads and quench their thirst, men swallowed the tepid water in their canteens, then next minute wished they had saved it. It was hard to believe that just taking position could be such torture. All in from its climb, the battalion found itself turning left to snake its way up the inner edge of a long plateau. In this exposed position, men waited apprehensively for enemy gunfire. But the area to the west remained ominously quiet as the artillery barrage from along the Matanikau beat noisily over it.

Everybody and his uncle were on the ridge, supervising this advancement of the line. There was Major General Alexander M. Patch himself, who, the men gathered, was in command of the Americal division to which they belonged, along with other old National Guard units like the 164th Infantry from the Middle West. The 164th was the first army regiment to arrive on Guadalcanal, having preceded the 182nd by several weeks.

Company F continued along to occupy the left flank, furthest inland, where the ridge curved back on itself toward the upper Matanikau. In front, down the height, lay deep jungle, with what a patrol reported might be a water hole. Next came Company G, with

E, which had been covering a knoll on the river's east bank to prevent infiltration, moving up to take over the right. Toward the sea where the ridge dropped down to the jungle there seemed to be no people at all to plug the gap, a circumstance which was driving Lieutenant Colonel Twombley nearly crazy. Marines, along with other units of the division, were supposed to be taking care of the swampy coastal plain and the beach itself.

Strung along the battalion line, the machine-gunners of H Company were setting up their eight emplacements — though you could scarcely dent the coral, and defenses had to be built up rather than dug down. Fortunately the enemy continued quiet. Because of the steepness of the inner slope, with dense, wet jungle below, the mortar men of H Company were obliged to place their four weapons close together on the only level spot, back of F Company, with Battalion Headquarters just to the right. The medics were setting up shop in the same area.

Communications Sergeant Mikey Lombardo, in charge of the company runners, wandered over for a glance at the mortars. One thing was certain; they had not been able to lug in enough ammunition to last very long at that rate of fire. Looking over the jungle below, he figured if one could get through diagonally to the footbridge, instead of following the crooked elbow, time could be saved in reaching the dump. There might be one or a thousand Japs in the murk down there, warned Captain Hutchinson. Mikey scraped together a group of volunteers from the personnel gathered at company headquarters, and started down.

Meanwhile, in the sun that hit like a blowtorch though its rays were beginning to slant from the west, water became a vital necessity. A detail was setting out from G Company's sector to where the water hole lay. Couldn't he tag along with Headquarters' canteens? suggested Dorsey King, easygoing, happy-go-lucky H Company runner, a Southern boy who had somehow strayed into this New England outfit. Hutchinson nodded. The runner, and a soldier from the mortars, stringing canteens all over themselves, joined the patrol. Just as Hutchinson, uneasy for the safety of the pair, calculated they should be returning, a terrific racket broke out, its sound somewhat muffled by the height of land. Machine-gun fire, small arms, everything blazing away. A call came for H Company's mortars to lob their shells beyond the melee. It was bad enough to have Mikey and his detail lost in the jungle. Now King and Charlie Rock were probably dead.

King's luck, however, stayed with him. Captain Hutchinson saw both coming back, their canteens dripping. Ambushing Japs had waited till most of the detail were in a bunch, then opened up. A platoon gone to the rescue was still pinned down. As it turned out, they were there for the night, with plenty of casualties and two officers haywire.

Mikey Lombardo, his jungle greens tattered, also got back. In fact, with his shorter route broken out, he led two more trips that brought the mortars all the ammunition needed. Captain Hutchinson resolved to see that Mikey was recommended for a citation. No casualties in the Company, thank God, but what a hell of a day!

It was astonishing how sleepless night could be. The thunderstorm which presently drenched the soldiers along the ridge, at the mortars, in the first-aid station where some of the wounded from the water hole lay wet and shivering in the coolness after the furnace-like day, was right in keeping with the din of the naval battle still ringing in men's ears. When the storm was over, nervous trigger-quick people would blaze away, the flashes from their guns all too likely to draw enemy mortar fire. Yet the moments of quiet were almost worse than the noise. Sand crabs and lizards — probably, though who dared be sure? — made a stealthy creaking like a Jap moving toward the sparsely strung wire.

Next morning brought an advance of some four or five hundred yards to the further side of the plateau, but when G and F Companies tried to reach the ridge beyond, they were pinned down by enemy machine guns from the ravine. Colonel Twombley, to save his men, stabilized the line at the second position while soldiers worked furiously to bore down deeper in the coral. Here the battalion stuck. Nothing seemed to dislodge the enemy's people from their hiding places — neither co-ordinated artillery and mortar fire nor bombing and strafing by our planes. You hardly ever saw a living Jap, though patrols beyond the line saw plenty of dead ones, killed by the artillery.

Infantrymen in other companies of the battalion had been getting hit, but H Company, manning its heavy weapons, stayed lucky. Early this Thanksgiving morning, November 26, that was something to be thankful for. Shortly after nine, the luck changed. Over on G Company's curve of the ridge, Sergeant Ken Dunn, section leader in charge of two Company H machine guns, died instantly, drilled through by a burst of enemy fire. Joe Viscariello, at the same emplacement, suffered a chunk of his heel ripped off. To the right, Amos Murray and Joe Yokum, whose gun team covered part of F Company's sector, had both been hurt, Murray badly. Joe's left cheek had been pierced by a fragment of mortar shell, which he spat out, along with a couple of teeth. The medical aide man who gave Murray plasma reported that unless they could take him out of there quickly he would not last. With gunfire all along the line, every team of stretcher bearers was busy elsewhere on the hard-hit sector. There might be difficulty in getting any other soldiers past the stragglers' line, set up by the military police along the river behind the zone of combat. Yet Murray must be kept alive. Captain Hutchinson asked Colonel Twombley for an order to take the boy out. A Company detail got the precious slip of paper.

The flash and crack of high explosive burst over the mortar pits. One of our own shells from across the Matanikau, guessed Hutchinson, must have fallen short. That can happen when men grow tired. Hurrying to the battery, he found the crew of one mortar flung all over the place like sacks of meal. A medical corpsman — where he had come from so quickly the captain could not imagine — was already applying a tourniquet to the spurting, shattered right arm of a soldier. Near the wounded man lay another, his face torn half away, the loose skin hanging. It was only from their dog tags you could be sure who they were.

As the captain of H Company quitted the aid station, he met the boys of the stretcher detail. They had put Murray into one of the ambulances waiting beyond the river, then come back. Nobody was going to call them yellow.

Five of the Company wounded, one killed — Thanksgiving was over.

Day after day on the ridge with no letup from the acute discomfort, the sense of danger. It was not just the enemy; the enemy was merely part of it. Mosquitoes, sure to be full of malaria, settled in waves. No larger than those in the river meadows back home, they were twice as persistent. Hands or feet blitzed by a scorpion stayed sore for a week.

Each night grew tougher on fraying nerves. Unlike normal men, the Nips seemed never to rest. They made the hours from sunset to sunrise the liveliest. During the darkness, a terrific racket was sure to burst from Henderson Field as antiaircraft gunners tried to pot down Washing Machine Charlie. Soon you would hear the slow, exasperating, labored hum of his motor as he cruised the area. Just before dawn, without knowing you were dropping off, you might snatch a little sleep. Waking at the bottom of a foxhole was part of the nightmare. All the realization of where you were would come flooding back. In the pain of unkinking its joints, your numbed and stiffened body seemed breaking apart. And the blistering, shadeless, drinkless day lay ahead.

For lack of water, nobody washed, nobody shaved. Captain Hutchinson's tangled red whiskers would have frightened the children back at Snow's drugstore where he used to dispense ice-cream cones between making up prescriptions. Sammy Hosmer's beard was the thickest and blackest. Though you got used to your own stench, your neighbor was offensive five yards away. Sores on hands and face from coral poisoning — each little scratch became infected — had a putrid smell of their own. All along the exposed ridge, men passed out from heat exhaustion. You could fry an egg in the sun — if you had an egg. The heat was as vicious as the enemy, though there were sections of the line where you could not raise a finger without having it shot at. A near miss sent Lieutenant Algeo's helmet sailing from his head.

On that exposed plateau, the Second Battalion felt more than ever out on a limb. The High Command had decided the Pacific War must wait. They must manage to hang on with what they had.

Three weeks now. No banzai attacks — though Colonel Whitney, with the First Battalion in the jungles on the right, had rallied his command after several assaults by the enemy. On the ridge, the thing itself was what beat you down — the heat, the noise, the killed and wounded, the lack of sleep, the smell and discomfort of one's body.

When a battalion of the Second Marines came up from defending the Henderson Field area, it was hard to realize this was really relief. The Marines were sore as hell. They had clung to the notion they were being taken off the island.

Their fatigue greens tattered and rotting with sweat, their hands and faces swollen from coral poisoning, the men of the Second Battalion, looking like a legion of the damned, recrossed the Matanikau.

Christmas morning dawned hot and clear, as the machine-gunners of H Company relaxed a bit at their emplacements along the battalion front facing inland back of Henderson Field between the

Lunga and Tenaru rivers. Saint Nick had not put in an appearance, but neither had the Japs, though they usually picked holidays.

General Vandegrift's commendation addressed to all military personnel on the island was an indication of improved conditions. "It may be that this modest operation," ran the letter, "has through your efforts been successful in thwarting the larger aims of our enemy in the Pacific."

Those final days before Christmas had been a good deal more easy, with time on one's hands. Mikey Lombardo of the Headquarters detachment, some of the cooks, the mortar men, the H Company boys at the motor pool, even a few of the machine-gunners, had managed to get down to the shore for a swim. What a feeling — thought Mikey — to bask on the sand, pushing away all other thought!

At one time or another, most of the Concord boys visited Dunnie's and Heyliger's graves. The folks in West Concord, they learned, had named a square for Dunn, and the Navy was going to christen a destroyer escort the *George Heyliger*. Sheltered under its grove of palms, the blue water of Tulagi Sound to the north, the hazy mountains of Guadalcanal behind, the cemetery seemed somehow out of this war, though so poignantly part of it. Like the others, the graves of the two Concord boys were marked with rough packing-box slats, painted green and nailed together in the form of a cross. Here and there you could see a Star of David.

"The three things which are of the most interest," wrote Corporal Bill Delaney, "are letters from home, the *Reader's Digest*, and the Concord *Journal*." Old Ed McKenna, though the boys knew he could ill afford to, saw to the *Digests*. He was sending ten copies a month to the Company. These passed from hand to hand till they turned to pulp in the rain and mud.

Since Sam Kent had hit on the scheme of mailing the *Journal* first-class, news came fairly fresh. Whitney Cook, reported the paper, was safe, but a prisoner in the Philippines.

When Christmas came, Mess Sergeant Leon Volta outdid himself with the dinner. Turkey with dressing, gravy, mashed potatoes, boiled onions, buttered peas, hot rolls, hot coffee, cranberry sauce, celery, pumpkin pie and plum pudding (one can to six men) were the incredible items. Also apples and oranges, candy, nuts, and cigarettes. At Company Headquarters, Pappy Brooks was figuring ways and means for the runners to bring the Christmas packages and cards to each gun crew along with its food containers. Many of the home-packed boxes had not weathered the journey. With identification labels gone, the smashed and broken cartons crawled with cockroaches and red and black Guadalcanal ants.

The coconut bugs that clung to each morsel of food were for once only a minor nuisance. The Japs remained unaccountably quiet. Machine-gunners watched the first Flying Fortresses soar off the island to head northwestward up the slot. Going to bomb Rabaul and Bougainville, they guessed, where most of the trouble came from.

At the mortar emplacements, Second Lieutenant Joe Wozinski's platoon fixed up a little palm tree with decorations cut from tin cans. They hung their mess kits in place of stockings, and Sergeant Maurice Dee led the gang singing carols. Was Concord having a white Christmas? That song had been haunting the island.

At H Company Headquarters, Lieutenant-Colonel Whitney and other invited guests hailing from Concord swapped talk and shared the festivities. Captain Hutchinson, however, did not feel much like taking part. He knew what next to expect — nausea, then fever, then the shakes. The regulation daily dose of Atabrine could not seem to check the malaria spreading through his system. Still, it had been a pretty good day — no air raid, not even the usual wetting by a thunderstorm. The starlight of the Christ Child shone over the palms.

One year later, the 182nd Regiment, with a Presidential unit citation for Guadalcanal and many individual awards, found itself fighting on Bougainville.

After Guadalcanal, Company H had been sent to Viti Levu, in the Fiji Islands, for recuperation and further training. Interesting at first, Viti Levu became merely another island to be sweated out. It became an island of sickness. When the doctors tried to cut down the Atabrine, a flare-up of malaria caught nearly one quarter of the command. Perhaps the sickest were the luckiest, since the medics sent them home. Captain Hutchinson left, Pappy Brooks, and a number of others. With replacements from all over the States, H Company was no longer predominantly Concord's.

Now it was Bunker Hill Day, June 17, with the Japanese nearly done for in the Solomons.

"We are gathered here today," the loudspeaker was blaring, "to pay tribute to the veterans of the Battle for Hill 260. We are dedicating this road to the men who fought and those who died on this Hill."

At a moment like this you recall all of the dead. Angelo T. Moscarillo lay buried near Dunn and Heyliger. He had started as a corporal with Company H. He had ended after promotion in the field as a second lieutenant with C Company. Charlie Tolman, in command of the *DeHaven*, lost with his ship off Guadalcanal. Letters and the papers from home kept adding to the number — Dick Howard, lieutenant in the Navy, missing in the North Atlantic, John Stephens, merchant marine, lost on the Murmansk run, Bob Egleston, whose B–17, leaving Greenland, was never heard from. And right here on Bougainville, the first to die was Dick Avery, from Thoreau Street, who lost his life while the Marines were capturing this beachhead at Empress Augusta Bay, with the Americal Division landing just before Christmas to relieve them.

When it fought at Bunker Hill — the speaker continued — this regiment was already one hundred and thirty-nine years old, having seen service through the French and Indian wars.

"Hill 260 will not be remembered among Americans as long as Bunker Hill. Yet those of us who fought there will never forget it. We paid a heavy price for this hill." Like Bunker Hill, it had become a symbol for courage. "And so we dedicate this road," the voice concluded, "as Bunker Hill Road, in respectful memory of the men of this regiment who died, not for two hills alone, but for America."

The rest of the time on Bougainville was like waiting overlong for the third act. More than ever, mail, with news about friends and home, remained a blessing. "Do us a favor, tell us one thing," wrote Bill Delaney, "is Main Street still in the same place?" "It is sure swell to see John Hutchinson out of uniform and back behind the counters at Snow's Pharmacy," wrote Sam Kent in his *Journal* column, "Oddi-torials." Like Lieutenant Samuel Melisi, who had commanded the Company on Fiji, John devoted a lot of time to letting families know how their men were doing. Whenever a letter came from overseas, Pappy Brooks, now a mail carrier in West Concord, delivered it to the boy's people even if it meant an extra trip.

It didn't do to let your mind dwell too much on the papers' accounts about all the boys being lost from the town, especially kids like Mert Sanborn, aviation cadet. Concord had buried him in

Sleepy Hollow, with a guard of honor, and planes from near-by
Bedford Field dipping their wings. Billy Emerson, just twenty years
old and recently married, had also been killed in a flying accident.
Thinking of Bill himself, few soldiers recalled this was the great-
grandson of the town's most distinguished citizen.

The mechanical Macones, reported the *Journal*, were at it again.
They had put together a synthetic motor-bike contraption capable of
making thirty miles on a pint of gas. There was quite a history of
the firm in the paper — how the grandfather, on coming from Italy,
had started a farm on Strawberry Hill which prospered so greatly
that his son Nic and the younger brothers had been able to set up
their Lowell Road garage. Nic now had six sons in the service, and
several nephews, so the older generation was again carrying on.

Gunder Hagg, Swedish runner in quest of the four-minute mile,
had spent a week in Concord, the *Journal* reported. The Office of
War Information had taken motion pictures of him at the bridge,
to be used abroad. A bunch of boys, gathered at random from the
Emerson playgrounds, were shown running beside him. Of Swedish,
Italian, Swiss, Norwegian, and Irish lineage, they would serve to
illustrate some of the racial strains which make up America.

Lots of other news, too. The Red Cross Blood Donors' Committee
was announcing new members of the Gallon Club. Kenneth Teed,
pastor of the Union Church at West Concord, had sent to the
Enterprise a letter from an absent member of his congregation.
"Maybe I was out of order," wrote this wounded soldier, "but as I
saw those bottles empty, all I could think of was, 'This is His blood
which was shed for you.' "

One Concord soldier had written in to complain that the *Journal*
never printed a picture of the Minute Man. Sam Kent obliged with a
big one — the official emblem of United States War Savings bonds.

Patriots' Day, April 19, was going on as usual. The *Journal* printed
Professor Carl Friedrich's talk in which he linked the War for Independence with the present war. A United States had grown from
that first upheaval. "Is it too much to hope that there will grow a
United World out of this great world revolutionary conflict?"

Pappy Brooks, who reveled in the gift of gab, was becoming quite
a speaker. What he said to the boys and girls at Concord High
School, felt his old companions, made pretty good sense. The war
for a lasting peace, he insisted, is the people's war, a war that the
leaders, no matter how great, can't fight for them.

Even the advertisements made popular reading. "I've done quite a bit of thinking about home repairs," wrote Frank Croft, after studying an ad by the lumber company offering to explain government building regulations. "Mine is a jungle home. I need new screens, as the snakes and lizards and mosquitoes, also the ants, are very bothersome. I figure that one roll of No. 16 copper screen, with tacks, etc., will be sufficient. I also need a bit of canvas roofing. Have Eddie Curran deliver it. I suggest he equip the truck with pontoons."

Marking their absentee ballots, service men were interested in two letters, run side by side in the *Journal* under the heading CHOOSE YOUR POISON — pro Dewey, by Charles W. Cheney, business accountant; pro Roosevelt, by Edward Loughlin, Clerk of the District Court, whom most of the boys thought of as head of the Playgrounds Committee. The foreign policy stand of both parties, favoring international co-operation, wrote Mr. Cheney, looks much the same, removing this important item as an issue. Thus, with the Democrats in so long, two-party government is a vital question. "Americans still have the right, but who knows whether they have the power, with any candidate, to 'kick the rascals out.'" . . . Dewey's speeches, wrote Mr. Loughlin, have for the most part consisted of accusations not supported by proof. And what did Mr. Dewey mean by saying with one breath, "Our military leadership has been superb," and with the next declaring "The war effort has been constantly hampered"?

> The very progress of the war in all theaters of action proves, beyond a cavil or doubt, that there has been a magnificent and successful prosecution on land and sea by our soldiers, sailors, marines, airmen, submarine men, Wacs, Waves, and Spars, not to forget the Merchant Marine, the Coast Guard, and the Seabees, under the leadership of capable officers appointed by the Commander in Chief, together with an unparalleled civilian production.

At strategic times and places, in every service Loughlin referred to, Concord, like all America, had her representative sons and daughters — at the African landing, the Sicilian invasion, the Normandy beachhead.

Lieutenant Margaret Thornton wrote to Cottage Street that she was finding it harder and harder, beyond Paris, as supply lines stretched, to keep her front-line hospital fed. Some tins of vegetables abandoned by the Germans were manna from heaven.

In late November, 1944, Concordians spinning their dials to catch the 8 P.M. news were electrified to hear how Captain Daniel French Keyes, his company surrounded by Germans, had held on at the village of Koslar till reinforcements cut their way through. True, the commentator pronounced it "Keys," but it was Danny, all right.

Then the Battle of the Bulge, to cast gloom over the holidays. Private William J. Witton killed four days before Christmas, the thirty-second Concord boy to die in the war.

Warsaw liberated on January 14, 1945, by the Red Army's winter offensive. "The greatness of their army stems directly from the unity and resolve of their people," wrote Major Sherman Hoar, bomber pilot on shuttle missions into Russia. "They look directly in one's eyes as they talk. They like laughter and fun. They are the first people with an American sense of humor that I have met."

"What a mess this place is," said a letter from Sergeant Jackie Clarkson, after the fall of Cologne. "I looked for an undamaged building but couldn't find one. Everything completely kaputt."

On March the seventh, Private First Class Johnny Nims was with the 104th Infantry at the crossing of the Rhine at Remagen. "It has been exciting, dull, dirty, unforgettable, tragic, trivial, and often funny," reported another soldier from inside Germany, "above all, it has been cold. Spring is still dawdling and delaying. I think the Germans will come to terms before the weather does." Yet in April, submarine warfare was picking up. Second Engineer Jim Lane of West Concord felt lucky to escape when his tanker went down off Point Judith.

"You can believe those atrocities all right," wrote an M. P. "I've seen them!"

"Roosevelt's death looks like a catastrophe," wrote a boy on April 12, as the news went out on the ship's loudspeaker. "I don't see how we'll manage without him."

From Czechoslovakia, Private First Class Raymond Cull, with the Ninth Armored Division, and a veteran of the stand at Bastogne, told about meeting the Russians. A Russian major had blown his squad to a party.

In Italy, on the "forgotten front," the Germans at last were apparently cracking, but only after having imposed vast suffering and injury on the land. In several families, Italy had never been out of mind. Men from Concord had died there — Private Natale Arena killed north of Rome, in his parents' native country.

In the final mud of that campaign, Private Dennie Volkmann, of the Third Battalion, 85th Regiment, Tenth Mountain Division, celebrated the tapering-off of hostilities in a soldier's way — by taking a bath in *two* helmets.

"No firing pistols into the air, no drinking in celebration," wrote Lieutenant Walter Renhult from the Pacific when he heard of Germany's surrender. "It seems very far away and quite unrelated to our war out here — which is NOT over."

Over only for the dead. Marine Sergeant Joe Sheehan, veteran of Guadalcanal and many another landing, dead of wounds when Peleliu was taken. Lieutenant George Adams Taylor, son of the moderator, killed during a kamikaze attack on the *Ticonderoga*. Marine Corporal Bob Field, killed in the recapture of Guam. Just a short while before, he and Corporal Joe Mara, and Marine Captain Mike Dee, Jr., had staged a reunion on Peleliu.

The last of the Concord boys left with H Company were again seeing action at Leyte, in the Philippines. The assault on the defensive heights of Cebu City, reported Fred Marshall, was the toughest assignment yet. Even Lieutenant General Robert Eichelberger, Eighth Army commander, admitted these positions the hardest to reduce he had ever seen.

In Manila, Lieutenant Letha McHaile, night supervisor at Emerson Hospital before the war, was freed after three years in Santo Tomás. Slight and trim to begin with, she had lost thirty pounds. But Whitney Cook was nowhere on the islands. Shortly before MacArthur's return, the Japanese herded a batch of prisoners into a transport. Not identified as a prison ship by any markings, she was bombed by an American plane and sunk close to the beach in Subic Bay. The Japanese machine-gunned survivors trying to swim ashore. On his return to the States, one boy, who escaped, made a special trip to tell Mr. Cook about Whitney. He had always made their lot easier for his fellow prisoners. His hope and courage never flagged.

Through April and May, Okinawa remained the vortex. After action ceased, Arthur Christian, of the Seabees, found time for a sightseeing trip with his fellow Concordian Bob Sawyer. You came on those cemeteries very suddenly, at some turn in the road — thousands of white crosses unbelievably close together in their geometric rows.

"With this new bomb, the war can't last much longer, nor the world either, for that matter," wrote a boy in August. "How does the use of it on Jap cities sit with the U. S.? Is there any suggestion in the papers that it is a little on the drastic side?"

Aboard the Carrier U. S. S. *Ticonderoga*, news came over the ship's squawker that the Japanese might surrender if they could keep Hirohito. But two days later, same as usual, found the fliers over Tokyo. A few nights afterwards, when Domei reports came through that a statement would be issued, flight officers were told this might just be a gag. At 3:45, Lieutenant Paul Boyd, of Lowell Road, mustered for briefing. At 5:15 his torpedo bomber took off. She was at eleven thousand feet, ten miles from land, and close to the target, when the receiver picked up a transmission. All planes were to jettison their loads and return to the ship.

Over the interphone, in good Brooklynese, came the voice of Waldo Waldinger, the turret gunner. He and the radioman, he said, were celebrating by sharing an orange.

Some thousand miles north, off the Kurile Islands, that same August twelfth, the Cruiser *Concord*, veteran of twenty-three years of service, was firing from the six-inch guns of her afterturret the last salvo of the war.

"I write this to the noise of an endless procession of planes going in and out of the conquered enemy's stronghold. The occupation goes on apace — above, about, and around me." The submarine U. S. S. *Hake*, Lieutenant Jack Edmands of Concord her executive officer, entering Tokyo Bay; Sandy Bowser, after the Aleutians and Okinawa, landing airborne near Fujiyama; three of the Flannery boys, from Lexington Road, in the Tokyo area. "These are, I suppose, thrilling days, but I have gotten far less enthusiastic about the war's end than I had supposed I would be. Maybe it's because the end has come after so long a time, and after so much suffering."

Men like Sergeant Emery Whipple, who served right through, knew about the suffering. At Iwo Jima, where Emery was a second time wounded, Chaplain Rowland B. Gittleson was speaker at the dedication of the cemetery: "Here lie officers and men, Negroes and whites, rich men and poor — together. Here are Protestants, Catholics, and Jews — together. Here no man prefers another because of his faith or despises him because of his color. Here there are no quotas of how many from each group are admitted or allowed. Among these men there is no discrimination, no prejudice, no hatred. Theirs is the highest and purest democracy. Any man among us, the living, who fails to understand *that*, will betray those who lie here dead."

Concord, too, kept its memorials.

The lilacs on the Communion Table this morning — said Parson Daniels in the First Parish Church — are in loving memory of Caleb Kendall Wheeler. They are from the farm he loved and on which he worked with his family.

He attended our local schools, then entered Bowdoin College, graduating well up in his class, for he was a conscientious student. He registered at the Harvard Graduate School, since he wanted to advance his education as far as possible before being called into service. He chose the Army Air Force. I well remember the day he came to ask me if I would be willing to write a letter of recommendation. Some months later he returned wearing proudly the wings of a Navigator, and on the steps of this meeting house he told me he was about to be married. Shortly after, he brought his bride with him, for it was his habit when home from college or on leave to attend the services of the church in which he had grown up and which he loved.

He was quiet and gentle, almost shy. What he accomplished he let speak for itself. His convictions were never lightly held and so it was not hard for him when the time came to offer his life for that in which he deeply believed. There was substance to him of the kind which makes us certain that, whatever the turn of fate, there will always be those to meet it and deal with it resolutely.

Late in December of that year of victory, another Concord boy, his tanker back from the Pacific and on the stormy Atlantic carrying fuel to England, was writing about the death of friends. News comes tardily to men at sea. "They helped accomplish a purpose, a great one," he wrote, "but surely there must be better ways than this of achieving a goal which even now I feel is on insecure ground. Already men are talking about the next war, when we live in caves. When people assume there will be another, they automatically help it along."

CHAPTER XXV

Preface to What?

WHEN one seventh of a community returns, there are bound to be hitches. But as Sammy Hosmer, late of H Company, remarked, getting back into the stream depends largely on one's attitude.

As descendant of an original minute man, Sam, his modern counterpart, had been interviewed in front of the statue on a nation-wide radio hook-up to spark the final Victory Loan campaign.

Take a good vacation, was Sam's advice, then get back to work or to school. From my own experience — he added — the more one hangs around, the harder it is to get started.

Concord itself was looking forward. A special Town Plans Committee, with a five-thousand-dollar appropriation for study and surveys, was drawing up suggestions for a ten-year program.

Frank and Tom McPhillips, Sam's comrades in H Company, were back in the trucking business. Mikey Lombardo was selling insurance. Peanut Macone was again setting up a bicycle and sporting goods shop. Jack Bent, Company H's former first sergeant, a building contractor by profession, got a loan through the Concord Co-operative Bank, under the G.I. Bill of Rights, to put up a house for himself at the corner of Emerson and Old Marlboro Roads. But many another veteran saw no prospect of finding a place of his own.

Lawyers were returning to the law; doctors and nurses were getting back to practice. Otis Whitney, with a silver star for valor, was once more an attorney, ready again to toss his hat into the political ring. Major Sherman Hoar, among the teachers, would take on German, history, and mathematics at Middlesex and lend a hand coaching football.

Sandy Bowser faced another year at school. Being a freshman at

Harvard, felt Paul Boyd's friends, would be no easy matter. It might take almost as much courage, of a different sort, as that he had shown in facing the antiaircraft fire that tossed his Grumman Avenger around till the bomber's torpedo smacked the Japanese battleship square in the middle and sent it down — an action that won Paul the Navy Cross. Concentration on Freshman Economics, Paul admitted, was difficult. That was no reason, he told himself, for passing up what, fifteen years hence, you'd kick yourself for having neglected.

But if you have no definite purpose or calling, and are not trained, what then?

Along with the agencies officially in charge of the problem, veterans' organizations, both old and new, had an eye to that. The Legion was eager to enroll members. But many service men found it preferable to remain on their own or found new units of established groups.

With Barney Rushe, of the Fighting First Division, at its head, a Concord Chapter of the Veterans of Foreign Wars was getting established. Wounded in the African landing, commissioned on the field, wounded again on D-day at Omaha Beach, decorated by General Eisenhower, Rushe should prove a popular commander. Help for disabled comrades locally was a chapter aim, along with the program for needy veterans and their families, carried on through the national organization.

Other veterans felt such limited objectives were not enough. Commander Albert Mason Harlow had studied the declaration of the San Francisco Conference: "We, the people of the United Nations . . ." He had read how Greenwich, Connecticut, responded to the prospect that the United Nations headquarters might find a site near by. When the *Concord Journal* reached him, Harlow discovered that various citizens of his native town had behaved in much the same inhospitable fashion while Concord itself was under consideration. "Did George Heyliger," he wrote to the editor, "ponder his own welfare in the invasion in which he and so many other United States Marines lost their lives?" Had Whit Cook thought only of his own comfort? How about Dominic Rizzitano, classmate at Peter Bulkeley? Dominic had lost his life in the Philippines when colored sailors, angry because white prison guards had beaten up one of their number, ambushed the first white man to come up the jungle path where they were waiting. Dominic was always gentle and friendly. At seventeen he had volunteered as a radio technician, having prepared himself at Boston Trade School where he got on well with other young Americans, among them Negroes and Jews. "He would be uneasy in his grave," Harlow concluded, "were he ever to learn that his own friends in Concord had put any obstacle in the way of better understanding and co-operation among the races and nations."

With the countries that had won the war drifting apart, once the goad of a common enemy was withdrawn; with America herself no longer sure of her purposes in this disillusioning aftermath — thoughtful servicemen felt it all the more imperative to hold on to this peace they had fought for. Famine, slaughter, and greed were yet loose in the world. Free again to voice their opinions, most found themselves united in at least one thing — they hoped never to have to fight again. They wanted no such amputation of normal living to be the fate of their children. Some saw in powerful national defenses the only security; others warned of an atomic armament race already begun, with distrust rising among nations till fear would push the button to end civilization.

Caleb Wheeler's brother Joe, out of the Army Air Force and once more at Bowdoin, admitted he was horrified by the way things were drifting. While a junior at High School he had been active with the Student Federalists campaigning for democratic world government. Since then, many of these schoolboys had fought a war.

Joe joined the American Veterans' Committee because he liked their approach. Members considered themselves obligated as citizens first, veterans second. Surely the United States was calling for an informed citizenry to solve its problems. From bitter experience, Joe, like the majority of veterans, recognized the need for international co-operation as the one best hope for a decent world in which to live. Most had no very clear notion how to further this objective — but a few felt sure. In *Yank*, in *Stars and Stripes*, later in the A.V.C. bulletin, they had read one another's views. "If from these years of toil and desolation and unlimited murder we have not learned how to live with others, our fathers and brothers have indeed died in the greatest farce in all history." Nor must young men, as they grow old, forget their youth and the fighter's realistic idealism.

Old patterns will bring new wars and new depressions. It is time for a change.

Before returning to college, Joe worked at the Student Federalist headquarters. There he learned that a youth conference was in the wind. Harris Wofford, Air Corps veteran, founder of the Student Federalist movement in 1942, had sent out a memo to student leaders — many returned veterans like himself — outlining his notion. Joe called Wofford's attention to his native town of Concord. Long ago, Concord farmers and their neighbors had rallied to democracy's cause. Illustrious Americans whose words helped shape the American way of thinking had lived at Concord. Joe felt sure that present residents would be willing to provide lodging for the eighty-five or so delegates of both sexes who might be expected to come.

Thus the conference was called. Among the arrivals at various households were Dorothy Nestler, founder of the Wellesley College committee for World Federation, and Wilder Crane, High School chairman of the Student Federalists, who in his junior year at Chippewa Falls, Wisconsin, came to Washington to manage the central office during critical months while older members were away. Ex-Lieutenant Cord Meyer, Jr., graduate student at Harvard, had served on Harold Stassen's advisory committee during the United Nations Charter Conference at San Francisco. Not that Cord gained much opportunity for advising. "Perhaps there should be a regulation that no one over thirty could sit at a peace table," wrote Charles G. Bolte, Meyer's colleague on A.V.C. Older delegates seem to be pushing a ponderous load ahead of them — a frontier to claim, oil fields to hold, a strategic base. Under thirty, there is no vested interest except an interest in peace.

From New Haven came Girvan Peck, founder of the Yale League for World Government. To a flyer like himself, veteran of bomber missions over Europe, the notion of a world of self-important sovereign states with uncrossable boundaries seemed very silly.

Charles Nelson, member of the executive body of A.V.C., was presiding chairman. Already the agenda committee, under Steve Benedict of Saint Johns College, Maryland, had worked out a smooth-running program. Then on the fifth day, at an open meeting for the public and press, five speakers in less than thirty minutes explained plans and purposes.

Clare Lingren, from the University of Minnesota, national president, read a statement unanimously adopted as the "Concord Charter."

We must make world citizenship a political fact. Existing governments have demonstrated they are incapable of preserving peace and protecting human rights in an interdependent world. The atomic bomb blasts forever the illusion that power politics can give us peace.

Only a new world sovereignty on the principles of federalism can destroy the irresponsibility of nationalism, while preserving national identity. The United Nations Organization is not a federal govern-ment. It has no authority over individuals; it can only make recommendations to member nations; and it cannot prevent secession of any nation. It will not be adequate unless it is capable of making, interpreting, and enforcing world law. Therefore, a federal world government must be created, either by calling a convention under Article 109 of the United Nations Charter or by other international action. We recognize frankly that the United States and the Soviet Union are the two chief obstacles to such action. Either is powerful enough to take the lead.

To awaken America, Student Federalists will stimulate thinking on the urgent need; educate our generation in the principles of federalism; find, train, and organize the necessary leaders; and support all steps which will lead to a federal world government.

A veterans' committee would explore the attitudes of other service men's organizations, urging them to exercise united strength in this cause — a strength commensurate with the sacrifices they had made. And like-minded civilian groups were urged by the young delegates to unite for the common cause, with a minimum of doctrinal conflict.

Perhaps — thought Joe Wheeler, back at Bowdoin — perhaps a new shot has been fired at the bridge.

"A few years ago, we were merely idealists. Perhaps we're the only true realists now." In the army, Joe had discovered how men, quite apart from army discipline, work together for common survival. The history of his little town, Joe knew, showed similar teamplay. Not that Concord always lived up to its name. Often there had been bickering and disagreements. Yet in the long run, the good of the many had prevailed.

Only thus could the peoples escape self-destruction.

Only in such a spirit can the world become one.

Bibliographical Notes
and Acknowledgments

THIS book is written from the records. I have depended throughout chiefly on the minutes of the town meetings of Concord, in manuscript up to 1836, printed annually thereafter. They are remarkably detailed and complete. Not just the articles of business voted on but often the debates themselves have been scrupulously set down by such Clerks of the Town as Ephraim Wood and the Heywoods. The records of the First Parish Church in Concord, along with other church documents, have proved valuable. Through their biographies of all deceased members, and their reference to other matters over a long period of time, the five volumes published by the Social Circle, the most recent in 1940, provide information on the doings of a small town and its inhabitants possibly unequaled anywhere else. Since 1817, Concord has never lacked one or more weekly newspapers. From that year, I have been able to draw on the local press.

Apart from the special materials used to reconstruct the American story through Concord, the following, among standard works of history and reference, have been especially helpful: *The Growth of the American Republic* by Samuel Eliot Morison and Henry Steele Commager, third edition, revised and enlarged, 1942; Edward Channing's six-volume *History of the United States* up to 1865; the *History of American Life*, edited by A. M. Schlesinger and D. R. Fox; the *Dictionary of American Biography*, edited by Allen Johnson and Dumas Malone; and the *Dictionary of American History*, edited by J. T. Adams. The most detailed local account available is Lemuel Shattuck's *A History of the Town of Concord, Middlesex County, Massachusetts, from its earliest settlement to 1832*, Boston, 1835. Since it is not entirely trustworthy as to accuracy, I have made it a rule, wherever possible, to go to the records on which it was based. Charles H. Walcott's *Concord in the Colonial Period*, Boston, 1884, while briefer and limited in scope, is a more reliable work. For the period before the Revolution, I should mention Charles M. Andrew's *The Colonial Period of American History*. For the Revolution, I owe a special debt to Allen French's *The First Year of the American Revolution*, along with his other writings on the general subject, because of detailed treatment of events in and around Concord.

For first hand materials, the great collections of the Sterling Memorial Library of Yale University have been invaluable to my purposes. I owe a similar debt to the Boston Public Library, and to Harvard University, especially to its Houghton Library, custodian of various manuscripts on which I have drawn. I wish particularly to thank Miss Carolyn Jakeman, of the Houghton Library, for kind assistance. To Charles B. Shaw, Librarian of Swarthmore College, and to Mrs. Catharine J. Pierce of the reference department, I am grateful for painstaking searches for rare books needed, which they obtained for me through interlibrary loans. And I am happy to thank Miss Sarah R. Bartlett, Librarian of the Concord Free Public Library, and her associates Mrs. Elinor Evans, Miss Charlotte Johnson, Mrs. Mildred L. Marsh, Mrs. Marian B. Miller, Miss Elizabeth R. Pickard, and Mrs. Louise C. Wood for their efficient helpfulness during my use of the books and manuscripts in their charge. I am also grateful to Mrs. Elsie E. Rose, Town Clerk, and to other members of the town's administration who have aided me.

For assistance in preparing this book for the press, I thank Miss Margaret Newell and Mrs. Cornelia T. Gourley.

CHAPTER I: Manuscripts in the Concord library, and probated wills and other documents among the Middlesex County records at Cambridge, have thrown light on the Bulkeley and Willard families. In this chapter, and throughout much of the book, Emerson's and Thoreau's books, journals, and letters have of course been stand-bys. With Emerson's journals, I have used both the originals and the typescripts made from them by the Emerson Memorial Association. The published *Journals* are considerably cut. *Pictures and Stories of old Concord Houses*, a compilation by Mrs. Ruth R. Wheeler prepared for the town's tercentenary in 1935, has been helpful in this and later chapters, and Mrs. Wheeler herself has been most generous in sharing with me the fund of information concerning Concord which her long interest in its houses and history has assembled. As a supplement to sources I wish to mention *The Fur Trade in New England,* by F. X. Maloney, Cambridge, Massachusetts, 1931. A Harvard undergraduate honors thesis, this little book, which presents clearly and briefly within its general subject the specific role played by Simon Willard in the fur trade, has greater value than many a more ambitious historical dissertation.

CHAPTER II: I have been able to supplement the familiar accounts of King Philip's War with manuscript town records and other documents. Concord was so much a storm center during the Indian trouble that its records are unusually complete. These, along with Bulkeley and Willard papers, also furnish considerable material for Chapter III.

CHAPTER IV: Until 1936, the commonly accepted date for Lovewell's Fight was Saturday, May 8, 1725. Then Miss Fannie H. Eckstrom, in her article, "Pigwacket and Parson Symmes," the *New England Quarterly,* IX, 378–402 (September, 1936), exposed the contrivances of Parson Symmes to cover up the fact that the fight actually took place on Sunday, May 9, 1725.

CHAPTER V: Reports of several Church Councils, during the period of Concord's early ecclesiastical difficulties, are among the manuscripts in the local Free Public Library. Others are in the collections of the Boston Public Library.

CHAPTER VI: William Emerson's diary, several of his sermons in manuscript, and various of his letters, drawn on in this and Chapters VII and VIII, are in the custody of the Houghton Library, Harvard University. For Concord's part in the Revolution, and in events immediately afterwards, described in these chapters and in Chapter IX, militia and minute men muster rolls and other documents in the local library have been useful, with the town records on meetings to consider constitutional matters especially informative.

CHAPTER X: Dr. Ripley's *Half Century Discourse,* passages from which are quoted throughout this chapter, was published in Concord in 1829.

CHAPTERS XI–XIV: In these chapters, among other sources, the testimony of Emerson, Thoreau, Alcott, Hawthorne, and their fellow Concord writers has been of great help. Especially in Chapter XIV, and also in XV, I have drawn heavily on Frank B. Sanborn's private papers (letters mostly) in the local library. The voluminous minutes of the Concord Farmers' Club, setting down such debates as that on employment of hired help, were of aid in writing the agricultural interlude in the latter chapter, as were Ephraim Wales Bull's private papers.

CHAPTERS XV–XVI: John S. Keyes's papers and diaries, still in private hands, have been of assistance in these chapters. For Civil War campaigns fought by Concord's soldiers, my chief source, in manuscript, has been a collection of diaries assembled by Grindall Reynolds, minister of the First Parish Church during the conflict, and similar materials and letters from collections in the local library and private hands.

CHAPTER XVII: As a supplement to original sources, a pamphlet by Roland Wells Robbins, *The Story of the Minute Man Statue*, presents information on the casting of the statue and on other details not heretofore uncovered.

CHAPTER XVIII: In my effort to give an account of the early days of St. Bernard's Parish, I received much help from Mr. Edward J. McKenna, whose memory stretches back to Father McCall's time. I regret that my acknowledgment of assistance from Father Quinlan, the rector, comes too late, since he died early in 1946. To the present ministers of Concord's other churches I am grateful for suggestions while writing various sections of this book.

CHAPTER XIX: In addition to other sources, I have been able in this chapter to draw on a detailed report covering the Spanish–American War issued by Concord's War Committee.

CHAPTERS XX–XXV: The local and national press have furnished a large part of the information here used. The records of various women's organizations in Concord supplied details concerning the suffrage issue locally. In Chapter XXI, I have drawn, among other sources, on J. M. Keyes's account of the reception of the Yankee Division after World War I. The members of Miss Gertrude H. Rideout's high school class in senior English, through themes written at her suggestion, after I had explained my problem to her, unknowingly furnished me with the sentences and phrases used at the conclusion of Chapter XXII. I wished to obtain as spontaneous an expression as possible. I hereby apologize to the class for not letting them in on the secret, and I acknowledge my indebtedness to them for their wise and honest judgments of life. For much of the material used in Chapters XXIV and XXV, I thank the various men of the services who have patiently answered my questions, helping me in my attempt to report — as far as a nonparticipant can — the nature of the ordeal they have been through. I should like to acknowledge by name my debt to each did I not know this would embarrass them. Among those who have assisted me, several replay their parts during the war in the pages of these chapters. To all I am very deeply grateful. I wish also to acknowledge the usefulness of certain on-the-spot reports by correspondents at Guadalcanal, especially those of Foster Hailey, in the *New York Times*. I have also used for reference the mimeographed *History of the Americal Division* prepared by Brigadier General Edmund B. Sebree, the *History of the 182d Infantry (Fifth Mass.) Regiment* prepared by the Office of Technical Information, Headquarters, Army Ground Forces, and *Guadalcanal Review* by First Lieutenant Charles W. Jamison. I wish to thank Lieutenant Francis Keppel, of the Information and Educational Division, War Department, Washington, for answering several questions. I am happy to acknowledge the debt I owe my friend, Colonel Kent Roberts Greenfield, former Chief of the Historical Section of the Army Ground Forces, for his aid with this and other sections of the book.

In conclusion, I wish to thank Swarthmore College for the time needed to write this book. The liberal grants of leave given me by the college made the work possible. I am also grateful to the John Simon Guggenheim Memorial Foundation for the assistance which enabled me to undertake this enterprise. And for astonishing patience and gracious helpfulness I thank the Town of Concord. The names of the inhabitants who in one way or another have assisted me with this book would make a sizeable town roll call.

Index

"What is the reason to be given for the extreme attraction which *persons* have for us, but that they are the Age?.....

HONOR ROLL

FAIRFIELD
BROOKFIELD
QUEBEC
BUNKER HILL
TICONDEROGA
BULL RUN
HARRISON'S LANDING
GETTYSBURG
UTUADO - PORTO RICO
CHÂTEAU-THIERRY
GUADALCANAL
OMAHA BEACH,
NORMANDY

Guadalcanal

CONCORD
American Town